CROSSROADS

A Popular History of
Malaysia & Singapore

Jim Baker

TIMES BOOKS INTERNATIONAL
Singapore • Kuala Lumpur

CONTENTS

ACKNOWLEDGMENTS

The publishers would like to thank Dato' Dr. Khoo Kay Kim, a retired professor of Malaysian history, and Desmond J.M. Tate, a Malaysian historian, for reviewing *Crossroads*. The author would like to thank Bob Dodge for his invaluable comments on the first draft of this book.

To Junia — wife, editor, critic, partner, and cheerleader.
Without her, this book would not have been possible.

INTRODUCTION

In the last quarter of the twentieth century, there has been much focus on what appears to be a shift in the world's economic and political power from North America and Europe to Asia. This is underscored by the increasingly prominent roles played by Asia both economically and politically, which impact not only on the region but also on the world at large. The change began with Japan's tremendous economic growth after World War II and was followed by economic booms in Taiwan, South Korea, Singapore, and Hong Kong. In the 1980s and 1990s, there was a third wave of growing economies in Malaysia, Indonesia, and Thailand. The final act in this economic renaissance of Asia will be the rise of two of the potentially largest world economies — India and China.

The economic downturn in the area in the late 1990s is no more than a temporary setback. Most economists believe Asia will emerge from the crisis to be just as important a player in the world economy as it was before the crisis.

There is a wealth of opinion and commentary about Asia's growth and its ramifications. A running theme is that the underpinnings of Asia's economic success are rooted in culture and values, that the rise of the East is driven by "Asian values," which create the climate necessary for these societies to compete successfully with the West. Evidence of this view is contained in popular commentaries on the economic conflict between Japan and the United States in the 1970s and 1980s. It is seen in the stated attempts by many Asian leaders to protect their societies from the influences of popular Western culture lest they corrupt the foundations of their success. And this view has been further advanced by cultural critics in the West who warn of economic decline because of current social conditions in Western societies.

The problem is that to define "Asian" values is virtually impossible, and for politicians to portray economic competition in today's world as one between geographic areas is a gross oversimplification. To see Asia as a monolithic cultural entity defies imagination. Who really believes that an Uzbeki Afghan shares common values with a Japanese in Yokohama, that the Malay living in a village in Kelantan views the world the same way as a factory worker in Seoul, or that a Chinese peasant farmer could share a similar value system with a Dani tribesman in Irian Jaya? Perhaps a reason why Asians were deeply shocked by their economic crises in the late 1990s was the overemphasis by their leaders on the uniqueness of their success. These leaders had indicated that growth was a result of strong Asian values, which blurred true economic realities and offered a false sense of never-ending growth.

Malaysia and Singapore are fascinating cases of the strengths and weaknesses of this ongoing debate. The Malay Peninsula is an area where not only has the East met the West but also where the East has met the East — a true crossroads.

This study of the history of Malaysia and Singapore offers a look at an area that contains cultural elements of many countries — the indigenous influences of archipelago Southeast Asia; the impact of Asia's cultural giants China and India on the area; the coming of Islam from western Asia by way of India; the contributions made by the West through European colonialism and economic exploitation; and finally, the impact of the process of globalization on the two countries in the late twentieth century.

The history of Malaysia and Singapore is more than two thousand years of cultural interaction, largely determined by the geographic positions of these countries. In the last sixty years, it is a history of three distinct groups of Asians — the indigenous Malaysians, Chinese, and Indians, all trying to find a common destiny. For it is in this sixty-year period that all three accepted the reality that they were going to live together permanently. The conflict, accommodation, and promise of this reality are vital elements of life in the area today.

This book, then, has two themes. One is the movement of culture, products, and people throughout the area, and the other is the people who stayed to create the modern nations. Economically, Malaysia and Singapore are rapidly developing, and perhaps by identifying the reasons for their success, these unique societies can give useful insight into some of the generalizations made about Asia today.

As political entities, Malaysia and Singapore are twentieth-century phenomena. As a result, looking at them historically must be in the context of the history of archipelago Southeast Asia. The two countries were in a community of Malayan people and culture until the nineteenth century, and modern Singapore's history in the nineteenth and early twentieth centuries was part of a Malaya created by forces from outside the archipelago.

In the course of reading this book, there will be vocabulary and references to terms that may be unfamiliar to some readers. Most of these are defined in the context of their usage, but Malays, Malaya, Malayans, Malaysia, and Malaysians are used frequently and do have different meanings. The Malays are a racial group, and Malay is their language. The Malays are the race that make up the majority of the population of the present-day Federation of Malaysia and a minority in the Republic of Singapore. Generally, the term includes a race of people who make up a significant portion of the population of southern Thailand and most of the populations of Indonesia and Brunei, as well as a minority in the southern Philippines. Collectively, they are the Malay people but only referred to in that way by the governments of Malaysia, Brunei, Singapore, and Thailand. The Malay language is spoken throughout the area but with significant differences in dialect. For example, the official languages, Bahasa Indonesia and Bahasa Malaysia, are quite similar.

Malaya was a British creation and refers to the states formerly controlled by the British on the Malay Peninsula. The formal use of the term came into being after World War II when the Federation of Malaya was created. This became an independent country in 1957. Prior to this, the area was often referred to as British Malaya and included Singapore for most of the nineteenth and twentieth centuries. In this book, Malaya refers to the area on the Malay Peninsula that eventually became British Malaya.

Malayans refers to the inhabitants of the peninsula and Penang, and later citizens of the federation, whether they be Malay, Chinese, Indian, or Eurasian.

Malaysia was created in 1963 with the merger of the Federation of Malaya, Singapore, Sarawak, and Sabah (formerly known as British North Borneo). Singapore left the federation in 1965, and today, Malaysia consists of the states of Penang, Perlis, Kedah, Melaka, Negri Sembilan, Johor, Pahang, Trengganu, Kelantan, Perak, Selangor, and the Federal District of Kuala Lumpur in the peninsula, as well as the states of Sarawak, Sabah, and the Federal Territory of Labuan in Borneo. Malaysians are citizens of this country, regardless of race. When the term Malaysia is used in this book, it refers to this area collectively.

There are developments that have taken place in the 1990s that may place some observations in this book in a different light — the economic crisis, ex-Malaysian Deputy Prime Minister Anwar Ibrahim's fall from power, the policies of the third generation PAP (People's Action Party) leaders, etc. These events are currently playing out, and to comment on them would move the realm of this book from history to current affairs. Before they are judged from a historical perspective, there needs to be a distance, perhaps in a revision five years hence.

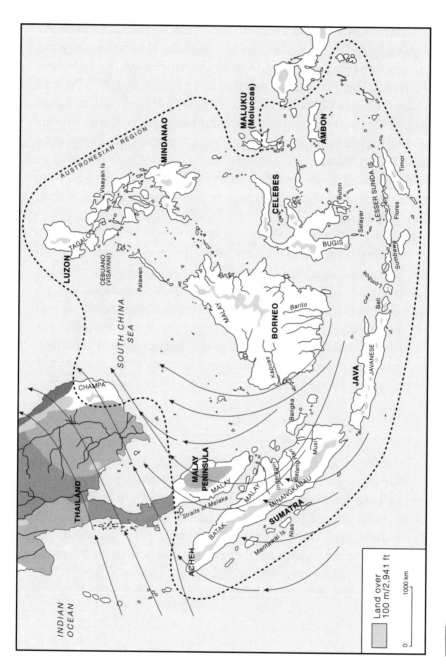

The Malay Mediterranean. The monsoon winds from the southwest blow from April through September. The northeast monsoon winds blow in the opposite direction during the rest of the year.

Chapter 1

EARLY MALAYSIA AND ITS INDIGENOUS PEOPLE

The most distinctive features of modern Malaysia and Singapore are their multiracial populations. The majority of the population, known culturally and politically as Malay, has inhabited the area for at least 2,500 years. The other two main races, the Chinese and the Indians, arrived in the area mostly in the nineteenth and twentieth centuries, although a small number of both immigrant communities can trace their roots back several centuries.

It is the Malays who inhabited the area when modern written history began, and it is the Malays who were influenced culturally by the geography of the area, as well as by the intermigration of people within archipelago Southeast Asia.

Climate and the Land

Climatically, Malaysia is part of what is often known as Monsoon Asia. Monsoons are strong seasonal winds that blow from the northeast from October to March, and from the southwest during the remaining part of the year. These winds bring tremendous amounts of rainfall. On the Indian subcontinent and mainland Southeast Asia, they bring about distinct seasons and significant changes in rainfall, on which agriculture is dependent. Malaysia, situated near the equator, has two seasons — a rainy season and a rainier season. The rain accompanying the winds is experienced throughout the year, although the northeast monsoon is more prevalent in terms of rainfall.

The monsoons have a dramatic impact on the people living along the eastern coast of the peninsula as well as on those living along the northwestern coast of Borneo. This is especially true for those in the northeastern states of Kelantan and Trengganu. These states feel the full brunt of the northeast monsoon from across the South China Sea. Many fishermen and farmers cannot count on any kind of regular life. Life, in fact, slows almost to a standstill during the months of December and January. For this reason, during the monsoons, some people in the northeastern areas devote their time to handicrafts such as woodcarving.

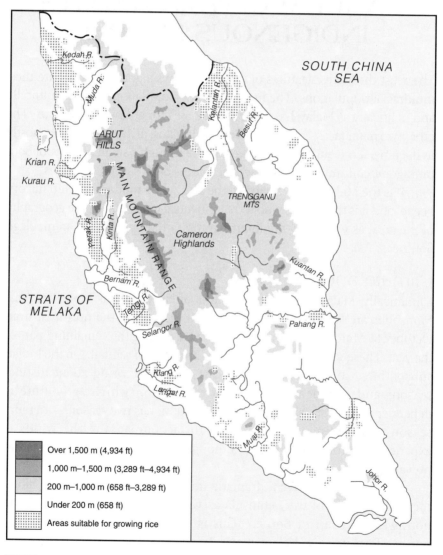

The topography of the Malay Peninsula, including the areas suited to growing rice.

While the western coast of the peninsula receives its share of the rainfall, it is protected from the southwest monsoon by Sumatra, and from the northeast monsoon by the main mountain range of the country. There are, however, some exceptions to the protection on the western coast. Freak storms sometimes occur together with the southwest monsoons on the Straits of Melaka, while winds called Sumatras occasionally rattle the homes of people from Johor to Perlis.

The differing impact of the monsoons on these two coasts has had an important influence on the development of the economy and population of the area. The northeast monsoon is one of the reasons for slow economic development on the eastern coast.

Since Malaysia, Singapore, and the rest of archipelago Southeast Asia are close to the equator, there is little variation in the average temperature throughout the year. Even in the states of northeastern Malaysia, which are very much affected by the monsoons, the temperature change is not significant.

To get a feel for the climate of the area, one only has to watch the weather report on television in Singapore. People from countries with distinct seasonal changes often smile at the monotony. Nearly every day, they listen to weather forecasts such as "occasional showers over parts of the island and temperatures range from 24 to 32° Celsius (75 to 92° Fahrenheit)."

One would think that the constant warm weather and abundant rainfall would make ideal conditions for agriculture. Actually, the reverse is true for Peninsular Malaysia. Many parts of Malaysia and Singapore have reddish brown soil with a high content of clay and iron. This soil is not conducive to the cultivation of food crops.

Parameswara, founder of the first Malay Empire in the peninsula, is said to have fought a battle there against the invading Javanese that was so brutal that the soil turned red from the spilled blood. Actually, the quality of the soil is a result of laterization, which comes about when temperatures average 75° Fahrenheit (24° C) or more, and the nutrients of the soil sink to lower levels. The Latin word *later* means "brick" and describes the hardness of the clay. This does not mean that nothing will grow; rather, it means the soil is not fertile.

15

Historically, as a result of this poor soil, Malaya was never able to support a very large population. As late as the turn of the nineteenth century, it was estimated that only 250,000 people lived in the peninsula. One reason that Malaya's greatest empire — Melaka — failed was that it could not feed itself.

In modern Malaysia, the harnessing of water and modern farming methods and fertilizers have somewhat improved the soil. However, not all of Malaysia has poor soil. Parts of the present states of Kedah and Perlis, the Pahang River basin, the Kelantan River delta, and the Kinabatangan River in Sabah are quite fertile, but they cover a relatively small area of the country. Thus, when the British introduced modern plantation crops, such as rubber, they were not taking away farmland from the people, unlike what the Dutch did in Indonesia for centuries, with catastrophic results.

Malay women in a rice field.

The climate of the region has had an impact on the attitudes and lifestyle of the people who lived there. It produced a slow paced life that reflected the heat and periods of inactivity caused by monsoon rainfall. The phrase "only mad dogs and Englishmen go out in the noonday sun" bears much truth. Like other cultures, such as Latin America, with its noontime siestas, and the Middle East, where life comes to a standstill during the hottest parts of the day, the traditional Malay lifestyle reflected an acceptance of the realities of nature. Among the Chinese immigrants and Europeans, it fed a stereotype that the Malays were lazy and easy going. It is not that they did not work hard; rather, they just had a different view of when and how to work. Anyone who has experienced the backbreaking non-mechanized labor of *padi*, or wet rice farming, knows that the stereotype is a myth, but it persists among some Singaporeans to this very day, perhaps to the point where they sometimes seriously underestimate the potential of their neighbors to the north.

The traditional Malay house is an example of the impact of geography on a way of life. It is built off the ground to avoid floods, as well as the insects, snakes, and animals that thrive in tropical climates. There are many windows, and the rooms open into one another to catch cooling breezes. A palm thatch roof absorbs the heat of the sun. Chinese immigrants who lived outside the urban areas did not copy this architectural style because they came from temperate climates. Until recently, the Chinese in the rural areas lived in houses built on the ground with cement floors and tin roofs, while the Malays preferred their traditional houses. These living styles were similar to patterns in other parts of Southeast Asia. For example, in Laos there are two words for house, one for the traditional Southeast Asian house and another for the type built by Chinese immigrants.

Further evidence of climatic influences can be found in such things as the clothes people wear. The *sarong,* or a skirt-like garment, is eminently practical for the circulation of air around the body and is worn by people throughout Southeast Asia and the Pacific. In fact, the only place in Southeast Asia where a sarong of some type is not the national dress is Vietnam.

At the Crossroads

The geographic entity known as Southeast Asia is divided into two somewhat distinct areas — mainland Southeast Asia, which includes Burma, Laos, Cambodia, Vietnam, and Thailand, and archipelago Southeast Asia, which includes Peninsular Malaysia (although it is physically attached to the mainland), Sabah and Sarawak in Borneo, Singapore, Indonesia, Brunei, and the Philippines. Being part of this geographic area and the geographic dimensions of the Malay Peninsula helped mold the Malay race and culture.

By far one of the most important geographic considerations in shaping Malaysian history has been its location. For Singapore, it is the most important consideration. Situated between the two giants of Asian culture and civilization — India and China — and atop the greatest source of spices in the world, the archipelago, Malaysia and Singapore were ideally placed to take advantage of and be influenced by the major commercial trends of the last two millennia.

Each·succeeding trading power that arose realized that the keys to controlling trade between the Pacific and Indian Oceans were the Melaka and Sunda Straits. Trade began through the area around the time of Christ, with India looking for markets for its products, such as cotton textiles, to trade for spices and straits produce, such as hardwood. As sailing technology improved, Malaya became a middleman for trade involving India, the archipelago, and China. The Europeans followed, searching for spices and to control trade with China. With the rise of British naval power, Malaya provided ports of call and military bases, and then became a source of raw materials itself.

In the days of sail power, Malaya's importance to commerce was not just its convenient location at the center of trading routes. The western coast of the peninsula was significant because the Straits of Melaka offered protection from the monsoons between Sumatra and the peninsula. It was where the monsoons met. Traders coming from both directions could sail with the prevailing winds, find shelter, conduct trade, and move on. Control of the straits meant control of the trade. The alternative to the straits was to go all the way south, virtually to Australia. Malaya could control the Straits of Melaka, and a naval base in Singapore could control both these straits and the much smaller Sunda Straits.

A further significance to Malaya's location culturally that went beyond its position astride these key straits was its access to and its integral position in archipelago Southeast Asia. G. Coedes compares this area to the Mediterranean. It is formed by the Straits of Melaka, the Java Sea, the Gulf of Siam, and the South China Sea. Much like its European counterpart, the economic, cultural, and racial interaction that took place within the archipelago was a key component in molding the society that would emerge in the peninsula and in Borneo.

This historical interaction continues to this very day. With the growth of the Pacific Rim economies, Malaysia and Singapore play important roles in the trade between the Pacific and the countries east of them. Both Malaysia and Singapore derive great benefits from the economic and cultural interaction that takes place as a result of their integration in the archipelago. Truly a crossroads.

Rain Forest and Topography

While much of Malaysia is not suited for food production, the interior supports vast areas of primary rain forest. Even today, after the clearing of large areas of jungle, what remains in the peninsula and Borneo supports the greatest diversity of flora and fauna in the world. The jungle provided products that the world wanted, such as hardwood, rattan, and beeswax, and the soil contained minerals, such as tin and gold, that formed the basis for trade for the Malays until the time of British colonialism.

For much of Malaysia's history, the jungle acted as a barrier to the growth of the population and hindered interaction among the inhabitants. The movement of the people, isolated from other Malays in the peninsula by the inhospitable rain forest, was along the rivers to the sea, where there was trade and arable land.

The jungle, however, did provide a sanctuary for the original inhabitants from succeeding waves of Malay immigrants. The aboriginal people of Malaya and Borneo were able to keep to themselves and preserve a primitive slash-and-burn culture well into the twentieth century and still do in Borneo and a few isolated parts of the peninsula. Indeed, the slash-and-burn form of cultivation was and still is used in Southeast Asia. Farmers cut and burn down the forest cover of the hillsides to provide the required minerals for the soil. After a year or two, the farmers move on to other areas because the ensuing tall weeds and leached soil make it difficult to raise good crops. It takes fifteen to twenty years for an abandoned clearing to return to full fertility. If tree roots are killed and new trees cannot grow, the area becomes covered with a course grass that cannot be re-cultivated except with sophisticated machinery.

The topography of the peninsula is characterized by a mountain range of 4,000–5,000 feet (1,215–1,520 meters), which runs down the length of the country for 300 miles (483 km), from the Thai border to a plain that makes up much of the state of Johor in the south. Numerous rivers flow out of this mountain range, the most important being the Pahang River (approximately 300 miles), the Perak River (250 miles/402 km), and the Kelantan River (150 miles/241 km).

These topographical features, coupled with the vast area of rain forest in the interior, created a coastal people whose population centers were situated at the mouths of major rivers or along them. Historically, these people had as much contact with the people in other parts of the archipelago as they did with people of their own peninsula or, in the case of Borneo, with the interior of their island. This had a dramatic effect on the evolution of the Malays and their culture. In the words of Charles Fisher, "the land divided and the sea united."

Further evidence of population patterns can be found in the Malay language. The modern Malay word for "city" or "town" is *bandar.* The original meaning of the word is "port," reflecting the fact that for much of Malay history, the two words were one and the same.

The People

Prior to the settlement of modern coastal Peninsular Malaysia, the area was inhabited by people who had been living there some thirty to forty thousand years. The descendants of these people, the Negritos, Senois, and Jakuns (Proto-Malays), still live in the interior of the country and represent a population of about eighty thousand. On the island of Borneo, indigenous groups, such as the Ibans, Kadazan-Dusuns, Bidayuhs (Land Dayaks), Muruts, and Melanaus, make up almost half of the population — over nine hundred thousand people. These groups predate the Malays by some two thousand years.

The Negritos, who today number in the thousands, have lived the longest in the country. Racially, they are Negroid and share a common heritage with groups as far away as the Papuans of New Guinea and the aborigines of Australia. The Senois and the Proto-Malays represent a later migration and share racial and linguistic similarities with the more modern coastal Malays. All three groups of *Orang Asli*, or Original People, were nomadic, jungle dwellers, although some Senois and Proto-Malays adopted more modern social and agricultural systems. The Orang Asli's impact on modern Malaysia has been very limited due to their small numbers and inability to hold their ground in the face of modern Malays. Succeeding waves of migrants forced the aboriginal people farther into the interior of the peninsula and into relative obscurity.

Today, the government encourages the Orang Asli to move into settled communities so they can have access to modern educational and social services. This encouragement, coupled with the clearing of the rain forest,

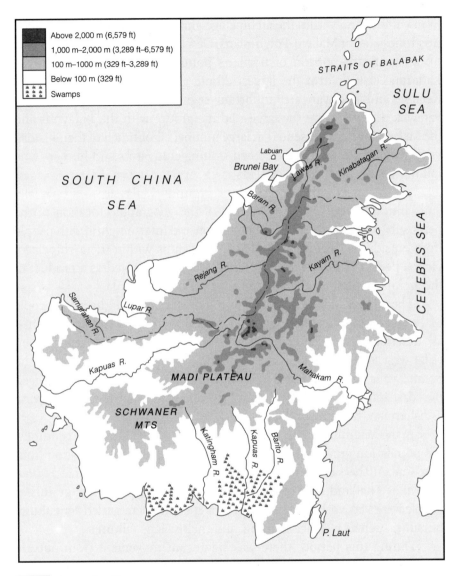

The topography of Borneo.

probably represents the end of their way of life, although some still hold out in the heart of the jungle.

In the Borneo states, the ancestors of the indigenous people were part of a southward migration from southern China and Taiwan that began some five thousand years ago. This was part of the movement of people from without and within the archipelago and who were collectively called Austronesians, or Malayo-Polynesians. Descendants of these people make up a significant portion of Borneo's population today. In Sabah, the Kadazan-Dusuns form the largest ethnic group, although the Muruts, Kelabit, and Kedayan are important segments of the community. In Sarawak, the Ibans are the largest ethnic group, with the Bidayuhs and the Melanaus also represented in large numbers. For much of their history, virtually all these groups have been shifting cultivators and hunters who followed communal social systems.

The Malays — the largest ethnic group in Malaysia — are racially and culturally very much a product of the geographic location of the peninsula. They are the result of migration and intermingling with people from outside the region, as well as from groups within the archipelago. Over a period of at least 2,500 years, the Malays evolved as a product of the archipelago rather than as a product of the peninsula.

The original Malays in Malaya were a mixture of the indigenous people of the area and Mongoloids, who had pushed south from Yunnan in China. We describe these Malays racially as Malayo-Polynesians, who can be seen as far west as Madagascar, which is off the coast of Africa; as far east as the South Pacific; and as far north as Taiwan. Originally, in Malaya, they hugged the coast and lived in villages around river mouths. They made their living as fishermen, hunters, and farmers.

In the first millennium, especially in the seventh and eighth centuries, the population grew and was influenced by a significant migration from Sumatra. At the same time, groups moved overland from what is now known as Thailand, and others sailed from the East. All these groups of people were Malayo-Polynesians and brought with them settled agricultural pursuits, such as wet rice farming, and their village cultures.

During this period, there was significant movement from outside the area in the form of Indian traders and missionaries, many of whom intermarried and settled, especially along the western coast of Malaya. This Indian influence had far-reaching consequences on Malay culture.

The second millennium saw further migration to Malaya. This came in the form of Muslim Indians, Arabs, and Persians (modern-day Iranians), who along with their religion, also intermingled on a limited scale with the population along the coast. Between the fifteenth and eighteenth centuries, there was continued migration from across the straits as in the form of the Minangkabau from central Sumatra, who settled in the areas now known as Negri Sembilan and Melaka. Some Minangkabau later moved across the peninsula to Pahang. Large numbers of people known as Bugis also migrated to Malaya from the eastern archipelago as a result of Dutch interference in their traditional trading patterns. The Bugis took up residence in Johor, Selangor, and Pahang. Two other groups from the Malay cultural area also left their imprint on Malaya in this era, albeit on a much more limited scale. Achehnese control of Perak during this time brought some settlers and cultural influence, and there is evidence of migration from Champa in what is today southern Vietnam, since Chams lived in Trengganu as weavers and in Pahang as miners.

This inter-archipelago migration continued into the twentieth century. Malaya was underpopulated, and there were large areas of undeveloped land to settle. British rule offered relative peace, security, and economic well-being, which contrasted with life in the Dutch East Indies (now Indonesia). This was especially seen in the significant numbers of Javanese who immigrated to the peninsula. Even today, this process goes on. Illegal immigrants still cross the straits from Sumatra to take advantage of opportunities created by Malaysia's relative prosperity, and a similar movement continues from Muslim Sulu in the Philippines to the Malaysian state of Sabah in Borneo. Nowhere is this inter-archipelago movement of people more evident than in Singapore's Malay community. There are ten identifiable groups from the archipelago within what is called the Malay community of Singapore, a proverbial melting pot of the Malayo-Polynesian people.

All these groups from the Malay Mediterranean made their contributions to Malay culture and language, creating regional characteristics in the relatively small area of land that is the peninsula. The people of Kelantan, for example, have significant differences in traditional law and language from those of the Minangkabau of Negri Sembilan. There was a degree of interaction and intermarriage in the peninsula, but until the last century, this was difficult because of Malaya's mountains and jungles.

A typical kampung.

Kampung Culture

Regardless of the regional differences within Malaysia, we can generalize and describe a Malay culture that evolved on Peninsular Malaysia and the coast of Borneo over a period of 2,500 years. Until the last couple of decades, it was a culture deeply rooted in the rural areas and the *kampung,* or village. While towns and trading centers did exist, for the vast majority of the Malays, their culture and values were molded in the kampung.

The major form of agriculture brought to Malaya by migrants from Sumatra and the mainland was wet rice cultivation. While many rural Malays today fish, cultivate coconuts, and grow rubber, the way of life, or rice culture, that evolved from wet rice agriculture provides insight into the values and outlook of most Malays. As mentioned earlier, large areas of Malaya were not suited for productive agriculture, but, in those areas that were fertile, wet rice grew well because of the large amount of rainfall and the availability of river water.

In the many villages of Malaya, life revolved around the cycles of rice growing. Seedlings were grown in nursery areas. When grown sufficiently, the fields were flooded, and the rice was transplanted by hand, shoot by shoot. The wet rice farming system never lent itself to mechanization, not even for harvesting, which was also done stalk by stalk. Traditionally, the final process of separating the grain from the chaff was done largely by hand. An important point to note is that this whole process was incredibly labor intensive. Your neighbor was an ally, and a lot of cooperation was necessary for the whole system to work in building and maintaining, for example, irrigation systems.

Prior to the twentieth century, before a modern infrastructure of roads and railroads was built, geographic realities contributed to the kampung culture that emerged. Communities were isolated and independent, and were primarily involved in subsistence agricultural pursuits. Mutual assistance was a necessity for survival.

The legal system of pre-Islamic times was indicative of the cooperative value system — the underpinning of kampung life. Although there were variations depending on what part of the archipelago the communities came from, *adat*, or traditional, law usually incorporated two key principles — compensation, which was preferred to punishment, and mutual responsibility.

Adat law recognized one of the dilemmas that faces more modern legal and judicial systems. When a criminal is punished, all the victim gets is revenge. If you are robbed or a member of your family is harmed, how does punishing the perpetrator compensate for the loss of productive resources? If a man kills another, is it better to put him to death or to force him to make up for the lost contribution to the victim's family? Under adat law, the latter alternative was preferred. Justice in the kampung was traditionally a search for compensation for the victim. The need for labor and the need to maintain harmony in a society that depended on cooperation made it imperative to have this outlook on crime and punishment.

This was further reflected in the belief that the group was responsible for the behavior of the individual — mutual responsibility. If a family member misbehaved, it was the family who was expected to compensate the victim. If problems occurred outside the village, the village itself was collectively responsible for the actions of its individual members. Once again, this reflected the view that life was a cooperative endeavor. People saw themselves as part of the group to the point that, in some adat systems, banishment from the community was considered the worst form of punishment possible. In the nineteenth and twentieth centuries, as rural communities began to produce for larger markets in the towns and cities, this group-directed behavior was seen as a barrier to free enterprise and capitalism among the Malays. If you worked hard and improved your economic situation, there was group pressure to share your good fortune. This served as a disincentive to individual economic advancement.

The impact of these rural societies manifests itself in behavioral expectations beyond the legal system. Most kampungs were relatively small, consisting of ten to twenty families. The ability to get along with neighbors was important to status in the community. The economic survival of the group was dependent on cooperation. Good manners were essential, and they became an important part of the Malay value system. Behavior or language that was confrontational or abusive was considered bad form in the kampung. The feeling was that they had to live and work together and thus could not afford vendettas or ill will, at least in public.

Unlike English or the Chinese dialects, the Malay language does not contain many graphic swear words. If you wish to insult someone in English or Chinese, you accuse them of unnatural sexual acts or compare them to parts of the body that are seen as unclean. The Malay language traditionally had no such vocabulary, although literal translations from English are slowly creeping into the language in the cities. The worst insult to most Malays is to be called *kurang ajar*, which means "lacking in manners." The phrase literally means "little teaching." Its use as an idiom reflects the cooperation and courtesy of kampung life. While all educational systems impart acceptable modes of behavior, to traditional Malays, manners are of utmost importance.

Malaysian Prime Minister Mahathir Mohamad, in his book, *The Malay Dilemma,* claims this created a society that valued form over substance and scorned assertiveness. As a result, when the cooperative Malay was confronted with other cultures, such as the competitive immigrant Chinese, his/her value system became unsuitable for success in a modern capitalist economy. Ironically, these very values were those that endeared the Malays to British civil servants, especially those from upper class backgrounds.

Before closing this look at village society and culture, some further insight may come from a distinctly Malay form of madness known as *amok*. The word itself is one of the few Malay words that has found its way into the English language.

Suppressing aggression, frustration, and anger were and still are important in Malay public behavior. Emotions must be controlled lest they impair relationships in the community and cause social disharmony. Periodically, this pressure becomes too great for an individual to bear, but to break away from the constraints of village society, the individual must choose insanity. Loss of honor, misfortune, or tragedy set him off, and he goes into a killing frenzy, attacking people around him indiscriminately. Amok occurs infrequently, but it does happen often enough for it to have become part of Malay folklore. To this day, articles with such headlines as "Amok kills six" occasionally appear in the newspapers.

There is a related occurrence among females known as *latah*. Women will fall into uncontrollable bouts of seemingly crazy behavior. Sometimes this takes the form of obscene language or endless giggling. Latah is most common among older women. This, according to some observers, is often the result of menopause, widowhood, or spinster status, which makes the women feel that they do not have a clearly defined role in society. The insecurity leads to what would normally be considered antisocial behavior, but in this case, they are merely viewed as insane. In recent times, the press has carried stories of female Malay workers running away from their factory jobs screaming and yelling. While this may not be latah in the traditional sense, it could reflect a reaction by rural women to an urban life that they do not understand. Traditional Malay culture offered no emotional outlet for the people. With no acceptable behavior available to the individual in society to deal with emotional problems, letting off steam this way was the only way to come to terms with such situations.

Another characteristic of traditional Malay rural society was the high status accorded to women. For example, Minangkabau society was matriarchal in most respects. Land ownership was passed from wife to daughter. As opposed to most societies, it was imperative for families to have daughters in order to ensure inheritance. When a couple married, the husband joined his wife's family and kampung. If he divorced her, he was expected to return to his own family. Women in Minangkabau villages could vote for tribal chiefs, and if their husband divorced them, they received custody of the children.

The majority of adat systems throughout the peninsula was patriarchal, but even in these, high status was still accorded to women. In the sixteenth, seventeenth, and eighteenth centuries, many of the archipelago immigrants to Malaya were Bugis, whose women had equal rights to property, participated in public affairs and government, and on occasion, were elected leaders of their communities and tribes. In Acheh, women traditionally enjoyed property rights equal to men, and in the seventeenth century, four consecutive rulers were women. This ended in 1699 in part because a legal recommendation from Mecca condemned rule by women as contrary to Islamic principles. Even in the twentieth century, Kelantan women have a large degree of control over family finances, run businesses, and enjoy employment outside the home.

These are only a few examples of rights and privileges enjoyed by Malay women that women in the West did not have until the twentieth century and which some societies do not have to this very day. Thus, by the time of the coming of Islam to the area in the fourteenth century, the communities of rural Malaya had well-developed systems of adat law. There were variations from place to place, and the characteristics varied by degree, depending on the migratory patterns of the people who settled there.

Islam

The conversion of the Peninsular Malays to Islam took place mainly in the fourteenth and fifteenth centuries and added another dimension to the nature of kampung life and Malay values. There are a number of reasons why the villages of Malaya embraced this foreign religion and forsook many of their animistic beliefs.

One reason was the Muslim belief in the community and equality of believers. Given the nature of kampung life and its sense of group-directed behavior, Islam was seen as a faith that bound the village even closer together, offering clearly delineated codes of behavior. It also emphasized the already existing desire for consensus and harmony.

As time went on, Islam not only provided greater unity for the village but also helped to create a sense of racial identity for all Malays, regardless of their origins or where they settled. This identity became even more important as foreigners, such as the Europeans, attempted to dominate the political lives of the Malays, and immigrant groups from outside the archipelago, such as the Chinese and Indians, came to settle and work in the peninsula and Borneo. In a period of a couple of centuries, the archipelago, from Acheh and Perlis to Sulu and the Celebes, had adopted this foreign religion, and this in itself reflected the cultural interaction that took place in the archipelago.

Another attraction was Islam's belief in predestination. For rural people, whose lives were controlled by the cycles and whims of nature and were already fatalistic, the idea of one God directing the daily fate of each member of society had great appeal. This was an aspect of the uncomplicated nature of Islam that was not evident in other religions and beliefs to which they had been exposed. The numerous gods in Hinduism, the stratified society it offered, and the endless cycle of rebirth, as well as the metaphysical aspects of Buddhism were not appealing. Islam was a religion that was relatively easy to understand. It fit their society.

The Islam that came to Malaya had already passed through India and Indonesia and thus was somewhat more accommodating and adaptable to the local culture than the Islam of the Middle East. It would seem that Islam would be in direct conflict with many traditional Malay beliefs, but the Malays found ways to accommodate the two. Islam weakened adat law but did not replace it. Islamic beliefs in punishment — for example, an eye for an eye and dismemberment for theft — were toned down and made to conform to village ways. Beliefs in polygamy, divorce on demand for males, and the separateness of women in the religion, such as the segregation of the two sexes in mosques, tended to give women a secondary role. In the archipelago, women had played too important a role in society to accept the subservient role that Islamic women had in Arabia. Therefore, for the most part, women were able to maintain property rights and take part in public affairs, albeit in diminished roles. After the coming of Islam, these women still had a much higher status than women in China or India.

Islam also placed new constraints on the behavior of the average Malay. New Islamic considerations, such as dietary laws, rules regarding dress and the relationship between the sexes, and prohibitions against gambling and usury, added to the expectations of what was considered proper or correct public behavior.

Contradictions, however, still remain. Prior to the coming of Islam, the Malays had a strong belief in the spirit world. Misfortune was caused by evil spirits or ghosts, and most communities had a medicine man, a *bomoh* or *shaman*, who could provide amulets or conduct ceremonies to protect villagers from disaster.

This belief persists to this very day. In the late 1970s, there was a newspaper story about how, because of a fear of rain, the organizers of the Malaysian Open golf tournament hired a bomoh to perform a ceremony to drive away the rain. A similar incident occurred when a school in Kuala Lumpur, attended by the children of foreign businessmen, called in a bomoh to exorcise the evil spirits on a newly built campus. This school had apparently been built on a former graveyard, and the local employees felt they needed help to ward off misfortune. These are enduring reminders that after Indianization, Islamization, colonialization, industrialization, and globalization, some aspects of the kampung still survive.

Chapter 2

INDIAN INFLUENCE AND EARLY EMPIRES

The influences that helped mold the value system of the Malays took place in what was basically a rural setting. This is important in understanding the Malays today, as rural life was a key element in their view of the world. Where they lived — the village — and what they did for a living — farming and fishing — were the entire universe for two-thirds of the Malay population until the last few decades. The Malay world around the time of Christ, that is before it absorbed much cultural influence from outside the area, was sparsely populated. People lived near rivers and river mouths. Some were fishermen; some were rice farmers. They lived in small villages, which were made up mainly of their relatives, and worshiped spirits under the leadership of their shamans.

However, one of the geographic influences mentioned in chapter 1 was Malaya's location and how the people who arrived there brought cultural and political contributions from outside the archipelago. Malaya was situated between two of the greatest civilizations of the time — China and India — but had little contact with them. This, however, changed in the first and second centuries A.D. The evolution of Malay society from small dispersed settlements into organized political states partially came about as a result of borrowing heavily from India. This process of Indianization was experienced by all the countries of Southeast Asia, except Vietnam and the Philippines.

In the first two centuries of the first millennium, a number of factors contributed to an Indian penetration of Southeast Asia. The first was a decline in trade involving China, India, and the Mediterranean. Rome was running a serious unfavorable balance of trade with India and China. Gold was exchanged for cotton, glass, and carpets from India, and silk and porcelain from China. In the first century A.D., in order to stem this drain of gold, Rome banned the export of gold coins. This brought about a need for new sources of gold and trade in order to make up for the decline in wealth caused by Rome's action. Secondly, as Rome weakened, and then fell apart, Persians and Arabs replaced the Indians as middlemen in the East-West trade.

China solved this problem through conquest in central Asia and Vietnam and through the use of overland trade routes. India looked east, searching for new trading partners. It had sailors who were willing to venture away from shore, while the Chinese had little inclination to trade by sea until much later. As trade and contacts between India and Southeast Asia increased, this stimulated demand for products from the area, such as spices and gold, as well as jungle produce, such as rattan, camphor, resins, and hardwood. This process accelerated over time as Buddhism and, later, Islam grew in popularity in India. These faiths offered their Hindu converts a means to circumvent the strict Hindu caste system that denied social mobility. Converts were free to seek new occupations and wealth.

Social and Political Changes

Over time, trade and cultural contacts between the Malay world and India had a profound impact on the people of the archipelago, especially on those who lived in or near important trading centers. Interaction with India brought about many social and political changes in the region.

Prior to the increase in trade between the archipelago and India, Malays lived in small, close-knit villages. Leadership consisted of village chieftains and medicine men. Their uncomplicated society did not require anything more. With trade came larger settlements at the river mouths — diverse populations that were no longer bound by family or clan. It also brought about a monetary economy and new forms of wealth. These economic and demographic changes demanded a more sophisticated form of government, which in turn led to social divisions.

The political leadership of Malay society understood the economic benefits of adopting Indian culture. Conversely, Indian merchants saw the advantages of marrying into the families of Malay leaders. The courts of the area also adopted the ceremonies and customs that set royalty apart from the common people. Indian royal models and Hinduism, which gave them religious and moral authority, transformed Malay chieftains into god-kings, reincarnated from Hindu gods with the divine right to rule.

The Indian merchants and Hindu priests who came with these leaders provided justification for this new aristocracy. Thus, not only did Malay leaders adopt Indian/Hindu models of government, they also introduced into Malay society significant social stratification within the royal towns and between the towns and kampungs. For example, the royal courts developed a language and vocabulary different from that spoken by the common people. Royalty "expired," but commoners "died," and royalty were "carried," while commoners "went" places.

While Indian/Hindu models had much appeal to the ruling classes, the religion had little success in the outlying areas. As time went on, people accepted the concept of royalty and some need for government, but within their own villages, their social institutions underwent little change. The communal and cooperative nature of kampung life did not require a formal and foreign government structure.

Language and Literature

India also had a dramatic influence on the Malay language. As new political and economic institutions developed, the language of fishermen and farmers proved to be inadequate. With the process of Indianization came a written language and a dramatic increase in the Malay vocabulary.

Prior to the industrial and technological revolutions, over half the words in the Malay language had their roots in Sanskrit, the language brought by Indian traders, priests, and entrepreneurs. The Malays did not have a written language until modern government and international trade made it necessary.

Sanskrit formed the basis of written Malay and provided the vocabulary needed for dialogue, positions in government, products, and laws. Richard Winstedt claims Malay had no vocabulary for abstract thought until the time of Indianization. Even when Islam came to the area and became the predominant religion, much of the religious vocabulary had Indian roots. This was because Islam came by way of India. Similar adaptations of vocabulary took place centuries later when the Malays needed words for European technology, products, and political systems. There are some who claim that there are few indigenous words in the Malay language, most of them having been borrowed from other languages as a result of Malaya's position in world trade.

Traditional Malay and Indonesian literatures are heavily laced with stories that have their origins in Hindu epics, such as the *Ramayana* and *Mahabharata*. The *wayang kulit*, or shadow play, is Malaysia's greatest theatrical tradition. The puppets perform as shadows cast by a lamp on a cotton sheet. The good and the noble, the kings and gods vie with demons, giants, witches, and villains in elaborate epics from the pre-Islamic roots of Malay culture.

Another example of Indian influence on Malay legends can be found in one of the Malay accounts of the history of Kedah, a Malay kingdom. The forerunner of Kedah was an Indianized Malay state on the Isthmus of Kra called Lankasuka. This state, according to the *Kedah Annals*, was founded by a tribe of tusked giants known as the *raksasa* — a cannibalistic tribe lifted from Indian mythology and ruled by one of the lesser Hindu gods. Over time, Lankasuka became Kedah, and the tribe of raksasa evolved into normal human beings. However, it was said that the people of Kedah were not able to eliminate their cannibal genes. The annals describe a later king whose cook cut herself and bled into his soup. The king enjoyed the soup so much that he insisted on knowing the new ingredient. Discovering it was the cook's blood, he demanded that all his meals contain human blood. Before long, he began to grow tusks and soon developed into a full-blown cannibal. The people of Kedah forced him to flee into the jungle where his ancestors had lived.

With the introduction of Arabic script and Islam, many of these stories were rearranged and given an Islamic twist. For instance, prophets were substituted for Hindu gods. The stories, however, are still readily recognizable as having their origins in Indian folklore. Yet another example of Indian influence on the history, literature, and mythology of the Malays is found in the story of Malay royalty. The story traces the lineage of all the kings of the Malay world to three Indian princes, who in turn were the heirs of Alexander the Great, a man seen by some as the greatest ruler of all time. Future Malay rulers, such as Parameswara and the sultans of the Malay kingdoms, would claim their royal legitimacy based on the following Muslim adaptation of an Indian story in the *Malay Annals*:

The city of Palembang in the land of Andelas [Sumatra today] was ruled by Demang Lebar Daun, a descendant of Raja Shulan. In the upper reaches of the Muar Tatang [river] was a river called the Melayu, and on the river was a hill called Si-Guntang Mahameru. In that region lived two widows, Wan Empok and Wan Malini, and the two of them had planted padi on Bukit Si-Guntang. It happened that one night they beheld from their house a glow as of fire on Bukit Si-Guntang. When day dawned, the two of them saw that their padi had golden grain, leaves of silver and stems of gold alloy. And as they walked along the hill they saw that the crest had turned into gold. According to tradition it has a color as of gold to this day. They beheld three youths of great beauty. All three of them were adorned like kings and wore crowns studded with precious stones, and they rode upon white elephants. And they asked the three youths, "Whence come you, sirs? Are you sons of genies or sons of fairies?" And the three youths made answer, "We are descended from Raja Iskandar Dzu'l-Karnain: of the lineage of Raja Nushirwan, Lord of the East and the West, are we. Our line springs from Raja Sulaiman." They then told of the marriage of Raja Iskandar to Raja Kida Hindi's daughter and of the descent of Raja Chulan into the sea. "These crowns that we wear are the sign that we are of the stock of Raja Iskandar and the proof is that because we alighted on this spot your padi has grain of gold." Demang Lebar Daun took the princes back with him to Palembang. Every ruler from every part of the country came to pay his respects to them. The eldest of the princes was taken by the people of Andelas to their country and was made raja at Minangkabau. The people of Tanjong Pura took the second to Tanjong Pura, where they made him raja. The youngest remained at Palembang as raja.

Much of the above story is lifted from Indian folklore, such as the undersea kingdom of Raja Chulan, but one probably wonders why Islamic Malays would trace their royal lineage to a Greek who lived in pre-Islamic times. The Raja Iskandar mentioned above is the Malay name for Alexander the Great. In actual fact, Alexander had taken on a significant role in Islamic history and legend as Islam worked its way east into Southeast Asia. His position was probably first put forward by Muslim Persians as a justification for their country's fall to the Greeks. They proclaimed

Alexander the first of the great kings sent by God to rule the earth, and therefore his conquests were considered divine intervention. Revisionist Persian historians made Alexander a follower of the one true God who met and was converted by the Prophet Khidir (some historians say Khidir was the prophet Elijah). Alexander's conquests in the Muslim world were justifiable because he was part of Muslim tradition. Thus, there are Muslim royal families in Malaysia who trace their heritage to the Greek, Alexander the Great!

Pattern of Indianization

The same Indian influences that were felt in the Malay world affected all of Southeast Asia, except for Vietnam and the Philippines. Indian political models, language, and religion became cornerstones on which pre-modern, pre-colonial society was built. Indian Buddhism sunk deep roots in mainland Southeast Asia and is the major religion in the area to this day. In archipelago Southeast Asia, any history is incomplete without studying the influences of India on the Malay Mediterranean.

It was the trade between India and China that brought the attention of the outside world to the archipelago. Originally, trade came from the Bay of Bengal to an area in the northern part of the peninsula near what is Kedah today. Goods were then transported overland to the eastern coast of the peninsula or vice versa and then sent on their way. Thus, originally, whoever controlled the Isthmus of Kra and the Gulf of Siam controlled the India-China trade. Because of this trade, the first significant Indianized states emerged in this area.

Funan

Sometime during the first century, the first significant Indianized state appeared around the area of the Mekong Delta in Vietnam today. According to legend, the state was created by an Indian prince whose personal genie appeared before him in a dream, presented him with a divine bow, and instructed him to embark on a sea voyage. The next day he found a bow at his temple and set out. The genie led him to what later became Funan. The natives, led by Queen Willowleaf, were not friendly and attacked his ship, but the prince fired arrows through the hull of the queen's boat. Duly impressed, she surrendered and agreed to marry the prince. This is how the royal line of the kingdom was supposed to have begun. In the Indian version of the founding of Funan, the natives did not wear clothes until the Indians introduced them to the concept, thus symbolizing the coming of civilization.

Funan was an example of the coming of Indian influence through trade. The royal court took on Indian political traditions and ceremonies and practiced a form of Hinduism in the worship of the god Shiva. The state's economic power and prestige were based on being the dominant force in the Malay Peninsula, which allowed it to control the portage trade across the Isthmus of Kra. Funan developed contacts with both China and India and thus became the prototype of the Southeast Asian middleman in the trade between the two great powers. Funan played this role until the sixth century when it was unable to stand up to the southern thrust of the Khmers (Cambodians) and was replaced by a kingdom known as Chenla. After the fall of Funan, no mainland power controlled trade as Funan had, and although the succeeding empires of Angkor and then Siam had impressive civilizations, they were founded on land-based power and agriculture, not trade.

The importance of the portage trade across the isthmus was further evidenced by the fact that the first known Malay states appeared in this area. Although records are sketchy, around the time of Funan there existed two Indianized states in what is Malaysia today — Lankasuka in the northeast and Kedah in the northwest. There are accounts by Chinese and Indian travelers of these two royal courts, which had adopted Indian royal systems. Their importance lay in the role they played in the East-West trade and their probably being vassal states of Funan. With the weakening of Funan, Kedah was absorbed into Sri Vijaya, a Malay maritime empire, and Lankasuka declined as a trading power

Champa

Another Indianized state that appeared in the area was Champa. It probably appeared as a state sometime late in the third century and lasted until the fifteenth century. It never achieved the power of Funan or Angkor, but it is of interest as part of the Malay racial and cultural world. Much of what is emphasized in Malay history took place in the western part of the archipelago around the Straits of Melaka and the Java Sea. There was, however, Malay interaction in the east, which is sometimes overlooked. Champa was a part of that.

The Chams were a people of Malayo-Polynesian stock who lived in the coastal area of what is southern Vietnam today. They were part of the movement of people, trade, and culture that took place among them, the eastern coast of Malaya, and the northern coast of Borneo. Originally, Champa was a Hindu state that made its living from trade and piracy. Later, around the same time as the rest of the people in the peninsula, its people converted to Islam. Women held high status in this community — they chose their husbands and inherited property. The Chams spoke a language close to the dialect of Malay spoken in Kelantan today.

Fierce enemies of the sinicized Vietnamese, the Chams managed to hold out against them until the late fifteenth century when they were finally conquered. At the end of that war, the Vietnamese killed about sixty thousand Chams and took another thirty thousand prisoners and slaves. From then on, the Chams slowly disappeared, some to other parts of the Malay cultural area, some to what is Cambodia today. The rest went into the interior of Vietnam. Except for a few isolated villages in Vietnam, there is little evidence today that Champa as a state actually existed.

Sri Vijaya

After the fall of Funan, forces at work in the sixth and seventh centuries transferred the center of Southeast Asian trade away from the northern peninsula and the isthmus to the Melaka and Sunda Straits. This was more than a geographical shift because it gave the maritime Malays an important role in the East-West trade for the next one thousand years. One reason for this shift was the growing popularity of sea routes over the overland portage system. Improvements in shipbuilding and navigation contributed to this. By the seventh century, for example, Persian ships were sailing all the way to China. The overland routes were time consuming and labor intensive, and sail power could deliver the traders much closer to the actual sources of the straits produce. There were still middlemen but not many of them.

Another factor was the tremendous increase in the volume of trade as a result of developments in the Middle East. With the establishment of the Islamic Empire in the seventh and eighth centuries, stability and

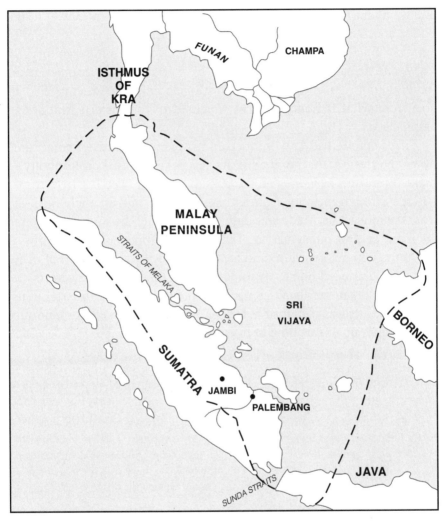

The Sri Vijaya Empire.

prosperity were brought to that area. The Arabs and Persians expanded their trade in the Middle East beyond India to China via Southeast Asia. Demand for straits products, such as spices and rain forest produce, increased dramatically.

Sometime around the seventh century, the empire of Sri Vijaya stepped in to take advantage of this change in trade patterns. Sri Vijaya probably arose out of the kingdom of Palembang in the southeastern part of Sumatra, and for about four or five centuries, it was the preeminent power in the Sunda and Melaka Straits. Its rise was paralleled by the rise of powerful agrarian kingdoms in central Java. Sometime in the ninth century, Sri Vijaya and the Javanese states appear to have been brought together under the mysterious Sailendra dynasty, creating an empire that controlled an area from what is now southern Thailand to the eastern Indonesian archipelago.

This empire had few products of its own to sell except what came down the rivers from the jungles. Its success was based on its ability to make huge sums of money off the passing trade. It offered relatively safe passage through the straits, ship repair facilities, and an anchorage safe from the monsoons. Trade was only "relatively safe" because the empire's ability to control piracy varied. The political support of coastal princes and ports was not constant, and Sri Vijaya's navy was made up of many men who had been pirates at some point in their maritime careers. Sri Vijaya's hold on the loyalties of these buccaneers was thus tenuous. Nonetheless, it was responsible for the area's most important emporium and entrepôt up to this time in history.

ONE MAN'S PIRATE IS ANOTHER MAN'S TAX COLLECTOR

The question of what constitutes piracy has long been a matter of interpretation by political leaders, merchants, and historians. *Webster's Third International Dictionary* defines it as "robbery on the high seas." Historically, on many occasions, there was a difference of opinion between those who were boarded and had their cargoes seized and those who did the boarding as to whether the act was piracy.

Astride one of the great arteries of world trade, there was bound to be conflict between the people of archipelago Southeast Asia who wanted to benefit from their geographical position and those from outside who plied this highway of trade. Prior to the colonial era, the kingdoms and empires of the area were alliances rather than political entities in the modern sense. In an era of loose and shifting loyalties, one man's tax collector was another man's pirate. Attacks on trade were seen as legitimate means of bringing revenue to the ports that controlled the shipping lanes. Those who tried to avoid their authority were fair game.

As competing factions fought for political control of the shipping lanes, one man's pirate was another man's naval officer. A European comparison would be the English "Sea Dogs" in the Elizabethan era. Were they pirates or part of the Spanish-English battle over trade and naval supremacy? The Spanish saw Francis Drake as a pirate, while he was a naval hero to the English. Elizabeth I invested in his voyages. The Spanish protested loudly when she knighted this "pirate."

As the Europeans moved in to control trade in the archipelago, a case could be made that one man's pirate was another man's freedom fighter. It was natural that the people of the area would fight to hold on to what had been theirs for centuries. Attacks on shipping in this case represented protests against foreigners who were displacing their legitimate position in their home waters. Thus, the term pirate should be taken for what it is, an ambiguous term that depends on whose eyes are viewing it.

Sri Vijaya was an Indianized state with its capital originally at Palembang and later at Jambi (Melayu). Its court ceremonies and legal system had Indian influence, and most of the ruling class had accepted Mahayana Buddhism from Indian missionaries and traders. In fact, some visiting Chinese pilgrims and scholars commented on the high standard of Buddhist learning and practice in the kingdom. The level of trade and learning is further evidenced by some historians who say that the first physical use of zeros came from Sri Vijayan inscriptions.

From the eleventh to the thirteenth centuries, the power and prestige of Sri Vijaya declined. Chola, a Tamil Empire in southern India, was a prime competitor for control of the East-West trade and in the eleventh century conducted a series of devastating raids along the coast of Sumatra and in the Malay Peninsula, from which Sri Vijaya never fully recovered. Second, given the basis of its power, Sri Vijaya would live and die with the volume of trade. Thus, in the thirteenth century, when China reduced its trade, Sri Vijaya suffered. Seafarers switched allegiance and revenue fell. Majapahit, a kingdom from eastern Java with a more diversified economy — it had significant agriculture — incorporated Sumatra into its empire.

Sri Vijaya is an important part of Malay history. This is evidenced by the story of the origins of Malay royalty earlier in this chapter. The ties across the Straits of Melaka go deep in terms of people — immigrants

41

have crossed over from Sumatra throughout Malay/Malaysian history; culture — the origins of much of adat law come from Sumatra, as did Islam later in history; and language — the modern Malay language probably has its roots in Sri Vijaya. It was the language of commerce adopted by most of the coastal ports in the straits. Sri Vijaya is also seen by many Malays as the forerunner of the Melaka Sultanate.

Melaka Empire

Sri Vijaya was taken over by a Javanese kingdom — Majapahit — sometime in the fourteenth century. This was resented by many in the old royal families, and it is unlikely there was much loyalty to the empire from Malays and their maritime allies, especially those from southeastern Sumatra and the islands south of Singapore — the Riau and Lingga Archipelagos.

In the latter part of the fourteenth century, a member of the Palembang royal family, Parameswara, assumed the leadership of those who opposed Javanese rule and declared himself the ruler of the Malays. In great pomp, this prince, whose name is one of the many names of Shiva, drew on the stature and tradition of Indianized court life and assumed the Lion Throne of the Malays. The Majapahit rulers, however, drove him out of Sumatra. He became a king in search of a kingdom.

Initially, he fled to Bentan in Riau where the queen apparently recognized his status and rolled out the red carpet. Riau was a fertile recruiting ground for Parameswara. The people who lived there had been an important part of Sri Vijaya's navy and had little loyalty or affection for the Javanese overlords. Because of its location at the mouth of the Melaka Straits, Riau was an ideal naval lair — it was a good place to prey on shipping and trade. For a while at least, it appears that Parameswara also made his living from piracy. Sometime in the 1390s, Parameswara and his followers from Sumatra and Riau set up a base on the island of Temasek (Singapore), where they staged a coup d'etat and murdered the ruler.

One explanation of how Temasek was renamed Singapore comes from a legend. As the Palembang Malays were exploring the island, they came across a great beast resembling the *singa*, or "a three-colored lion," from Hindu mythology. Together with another word *pura*, which means "city," the name Singapura came into being. A more likely story is that court historians in the *Malay Annals* changed the name to glorify Malay royalty. The historians did not want the founder of the Melaka Sultanate and the holder of the Lion Throne to rule a place with a name as mundane as Temasek (literally "sea town").

After becoming "king" of Singapore, Parameswara used it as a base to prey on trade entering the Straits of Melaka, a role that the island continued to play for centuries. Depending on which account one believes, either the Siamese or the Javanese, both of whom continued to be his enemies, did not take kindly to the killing of their vassal ruler on Temasek or to Parameswara's subsequent activities. They mounted an attack on the island to force Parameswara and his followers to flee.

The *Malay Annals* describe Parameswara's move north along the western coast of the peninsula in search of a new site for the capital of his Malay Empire. He chose Melaka because of what he saw as a sign that it would be a suitable place. As he was hunting with his hounds one day, they came across a *pelandok* (a mouse deer the size of a big cat). The deer, instead of fleeing from the dogs, turned and fought. According to the annals, Parameswara decided that this place would be his capital as even the mouse deer were fierce. The town was named after a tree that grows there.

Going beyond the legend, once Parameswara found a suitable place to establish his kingdom, he was able to lay down the foundations for an emporium and entrepôt that was equal to if not greater than that of Sri Vijaya in power and wealth. For a period of about a century, from the turn of the fifteenth century until 1511, Melaka played an important role in the trade among Europe, the Middle East, India, China, and the archipelago.

PERANAKAN CHINESE

The Chinese who settled in Melaka in the fifteenth century were the forefathers of a distinctly Malayan Chinese community, the Peranakans. This minority within the Chinese community has deeper roots in Malaya than the vast majority of Chinese who arrived there in the nineteenth and twentieth centuries. Unlike the later group of immigrants, the first wave of Chinese did not live apart from the indigenous community. As a result, they incorporated a Malay dimension into their culture.

Chinese males who married local women because of the absence of Chinese women started the first generations of Peranakans. The female children from these unions were not allowed to marry Malays, and this created a pool of wives for Chinese men. By the middle of the eighteenth century, Dutch census figures showed some two thousand living in Melaka.

While racially Chinese, this group adopted much from the Malay community, such as the following: Malay language — a unique Peranakan patois developed, which was a mixture of Hokkien and Malay, after their small group was forced to communicate with the larger Malay community; food — there is an identifiable Peranakan cuisine, which borrowed much from Malay food, such as the use of spices, curries, and coconut milk; dress — Peranakan women adopted the sarong as their main dress and wore blouses that retained some Chinese influence; and power — women in the Peranakan community enjoyed greater power and freedom than they did in China, especially in economic matters.

Some of the Chinese culture they retained was itself modified from that of China. Chinese religion became a Peranakan religion. Great emphasis was placed on the ceremonies connected with funerals, festivals, and ancestor worship. This may have come about because in Malaya they were prosperous and could afford such ceremonies.

With the arrival of the British, the Peranakans were absorbed into a larger Straits Chinese community, and shared this description with the Chinese who settled in the area in the nineteenth century. The Babas, as male Peranakans are called, had long-standing commercial contacts in the area and spoke the language, becoming valuable middlemen for British interests. Many Peranakans were English-educated, along with the other Straits Chinese, which further solidified their position in the colonial economic structure. Through all these changes, much of their culture was preserved and a people created who had their feet in three worlds — China, Malaya, and the West. True products of the crossroads.

A lot of what historians know about Melaka is drawn from the accounts of Chinese, Indian, and Portuguese observers in the fifteenth and sixteenth centuries. Another source of Melaka's history is the *Malay Annals*, one of the first historical accounts of the area written by the Malays in their language. As a reliable history, it is sadly lacking, but it is a rich source of Malay tradition, culture, and legend. There are tales of great rulers, such as Parameswara and Mansur Shah, who perform heroic deeds and have at their sides invincible warriors. All these men flourished during Melaka's glory days.

These accounts of Malay success and prestige were written in the early seventeenth century, that is, after the fall of Melaka to the Portuguese. They were primarily an attempt to glorify the Johor royal family, who were the descendants of the Melaka royal family. By that time, these descendants were fighting for survival against the Achehnese and Portuguese from makeshift capitals along the Johor River. Court scribes wrote the *Malay Annals* to tie these desperate leaders to a time of greatness, to reinforce the *daulat,* or divine right, that they carried and to prove that they were the true heirs to the glory of Melaka, the coming of Islam, and the rightful leaders of the Malay people.

Growth of Melaka

The success of this unlikely group of empire builders was partially due to Melaka's geographical position. Situated in the Straits of Melaka, it was where the monsoons met. Ships sailed to China with the southwest monsoon and returned with the northeast winds. The port itself was at the narrowest point of the straits and had a well-sheltered anchorage. It was hard to pass the port without dealing with the officials there, so it made sense to stop. Yet another geographic reason was its proximity to the products of the archipelago, especially tin, spices, hardwood, camphor, rattan, beeswax, and forest resins.

Geography alone could not account for its success. There were other ports with similar advantages. Perhaps it took an old political refugee to understand the needs of traders and shippers. Parameswara, together with his heirs, came up with an answer that is one of the keys to Singapore's success today — an infrastructure conducive to trade. A bureaucracy was set up with the needs of visitors in mind. Port fees were kept low and consistent, and each of the major trading groups had a *shahbandar,* or port official, of their race who spoke their language and was responsible for their well-being. For example, a Chinese official looked after Chinese interests and collected fees from them.

An effective navy under the leadership of a *laksamana,* or admiral, ensured safety on the sea lanes and kept them relatively free of piracy. A police force led by the *temenggung,* or Malay chief of police, maintained law and order in the city. All these officials were in turn responsible to the *bendahara,* or chief minister, whose job was to make sure that the government responded to the needs of commerce. Over the years, it was the bendahara and his ability to make the system work that ultimately determined the economic health of the sultanate.

As the port grew, it attracted men of stature and ability, improving the quality of the services it offered. Melaka eventually became the main center of trade in the area. Any product imaginable was available there, and the facilities for ship repair, building, and provisioning made trading elsewhere unnecessary.

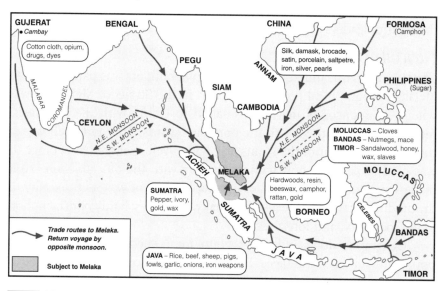

Melaka's trade in the fifteenth century.

Key elements of Melaka's success were the alliances it formed with others. Parameswara was fortunate in his timing as the creation of Melaka coincided with one of China's periods of interest in the outside world. For the first thirty years of its history, Melaka successfully courted the recognition and protection of China against the understandably hostile Siamese and Javanese, who coveted the trade of Melaka. Chinese fleets, such as those led by the eunuch Cheng Ho, regularly called at the port and helped eliminate piracy, including the base, ironically enough, at Palembang. Parameswara and his two successors visited China to pay tribute to the emperor. It is said that Parameswara married a daughter of the Chinese emperor. He did return with a Chinese wife, but it is doubtful that the emperor would have permitted a union with his daughter.

The Chinese community in Malaysia can trace its roots back to this time when some Chinese came and settled, although it was only in the nineteenth century that they came in large numbers. In the heart of Melaka today, there exists the oldest Chinese cemetery outside China — Bukit China — with graves dating back to the time of early Melaka.

The Coming of Islam

Melaka also courted the friendship of the Muslim rulers and traders of India, the Middle East, and the archipelago. In fact, in the 1430s, when it became apparent that China was going to turn inward again, Parameswara's grandson, Muhammad Shah, made a sudden conversion to Islam. This was the result of a dream in which an angel appeared before him. When he woke up, he could quote the holy Koran word for word. The miracle probably took place in China, where he was stranded for a year in the mid-1430s because the emperor had ended the sailings of Chinese fleets. Muhammad Shah realized his political survival depended on new alliances.

Ordinary Malays converted to Islam because it provided unity and a sense of identity, but the leaders in the business community initially converted for political and economic reasons as well. Within Melaka, a large number of people involved in business were already Muslims, each with his own shahbandar. The trade that stretched from the Mediterranean to the Spice Islands (the Moluccas) was controlled by Muslim Arabs, Muslim Persians, and Muslim Indians. The economic livelihood of the community depended on close relations with these people.

The coastal areas of the archipelago underwent a period of rapid conversion to Islam. Across the straits in Sumatra, states such as Acheh and Pasai had already embraced Islam. The Javanese, who controlled much of the spice trade as well as being an important source of food for Melaka, also forsook their Hindu and Buddhist traditions. It has been said that "Java was converted in Melaka." Kedah in the peninsula, which guarded the mouth of the straits and was another source of food for Melaka, was Islamic.

HANG TUAH AND HANG JEBAT

During the fifteenth century reign of Mansur Shah, great warriors were given the title Hang. The greatest of these warriors was Laksamana Hang Tuah, and his exploits in battle were famous throughout the Malay world. People believed it was impossible to defeat him because of his bravery and magic *kris,* or a curved dagger. Because of his good looks, the *Malay Annals* describes women running to embrace him as he walked down the street.

Hang Tuah's popularity and fame upset the sultan. It seemed that the public put him on a higher pedestal than the sultan. When rumors spread that Hang Tuah was visiting the sultan's harem, the sultan used this as a pretext to accuse Hang Tuah of treason. He then ordered the bendahara to execute Hang Tuah and insisted he bring back Hang Tuah's heart as proof. Hang Tuah could have fought back, but he submitted to his sultan in deference to his daulat. He gave his magic kris to his best friend and fellow warrior, Hang Jebat.

The bendahara, realizing the potential loss of this great man to Melaka, took Hang Tuah into the jungle and told him to lie low. The bendahara then returned with the heart of an animal to placate the sultan, biding his time until he could reinstate Hang Tuah.

Meanwhile, Hang Jebat rose up in rebellion at the injustice done to his best friend. Armed with Hang Tuah's kris, he ran amok in the palace, causing death and destruction. No one dared fight Hang Jebat because of his state of mind and the magic kris.

The sultan lamented his stupidity in executing Hang Tuah. The bendahara asked, "If Hang Tuah were alive, would you pardon him?" The sultan said "Yes." The real story behind the cover-up then unfolded. Hang Tuah was restored to his position and sent to subdue Hang Jebat. An epic battle ensued. The opponents were equal because Hang Jebat had the magic kris and Hang Tuah had been weakened by his time in exile. Hang Tuah was exhausted and prevailed upon his friend that they drive their daggers into a wooden wall and take a breather. Hang Jebat agreed, and when he put his weapon up, Hang Tuah grabbed it and killed his friend.

The story of Hang Tuah is found in many other Malay accounts of this time, with some variations but with a central theme. Hang Tuah was loyal to his sultan to the point of accepting execution and then returning to kill his friend. In court histories, Hang Tuah is the hero of the story because he recognizes the sultan as God's representative on earth, someone who commanded complete loyalty. Other versions see Hang Jebat as the hero of the story because he rose up against the injustice and vanity of a bad ruler.

Thus, by the middle of the fifteenth century, relations among all these groups improved through the shared faith of Islam. This conversion of the Malay people to Islam also strengthened the bond between ruler and subjects. Not only did they share a common religion, but that religion was used as a basis to uphold the legitimacy of the Malay royal class. Introduced into the Malay political tradition was the concept of daulat. Allah had placed these families on the throne, and thus they received his divine sanction to rule.

Melaka probably achieved the height of its power and influence during the rule of Mansur Shah (1459–1477). It is questionable how much he was responsible for Melaka's achievements because much of the credit for turning Melaka from an important port into an empire should be given to a bendahara by the name of Tun Perak, who held the office from 1456 to 1498. It is during this period that Melaka became an aggressive political and military power. Under his leadership, Melaka's forces successfully held off the Siamese and were able to bring about peace from a position of strength. Melaka's armies and navies conquered most of the Malay Peninsula, large areas of Sumatra, and the islands south of Singapore. This was also the time Hang Tuah was said to have accomplished great feats as laksamana.

Parameswara's dream of a new Sri Vijaya came true. It was, however, not just a trading empire — it became a conduit of culture as well. The ruling class may have had ulterior motives for its original conversion to Islam, but under Mansur Shah and Tun Perak, Melaka became a center for Islamic literature and theology. Melaka played a key role in the spread of Islam through its support of missionary work in other parts of the archipelago. Melaka also contributed to expanding Malay as the common language of trade, which had its beginnings in Sri Vijaya. New vocabulary was introduced from the Middle East. Malay scholarship was encouraged, and the language increasingly became the lingua franca of both sides of the straits and of the archipelago.

As long as Melaka had such strong leaders as Tun Perak, the system worked. Without them, there were inherent flaws that eventually brought about the fall of the sultanate in the early sixteenth century. By drawing foreigners to its capital, Melaka amassed great wealth but also encountered a few major problems. One was that many of the people who prospered were outsiders, and when Melaka was threatened by the Portuguese, they left and did business elsewhere. In addition, few among those in the indigenous population benefited from the power and prosperity. They too had little inclination to fight when challenged by foreigners in the sixteenth century.

Melaka produced little of its own, especially food. It was dependent on the sale of services to buy rice from others, such as the Javanese. If trade was interrupted, it spelt doom for them. This is exactly what happened.

Lastly, the bureaucracy and port facilities offered by Melaka depended on good government, and after the death of Tun Perak, corruption and incompetence set in. When the Portuguese arrived in the early sixteenth century, Melaka was in decline. Foreigners who prospered from Melaka's success had little loyalty to the sultanate; continuous court intrigue sapped the vitality of the government; and government officials lined their own pockets and cared little for the success of the state. Contrary to the story cited in the *Malay Annals* in the next chapter, Melaka became easy pickings for an aggressive power — the Portuguese.

Melaka holds a special place in the history of the Malays in the peninsula. In many ways, it is the historical origin of the Malay kingdom. With the *Malay Annals*, it represents the legacy of Malay written history. The Melaka sultans represent the origins of their lineage and, in turn, of their kingdoms. The coming of Islam and the subsequent racial and cultural unity it has since provided for the Malays are closely associated with Melaka. And finally, the Melaka Sultanate is seen as a time of great Malay civilization. It was a time in history that the peninsular Malays can look back on with great pride, perhaps a Malay Camelot.

Chapter 3

EUROPEANS IN
THE ARCHIPELAGO

"THE FALL OF MELAKA"*

Here now is a story of Fongso d'Albuquerque. At the end of his term of office as viceroy, he proceeded to Pertugal (Portugal) and presenting himself before the Raja of Pertugal asked for an armada. And when he reached Melaka, there was great excitement and word was brought to Sultan Ahmad, "The Franks are come to attack us! They have seven carracks, eight galleasses, ten long galleys, fifteen sloops and five foysts." Thereupon Sultan Ahmad had all his forces assembled and he ordered them to make ready their equipment. And the Franks engaged the men of Melaka in battle, and they fired their cannon from their ships so that the cannon balls came like rain. And the noise of the cannon was as the noise of thunder in the heavens and the flashes of fire of their guns were like flashes of lightning in the sky; and the noise of their matchlocks was like that of groundnuts popping in the frying-pan. So heavy was the gunfire that the men of Melaka could no longer maintain their position on the shore. The Franks then bore down upon the bridge with their galleys and foysts. Thereupon Sultan Ahmad came forth, mounted on his elephant Jituji.

When day dawned, the Franks landed and attacked. And Sultan Ahmad mounted his elephant Juru Demang, Tun Ali Hati balancing the king on the packsaddle. The Franks then fiercely engaged the men of Melaka in battle and so vehement was their onslaught that the Melaka line was broken, leaving the king on his elephant isolated. And the king fought with the Franks pike to pike, and he was wounded in the palm of the hand. And he showed the palm of his hand, saying, "See this, Malays!" And when they saw that

---

*As described in the Malay Annals.

51

Sultan Ahmad was wounded in the hand, the war chiefs returned to the attack and fought the Franks.

And Tun Salehuddin called upon the Orang Kaya (nobles) to fight with the Franks pike to pike. And Tun Salehuddin was struck in the chest and killed, and twenty of the leading war chiefs were killed. And Melaka fell.

In the sixteenth century, the archipelago faced a new challenge that was vastly different from its previous contacts with civilizations beyond the Malay world — Europe. India had come to the region to trade and had brought the culture as well as the tools Southeast Asians would need to be partners in a new economic world. The Indians, however, did not make any serious attempts to translate trade into political dominance of the area.

The archipelago's experience with China was even less dramatic. With periods of contraction and expansion of trade, it was not significantly affected, either politically or culturally. For example, between 1403 and 1430, the Chinese sent seven maritime expeditions into Southeast Asia. Each carried 27,000 men, but there was no attempt at conquest nor any attempt at influencing the culture of the area. Nor was Chinese culture easily exportable. Its philosophy/religion was deeply embedded in race and tradition. The mixture of Taoism, Confucianism, Buddhism, and ancestor veneration was hard to graft onto another culture without a revolutionary change in the social system. The Chinese felt that China was the center of the world, and other races would fail if they tried to duplicate their sophisticated culture.

The Europeans, on the other hand, did not just want to trade with Southeast Asia — they wanted to physically control that trade, and later, the people and their lands. Over a period of about three centuries, the people of the Malay world felt the impact of Western science and religion. Their social structures were shaken, and their economies were revolutionized.

There were three main stages of European expansion of power and influence in the area. In the sixteenth and seventeenth centuries, Europeans gained a few footholds on the coastal areas and islands in the strategic sea lanes. These were basically fortified trading posts. In the eighteenth century, the Dutch and Spaniards expanded their bases to control the hinterlands beyond the centers. In this second stage, there was still significant participation by local rulers and traders. By the end of the nineteenth century, virtually all Southeast Asia, except Thailand, was divided among European powers. When this happened, the role of the people from the archipelago in trade virtually ceased, except in coastal shipping and in the provision of labor to produce or extract what the Europeans wanted from the area.

Many forces at work in Europe shaped the motivation for and the nature of European expansion. In the sixteenth and seventeenth centuries, there was the rise of the nation state in Europe. Portugal, Spain, England, the Netherlands, and France were solving domestic problems and creating stronger central governments, governments that would martial greater economic and military power to achieve national goals outside their countries. This strong nationalism also meant there would be political and economic rivalries that would manifest themselves in the dominant European economic system of the time — mercantilism. The system was based on the premise that nation states were in competition for their share of the world's wealth. So, each nation needed to restrict trade to its country and colonies. This idea of "my gain is your loss" and vice versa was bound to lead to conflict.

Another economic force that contributed to Europe's outward expansion was the commercial revolution that took place around that time. New products created the need for new markets and new sources of wealth. Tea, spices, silk, cotton, tobacco, and coffee became increasingly in demand, and fortunes could be made in supplying these goods. This created wealth and capital beyond the traditional sources of land and its returns. At the same time, new forms of business organizations, such as the joint stock company, offered avenues for men in commerce to pool their wealth to embark on large business ventures. Access to these new products were controlled by a pipeline of Indian, Middle Eastern, and eastern Mediterranean merchants. If the European nations could circumvent these middlemen, there were unlimited opportunities for their businessmen and monarchs.

As a result of these forces, the first two European countries that came to Southeast Asia were the Spaniards and the Portuguese. They were followed by the Dutch and the English in the later part of the sixteenth century. As a result of the Treaty of Tordesillas, which was brokered by the Catholic Church, Spain and Portugal had literally split the world in half. Spanish voyages of exploration and conquest sailed west from Europe across the Atlantic, while the Portuguese moved east around the Cape of Good Hope.

For Gold, Glory, and God

It is remarkable that Portugal, a relatively small country of a little over a million people (most of whom were farmers and fishermen), had such an impact on the world in general and Asia in particular in the sixteenth and seventeenth centuries.

Portugal's goal was to circumvent and end Muslim control of the trade between Asia and Europe by moving it away from the Mediterranean to a route around the Cape of Good Hope. If it could monopolize the trade in spices from the archipelago and luxury goods from China and India, there would be great economic benefits to the crown and state.

Their motivation was also religious and aimed at those who controlled the trade — the Muslims. The Portuguese were tough, nationalistic, and used to adversity. Their battle for survival as a state had been against the Muslims, and the last of the Islamic invaders had only been expelled from the Iberian Peninsula in 1492. These battles, coupled with memories of the crusades, fueled their desire to punish the Muslims and convert the people of the East to Christianity.

The Portuguese possessed the means as well as the motivation to embark on this endeavor. In their voyages to trade with the East, the Portuguese took advantage of and made dramatic new strides in naval technology. As a result of new shipbuilding methods and sail design, the Portuguese could sail closer to the wind and generate more speed and maneuverability than their Eastern competitors. New navigational techniques freed their dependence on the prevailing winds. New advances in naval gunnery provided deck-mounted cannons that had a much longer range and better accuracy than those of the Indians and Malays. Their naval technology and the sailors' fervor to conquer and convert Muslims made them formidable opponents who required less manpower and fewer ships than the Eastern powers to accomplish their goals.

Much of this advancement in maritime prowess can be attributed to the vision of Prince Henry, the Navigator. Through his efforts, Bartolomeu Dias rounded the Cape of Good Hope in 1488, and Vasco da Gama reached India in 1498. These voyages paved the way for the development of the Portuguese trading empire in the sixteenth century.

FIRST TO CIRCLE THE GLOBE

Sailors in the Spanish expedition (1519 to 1522) led by Ferdinand Magellan are usually credited with being the first to circumnavigate the world. In actual fact, the first man to circumnavigate the world was a Malay.

Magellan was originally from Portugal, and his early seafaring career was in service to the Portuguese crown. While in Portuguese Melaka, he purchased a Malay slave from Sumatra, whom he called Enrique.

Enrique accompanied Magellan back to Europe from Southeast Asia. Shortly after his return, Magellan switched allegiance to Spain and renounced his Portuguese citizenship. In Spain, he convinced the crown to back an expedition to the Spice Islands by sailing west from Spain at a time when the Portuguese were sailing east, thus circumventing the Treaty of Tordesillas.

When Magellan arrived in the area that is now the Philippines, Enrique was invaluable to Magellan's efforts at converting the people to Christianity and conquering the area. This was because of his language skills in a language similar to Malay. After Magellan's death at the hands of enraged islanders, who were retaliating against the mass rape of their women, the remainder of the Spanish crew escaped. When the expedition arrived in the straits area, Enrique became the first person to have sailed around the world, although the credit went to the remnants of the expedition when they arrived back in Spain.

The Portuguese wanted to establish a series of naval fortresses from Lisbon to the Spice Islands in the archipelago in order to dominate the sea lanes, control the East-West trade, and deny alternative routes to those trying to avoid their system. They established bases in the Cape Verde Islands, Angola, and Mozambique to provide ports of call around the coast of Africa, a fortress at Socotra to dominate the entrance to the Red Sea, and a base at Ormuz to guard access to the Persian Gulf. On the western coast of India, they seized Goa, which became the headquarters of their trading empire in the East as well as a source of Indian goods, mainly cotton cloth, to trade with Southeast Asia.

The capture of Goa is a clear example of the religious dimension of Portuguese expansionism. Admiral Albuquerque put its entire Muslim population to the sword, butchering thousands of people. He then created a new Christian population by marrying non-Muslim Indians to Portuguese sailors from his fleet. This massacre of Muslims would be repeated later in Melaka. As a result, most Arab traders in the area fled the western coast of India. The establishment of a base at Goa served as a springboard for Portuguese expansion into the archipelago.

Fall of Melaka

Portuguese ships first called on Melaka in 1509, asking for trading privileges and the right to build a fort. The Malays attacked the Portuguese fleet and seized some twenty sailors. The Portuguese responded two years later when Albuquerque returned with a much larger fleet and a thirst for vengeance. Although the Portuguese were outnumbered 25 to 1, they won because of their superior artillery and the internal weakness of Melaka. In the ensuing battle, Albuquerque's guns destroyed all the Muslim shipping in the harbor. The ruling family of Melaka fled east to Pahang and eventually established a new Malay kingdom in Johor and the Riau Islands.

The Portuguese continued to establish outposts in the Spice Islands — at Ternate, Tidore, Ambon, and Timor — and a port in China near Canton, Macao. Thus, by the middle of the sixteenth century, the Portuguese trading empire stretched from China and the Celebes through Melaka and India, and around Africa to Lisbon, which became the distribution point for much of the eastern produce in western Europe.

This great empire brought much wealth to Portugal. To give an example, US$45 worth of spices bought in the Celebes could be sold for US$1,800 in Lisbon. However, the original objectives of the Portuguese were never really fulfilled to the extent that they had hoped. Melaka is an excellent case in point of dreams failing to measure up to reality. In fact, it is surprising that the Portuguese occupation of Melaka lasted as long as it did.

The Portuguese wanted to control of the Straits of Melaka and the trade that passed though it. Second, they wanted to take over Melaka's role as the collection site for the produce of the archipelago and its position as the principal center of trade for eastern goods. Third, they aimed to spread Christianity. However, Portugal never really met its goals in any of these areas. Portugal was a small country and its trading empire was too far flung. Portugal was never able to control the straits completely because its navy was constantly going through some form of crisis. As a result, Melaka under Portuguese rule spent most of its history fighting off attacks by the Javanese, the Achehnese, and the Johor Malays in 1513, 1537, 1539, 1547, 1551, 1568, 1573, 1574, 1575, 1586, 1587, 1606, 1616, and 1639.

They were fortunate that the Achehnese and the people of Johor disliked each other as much as they disliked the Portuguese and did not join forces against Portugal. The problem was that Portugal did not have enough ships to make a large enough presence to achieve its goals. The Portuguese fortress A Famosa (The Famous) in Melaka, with its eight foot walls, made it possible to hold off their enemies until help arrived each

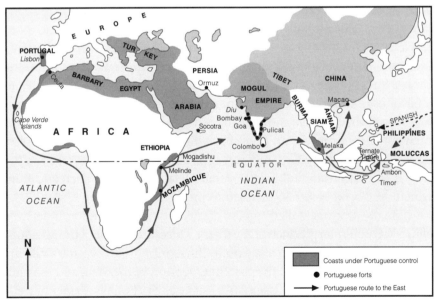

The Portuguese Empire in the sixteenth century.

57

time from Goa or the Spice Islands. Added to this was their inability to control the Sunda Straits, which meant traders could use western Java and avoid the Portuguese.

Portuguese Melaka never achieved its goal of becoming a trading center for a number of reasons. The Portuguese had originally intended to recreate the system and services provided by the former sultanate. The problem was that Melaka did not attract Portugal's best and brightest administrators. Most of the Portuguese who went there were military men and soldiers of fortune. The result was a system run by barely literate men that was rife with corruption. The officials who presided over Melaka's administration were primarily interested in their own personal gains. As a result, much of the revenue that was supposed to go to the crown and to run the port was mismanaged. Melaka could not pay its own way. As time went on, rather than enriching the royal Portuguese coffers, it became a liability. This in turn made Goa and Lisbon unwilling to provide the resources necessary to make the port a viable concern.

Given the crusading reputation of the Portuguese, no Muslim was going to trade there. This resulted in many Muslims from India trading with Acheh, Pasai, Riau, and Java. A general lack of discipline among Portuguese officials led to corruption, inadequate facilities, and poor services, turning away many non-Muslims. The volume of trade never increased, and Melaka became more of a garrison town than a trading center. It was of use to the Portuguese trading system as a port of call and a naval base to protect their shipping and trade. Ships going west from Macao in China with tea and silk stopped there, while Portuguese captains carrying silver from Japan and spices from the archipelago had a safe haven on their way to Goa and Portugal. This was useful but far from the role as an emporium and entrepôt that Melaka had once been and from which the Portuguese had planned to profit.

Finally, Portugal failed to convert people to Christianity; in fact, its efforts were counterproductive. By their ruthless treatment of the Muslims, the Portuguese drove them away from Christianity. Islam became a rallying call for those opposed to European intervention in the area, and the faith grew as a result. Great missionaries, such as St. Francis Xavier, gave it their best in Melaka but left in frustration. The only converts the Portuguese won were the wives and children of the locals who married Portuguese sailors and soldiers. The descendants of these people and the few Portuguese words that had crept into the Malay language are the only lasting heritage of Portuguese presence in Melaka.

The impact of the Malay world's first encounter with a European power was essentially negative. Portugal ended the Melaka Sultanate and its efforts to create greater political and cultural Malay unity. Although Johor would carry on the royal lineage of Melaka, the Malay political world was moving toward greater political fragmentation — something that made standing up to future European expansionism even more difficult. The presence of aggressive outside powers, such as the Portuguese, disrupted and dwindled the wealth that the peninsula derived from its strategic position in the East-West trade. Portuguese rule in the area was an omen of things to come.

By the last decade of the sixteenth century, it became increasingly apparent to other European trading nations how tenuous Portugal's hold over its Asian trading empire actually was. In particular, the Dutch and the English began to challenge its routes and sources, determined to take over the trade in the East and enjoy the wealth gained from it.

Dutch Challenge Portuguese Trade

The two largest ports in the world today are Singapore and Rotterdam. By collecting and selling the goods of other countries, both have used their geographical locations to become centers of trade. Rotterdam sits at the mouth of the Rhine River, which flows from the North Sea through the heart of western Europe to Switzerland. The Dutch made their living on the trade that flowed up and down this river. They also worked as coastal traders and fishermen in the Baltic Sea and the English Channel. The sea and trade were very much part of their lives.

In the sixteenth century, the Netherlands was part of the Spanish Empire. When the Protestant Reformation took place in Europe, many Dutch left the Catholic Church and became Protestant. This religious change was a rallying point in a Dutch rebellion against Catholic Spain. In 1580, the kingdoms of Spain and Portugal merged, and the Spanish crown, in an attempt to bring the rebellious Dutch in line, closed the port at Lisbon to Dutch traders and shipping. This was an attack on the lifeblood of the economy of the Netherlands. While the Portuguese and Lisbon were the source of products from the trade to the East, it was the Dutch who distributed these products in western Europe. The ban on access to some of their most lucrative trade became a primary motivation in the Dutch desire to cut out the middleman and seize control of the commerce from the East, especially that of the archipelago.

The Portuguese had built their trading success in part on maritime technology. Many Dutchmen had sailed with the Portuguese and visited the East. This gave them exposure to Portuguese navigational and sailing methods. During these voyages, the Dutch also observed that Portuguese control over their trading empire was actually very weak. The secret was out — Portugal was vulnerable and unable to muster the resources to defend its far-flung empire. This knowledge and Dutch advances in naval technology gave them the tools to challenge Portuguese trade between Europe and Asia. Thus, by the end of the sixteenth century, a mix of nationalism, economic necessity, and maritime knowledge created a new player in the trade of the archipelago — one much more formidable than the Portuguese.

The vehicle for the creation of Dutch trading dominance was a joint stock company called the United East India Company (the VOC). The Dutch movement to the East was thus financed and controlled by private investment. The Dutch government granted the VOC a monopoly on the trade with the East and the virtual powers of a government. The company had the power to make laws, appoint judges, set up courts and police forces, and administer any territories it seized.

The VOC also had the authority to establish its own army and navy. By the second half of the seventeenth century, it was a private company with an army of 10,000 men and an armed fleet of hundreds of merchant and naval vessels. In today's world, a comparison would be to allow either Mobil or Esso recruit its own army and navy and then give it total control over all the oil coming out of the Persian Gulf. At the same time, the company would be allowed to make its own laws and treat the rulers and people the way it wished. The VOC had this arrangement for the spice trade in the seventeenth and eighteenth centuries.

The VOC realized that the key to profitable trade meant controlling the supply of the product at its source, not just controlling the distribution but the actual amount placed on the market. The Dutch also realized that religion and politics do not mix well. They wanted to make money, not save souls or punish Muslims. By avoiding the mistakes the Portuguese made, the Dutch were able to make deals with local Muslim rulers and interfere in local battles over thrones without the Muslim/Christian issue. In Java and Sumatra, Dutch military support became important in tipping the scales in favor of competitors for royal power.

It did not take long for the locals to realize that the Dutch monopoly on trade was detrimental to the archipelago's economic health. As the seventeenth century progressed, Dutch policy became increasingly ruthless. Local leaders and populations in the Celebes and Moluccas who did not go along with Dutch demands faced fearful consequences. On Lontor, the entire population was wiped out because of its defiance of the Dutch; on Run, the local population was removed and sold into slavery. In Ternate in 1650, Bachan in 1656, and Timor in 1667, native spice crops were burned because too much had been grown, and the surplus could not be absorbed by the Dutch. As demand for coffee and sugar increased, local populations were forced to grow them in lieu of traditional crops or, in some cases, food crops.

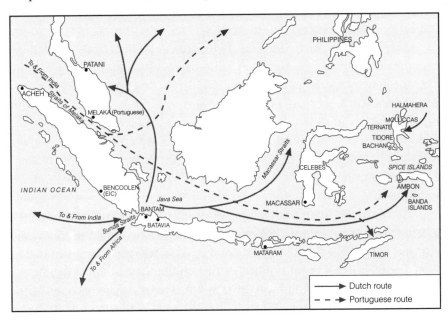

Portuguese and Dutch trade routes in the seventeenth century.

Control of the sea lanes was a necessary ingredient in the VOC's ambitions. To this end, the Straits of Melaka posed a problem. Acheh was at the northern entrance, while Johor was in the south. The Portuguese were in Melaka. The Dutch sidestepped the problem by establishing a new trading center in the western part of Java — Batavia. By utilizing the Sunda Straits as a shipping route, they avoided the Portuguese navy and moved their commercial collection point closer to the source of the product they were most interested in — spices. Batavia was established in 1619 on the site of a town the Javanese had called Jacatra. It was a new city built on a Dutch model, a bit of Europe in Southeast Asia. Batavia was meant to be the new Melaka.

The Portuguese and the local powers, especially the Javanese, fought tenaciously throughout the archipelago, but the Dutch slowly established their supremacy in Ambon and the Banda Islands (1621), Macassar (1667), Ternate (1677), Mataram (1682), and Bantam (1684). However, as long as the Portuguese held Melaka, Dutch control of the spice trade was under threat. Thus, in 1639, the Dutch joined forces with Johor to make a final attack on the port. As a result of the fighting spirit of their soldiers and the strength of A Famosa, the Portuguese held out for almost two years until they finally surrendered in 1641.

This alliance with the Dutch to attack Melaka was a learning experience for Johor. The people of Johor had planned to reoccupy Melaka after the Portuguese defeat and reestablish their former power and prestige. The Dutch wanted control of the straits and were not interested in Johor's plans. It began to dawn on the local powers that the Dutch objectives were to monopolize the trade in the area, and anyone who got in their way was bound to feel the wrath of their sea power. The Dutch were becoming a much bigger threat to Malay power and prosperity than the Portuguese had ever been.

As a result of Dutch occupation, Melaka declined further in importance as a trading center. Its role became negative — to deny its use to anyone else and to force the trade south to Batavia. Although the Dutch still had to fight the local powers for control of the straits, they negated the straits' importance as a major highway of trade. It is ironic that the only major non-Dutch power to use Melaka after its fall to the Dutch were the Portuguese. They needed a port of call between Macao in China and Goa in

India. A secondary role for Melaka under the Dutch was as a collection point for tin and to enforce Dutch monopoly of the produce coming out of Perak, which was not very successful. Thus, in the seventeenth and eighteenth centuries, the Melaka of Parameswara, Mansur Shah, and A Famosa became a secondary naval base in the VOC trading empire.

The English Join In

Another Protestant country that made an attempt to establish itself in the archipelago trade in the seventeenth century was England. In many ways, the Dutch and the English had much in common. Both were religious enemies of the Spaniards and Portuguese, and their commercial interests were in direct conflict with those of their Catholic competitors. Both were seafaring nations. Through the voyages of captains, such as Sir Francis Drake who had circumnavigated the globe (1580), the English had made their own contributions to the advancement of maritime knowledge. The English defeat of the Spanish Armada in 1588 had established them as a naval power. In Europe, England and the Netherlands had common strategic interests and were often allies against the Catholic powers. In fact, the English blockade of Lisbon in 1599 was of immense help to the fledgling VOC endeavors in the archipelago.

England's interests in Southeast Asia were also represented by a joint stock company — the English East India Company (EIC). This led to a conflict of interests between England and the Netherlands. While the two countries may have had common national interests and governments that looked at the Western world in a like manner, the EIC and the VOC were two competing private companies whose goals lay in profits and markets. Their loyalties were as much to the people who had invested in their companies as to their respective countries.

A combination of factors made the English company a relatively minor force in the archipelago trade until the second half of the eighteenth century when they made their presence felt with a vengeance. The first was the VOC position that it had developed the spice trade, and if the English wanted a piece of the action, they would have to pay for it. Even after the governments of England and the Netherlands had agreed on a formula in the Anglo-Dutch Treaty of 1619, the VOC still fought English participation. Because of its power in the East, it could defy the government and get

63

away with it. In 1623, the Dutch tortured and then killed a third of the English trading community in what became known as the "Massacre of Ambonia." The Dutch claimed the English had been conspiring to capture the fortress there. Faced with this kind of hostility, the English, for the most part, withdrew. They retained Bencoolen, a fort and trading center on the western coast of Sumatra, and developed contacts with Burma and Siam but maintained a relatively low profile in the archipelago.

Another reason why the EIC was willing to withdraw was that it was more interested in developing its trading empire in India. Its capital resources were less than those of the VOC, and it was pointless to overreach itself. As a result, English trade in the archipelago was left to country traders. These were private merchants who either owned their own ships or were masters of vessels owned by companies based in an EIC port in India and operating under the EIC's license.

In many ways, the seventeenth century was a Dutch century in the East Indies. The VOC made fabulous profits, and the people who worked for them in the East led a luxurious lifestyle with slaves, beautiful homes, and a standard of living far beyond what they would have enjoyed in the Netherlands.

Except for a few buildings in Melaka today, there is little evidence that the Dutch spent 150 years there. The true Dutch legacy to the history of Malaysia was its impact on the Malay Mediterranean as a whole. As a result of their interference in the economy of the area, the lives of large numbers of people in the Malay cultural world had changed. For many there were serious reductions in living standards as a result of Dutch policies and profits. For others, such as the Bugis, being excluded from their traditional trading patterns created large-scale migrations throughout the archipelago. The Malay Peninsula and Borneo were the eventual recipients of many of these displaced peoples. The Dutch also began a process, which over the next couple of centuries, forced many in the archipelago away from their traditional seafaring occupations to agricultural pursuits. Outgunned and outmaneuvered, farming became a more attractive option.

Chapter 4

THE MALAY WORLD (1500–1700)

The English, Dutch, and Portuguese were newcomers who affected the interplay of forces within the cultural area of the archipelago. The Europeans, like the Indians and the Chinese, represented influences from outside the area that came about because of its geographical location. While the Europeans were able to establish naval superiority, influence the trading patterns, and meddle in the politics of the archipelago, the process of cultural and racial exchanges in the period 1500–1700 continued as it had for the previous 1,500 years. Of interest in this period is how the European intrusion affected Acheh in Sumatra, the sultanates in the peninsula that had made up the old Melaka Empire, and the Bugis of the eastern archipelago.

The Rise of Acheh

Until the coming of the Portuguese, Acheh was a relatively minor state at the northern tip of Sumatra that survived off piracy and the sale of pepper. This Muslim state was one of the main benefactors of the exodus of Muslim traders from the Christian takeover of Melaka in 1511. The increase in trade and wealth generated from these traders made Acheh the dominant Malay power in the western archipelago in the century following the fall of Melaka.

Under the leadership of Sultan Alauddin Riayat Shah Al-Kahar, who ruled from 1537 to 1568, Acheh combined a religious fervor and a formidable military machine to achieve success. Acheh had accepted Islam in the fourteenth century and in the sixteenth century used the religion to unite under its rule those areas of Sumatra that were already Islamic. Missionary zeal accompanied by the sword made it possible to convert and conquer non-Muslims as well, such as the Minangkabau. Acheh assembled the most modern non-European military force in the area, with Turkish mercenaries providing advanced gunnery skills. The artillery capabilities of the Turks (who also hated the Portuguese), coupled with his fiercely loyal Achehnese, gave Alauddin an awesome force.

Acheh conquered much of the western coast of Sumatra and was successful in establishing control of the Sunda Straits for a while. This meant it was able to offer an alternative route to those who wanted to avoid the Portuguese in Melaka. Achehnese fought the Portuguese for a

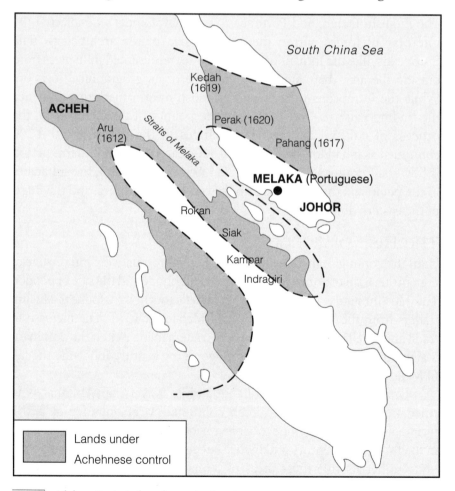

The Achehnese Empire in the early seventeenth century.

century, trying to wrest control of the Straits of Melaka and push them out of the area. In the end, they failed to defeat the foreigners primarily because of the more advanced Portuguese navy and the impregnable fortress at Melaka. Acheh did capture the sultanate of Perak and its tin deposits. The state would dominate Perak for almost a century, thus introducing a new group into the Malay cultural mix.

Acheh reached the height of its power under the rule of Sultan Iskandar Muda, who reigned from 1607 to 1636. During this time, Acheh extended its control over most of the Malay Peninsula, capturing Pahang in 1617 and transporting 1,000 of its inhabitants back to Acheh as slaves. The Achehnese seized Kedah in 1619 and turned the royal family of Johor into a band of refugees, constantly on the run from the repeated sacking of their capital. All that stood in the way of Sultan Iskandar and the recreation of an empire on the scale of Sri Vijaya and Melaka was the Portuguese garrison.

In 1629, Acheh assembled an army of 20,000 men and 200 ships to conquer Melaka. This was an incredibly large force for a trading empire to put together, and Iskandar threw a large portion of his resources into this battle to seize the straits. He came very close to achieving his aim. His troops fought almost to the heart of the city, but reinforcements arrived from Goa in time to tip the scales. In the Portuguese counterattack, the Achehnese suffered huge losses. Estimates by historians on the number of Achehnese killed in this battle vary from 10,000 to 19,000. Whatever the figure, this was devastating for a society the size of Acheh.

This debacle and the wars that preceded it decimated a generation of young males in Acheh and forced its withdrawal from many of its conquered lands. Although their power was checked, the Achehnese have a reputation of being a fiercely independent people, devout in their religion, and brave in war. In the nineteenth century, when the Netherlands extended its control over what is known as Indonesia today, Acheh was the last to be subjugated. The Dutch fought a twenty-five-year war with Acheh (1873–1898) and never really established effective control over these people. In fact, to this very day, the Achehnese remain a fiercely independent people and continue to resist the domination of the Indonesian government.

Johor and the Royal Family

Although Acheh was the heir to Melaka in terms of power and trade, Johor, in the eyes of many Malays, was the legitimate heir to the lineage of Sri Vijaya, Parameswara, and Melaka. The story of this royal family begins with the last days of Melaka.

Much of the success of Melaka had come about as a result of the ability of the bendahara and the government to provide a conducive place for business. The successor to Tun Perak was Bendahara Mutahir. He publicly flouted his political power and wealth, some of which was augmented by bribes. This caused Sultan Mahmud (1488–1530) to lose considerable face. Apparently, Mutahir had a beautiful daughter, and it was the custom for a bendahara to offer his daughter in marriage to the sultan. Mutahir did not do this, which further strained relations between the palace and him.

When a trade dispute broke out in the Tamil community between one of the leading merchants and the Tamil shahbandar, the bendahara, after the appropriate amount of money had changed hands, sided with the merchant. The shahbandar, understandably upset, went to Laksamana Hang Nadim (Hang Tuah's son-in-law) and told him that the bendahara was plotting to overthrow the sultan. The laksamana reported this to the sultan, to whom this was the last straw. He had the bendahara and his family put to death, except for his daughter whom he married. Unfortunately, in the family that was murdered was the state treasurer and chief of police. The sultan had crippled his administration, and when the truth emerged that there had been no plot, the bendahara's daughter made his life miserable. The sultan then had the Tamil shahbandar put to death and Hang Nadim castrated. He turned the throne over to his son Ahmad and withdrew from public life.

After the Portuguese captured Melaka, Sultan Ahmad and his father beat a hasty retreat to Pahang. Sultan Mahmud, having observed his son's ineptitude in crises with the Portuguese and upset with Ahmad's deviant and toadying entourage, eventually had him murdered and reclaimed the throne, not trusting the future of the Melaka royal family in Ahmad's hands.

To reestablish the prestige of his court, Mahmud settled in Riau on Bentan. Like his forefather Parameswara, he turned to the local

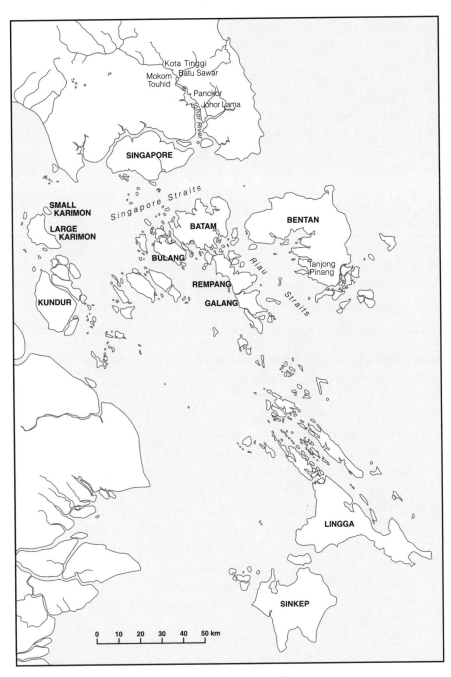

Johor River and the Riau and Lingga Archipelagos (1500–1700).

community, the Orang Laut, for the support and manpower he needed. The inhabitants of Riau had a great affection for this royal family that dated back to the time of Sri Vijaya. Riau and its neighbors, including Temasek (Singapore), were strategically close to both the Melaka and Sunda Straits, ideal trading centers.

The sixteenth century was a time of three-way competition for control of the straits and trade in the western archipelago among Acheh, Johor, and Portugal. Johor was constantly on the losing end of conflicts with its two more powerful opponents. It has been said that Johor's capital was burned down and sacked so often that the followers of the sultan became construction experts by rebuilding it.

Initially, Mahmud's plan was to raise an army and retake Melaka. Virtually all the peninsular states had ties through marriage with the Melaka royal family, and there was hope that an alliance among the states, the Orang Laut from Riau, and the remnants of the old empire could defeat the Portuguese. Johor would pay a heavy price for this belief.

In 1526, the Portuguese burned Bentan in retaliation against an attack on them by followers of the sultan. The royal court was then moved to a site up the Johor River. In 1535, the Portuguese destroyed the new capital. By the 1540s, because of its inability to fight off the Portuguese and Achehnese, Johor ceased to be the heir to Melaka in the eyes of some of the other royal families, particularly in Sumatra. However, its overlordship continued to be recognized in many parts of the peninsula up until the nineteenth century.

Riau and Johor spent the rest of the century on the defensive, as Acheh grew in power and became increasingly hostile to Johor. Johor made an alliance with the Portuguese who also wanted to check the power of Acheh. The sultan made a state visit to Melaka — the first member of the royal family to set foot in Melaka since 1511 — to consummate the alliance. However, a successful campaign against Acheh fueled Johor's ambition, and it attacked Melaka, while Portugal was sidetracked by Acheh. In 1587, the Portuguese retaliated, and the royal court moved farther up the river to Batu Sawar.

Acheh occupied the Johor capital in 1613 and took the royal family prisoner. It put the half brother of the sultan on the throne with the support of Achehnese troops, but Sultan Hammat Shah proved to be no puppet and removed the royal court into the Orang Laut heartland in the Riau and Lingga Archipelagos. In retaliation against his perceived treachery, Acheh pillaged and burned the capital at Lingga. This was, no doubt, one of the low points for the descendants of Parameswara. The sultan went into hiding; Johor faced the prospect of political and economic obscurity.

Johor's fortunes changed with the arrival of the Dutch. Both Acheh and the Portuguese were natural enemies of the Dutch. Acheh controlled the Sunda Straits, and the Portuguese stood in the way of Dutch trading ambitions. Thus, the Dutch were willing to help Johor stand against these two. The Dutch had little interest in the political affairs of the peninsula outside of Melaka, and as Johor expanded its influence northward, they were perfectly happy to stay out of the way. Friendly relations with Johor were in the interests of the Dutch because of the havoc Johor's sailors could wreak on Dutch shipping from their bases in Riau. As a result of Dutch victory over the Portuguese and the check they placed on the weakening Achehnese, the people of Johor were able to move their capital back to the mainland and establish the kingdom along the Johor River under the leadership of Sultan Abdul Jalil Shah II (1623–1677).

Over the next fifty years, Johor was once again the strongest power in the peninsula. It reestablished influence over much of what had been Melaka's territory and made alliances with sultanates in Sumatra. The Johor River and Riau once again became important entrepôts. Although much of the trade was with the Dutch, there are numerous accounts of a bustling, successful trading economy that was the outlet for the products of Malaya, such as pepper, hardwood, camphor, rattan, and tin. That Johor could achieve this after its losses to Acheh and Portugal was because of the system of government inherited from Melaka. This system, which was described earlier, was portable and friendly to commerce.

If Johor had not become involved in a disastrous war with Jambi in Sumatra in 1673, it might have remained a prosperous kingdom with economic and political independence. The war was a result of royal marriage politics. The sultan of Jambi pledged his daughter to the crown prince of Johor. The laksamana of Johor, Abdul Jamil, feared that both his and Johor's power would be diluted by this alliance and wanted his own daughter to marry the prince. The sultan of Jambi took this as a personal slight and an insult to his people and proceeded to raze the capital.

Johor eventually won the war but, in the process, lost political control over its own government. Weakened by the destruction of the capital and in the face of superior forces, the laksamana moved his base to Riau and enlisted the help of Bugis mercenaries from the eastern archipelago. The Bugis tipped the scales in favor of Johor, but at the end of the war, they refused to go home. Not having the military power to force them to leave, Johor was forced to invite into its midst a tough, cohesive people who

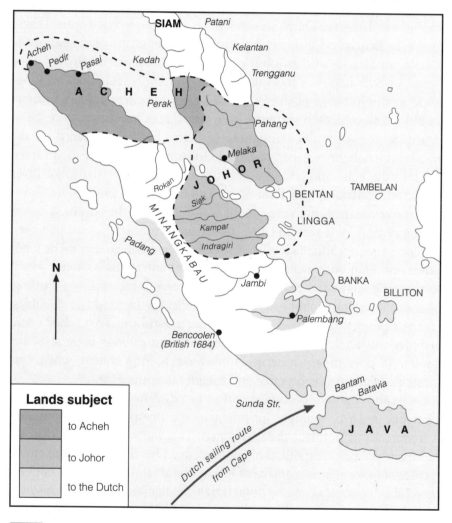

Acheh, Johor, and the Netherlands in the late seventeenth century.

would dictate the future of the sultanate. Another result of this war was Johor's loss of control over the Sumatran Minangkabau who no longer feared Johor's power. With settlements on both sides of the straits, the Minangkabau would later become a formidable opponent.

Johor's loss of independence came about during the reign of Sultan Mahmud (1685–1699). A seven-year-old at the time of his ascension to the throne, he was dominated by the family of Laksamana Abdul Jamil, who for all practical purposes ran the country. When Sultan Mahmud came of age, it became apparent that he had some serious personality flaws and was not suitable to be a Malay sultan. He was a sadist and a pervert, as well as a homosexual. It was said that he once used members of his court for target practice when he was trying out a new set of guns. Another time, he was said to have ruthlessly punished the pregnant wife of one of Johor's leading citizens for stealing fruit from his orchard by having her disemboweled in public.

The sultan posed a problem for the merchants and officials of Johor. They wanted him dead, but the Malays believed that the sultan was God's representative on earth. Sultans had been killed in the past but only because of royal intrigue. For commoners to kill the sultan was a threat to the legitimacy of the crown. If they could overthrow the crown, where was the daulat of the sultans? But they did — leaders in the merchant community jumped the sultan in the marketplace and stabbed him to death.

Although Johor prospered for a short while under Sultan Abdul Jalil Riayat Shah III, who as bendahara had been one of the conspirators, the murder of Sultan Mahmud ended a royal line that stretched back to the divine creation of the Palembang monarchy. His murder weakened the loyalties of many of the people in the area, especially the Orang Laut. Secondly, questions were raised over the divine legitimacy of a ruler. These factors caused fights between the Bugis and the Minangkabau for the power vacuum that existed.

Bugis Dominate in the Eighteenth Century

In the eighteenth century, the political life of the peninsula was dominated by the Bugis. This group of people had traditionally played a key role in the spice trade of the eastern archipelago. Skilled sailors, boat builders, and traders, they were adversely affected by European efforts to dominate the trade of the area and by the political problems caused by interference from these outside powers. As the Dutch increased their power and influence, many Bugis migrated west in the archipelago. Bugis participation in trade declined, as Dutch control over the area grew. The movement west was also caused by political refugees forced to flee because of civil wars that had erupted as a result of Dutch manipulation of local rivalries.

While the Bugis heartland would always remain in the eastern archipelago, in the seventeenth century, many displaced Bugis began to sell their mercenary skills. As ruthless fighters in the employ of the Portuguese, the Dutch, and later the kingdoms of the western archipelago, the Bugis were feared by all. From fighting alongside the Portuguese and Dutch, they learned the use of modern weaponry. They would sign on with anyone who could meet their price.

Their prowess as fighters was an important ingredient in the power they had in the straits, but it was more than their martial skills that made them powerful. The Bugis were not individual mercenaries but organized military and social units that had clear lines of leadership and

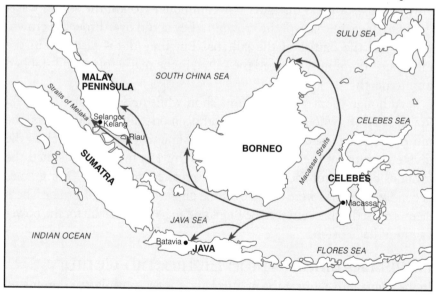

Routes showing Bugis migration.

74

group loyalty. They literally brought their government with them as they migrated, and each group was a part of a larger Bugis culture from which it could draw assistance.

In the eighteenth century, a well-connected series of Bugis settlements stretched from the Celebes to the southern entrance of the Straits of Melaka. It is estimated that, if necessary, the Bugis could mobilize over twenty thousand men from their bases in Selangor, Riau, Borneo, and the Celebes. Discounting their great fighting abilities, this was a tremendous force at that time.

A final reason for their success was that they were willing to work within the local political institutions. For example, in Johor, they operated as powers behind the scenes and maintained the traditional structure of the sultanate and its symbolic position in the eyes of the local inhabitants.

In the Malayan area of the archipelago, some Bugis settled in the uninhabited areas of Selangor and Linggi. Others signed on as soldiers in Johor and established themselves in the Riau and Lingga Archipelagos. It is from their bases in these areas that they rose to power in the Malay sultanates.

In the early eighteenth century, the battle for control of Johor passed from internal competing factions to outsiders. The decade and a half of peace and prosperity after the assassination of Sultan Mahmud ended with a battle between the Bugis and the Minangkabau for control of the Malay kingdoms in the peninsula.

In 1716, there appeared a Minangkabau prince from Siak in Sumatra. A new claimant to the Johor throne, Raja Kecil claimed that he was the son of the last legitimate sultan — Mahmud. His somewhat farfetched story was that his mother smuggled him out of the country, and he was born after his father's murder. His claim was backed by his origins in Minangkabau and the support of their religious leaders, who traced his legitimacy back to the three princes who were the original rulers of the Malay lands. Raja Kecil was able to rally the support of many Orang Laut and Johor subjects who felt that Sultan Abdul Jalil's throne was illegitimate. Raja Kecil invited the Bugis from Riau to join him in restoring his family to the throne. However, fearing the consequences of Bugis demands in the wake of a victory, the Minangkabau staged a preemptive strike on Johor's capital and installed Raja Kecil as the sultan of Johor.

Raja Kecil outwitted himself because the Bugis felt that the coup was an act of treachery. A five-year war ensued. The Bugis gained control of Johor and put the son of Abdul Jalil on the throne. Sulaiman was meant to give the government a veneer of legitimacy, while the Bugis filled the key positions of power. An eighteenth-century Bugis chronicle observed that "The sultan is to occupy the position of a woman only; he is to be fed when we choose to feed him; but the (Bugis) is to be in the position of a husband; his will is always to prevail."

How much the Bugis cared about the day-to-day affairs of government in the peninsula is questionable. What they really wanted was a base in Riau free from interference from Johor so as to extend their power and influence throughout the region. They gained power by intervening in the competition for the thrones of the sultanates. The fights over succession to thrones had by then taken on epidemic proportions. In Kedah and Perak, the Bugis and Minangkabau sided with competing factions for the control of their governments, and in the ensuing warfare the Bugis came out on top.

Selangor was an exception to the Bugis practice of ruling through puppet sultans. In the eighteenth century, the interior of Selangor was virtually uninhabited, and when the migration of Bugis from the east took place, many settled there. During the period of conflict between the Minangkabau and the Bugis, Raja Kecil invaded Selangor. The Bugis eventually drove the Minangkabau out in 1742 but realized they needed to give the settlements there a governmental structure. To that end they established the sultanate of Selangor, only this time a Bugis family held the title. A Bugis prince, Raja Salehuddin, began a dynasty that has passed down directly to the present sultan of Selangor.

By the middle of the eighteenth century, the Bugis had established an impressive area of control that included Johor and with it the allegiance of Pahang and the strategic Riau Islands, Kedah (the largest rice growing area), Perak (the largest source of tin), Selangor (a base on the Straits of Melaka), and the Bugis homeland in the Celebes (a source of manpower). The only local threat was the Minangkabau, but they had become somewhat docile after being defeated so often by the Bugis.

The Bugis/Dutch Conflict

Eventually, the Bugis came in conflict with the Dutch because their goals were the same — to dominate the trade and commerce of the archipelago. As long as the Bugis stuck to the political infighting of the peninsular sultanates, the Dutch had little interest in clipping their wings, but by the middle of the eighteenth century, they were on a collision course.

Demand for tin in Europe and China had risen rapidly, and Bugis control over most of the tin-producing areas in the peninsula threatened Dutch access to and control of this lucrative commerce. The Bugis/Malay entrepôt in Riau was a thriving concern. It drained trade away from Batavia. What the Dutch saw as Bugis piracy also contributed to increased confrontations. At heart, most of the Bugis were warriors, and as Dutch shipping and trade increased, their ships were too tempting to ignore. The losing sides in political battles in the peninsula also involved themselves in these attacks on the Dutch.

This combination of commercial competition and mayhem on the high seas drew the Dutch into armed conflict with the Bugis. In the 1750s and 1780s, actual warfare took place, culminating with a Bugis attack on Melaka in 1784. The Dutch victory and the ensuing counterattack seriously curtailed Bugis power and influence. Caught between the Dutch fleet and the walls of A Famosa, the Bugis incurred heavy losses. After their victory at Melaka, the Dutch attacked Selangor and forced the Bugis sultan to flee temporarily to the eastern coast. They then attacked and occupied Riau, taking over the administration of the government. It is ironic that although the Dutch successfully destroyed Bugis power in the area, it was the British who benefited from it

With the end of Bugis power in the peninsula, there was no longer a dominant local power. This gave areas that had been under the domain of the Bugis or Johor or Acheh the opportunity to reassert their sovereignty.

The period 1500–1700 is a vivid picture of the spread of cultures that made up the archipelago: the Achehnese in Perak; the Bugis in almost all parts of the area; the Minangkabau in Negri Sembilan, Melaka, and Pahang; the Chams in Trengganu and Pahang; and the Orang Laut along the coasts of Johor. All these groups intermingled with local populations, leaving their cultural imprint. A new race of people emerged, representing an amalgamation of groups from across the archipelago.

In the nineteenth century, there was a distinct demarcation in the history of Malaysia. Prior to this time, the history of the Malays and Malaya could not be divorced from the history of the greater archipelago. The sultanates were not modern states with fixed borders but river and coastal royal courts that came and went with the fortunes of trade and manpower. With the coming of the British, more modern, stable states were created, and the history of Malaya became a history of the peninsula.

Chapter 5

BRITAIN TAKES CONTROL OF THE CROSSROADS

Britain's emergence as the world's premier economic and naval power in the nineteenth century had a dramatic impact on Malaya and the Malays. The British imposed a future on the peninsula that would be different from the traditions of the archipelago. By creating a new economic and political world, they brought Malaya into a worldwide imperial system, which the Malays came to share with people from outside the archipelago. By the end of the nineteenth century, the Malays lived in a society ruled by cultural outsiders — the British — and shared their lands with other cultural outsiders, the Chinese and Indian immigrant communities.

Renewed Interest in Asia

In the seventeenth century, the English had virtually withdrawn from the archipelago as a result of Dutch hostility. They also wanted to concentrate their resources on developing their trade and influence in India.

There were a number of reasons for renewed British interest in the area in the late eighteenth and early nineteenth centuries. The first was a result of its battles with France for international naval, economic, and colonial supremacy. Between 1689 and Napoleon's defeat at Waterloo in 1815, the British and French fought seven world wars, that is, wars that took place on multiple continents. It could be argued that World War I and World War II were misnomers — they were more like World Wars VIII and IX. Out of a period of 126 years, eighty were consumed by all-out warfare. Some historians call this time period the Second Hundred Years' War.

For the most part, wars between these two competing mercantilist systems revolved around control of North America and India. The conflict over North America ended with the Seven Years' War (known as the French

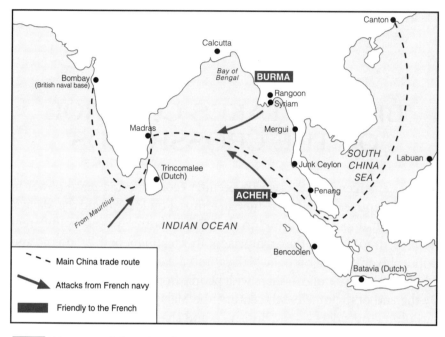

British position in the late eighteenth century.

and Indian War in the United States), when in 1763, the French were forced to cede Canada to the British.

After the North American war, the conflict between the two countries centered on trade in the East, especially around the Bay of Bengal. Ships traveling from China to India took advantage of the northeast monsoons to cross the Bay of Bengal and were especially vulnerable to French attacks during that time. The main British naval base was on the western coast of India — Bombay (now Mumbai) — and ships facing rough seas and the prevailing winds on the eastern side needed a base.

During the American Revolution (1775–1783), the French and Dutch allied with the colonies in an attempt to curtail Britain's rising naval and commercial power. Using bases in Dutch areas of control in the archipelago, they wreaked havoc on British East-West trade, closing their ports to the British and attacking their ships. It became imperative for Britain to establish naval bases in the eastern archipelago. This change in policy was reinforced by the fact that in the next two wars — the French Revolution and the Napoleonic War — the French would occupy the Netherlands and once again have access to the Dutch bases and fleet in the East. The British needed a year-round naval presence east of the Bay of Bengal.

Another reason for active British intervention in the archipelago was the dramatic increase in trade and wealth from China and Southeast Asia. Chinese tea, for instance, increased in demand. In 1785, 16 million pounds (7.3 million kilograms) of tea were imported into Britain. In the next three decades, that amount doubled. The potential profits for the EIC, which held a government granted monopoly on the tea trade, were huge, and the revenue collected from the tea tax benefited the British government. At the same time, demand for produce from the straits increased, especially for tin. Although the EIC had withdrawn from the archipelago, with the exception of Bencoolen, a growing number of independent British merchants, or country traders, began operating under licenses from the EIC to bring trade from Malaya to India.

The nagging problem was what to trade in exchange for tin and tea. There was little Britain had that China wanted, either from Europe or India. Traditionally, in Southeast Asia, cotton textiles from India were traded for straits and Chinese goods, but the competition was fierce because the Dutch and Muslims were also involved in the textiles trade. Thus, the British had to pay for tea and tin with silver, which caused a drain on Britain's wealth. This was counterproductive to the entire idea of a mercantilist trading empire.

In the eighteenth century, this problem was solved when the EIC went into the opium business. Opium had been a trading commodity for some time but on a relatively minor scale. What the EIC did with opium would make the Colombian drug deals of the 1990s seem almost insignificant. They did it legally, had an army and navy, and had government control over the areas in India that grew it. By paying Indian farmers to grow opium and promoting the trade by giving credit facilities to country traders, the British had the perfect trading commodity — one that would create a demand for more and on which they had a monopoly.

The combination of European power rivalries, the general increase in trade, and the boost given to trade through the sale of opium created a need for a base and port in the archipelago. The British needed a place to collect the produce of the area (tin and spices), a port of call in the trade between India and China, and a naval base to protect that trade.

81

The final reason for the British return and subsequent dominance of Malaya was the weakening of opposition to their entry. While Britain's power and prestige increased in the eighteenth century, that of the Dutch and the VOC waned. The Dutch had superior military strength against local powers, such as the Bugis, but not against a country that was as strong and committed to its course as Britain was. In the second half of the eighteenth century, the VOC began to face serious problems.

The Netherlands was not a large country, and as it expanded its activities in the archipelago, it became increasingly difficult to find people to maintain its trading empire. The administration became inefficient and corrupt. The Dutch paid their top officials low salaries and as a result, indirectly encouraged them to skim money from the company or to go into business for themselves. This, and the life of ease they led in the East, meant that officials were not inclined to work hard for company profit. Lower level officials and personnel to man the VOC army and navy were difficult to find and often were recruited from the criminal classes in the Netherlands. The weakening of the company impeded its ability to keep the local princes and chieftains in line and enforce its monopoly on the produce. Debts to the VOC were not paid, and smuggling and piracy became rampant.

By the time the French occupied the Netherlands at the end of the eighteenth century, the VOC was a spent force in Southeast Asia, unable to stand in the way of the British. In addition, any Malay opposition to the British was bound to fail because of the chaotic and ongoing political problems in the peninsula. The stage was set for British acquisition of Penang, Melaka, and Singapore, as well as their subsequent control of commerce in the archipelago.

The Founding of Penang

It was one thing to recognize the need for a base in the archipelago but quite something else to operate it. The EIC was the agent responsible for setting up the base and for its defense. It was first and foremost a commercial enterprise, which had the responsibility of providing profits for its shareholders. It, therefore, did not want to be drawn into any ventures that would require expenditures for military campaigns. Nor did the British government want the EIC to get involved in local military conflicts. The irony was that, given the political situation in the archipelago in the eighteenth century, the British would not get a base unless they helped some local ruler ward off his enemies.

In many ways, the founding of Penang was a microcosm of the problems and promises of a British base. The man responsible for the founding, Francis Light, was a country trader. He and others like him had developed close contacts with many of the local royal courts, spoke Malay, and wanted the British to bring order to the area. Like many of his counterparts, Light saw a bright future for Britain in the area, especially in the western archipelago.

In 1771, the sultan of Kedah had offered the British a base provided they gave him protection from the Selangor Bugis. Light passed this information on to the EIC, which was eager to set up the base but did not want to provide protection for the sultan. Light continued to lobby the EIC, while it tried to establish alternative bases in Borneo, Riau, Acheh, and Sulu, all of which failed miserably.

At the end of the American Revolution, the EIC and Britain became more serious in their search for a base, and once again, the sultan made an offer through Light. The sultan was now threatened by the Siamese, who had been gaining power throughout the eighteenth century. They forced the northern Malay states to pay tribute and declare their loyalty to the Siamese throne. If they refused, the Siamese destroyed their towns and villages. Light accepted the sultan's offer. The EIC went along with his plans, although it had no intention of fulfilling its side of the bargain by helping the sultan fend off his enemies.

Many Malay rulers hoped that the British would be their ally against the Siamese in the north and the Dutch in the south. Their experiences with the British country traders had been positive. They traded freely and fairly, gave good advice, and along with the Americans, were willing to sell them modern arms. But help from the British was not to be — the British were there to trade and protect shipping lanes. The only interest they had in involving themselves in the affairs of the Malay states was to step in if trade or the shipping lanes were threatened in some way.

In 1786, Light hoisted the Union Jack in a settlement on Penang Island, which he called Georgetown after King George III. Britain had its first foothold in the Straits of Melaka. It is said that Light paved the way for British occupation by using cannon shot of silver dollars to clear the jungle of unwanted growth and gain the goodwill of the local Malays.

Both in terms of trade and population, Penang grew rapidly and soon became the British entrepôt Light had envisioned. Products from Britain and India, such as opium, textiles, steel, gunpowder, and iron goods were sold in Penang to merchants, who distributed them throughout the archipelago. In return, British merchants bought straits produce, such as rice, tin, spices, rattan, gold dust, ivory, and hardwood.

During the French Revolution, when France occupied the Netherlands, Penang proved its usefulness as a base. The port was used as a naval staging area to deny the French access to Dutch colonies.

British order and protection drew merchants and immigrants from all over the archipelago to Penang. In what was to be indicative of future British settlements in the area, large numbers of Chinese moved to the port to work and trade. Within eight years of its establishment, over three thousand Chinese had come to live in Penang. They constituted the single largest community. The port also drew Arabs, Bugis, Indians, Americans, Persians, Siamese, and Malays from the mainland.

The sultan of Kedah was not particularly happy about the success of Georgetown. He felt the EIC had obtained the port under false pretenses. He received a yearly pension, but it was apparent that the British had no intention of protecting his people from the Siamese. In 1791, he assembled a force to attack the British. The British, under Light's leadership, staged a preemptive strike and destroyed the sultan's fleet at Prai, directly opposite Penang Island. In order to prevent future such incidents and to obtain an area in which to grow food for the island, the British purchased the district of Prai from the sultan. They named it Province Wellesley. It gave them control of a piece of the mainland facing the island and created close physical links with Kedah.

Penang never really lived up to Light's hopes for the colony. Situated at the northern tip of the Straits of Melaka, its strategic value was limited by its distance from the Sunda Straits. Also, it was too far away from the sources of much of the straits produce. As a naval base its use was limited because it could not provide the kinds of wood necessary for ship repair and experienced difficulty in building dockyards. Whatever importance Penang had was later eclipsed by the success of Singapore.

Penang, however, was successful as a model for the future. Stamford Raffles, the founder of Singapore, was stationed in Penang as an official of the EIC and saw the potential for a similar port that was more strategically located. A good case can be made that without Light's vision for Penang and the example it set, there would have been no British Singapore.

Melaka

As a result of the French Revolution and its attack on the institution of the monarchy in Europe, in 1793, Britain joined forces with other European monarchies to try and roll back the republican tide. In 1795, the French created a puppet republic in the Netherlands, and the Dutch king fled to Britain. As the war spread and involved more countries, the British, fearing that the French would use Dutch possessions in Southeast Asia to attack their empire and commerce, convinced King William to order Dutch officials to allow British occupation of their overseas territories. In 1795, after token resistance, Melaka changed hands once again and was occupied by EIC forces.

Under the Dutch, Melaka had declined in importance as a trading center, but it still provided the Dutch with a strategic presence in the Straits of Melaka and with a base that forced the Malay states to trade their tin with the VOC. The EIC, knowing that when the war was over they would have to hand Melaka back, had plans to make it useless to the Dutch. Their intention was to move the entire population of 15,000 to Penang and return an empty city to the Dutch. They hoped the Dutch would then abandon it. To reduce Melaka's usefulness to the Dutch, the British undertook the demolition work of the old Portuguese fort, A Famosa. Between 1806 and 1807, the most significant building in the peninsula, if not the only major stone building, disappeared. Only one of the gates, which has survived to this day, was left standing.

Around this time Stamford Raffles made his first impact on British policy in the area. Raffles and Light were similar in many ways. Both men were from relatively humble backgrounds and rose to positions of responsibility through hard work and force of intellect. They represented a unique breed of Englishmen who felt that Britain and its empire had a mission that went beyond gaining wealth and power. The empire should establish institutions that benefited the inhabitants of the lands that came under it. Both men took the trouble to learn the language, history, and customs of the area, and neither of them amassed great personal wealth. However, one should be careful in praising such men. Questions will always be asked about how much any country benefits from being conquered and subjugated by another. Suffice it to say that if someone was going to take over a country and make it part of an empire, these men would be the best to do it.

Raffles was instrumental in convincing the EIC to change its plans in regard to the future of Melaka. In 1808, while on leave from his job in Penang as secretary and Malay interpreter to the government, he paid Melaka a visit. He had picked up a tropical illness and spent the time recuperating there. When he realized what the repercussions of EIC policy would be, he argued against their implementation.

Raffles had a number of reasons for keeping Melaka intact. He argued that it would be inhuman to force Eurasians, Chinese, Indians, and Malays who had lived in Melaka for hundreds of years to move to another place. Most would resist the move, and it would be absurd to force them to do so at gunpoint. Secondly, Melaka was no threat to Penang commercially, but if abandoned, anyone could move in and threaten British strategic interests. Hinted at here was Raffles' belief that Melaka was only the first step in pushing British interests farther south and incorporating all the Dutch possessions into the British Empire. Thirdly, Melaka's population of 15,000 had a sufficient tax base to pay for its administrative costs and defense, something Penang and Singapore were unable to do for a long time, so it would not be a financial drain on the EIC. Finally, he argued that Britain could not destroy a city after it had promised to protect the people in it. Britain and the EIC would loose their credibility in the area.

Raffles prevailed, and the EIC did not destroy Melaka. The settlement remained under the British until 1957, except for brief periods of occupation by the Dutch (1818–1824) and the Japanese (1942–1945). Raffles also managed to save the last of A Famosa, which today is one of the oldest man-made structures in Malaysia. Had the EIC gone ahead with its plans, the historical city of Melaka would probably not exist today. The mixture of Dutch, Portuguese, Chinese, Indian, Malay, and British influences on this city over a period of five hundred years makes it a unique Malaysian national treasure.

Raffles and Singapore

Raffles' efforts attracted the attention of the governor-general of India, Lord Minto, who recalled him to India to act as an advisor on the archipelago. During the Napoleonic Wars, Britain had seized and occupied all the Dutch possessions, except Java. This continued to be administered by the Dutch, who owed allegiance to France at that time. Lord Minto, who was organizing a force to invade Java, wanted Raffles as an aide because of his extensive knowledge of the area. In the period 1810 to 1811, the British assembled their invasion army at Melaka. In 1811, they successfully invaded and occupied Java.

Raffles was made the head of the British administration in Java. He spent five years in Java trying to reform the excesses of Dutch rule while, at the same time, fighting hard to convince his superiors in India and London that when the war was over, Britain should hold on to all the Dutch possessions in the archipelago. The archipelago might be a far different place today if his efforts had been successful, and Java had been part of the British Empire.

While in Java, Raffles wrote *A History of Java*, a classic piece of scholarship. For this and his efforts on behalf of the empire, he was knighted Sir Stamford Raffles in 1816.

The future of the area was to be determined by European considerations rather than by the opinions of such men as Raffles who were already present in Southeast Asia. When the Napoleonic Wars ended, it was the intention of the British government to build strong counterbalances to France in Europe to prevent future French aggression. The Netherlands was an important ingredient in this plan, and the British felt that the Netherlands could only be strong if it had an overseas empire. The British had already decided to keep the Dutch colonies they had seized on the cape of Africa and in Ceylon (now Sri Lanka). Thus, if the Dutch were going to have any empire left, Dutch possessions in the archipelago would have to be returned.

It was not the VOC that reoccupied the Dutch East Indies after the war because the company had gone bankrupt. Instead, the Dutch government took over the administration of the area, intent on restoring its monopoly on trade. British ships were banned from all ports except Batavia that were under Dutch control, and this ban was enforced by the Dutch navy and army.

In 1818, Raffles returned to the area as head of the British colony of Bencoolen. Situated on the western coast of Sumatra, it was a relatively insignificant assignment, but he had his foot in the door. It was from this base that Raffles would establish modern Singapore but that, in itself, was not his greatest contribution to the history of Malaysia and Singapore. Singapore was a means to an end, that end being British control of the straits and the trade that flowed through it. Ultimately, Raffles' move on Singapore would lead to British control of the destiny of the entire Malay Peninsula.

Raffles feared that, with the Dutch return to Batavia, Riau, Melaka, and ports on the eastern coast of Sumatra, it would only be a matter of time before they dominated the entire archipelago, especially given the vigor with which they were reestablishing themselves in the area. He felt that Britain had to find a trading and naval base farther south of Penang to thwart Dutch intentions. The problem was that the British government did not want to upset the Dutch, and the EIC, Raffles' employer, did not want to take on costly military or administrative actions. Raffles understood that the consequences of their inaction would be Dutch dominance of the archipelago. He finally convinced Lord Hastings, governor general of India, to allow him to search for a British base in the area of Riau. It was, however, conditional on avoiding conflict with the Dutch. This was a tall order he proceeded to ignore, because anything he did would bring him into conflict with the Dutch.

Raffles sailed from India in December 1818, and there is little doubt that Singapore was the site he had in mind for a British port and base. It was an ideal site — it had an excellent natural harbor, ample timber supplies, and fresh drinking water. Moreover, it sat astride some of the busiest shipping lanes in the world.

When he arrived in January 1819, the island was basically a base for pirates. Singapore had been significant in Malay history during the time of Parameswara and had regained some stature as a trading center during the height of the Johor Empire in the seventeenth century. However, in 1819, all it had was a settlement around the mouth of the Singapore River ruled by the temenggung of Johor, who apparently had hereditary rights to the island. Traditionally, the temenggung had been an important official in the court of Malay rulers, but with the demise of the Johor Empire, he was not much more than a village chieftain. There were some Chinese on the island who had spice plantations around the area where downtown Singapore is today. And there were groups of *Orang Laut*, or Sea Gypsies, concentrated around the mouths of the Singapore, Kallang, and Seletar Rivers. Together, these people constituted a population of about a thousand.

SEA GYPSIES

An article in the *Sunday Star*, October 19, 1997, describes a Penang correspondent's observations of Sea Gypsies in 1927:

... As a ship drew near the peninsula, it would be possible to see half a dozen little brown sails of low crafts hastening into some torturous channel between the islands. These were tiny dugouts, whose sides had been built up with yellow bamboos in such a way as to preserve 12 to 18 inches (30 to 45 centimeters) of free-board between the *rotan*, or rattan, deck (on which squatted the crew) and the water.

Sea Gypsy houseboats.

A typical boat was usually about 10 feet (3 m) in length, accommodating seven to eight people besides their scanty property. At the bow a youth could be seen "paddling vigorously, with a peculiar, jerking movement of the arm and shoulders that one will see nowhere else in the world."

A little farther aft, there could be a couple of girls bending over a cooking pot and a woman squatting under a palm-thatched shelter, cuddling a baby. Near the stern, a man (father of the family) tended to the sail and steering.

All of them were dark, with woolly Negroid hair, thick lips, and short sturdy limbs. A yard of cloth, it appeared, provided clothes for the entire family — or at least for two or three older members who bothered to wear diminutive skirts ...

Fish was often eaten raw; their entrails were cast into the bottom of the boat for, if thrown overboard, it would attract the sharks, which would prove hazardous to the gypsy children who spent a great deal of time swimming ahead, around and under the boat.

The gypsies usually sailed in fleets of six to a dozen boats. Crime was practically unknown, warfare unheard of, and morals impeccable. Their language contained but a few hundred words. Believing in the afterlife, they would reply when anyone of them was asked for his name: "The name of my body is this, or that, but the name of my soul I know not."

With no written law, they were ruled rigidly by custom. When a youth and a maid evinced an affection for each other, their families seldom interfered and, once mated, infidelity was unknown. The birth of a child meant a day's illness, scarcely more. Death was little dreaded. The corpse was usually buried in some island reserved for the purpose, or was placed on a platform and left to the mercy of the sun, the wind, and the rain. Sometimes, the dead man's boat was cut in two and became his shroud.

Munshi Abdullah, who taught the Malay language to the British and wrote some interesting accounts of the straits area in the early nineteenth century, described Singapore as follows:

> Now, at this time, the seas round Singapore so far from being navigated freely by men were feared even by *jinns* [demons] and devils, for along the shores were the sleeping-huts of the pirates. Whenever they plundered a ship or a ketch or a cargo-boat, they brought it in to Singapore, where they shared the spoils and slaughtered the crew, or fought to death among themselves to secure their gains. All along the shore there were hundreds of human skulls rolling about on the sand; some old, some new, some with hair still sticking to them, some with teeth filed and others without. News of these skulls was brought to Colonel Farquhar [the first resident of Singapore] and after he had seen them, he ordered them to be gathered up and cast into the sea.

Raffles faced a few key problems in bringing his plans for Singapore to fruition. He had to provide some legal reason for British occupation of the island. He also had to keep the Dutch at bay and to keep his critics in Penang, India, and London from interfering before Singapore was a going concern.

The political situation in Johor, which ruled the island, was pretty hazy around this time. In the eighteenth century, much of the real political power in Johor had been usurped by the Bugis who had allowed the sultanate to decline in importance. In the 1780s, the Dutch had occupied Riau and signed treaties with the Johor sultan and the Bugis. When the British occupied Melaka in 1795, the absence of the Dutch had created a power vacuum, with both Sultan Mahmud and the Bugis fighting to fill it. The sultan had two sons, and when he died in 1812, *Tengku*, or prince, Hussein was out of the country, so the Bugis put his younger brother Tengku Abdul Rahman on the throne, believing he would be easier to control. Both the Dutch and the British recognized Abdul Rahman as the rightful ruler of Johor and thus the ruler of Singapore.

Raffles was faced with a dilemma. The Dutch and the Bugis occupied Riau and controlled Abdul Rahman. There was no way they would allow a British presence in Singapore. Tengku Hussein was living in poverty and in exile on one of the Riau islands, and Raffles conspired with the temenggung to bring the prince to Singapore. The deal was that if Hussein signed a treaty giving the British rights to Singapore, Raffles and the temenggung would recognize Hussein as the rightful sultan of Johor. The EIC would then pay both the prince and the temenggung a yearly salary. The promise of a stable income made Hussein more than willing to sign a treaty with Raffles.

These negotiations far exceeded any instructions or authority that Raffles had, but his superiors were far away, and he hoped that it would be too late by the time they objected. The Dutch were much closer than Raffles' superiors, and it did not take long for them to protest against this British threat to their area of influence and control.

Raffles left Singapore for Bencoolen soon after the settlement was established and left Major William Farquhar in charge, with instructions to set up a free port and build defenses against a Dutch attack. The first part was practicable, but the second was more difficult. Facing an imminent Dutch attempt to take control of the island, Farquhar had a cruiser that was beached because it was full of termites, some British artillery, and an Indian regiment, which was close to mutiny because the soldiers had been forced to accompany Raffles when they were meant to go home to India. Farquhar appealed for help from Penang, but it was turned down. Reinforcements finally arrived from Bencoolen in April 1819, and the crisis was averted.

After this, Dutch attempts to dislodge the British moved to Europe and to the diplomats. The Dutch had considerable support. There were members of the British government who saw Raffles' actions as a violation of government policy. Within the EIC, there was significant opposition — from Penang, whose officials felt that Singapore was a threat to their future, and from India, which thought it was a costly venture that would drag the company into a profit draining conflict with the Dutch. If there had been modern communication at the time, Singapore probably would have been returned to the Dutch.

What saved Singapore was its success. While diplomats, bureaucrats, and company officials argued, Singapore's fate was already being determined. The offer of free trade and the opportunity to avoid the Dutch monopoly had an effect on immigration and commerce much like it had on Penang but on a much more impressive scale. By 1821, Singapore's population had increased to 5,000, and by 1824, it was over ten thousand. Like Penang, it drew people from all over, especially the Chinese, who from the very start made up the majority of the population. In its first year of existence, Singapore conducted over $400,000 in trade. In 1821, this increased to $8 million and in 1823 to $13 million. By 1825, the trade figures for these British ports were Melaka $2.5 million, Penang $8.5 million, and Singapore about $22 million.

Singapore had become too important a port for Britain to return it to the Dutch. By 1821, the EIC had changed its tune and favored keeping Singapore. By 1822, the British government made it clear to the Dutch that they were there to stay, and it was time to negotiate the future of the Dutch and the British in the archipelago.

It is impossible for any visitor to Singapore today to avoid the apparent importance of Sir Stamford Raffles to the history of the island. To twist a phrase by Winston Churchill, never in the course of human events has so much been named after a man who spent so little time in a place. Three of Singapore's premier schools are named after him; a number of roads bear his name; Singapore's most famous hotel is the Raffles Hotel; there is Raffles lighthouse and Raffles Country Club; Raffles City is a hotel as well as a shopping complex; and there is even a beer called Raffles Light. Yet, he spent only nine to ten months in total on the island.

There is ample evidence that his vision and determination were responsible for the creation of modern Singapore, but the man who was largely responsible for turning his dreams into reality was William Farquhar, a man largely ignored in the history of the country. It takes a dedicated searcher to find the one short lane that bears the name of the man who actually ran Singapore in the key years from 1819 to 1823.

Farquhar spent over thirty years working in the Far East for the EIC. In the years 1795 to 1818, he was chief administrator of British-occupied Melaka. While there, he learned the Malay language and married a Malay woman. His knowledge of the area, the people, and the language made him an important part of a number of British expeditions in the area, including the invasion of Java in 1811. Farquhar and others even claim it was actually he who convinced Raffles to fight the destruction of Melaka.

In the early years of Singapore, it was Farquhar who had to grapple with the day-to-day problems of this new outpost of the empire. The EIC did not want to spend much money to support the venture, and Raffles had decreed it a free port. In the wake of these financial constraints, Farquhar had to find the money to run the place. For example, when Raffles returned to Singapore in 1822, he was critical of Farquhar's decision to legalize gambling. Raffles saw it as a social evil; Farquhar saw it as a way to obtain revenue for the government. Besides, Farquhar knew it was impossible to stop gambling, given the government's inability to communicate in Chinese and the limited resources or police to control a rowdy, growing population. Professor Mary Turnbull points out that more was spent on salaries in the backwater colony of Bencoolen in a month than was spent by booming Singapore in a year. Bencoolen was Raffles' official base of operations.

It appears that Farquhar's tenure in Singapore won the respect and affection of the local population. Munshi Abdullah describes a scene in 1823 when thousands of Singapore residents turned out to bid Farquhar an emotional farewell. Raffles was responsible for engineering the man's dismissal from his post in Singapore. He felt Farquhar had not carried out his plans for the city that he left behind in early 1819. Raffles also felt that Farquhar had become too close to the local population. In the language of the British Empire, Farquhar had "gone native." Apparently, Raffles wanted the British to "uplift" the people in the area but not become too friendly with them.

CAMPAIGNS AGAINST RATS AND CENTIPEDES

Modern Singapore is famous for its campaigns to improve civil life. Some examples include the courtesy campaign, the anti-smoking campaign, and the save water campaign. Munshi Abdullah, Raffles' secretary and interpreter, describes the earliest campaigns:

There were thousands of rats all over the district, some almost as large as cats. They were so big that they used to attack us if we went out walking at night and many people were knocked over. Colonel Farquhar made an order saying "To anyone who kills a rat I will give one *wang,* or coin." When people heard of this they devised all manner of instruments for killing rats. At first the rats brought in every morning were counted almost in thousands, and Colonel Farquhar paid out according to his promise. After six or seven days a multitude of rats were still to be seen and he promised five *duit,* or a smaller coin, for each rat caught. They were still brought in thousands and Colonel Farquhar ordered a very deep trench to be dug and the dead bodies to be buried. Finally the uproar and the campaign against the rats in Singapore came to an end, the infestation having completely subsided.

Some time later a great many centipedes appeared, people being bitten by them all over the place. In every dwelling, if one sat for any length of time, two or three centipedes would drop from the atap roof. When the news reached Colonel Farquhar he made an order saying that to anyone who killed a centipede he would give one wang. Hearing this people searched high and low for centipedes, and every day they brought in hundreds which they had caught by methods of their own devising. So the numbers dwindled until once in two or three days some twenty or thirty centipedes were brought in. Finally the campaign and furore caused by the centipedes came to an end, and people no longer cried out because of the pain when they got bitten.

In the years following Farquhar's return to Britain, his role in the success of the Straits Settlements became a matter of public debate, both there and in Singapore. Farquar, in word and in print, tried to gain acceptance for his contributions to the area. The supporters of Raffles, including his widow, fought hard to make sure that Raffles was the dominant figure in the empire's history of the region. A century and a half later, it is quite obvious who won the argument.

In 1824, Britain and the Netherlands came to an agreement on the future of their interests in the area in what was called the Anglo-Dutch

Treaty. By the treaty, they agreed that Singapore was recognized as British and Riau as Dutch. By drawing a line down the middle of the Straits of Melaka, it was recognized that everything north and east would fall under British influence and everything south under the Dutch. Britain was recognized as the sole power in the peninsula but gave up all claims to Sumatra and thus transferred Bencoolen to the Dutch.

The results of this treaty had far-reaching implications for the future of the people in the archipelago. The destinies of the people in this area called the Malay Mediterranean were now separated. For example, Riau, which had been part of Johor, Melaka, and Sri Vijaya, was now cut off from the peninsula. The treaty was really the beginning of what would be Indonesia and Malaysia, but it was formulated in Europe without regard for the traditional flow of people and cultures. Further, it established Britain as the unrivaled trading power in Asia. Between its navy and the occupation of Penang, Melaka, and Singapore, Britain controlled the shipping lanes between India and China, as well as the entrepôt for produce from the archipelago.

The British and the Chinese, who were flocking to these colonies, had taken over the trade in which Malays had previously been an important part. Increasingly, the vast majority of the Malays were being pushed into a rural, agricultural life and cut off from the centers of commerce they had dominated for so long. As the nineteenth century progressed, the Malays were facing a new world over which they had little control.

Chapter 6

SINGAPORE IN THE NINETEENTH CENTURY

The Anglo-Dutch Treaty of 1824 officially recognized British sovereignty over Penang, Melaka, and Singapore, and in 1826, these three territories became one administrative entity called the Straits Settlements. British rule drew them into the world's premier commercial and trading empire. By the turn of the twentieth century, Singapore had become one of the world's most important ports. The Straits Settlements had recorded impressive growth in wealth, trade, and population. British policies had created two predominantly Chinese cities — Penang and Singapore — at the two ends of Asia's highway of commerce, the Straits of Melaka. They were Chinese cities ruled by the British in a Malay world.

Economic Growth

The reasons for Singapore's growth as a port city are most importantly geographic ones, but the people who colonized Singapore played an important role as well. If the Dutch had beaten Raffles to the punch, Singapore would be a vastly different place today. Contrasting Dutch commerce and trade in the archipelago in the nineteenth century with that of the British gives an insight into why this is true.

The trade for the products of China, the archipelago, and Europe had been financed by trading Indian products (especially cotton textiles) or silver for spices and tea. The drain on Britain's silver supply had led to its entry into the opium trade. The Dutch did not have to use their country's hard currency because they sold the products of the archipelago throughout Europe for German, French, and Swedish gold and silver. This wealth was the driving force behind the Dutch desire to monopolize trade in the areas they controlled. When the Dutch returned in the nineteenth century, they continued to control the sources of their products in Indonesia and peddle them to the rest of Europe. It was such a lucrative trade that they were able to pay off their national debt from the Napoleonic Wars and build a national railway system from the profits they made between 1820 and 1850 alone. It was a policy of restricted trade controlled by the Dutch government and imposed on the Indonesian people.

For Britain the economics of trade in the nineteenth century was vastly different from that of the Dutch. The Industrial Revolution had come to Britain first, and the emphasis of its trade policy changed accordingly. Britain was the world's premier industrial power and was looking for markets in Asia for its manufactured goods. The hundreds of millions of people in India, Southeast Asia, and China represented untapped markets to expand the sales of British goods. Cotton textiles, which was one of the mainstays of trade in the area, could be produced inexpensively and in greater quantities in Manchester than in India. Metal products, such as tools, pots and pans, and weapons, poured out of British factories and were more competitively priced than those of other manufacturers.

These considerations resulted in the British moving away from their mercantilist policies to free trade. When a country can produce more goods inexpensively than its competitors, free trade is definitely to its advantage.

Singapore and, to a lesser degree, Penang benefited from the free trade tremendously because the Straits Settlements were open to anyone. The lack of restrictions on trade acted as a magnet for trade and commerce. This was reinforced by the presence of the Royal Navy, which was responsible for keeping the sea lanes open and expanding opportunities for free trade for the merchants of British territories.

The policy of the British was not unlike the US trade policy after 1945. In the past three decades, the United States has become a convert to the gospel of free trade. Much US energy and wealth has been spent trying to convince others to end trade barriers, open up markets, and make the world's shipping lanes open to all. This is a relatively new outlook for the United States. Until World War II, much of its industrialized economic power had been built behind closed US markets and tariffs, but after the war, Americans found themselves in much the same position as the British after the Napoleonic Wars — they could only benefit from free trade because they were the premier economic and military power.

Singapore's free port reflected the views of men such as Raffles who felt that open trade was in Britain's best interests. Two other specific examples in the first half of the nineteenth century illustrate how Singapore was in a position to grow as a result of Britain's move toward nonrestrictive trade policies. The EIC, like the VOC, had been granted monopolies on trade in the Far East, and one of these was on tea. The EIC could manipulate the price of tea by controlling the amount placed on the market in Britain. In 1834, the British government ended this monopoly. New British competitors quickly entered the market, and the amount supplied to Britain increased. This brought down the price of tea and, in turn, increased the amount of tea sold in Britain. Singapore benefited directly from this through an increase in shipping traffic and traders' need to find straits produce to trade for tea.

The opening of Chinese ports to foreign trade other than opium as a result of the Opium War of 1839–1842 and the subsequent Unequal Treaties that followed were also significant for Singapore. These treaties not only increased the level of trade through Singapore in the long run but also completed a British trading empire that stretched from London to the newly acquired colony of Hong Kong in China in 1842. This enhanced Singapore's importance as a naval resupply center and base for the Royal Navy, whose presence had been beefed up to take responsibility for an expanded empire and to protect the increasing volume of shipping and trade. The opening of Chinese ports not only meant an increase in trade of manufactured goods but also greater access to the Chinese markets for products from the archipelago.

There were other developments in the second half of the nineteenth century that contributed to Singapore's growing importance as an international port. The advent of steamships and the opening of the Suez Canal in 1869 revolutionized trade between Europe and Asia for both the consumer and the merchant because the time that a merchant's money was tied up in goods moving between ports was reduced dramatically.

Prior to steamships and the opening of the canal, the record for passage between Singapore and London was 117 days. After the opening of the canal, the average was forty to forty-five days. The ship in which a person invested could make three trips a year as opposed to one for a ship sailing around Africa. This speed, coupled with the increased capacity of steamships, lowered the cost of freight significantly. It has been estimated that the cost per ton of freight between Singapore and London by clipper ship in the 1860s was about $100 per ton, but by 1887 had dropped to about $8 per ton. This drop in freight costs not only meant increased profits for the merchant but also meant less expensive goods for the consumer in Europe and Asia. Goods previously considered luxury goods became affordable for the common man on both continents.

In Singapore, the volume of trade grew exponentially. In 1860, the tonnage of ships using the port was 500,000 tons; by 1878, this had quadrupled to 1.6 million tons. Steamships needed fuel, and Singapore was ready to provide that service first as a coaling station and later on as an oil bunkerage, a role it continues to play today.

It was not just trade with Europe that increased. Singapore's trade with the United States also boomed. One reason was the general growth in the US economy, but more specifically, a second factor was the completion of the transcontinental railroad (1870) in the United States, which opened up the US market to straits produce. The United States had been buying products, such as tin, rattan, coffee, and spices, for some time, but shipping to the larger markets in the eastern and mid-western United States was expensive. The steamship and the railroad changed that. For example, in 1864, Singapore exported 700 tons of rattan to the United States, and in fifteen years, this more than tripled. The Americans made a further contribution to trade from the area with the widespread use of the tin can during the American Civil War (1861–1865). The war increased the demand for tin in the United States as well as in the rest of the world.

THE OPIUM WAR (1839–1842)

The war between Britain and China from 1839 to 1842 is called the Opium War because the Chinese government's seizure of British opium in Canton sparked it off. The war was really about a much bigger issue — China's trading relationship with Britain in particular and the West in general.

Opium was originally traded by Westerners to obtain Chinese goods, but by the 1820s, demand for it in China had outstripped what the Chinese had or were willing to trade. This unfavorable balance of trade was siphoning silver out of China at an alarming rate, putting its monetary system at peril. Along with this, the coastal areas of China were facing a drug problem that affected all levels of society. These social and monetary factors prompted the Chinese government to try to put an end to the opium trade.

For the British, Chinese attempts at curtailing the opium trade were part of a larger issue. China was trying to control and limit its trade with the West, and Britain wanted trade conducted on a regular basis with set tariffs and equal access. The hundreds of millions of Chinese were the ultimate market for British manufactured goods. The opium trade was Britain's most profitable venture, and it made its shareholders wealthy.

A typical opium smoker of the nineteenth century.

The war itself was a debacle, as the Chinese used fifteenth-century tactics and weapons. It is one of history's ironies that the Chinese invented gunpowder, but the Europeans developed its deadly use in weapons.

The war ended with the Treaty of Nanking in which China ceded the island of Hong Kong to the British, opened up five ports to British trade in southern China, compensated the British for the opium seized, and granted extraterritorial rights to British subjects in China.

This was the first of what became called the Unequal Treaties signed between China and the West. In these treaties, China's coastal ports were divided up among the West as virtual colonies. Westerners were granted immunity from Chinese law, and the West dictated the terms of their trading relationship.

Nature of Singapore's Population

Singapore is a unique Southeast Asian country in that the vast majority of its population is not from Southeast Asia. In the nineteenth century, everyone who lived in Singapore came from somewhere else. It was a society of immigrants and migrants.* Some were sinking roots and experiencing a challenging immigrant experience, much like the immigrants in the United States or Australia, but the vast majority were just passing through or thought they were. These two groups were key ingredients in both the success and problems that Singapore faced.

Although virtually all the Chinese who came to Singapore were from southern China, the Chinese community of the nineteenth century is probably best characterized as divided and disorderly. The first Chinese to settle in Singapore were Peranakan Chinese who moved there from Melaka and Riau. These people were descendants of the Chinese who had immigrated to the area previously, had married local women, and had sunk roots, some of which went back hundreds of years. They essentially made up the Chinese merchant class and came to take advantage of increased trading opportunities in Singapore. These early Chinese played an important role in Singapore's early success because of their knowledge of the area and the commercial contacts they had developed in the straits over the years. Much of the coastal trade that brought straits produce to Singapore was dominated by this community.

The Peranakan community was quickly dwarfed by the thousands of uneducated laborers who poured in from southern China in the remainder of the century. This migration was part of a much larger movement, in which large numbers of Chinese fled rural China to settle in the United States, Malaya, Borneo, Thailand, and Indonesia.

The Chinese government had traditionally opposed the migration of its citizens. The Manchu government feared that overseas Chinese communities over which they had little control would become hotbeds of anti-government activity. In addition, the Chinese were reluctant to leave China because of strong cultural ties to the family and their ancestors. Ancestor veneration and the ceremonies that went with it were important

---

* *Throughout this book, a migrant is defined as a person who moves to another area to find work. An immigrant is defined as a person who moves to another country for the purpose of permanent residence.*

parts of Chinese culture. To move to another part of the world weakened these ties and was a traumatic experience for most Chinese.

However, in the nineteenth century, a number of factors worked together to overcome these barriers. Some were domestic — southern China's huge population explosion in the eighteenth and nineteenth centuries created small and inefficient farm units, as each generation grew and divided the land. Added to this were natural disasters that caused cycles of famine and poverty, making life unbearable. The ruling class of China did not know how to deal with these challenges because, as the general population fell into greater economic distress, the people at the top became increasingly corrupt, incompetent, and backward looking. As conditions worsened, the government of China resorted to oppression, force, and cruelty to keep order in the country. The resulting disorder, civil strife, and war added pressure on many Chinese to escape and seek opportunities elsewhere.

Meanwhile, the West was trying to get China to open up its ports and markets. The Opium Wars and the Unequal Treaties gave the West virtual control of many southern Chinese ports and thus provided a gateway for those who wanted to escape the conditions of nineteenth century China. As the Chinese left, a pipeline formed back to their villages and families, ensuring that future migrants would follow in their footsteps to the same places.

A system similar to indentured labor, known as the credit ticket system, developed. Laborers would board a ship in one of the southern ports and when they arrived in Singapore or Penang, Chinese merchants would buy them from the ship's captain. The migrants were then obligated to work for the merchants until they paid off the original investment. The Chinese hoped that they could then find work, send money home, and eventually save enough to return home. Most sent money home, but few returned to China wealthy. For some of those who migrated to Singapore, the journey did not end there. Because of a lack of government supervision and regulation in Singapore, many migrants were practically sold into slavery as coolies in other parts of the archipelago. Singapore was no workers' paradise, but the conditions for coolies in areas such as Sumatra were far worse. The abuses of the coolie trade brought some criticism from the press in London, but the lack of regulation was symptomatic of the laissez-faire attitude of the government and its inability to either communicate with or control the excesses of its alien population.

In the nineteenth century, two Chinese societies developed in Singapore, one of immigrant Chinese and one of migrant workers. Until 1863, the Chinese government banned the migration of Chinese women, and thus the vast majority of migrants in Singapore were male. In 1830, the ratio of males to females was 8 to 1. Even when the government lifted the restriction on women, the ratio remained high because most Chinese felt that their stay in Singapore would be temporary.

The growth of a society that saw Singapore as home was something that would only take place in the twentieth century, although there was a segment of the population that did settle and become true immigrants in the nineteenth century — the Straits Chinese. These included the Peranakans and then, as time went on, migrant workers who married local Chinese and raised families. After a generation or two, the non-Peranakans as well as the Peranakans created a distinct community. Many adopted an Anglicized lifestyle. They ran businesses, went into the professions, worked for British and Chinese firms, and became citizens of the British Empire. In the twentieth century, when large numbers of Chinese women moved to Singapore and the migrants began to settle there, the newcomers remained separate from this group of mainly English-educated, middle class, Westernized people.

Another factor that divided the Chinese community was dialect. While China has a common written language, it has numerous oral dialects, which are distinctly different from one another. The migrants from southern China, depending on where they came from, spoke Hokkien, Cantonese, Teochew, Hakka, and Hainanese and literally could not understand one another. Each dialect group clung together, forming associations, clan organizations, and secret societies. In many cases, there were prejudices and animosities that went back centuries. These divisions were reflected in what people did for a living, and each group attempted to advance its members at the expense of other dialect groups. Most who came to Singapore as laborers were Hakka; businessmen and shopkeepers generally were Hokkien; artisans tended to be Cantonese; farmers and some shopkeepers were Teochew; and the Hainanese were often servants, waiters, and seamen. On occasion, these differences caused violence, such

CHINESE DIALECT POPULATION IN SINGAPORE, 1881				
Group	Male	Female	Total	Percentage
Hokkien	23,327	1,654	24,981	28.8
Teochew	20,946	1,698	22,644	26.1
Cantonese	9,699	5,154	14,853	17.1
Hainanese	8,266	53	6,319	9.6
Hakka	5,561	609	6,170	7.1
Others	259	13	272	0.3
Straits Chinese	4,513	5,014	9,527	11.0
TOTAL	**72,571**	**14,195**	**86,766**	**100.0**

as in 1889 when the Hakkas and Teochews battled it out in Chinatown with scores of casualties.

Government and Social Conditions

In the first half of the century of British rule, Singapore for the most part was administered by the EIC as a division of India. This long-distance government was weak and ineffective, and had little knowledge of or control over its people. In the early years, there had been some administrators with experience in the area and some knowledge of the languages, but by the 1830s, they had retired and were replaced by EIC employees from India who were not interested in learning about the area or the Chinese culture. It was rare that any spoke even one Chinese dialect. An example of their ignorance of Chinese customs was when it was proposed that the government abolish gambling but make it legal for fifteen days around the time of the Chinese New Year. The British thought it was part of the Chinese religion.

Because it was a commercial concern, the EIC had no interest in investing the money necessary to provide the settlement with the administrative structure it needed to rule effectively. While the company benefited from the port in terms of trade, there was not much revenue because Singapore was a free port. Rather than take a loss, they just scaled back expenditure on administration. In 1850, for example, the city had 59,023 people, but the police force consisted of only twelve constables and the governor doubled as the chief of police. The police were all Indians from Bengal, who had no idea as to what went on in the Chinese community. The attitude was that as long as the problems in the Chinese community did not spill over into the community at large or threaten the economic health of the port, the Chinese could do what they liked. This was fine with those who were the movers and shakers within that community — the gangsters.

In the middle of the nineteenth century, Singapore was a city of predominantly single men who did not have the responsibilities or the moral constraints that families place on men. It was a port city with all the problems that come with sailors who have been out at sea for long periods of time. Only a small minority looked on Singapore as home and felt any civic responsibility toward it. Its ineffective government was out of touch with its inhabitants. Prostitution and gambling boomed, as did all the abuses that went along with a relatively lawless town. For men who worked in mind-numbing physical labor, opium smoking became a popular diversion. It was estimated by a newspaper of this time that 20 percent of the total population and half of the adult Chinese were opium addicts.

The government and the EIC were active participants in gambling and opium activities. British administrators, desperate to find sources of revenue due to the EIC's neglect of their needs, sold gambling franchises, and the revenue from opium sales became their largest single source of income. The Straits Settlements had become the EIC's best customers for opium after China.

Prostitution, drugs, and gambling with little government interference, and in some cases encouragement, created a perfect environment for organized crime. This environment opened the door to Chinese secret societies, known as *hui*, which went back many centuries in China. Originally religious or fraternal organizations, their influence was relatively benign until the Manchus took over China. During the eighteenth and nineteenth centuries, they took on a more political dimension, participating in the numerous anti-government and peasant rebellions that culminated in the Taiping Rebellion (1850). As southern China slipped into greater disorder in the nineteenth century, the societies fragmented and began to attract criminal elements. In the wide-open treaty ports, such as Canton and Shanghai, they degenerated into criminal gangs.

REVENUE FROM OPIUM IN THE STRAITS SETTLEMENTS

Year	Total Revenue	Total Expenditure	Revenue from Opium	Percentage of Total
1898	5,071,281*	4,587,366	2,332,186	45.9
1899	5,200,025	5,060,523	2,333,426	44.8
1900	5,386,556	6,030,739	2,333,300	43.3
1901	7,041,685	7,315,000	3,747,269	53.2
1902	7,754,733	7,600,734	3,746,729	48.3
1903	7,958,496	8,185,952	3,746,659	47.1
1904	10,746,517	10,848,988	6,357,727	59.1
1905	11,657,423	10,976,525	5,368,939	46.0
1906	9,618,312	8,747,819	5,125,506	53.3

* All figures in US dollars.

As there were no restrictions or regulations on immigration to the Straits Settlements, along with the laborers came China's secret societies. Few aspects of Chinese life were immune to the influences of the hui. The brothels, gambling dens, and opium were either controlled by them or paid them "protection." Large segments of the Chinese community became members out of fear, dialect loyalty, and the inability of the government to restrain hui activities. As new immigrants arrived in the settlements, one of their first contacts was with the hui. For newcomers in a strange country, the hui offered the opportunity of social contact with their own dialect group as well as help in adjusting to their new surroundings. The alternative was persecution and violence. Once initiated into the society, oaths of loyalty that drew on cultural loyalties and fear of retribution kept the members in line.

These societies were able to mobilize 10,000 to 20,000 members for inter-gang warfare. As time went on, disputes over turf became a threat to life and public order. In the 1850s and 1860s, there was, on occasion, serious disorder that bordered on civil war. In 1851, there were riots against the Chinese who had converted to Christianity to escape the clutches of the hui. By the time order was restored, about four hundred converts had been killed. In 1854, a conflict between the Cantonese and Hokkien hui spread throughout the city, with other hui choosing sides, looting, burning, and killing. It took the military, armed Europeans, and even men off the ships in the harbor to restore order, but not before hundreds had been killed and thousands injured.

The problems of law and order were not confined to the islands of Penang and Singapore. They extended to the shipping and trade routes in the form of piracy, which had a tradition that went back centuries in the area. Political leaders in the archipelago often gave official sanction to piracy in bad times or as a tool against their enemies. As the European powers expanded their control of trade, piracy became the only avenue for Malays to participate in the trade that had been part of their economy for centuries. The Orang Laut, Parameswara, the Chams, and the Bugis are all examples of the fine line that existed between piracy and the legitimate control of trade. Many times, what was viewed as piracy by the ship that was attacked was viewed otherwise by the followers of local rulers. By drawing trade to their ports or areas of control, they saw piracy as a perfectly legitimate way to increase the power and prestige of their leaders.

It is ironic that the creation of the port of Singapore by the British and its subsequent success actually increased piracy in the nineteenth century. One reason was the sheer volume of trade that took place. Penang and Singapore became collection points for the produce of the archipelago, and most of this trade was conducted by the Chinese or local coastal traders. As demand for tin, spices, hardwood, rattan, beeswax, resin, and camphor increased in Europe and the United States, the opportunities for Malay pirates increased.

The entrepôt trade of the area had passed from the hands of the Malays to the British, and no local port could compete with the Straits Settlements as a center for trade and transshipment. Thus, the effect was not much different from how Dutch intervention in the eastern archipelago had affected the Bugis. Communities and sailors who had depended on legitimate commerce were displaced by these big ports. The loss of revenue from the archipelago trade further weakened the rulers' ability to control their chaotic domains and subjects. Young princes and leaders had no empires and thus turned to more violent endeavors to seek their fortunes and those of their followers. Attacking from the many river mouths and mangrove swamps, they preyed on the small coastal traders who did not carry heavy armament. In the 1850s, the press in Singapore estimated that half the local coastal trade was attacked by pirates on its way to Singapore.

A Crown Colony

Singapore in the nineteenth century was a society that saw dramatic growth in trade and economic importance. At the same time, however, it faced serious social and administrative problems. There were members of the Singapore community who agitated for change, especially after the riots of the 1850s. Among the Straits Chinese and the European merchant communities, there were many who spoke out, demanding reform before Singapore sank into a society controlled by lawless elements.

As long as Singapore was run by employees of the EIC from India, there was little hope for change. Singapore had to be run by administrators whose main interest was in local affairs. Movement in this direction began after the Indian Mutiny in India (1857–1858) when the EIC was abolished. Singapore was no longer under company rule but under British Indian rule. But Singapore's merchant community wanted the Straits Settlements to be a separate colony and lobbied heavily for this in London. In 1867, the British government established the Crown Colony with its own government and administration based in Singapore. This reflected the recognition of the government in London of Singapore's importance as a port and a naval base.

Becoming a separate colony meant the creation of a Straits Settlements civil service, which could be trained to deal with conditions in the territories. Its members could be required to learn Chinese and Malay in order to extend government influence in the Asian communities. Another change was the establishment of a Singapore legislative council as a lawmaking body. Although this council was not democratically elected, those appointed to it could raise issues and propose legislation reflecting the concerns of at least some of Singapore's population. By the twentieth century, half the members were colonial administrators and the other half consisted equally of members of the British business community, as well as Asians who represented the Straits Chinese and commercial interests. The governors still held veto power over the council and echoed the aims of the British government who appointed them. Nevertheless, the creation of the council was an important step forward in Singapore's political development.

The first Asian to sit on the executive council was Hoo Ah Kay, also known as Whampoa. He came to Singapore from China in 1830 and quickly became a leading businessman, who was active both in the community and in government service. He was a member of the legislative council, and in 1869, he became an extraordinary member of the executive council, the only Chinese ever to hold this position.

In the last quarter of the nineteenth century, this new governmental structure began to address some of the serious social problems plaguing Singapore. An important action was the creation of a government department known as the Chinese Protectorate in 1877, which was meant to act as an intermediary between the Chinese community and the government. Under the leadership of its first Chinese-speaking director, William Pickering, the protectorate's role was to attack some of the abuses brought about by the nature of the nineteenth-century Chinese society in Singapore. It had the power to enforce legislation that had been passed in 1873 to register and regulate Chinese immigration. This was a key weapon in combating the abuses of the coolie trade. There was better record keeping as well as an agency that had the power to board ships and ensure that migrant workers were not forced to do the bidding of the hui.

The protectorate was also given the authority to implement laws to register brothels and prostitutes. It would have been difficult to end prostitution, but government regulation could curb the disease and near slavery that came about as side effects. In 1890, the protectorate's activities were broadened to include the registration of all societies in Singapore. This ended the laissez-faire attitude toward the hui.

These actions were not real solutions, although they were steps in the right direction. A Western civil service could not really solve problems within the Chinese community, a task that in the long run could only be dealt with by Chinese Singaporeans. For example, the government reduced the power and influence of secret societies, but no Englishman was going to be able to infiltrate these illegal and secret organizations. Only when Singaporeans took control of the police and government were the backs of these gangs truly broken and even then, in spite of every effort, some secret society activity exists to this day.

A few other developments in the latter part of the nineteenth century affected the social stability of Singapore. One was the Chinese government's lifting of the restrictions on female immigration in the 1860s. Women came to Singapore and as a result there were more families and native-born Chinese. The process was slow — in 1884, a third of the women coming to Singapore were prostitutes — and did not make a dramatic impact until the twentieth century. More and more Chinese were sinking roots and becoming immigrants in the true sense of the word.

A desire on the part of Great Britain to create a more stable and orderly Straits Settlements was further reinforced by British intervention in the affairs of the Malay states in the latter part of the nineteenth century. British Malaya was to increase the political and economic importance of Singapore as an administrative, banking, and military center for the area. All this required British commitment to the area in terms of resources for infrastructure and law and order.

TAN TOCK SENG (1798–1850)

Tan Tock Seng was born in Melaka in 1798 and traveled to the bustling new port of Singapore to seek his fortune as a young man. He sold fruit and vegetables door to door, then opened up a shop, and eventually became one of the richest Chinese in Singapore. He was a generous man, helping poor Chinese immigrants with money and advice and was known as the "Captain of the Chinese." Tan was one of the founders of the Thian Hock Keng temple, a meeting place for the Hokkien community. The British government recognized his contributions by appointing him the first Asian justice of the peace.

Tan is most remembered for donating $5,000 to the Chinese Pauper's Hospital in its efforts to build a new hospital. The hospital was run by donations from the Chinese community, Tan's family, and other community members, including Syed Ali bin Mohammed al Junied, a wealthy Arab merchant. The Tan Tock Seng hospital exists to this day, although at a different location.

His final legacy was his family. His son Tan Kim Ching was a wealthy merchant and one of the earliest importers of Chinese silk. He was the first president of the Hokkien Huay Kuan, a clan association, the most powerful financial organization in Singapore at that time. He was noted for settling a dispute between Siam and Perak. He also sought government action against pirates, was a justice of the peace, and fought for protection against the kidnapping of Chinese immigrants.

Another son, Tan Teck Guan, was a prominent member of the Chinese community in Melaka. He was a scholar and known for his knowledge of botany.

Apart from being a justice of the peace, he contributed to the education of the Chinese.

The grandsons of Tan Tock Seng all became well-known figures in Singapore and Melaka as leaders and supporters of reforms and progress for the Chinese community.

Malays in Singapore

Nineteenth-century Singapore also had a Malay community that was evolving in this bustling entrepôt. The city was predominantly Chinese, but its unique Malay community reflected the cosmopolitan nature of Singapore. By the turn of the twentieth century, there were some 35,000 people living in Singapore who were classified as Malays, but within that group, there were ten subgroups identified by the government. These included the Bugis, Achehnese, Minangkabau, Javanese, Boyanese, Bidayuhs, Peninsular Malays, Madurese, Orang Laut, and Arabs. Singapore was a Malay melting pot of the archipelago.

People from all over the archipelago came to settle in Peninsular Malaya, but this process was different from the development of the Malay community in Singapore. The movement of the Bugis to Selangor and Johor; the Minangkabau to Negri Sembilan, Pahang, Melaka, and Johor; and the Achehnese to Perak took place over time and in a rural context. Each group intermarried with the local inhabitants and developed ties as a part of the community or village in which they settled. The end results were societies in which cultures and ways of life were adapted and assimilated usually in one-on-one situations.

The kampungs of Singapore were part of an urban society and contained diverse groups of people from all over the peninsula and archipelago. While the kampung in Malaya was bound together by deep ties of family and community, in Singapore what drew Malays together were ties of language and religion in the face of the more alien Chinese and Indians. While the kampung in Malaya revolved around the needs of an agricultural society, in Singapore, the people were merchants and wage earners working away from the community and faced with a barrage of cultural influences unknown to the rural villages of their homelands.

Given what bound these Malays together in Singapore, it is not surprising that in the late nineteenth and early twentieth centuries,

Singapore was a significant center of scholarship of the Malay language and Islam. Much new vocabulary entered the Malay language through Malay newspapers and journals. In Singapore, the Malay language was confronted for the first time with the world of Western commerce and industry, and the world of Western government and law. The process was not unlike what had taken place as a result of Indianization. The Malay world at that time had felt the impact on its language, but it took the cosmopolitan worlds of Sri Vijaya and Melaka to solidify some common usage in the wider Malay world. Singapore, because of its position in the crossroads of the archipelago and the presence of its diverse community of Malays, played a similar role in adapting language to the new world created by Europe's economic and political domination.

Singapore also acted as a conduit for closer Islamic ties with the Middle East. There was already a strong Arab community that reinforced Singapore's trade ties with the Middle East. Other factors that brought closer ties with the Middle East were the opening of the Suez Canal and the introduction of the steamship, which made it less expensive for increasing numbers of Malays to go on the Haj. It was possible for Muslims to go to Singapore, find jobs, and earn enough money to go on the pilgrimage. Prior to this, the Haj was only open to the wealthy. Many Muslims from areas of Dutch control took advantage of the openness of Singapore to do this. The Dutch actively discouraged participation in the Haj because of the subversive influence they thought it had. Singapore also served as a connection for Muslims who wished to go to places like Cairo to study in Islamic universities.

As Malaya was opened up to economic development in the twentieth century, Singapore's position as an Islamic center declined somewhat. There was, however, a period of some fifty or so years when Singapore played a role not unlike Melaka's in the fifteenth century. It was a center for Islamic contact and dissemination of Islamic thought, as well as an entrepôt of ideas and trade.

Chapter 7

THE MALAY PENINSULA UNTIL 1874

The Anglo-Dutch Treaty of 1824 put an official European stamp of approval on the change in the control of archipelago trade, which had been taking place since Francis Light hoisted the Union Jack on the island of Penang in 1786. The treaty and the subsequent creation of the Straits Settlements in 1826 symbolized the end of direct Malay participation in international trade that had stretched back centuries to Selangor, Trengganu, Riau, Johor, Melaka, Sri Vijaya, and Kedah.

In the nineteenth century, trade to and from the Malay Peninsula was dominated by foreigners from outside the archipelago and funneled through the ports of the Straits Settlements for the benefit of outsiders. The power and prestige Malay rulers and traders derived from their positions astride one of the world's most important trading routes was gone. Instead of being partners and participants, the Malays were relegated to the role of spectators. The treaty also symbolized international acceptance that Britain would determine the future of the Malay states in the peninsula. Siam did not actually agree to the treaty but eventually bowed to its reality.

The relegation of the people of Malaya to minor positions in the international maritime trade created a nineteenth-century Malay political world characterized by fragmentation, instability, and weakness. Malay leaders had dealt with foreigners before, and intrigue and shifting political loyalties had been hallmarks of their history. The rules of the game, however, were changing. The traditional power of the Malay sultanates had been based on three factors, which for the most part were interrelated: their ability to obtain revenue from the trade and shipping that passed through the straits and up the rivers to the royal capitals; their ability to

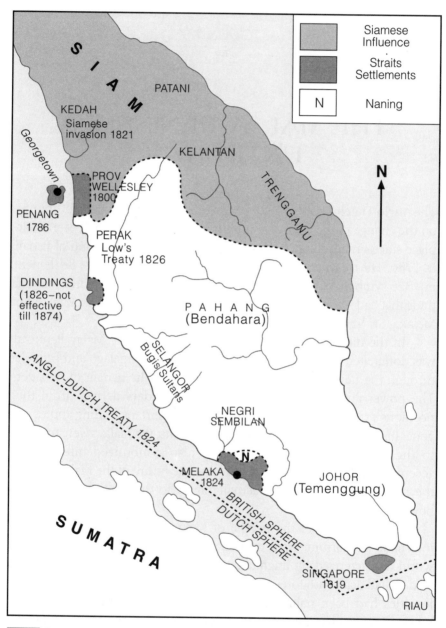

Malaya in 1826, showing the division between the Malay Mediterranean by the Anglo-Dutch Treaty of 1824. The islands near Dindings were ceded to the British in 1826, the mainland in 1874, and were part of the Straits Settlements. Dindings was not used by the British, except as a small base for the suppression of piracy, and was returned to Perak in 1935.

create alliances with other states and groups within the trade routes or with those who used the trade routes, such as the Chinese and Indians; and their ability to mobilize manpower to control the revenue and alliances.

In the post-1824 world, the scope of the royal courts to wheel and deal in the ways of their forefathers had eroded significantly. The Dutch moved steadily to establish political control over the Malay states in Sumatra. Politically, this effectively cut off the peninsular states from areas that had ties of history and blood that went back to Sri Vijaya. The treaty also isolated the peninsula from political ties with Riau, which had always been a fertile source of manpower, such as the Orang Laut and the Bugis. The Indians and Chinese were no longer viable sources of support because India was controlled by the British, and China's foreign trade was dominated by the West.

The Malay states still had produce the world wanted, but this trade was reaching the world markets through coastal traders, a large number of whom were foreigners who sold their products in the British settlements. The weakening of their power base also made it difficult for the coastal royal courts to exercise control over the sources of the produce in the interior of the country. After the establishment of the Straits Settlements and the demarcation of the archipelago into Dutch and British spheres of influence, no Malay port in the peninsula, including Melaka, achieved any level of importance until the latter half of the twentieth century.

In the past, when Malay leaders faced political adversity or a decline in their fortunes, they often turned to piracy as a means of survival until they or their descendants could rebuild alliances and draw sufficient manpower to stage a comeback. For a while in the nineteenth century, the Malays turned to piracy, but this avenue was eventually blocked by Western military power and technology. The presence of the Royal Navy in the straits was no doubt important in reducing piracy directed at trade in the area. In any direct confrontation, the superior firepower of British ships was an awesome deterrent. Although the river mouths and mangrove swamps of the area gave great cover to small Malay crafts, which could outmaneuver the larger naval vessels, this changed with the arrival of the steamship in the middle of the century. The British navy could move faster against the wind, making piracy a much more risky business than it had been in the past.

The impact of a steamship on those who had never seen one is aptly portrayed in the story of the HMS Diana. In 1837, a group of Malay pirates saw smoke coming from the ship as it entered Malayan waters and thought it was on fire. They mounted an attack on what they thought was a crippled ship, but instead their flotilla was destroyed by the Diana.

The political situation in the Malay Peninsula was in considerable flux. The underpinnings of the old feudal Malay states of Perak, Selangor, and Negri Sembilan were seriously weakened, and until formal British intervention in the last quarter of the nineteenth century, there appeared to be few viable alternatives to disorder and political instability. Politics in the northern states was also complicated by Siam, which emerged from its eighteenth-century wars with Burma stronger, more united, and more aggressive. The Malay states had to contend not only with the consequences of the Anglo-Dutch Treaty but also with a northern neighbor that wanted to dominate them. Johor was an exception to this instability because of its strong leadership and its proximity to Singapore.

The majority of the Malay population, or the common man, experienced little change in this century. Life in the kampungs under village leaders continued to revolve around subsistence agriculture and fishing. The peninsula was still sparsely populated, with a Malay population of about 300,000 people in the 1830s. While the rural population grew during this period as a result of further emigration from the archipelago, especially from Sumatra, the growth did not represent a significant source of political support or manpower to restore the fortunes of its rulers.

The villages were portable and rebuildable. Villagers had few material possessions and limited loyalty to their sultans. Thus, if the demands of the political leadership were too great or economic times were bad, the people moved on. Their way of life was village based and could operate in any place where land was available. In the early nineteenth century when Kedah went to war with Siam, a large part of the rural population upped and left for the relative security of British-ruled Province Wellesley, reestablished their villages, and continued their agricultural pursuits. In the second half of the century, when famine hit Kelantan, a large number of farmers moved to the south and west of the peninsula.

Non-Intervention

The problems of the political leadership of Malaya were further compounded by the nature of British policy for the first three quarters of the century. While Malaya fell within a British sphere of influence, until 1874, the British pursued an ambiguous policy of non-intervention in the affairs of the Malay states. While the British revolutionized the Malay political world by controlling the straits and trade, they did not want to interfere in the internal affairs of the peninsula. This in itself was an unrealistic policy. The instability could not be ignored and from time to time the British were forced to interfere.

The policy created a sort of political limbo in which Malay leaders did not know whether the British would interfere in or ignore a crisis. Additionally, Malaya, like the Straits Settlements, had to deal with the fact that until 1858, this power was not the British government but rather a private company, the EIC, whose policies were formulated in India. To the EIC, the purpose of a British presence in the area was driven by three considerations — to keep the shipping lanes open, to provide ports of call for the India-China trade, and to obtain produce that could be used in trade between these two areas. What happened in the peninsula was of little concern unless it interfered with these goals.

Any involvement in the affairs of the Malay states ran counter to the interests of the company, and any expansion of British involvement carried with it expenses that could affect the profit margins of the company. An example of the heavy cost of interference was the Naning War of the 1830s. Naning was an area adjacent to Melaka and was settled by the Minangkabau. To call it a state would be a misnomer. It was a collection of villages stretching over an area of about 200 square miles (518 square kilometers) and owed allegiance to a *dato penghulu*, or hereditary chieftain. In the early days of the Dutch occupation of Melaka, Naning accepted the control of the VOC government. For a while in the seventeenth century, it apparently paid a tax amounting to 10 percent of its crops to the Dutch. Over time, the Dutch stopped collecting the tax because it cost them more to enforce payment than what it could collect in actual revenue.

As time went on, the people of Naning, like the other Minangkabau "states" in what is now the state of Negri Sembilan, came under the control of the Johor Empire. Naning remained a vassal state to Johor until the latter half of the eighteenth century. As Johor began to disintegrate, a situation developed in Naning that was typical of the political problems faced by the Malay states in the nineteenth century. Because of the lack of any kind of central control, political leaders of small districts began to assert their authority. In Naning, Abdul Said, the hereditary chieftain, began to take on the trappings of Malay royalty, passing out noble titles and assuming the divine authority claimed by traditional Malay courts.

Given the insignificance of the size of the state he ruled, Abdul Said's leadership would probably not have posed much of a problem, but it did when an EIC civil servant, sifting through Dutch records, discovered the old connection with Melaka. In 1827, the civil servant made a case to Governor Fullerton of the Straits Settlements that Naning should be part of the Melaka that the EIC had inherited from the Dutch. Fullerton accepted the claim and its vastly inflated promise of a revenue of $4,500 a year, and proceeded to push for British control over the area. Naning and its ruler rejected the argument with good cause, considering the tax had not been collected for 150 years. Problems of face developed on both sides. Abdul Said refused to give up his independence, and the EIC did not like being defied by a relatively minor Malay political leader.

At this point, the nature of the EIC rule came into play. For a couple of years, the argument went back and forth between EIC headquarters in India and its representatives in the straits. Abdul Said misread the inefficiency of the EIC for lack of will and decided to dig in. The Malay leader was encouraged to stand up to the British by Dutch merchants in Melaka, who were more attuned to the slow pace of the decision-making process of the EIC and sensed the possibility of a war. There was money to be made if a conflict ensued, and the Dutch were more than happy to do their part to help make this happen.

Eventually in 1831, 120 EIC troops were sent to collect the tax. The state had no roads, and the British Indian troops became bogged down in guerrilla warfare in jungle tracks and lanes between rice fields. In the end, they were forced to withdraw, giving Abdul Said a great victory. Embarrassed by its loss, the EIC eventually sent in a military force amounting to about a third of the entire population of Naning. This, with the help of other Minangkabau who wanted to cut Abdul Said down to size, ended the Naning War. The conflict is a vivid example of Malay leaders who did not tamely acquiesce to the imposition of British control over their land and independence, a fact further borne out by later violent reactions to British rule in Perak and Pahang.

The campaign cost the EIC $600,000 to obtain a tax revenue that was worth some $600 a year. The directors of the EIC in London and India, instead of seeing the war as an example of bungling local officials, saw it as evidence of why they should stay out of local affairs. The irony was that Abdul Said was captured and forced to live in Melaka on a pension that was far greater than any potential tax revenue from Naning. He used it to a lead comfortable life in Melaka. The British treatment of Abdul Said gained them respect in the eyes of some Malays. To them this seemed to be a civilized way to treat the loser in a power struggle.

Incidents such as this and the lack of understanding of what was going on in the peninsula convinced the EIC that intervention in disputes between local rulers was a costly path to take. They overlooked the fact that they had obtained Singapore through Raffles' intervention in local disputes. They were a company interested in profit, not people, and were not even satisfied with the Straits Settlements because the administrative costs were greater than the tax revenue. Professor L. Mills called this a policy of harakiri because Britain had the opportunity to extend its influence and trading empire but chose not to.

A final reason the EIC wanted to stay out of the affairs of the Malay states was its intention to maintain friendly relations with Siam, which claimed authority over Kedah, Kelantan, and Trengganu. The EIC felt that any intervention in the northern states could lead to a costly military confrontation with the Siamese. Also, the company felt there were greater opportunities for trade with Siam than with the Malay states. Many of the British traders in the Straits Settlements argued vigorously that the potential for profit from the Malay states was great enough to support intervention and that intervention was inevitable. For example, Singapore's trade with the eastern coast of the peninsula alone was greater than the EIC's trade with Siam and remained so until the abolition of the company in 1858.

The result of this policy was that the EIC and the Siamese negotiated the Anglo-Siamese Treaty of 1826 (Burney's Treaty), which recognized Siamese sovereignty over Kedah and Siamese influence in Kelantan and Trengganu. In return, the Siamese gave up any claim to other parts of the peninsula and agreed not to interfere in the affairs of the other Malay states. The Siamese also granted the British trading privileges in the northern states and in Siam. Given Siamese aspirations in the peninsula, the treaty was unrealistic. The attitude of the Siamese was that if the British refused to intervene in the affairs of the Malay states, it left the door open for them to do exactly that.

The Anglo-Siamese Treaty sent the northern Malay states down a different path from that of the rest of the peninsula. Kedah, Kelantan, and Trengganu spent the next seventy-five years trying to avoid Siamese control over their affairs. Islam, the Malay language, and Malay culture were unifying factors in the face of Siamese attempts to dominate the people and draw them into a Siamese/Buddhist state. As the rest of the peninsula was developed and made part of British imperial commerce, the northern states became more insular and self-reliant. The states avoided the social dislocation that came with the economic development and immigration caused by British influence in other parts of the peninsula.

In the early twentieth century, the British renewed their interest in these states and eventually brought them under their control, but the seventy-five years the states spent under the terms of the 1826 treaty had a marked impact on them. Because they did not participate to any great extent in the nineteenth-century economic development of the peninsula, the northern states maintained a more traditional Malay culture. The states did not draw many immigrants, and as a result, their societies were much more homogeneous. There were few urban centers, and subsequently they were court and kampung societies, a culture that was passing rapidly.

Thus, the British policy of non-intervention in the affairs of the peninsula was formulated on the basis of commercial concerns. For fifty years after the signing of the Anglo-Dutch Treaty, Britain tried to adhere to this policy with mixed results. Eventually, it abandoned the policy because of the political and economic realities of the peninsula.

After 1858 and prior to the official reversal of the policy in 1874, the British government found it difficult to follow a consistent policy for a number of reasons. One was the question of geography. It was difficult to maintain a hands-off policy in those areas that were in the immediate vicinity of the Straits Settlements, as problems there could spill over and spark off a reaction. Events elsewhere in the peninsula could also affect British economic interests and those of the inhabitants of the Straits Settlements. Finally, it was difficult to control the actions of the British officials living in the archipelago because of the distance between the men implementing the non-intervention policy and those who formulated it in India and London.

Kedah and Siam

Kedah is a good example of how proximity to the Straits Settlements made it difficult for the British to follow a consistent policy of non-intervention. In the eighteenth century, Kedah came under the political influence of Siam. The state paid an annual tribute in gold to Siam, and for the most part, the Siamese let it run its own affairs. In 1786, Sultan Abdullah, fearing the Siamese would change the relationship to one of more direct control, had offered Penang to the EIC in return for protection from Siam. The officials in India rejected the protection from Siam but kept Penang.

In the early nineteenth century, Sultan Abdullah's fear became a reality. Five years after his death, Abdullah's son Ahmad Tajuddin won the throne with the help of Siam. The Siamese, looking for wealth and allies in their conflict with the Burmese, called in the debt by asking Ahmad to invade Perak so Siam could control its rich tin deposits. Sultan Ahmad appealed to the EIC for help. The British in India refused despite the fact that there was significant support in Penang for intervention because Kedah was an important source of food for the island.

The sultan's continued attempts to promote his independence from Siam eventually provoked the Siamese. Without fear of a British reaction, Siam invaded Kedah in 1821. The sultan was forced to flee to Penang. Siam's war against Kedah was especially brutal and destructive. Villages and crops were torched, women were raped, and homes looted. Thousands of refugees poured into Province Wellesley and Penang, forming the nucleus of what was to become a holy war as the Malays in Kedah fought to recapture their state from the Siamese.

Much of the warfare was hit-and-run in nature, but, on at least three occasions, the EIC intervened on the side of the Siamese. In 1831, about three thousand Malays crossed the border into Kedah and forced the Siamese garrison to flee. In the ensuing Siamese counterattack, EIC ships blockaded the coast to keep the rebels from being resupplied by sympathizers in Penang. It was significant that a large amount of financial and material support for the Malay invasion came from the British and Chinese business community on the island.

After the Siamese put down the revolt, Sultan Ahmad was forcibly moved from Penang to Melaka because he had not informed the British of the Malay attack and also to remove him as a rallying center. In 1836, the sultan assembled another force in Perak to try and recapture his throne. The British sent warships that destroyed his invasion fleet and dragged him back to Melaka. A repeat of the 1831 invasion took place in 1838 when a force of Kedah refugees from Province Wellesley supported an uprising against the occupiers. Once again, they defeated the Siamese army stationed there. As in 1831, they did it with the support of the Penang mercantile community. When the Siamese counterattacked to prevent the rebels from obtaining reinforcements and arms, the British again intervened.

The struggle ended in 1842 when British diplomats took advantage of Siam's war fatigue and Sultan Ahmad's desperation to hammer out a peace settlement. The Siamese withdrew their military forces from Kedah and restored Ahmad to his throne. The price Kedah paid was that that part of the state bordering Siam was sliced off to create the state of Perlis and another part was annexed by Siam. Both Ahmad and the new royal family of Perlis agreed to be Siamese tributary states.

Three decades of the policy of non-intervention by the EIC had far-reaching consequences on the sultanate. Ahmad presided over a smaller, poorer state. Kedah was devastated by two decades of war, and the state took close to thirty years to recover from the effects of the war. The entrepôt trade it had participated in for centuries was controlled by the British and Chinese in Penang. The royal family's primary source of income was the yearly payment they received from the EIC for giving them Penang and Province Wellesley. The end result of non-intervention meant that the royal family was paid by the British to be a vassal state of Siam. All this was a far cry from what Kedah thought would happen when it made the original deal with Francis Light.

Johor and Singapore

Johor is another example of a Malay state that drew British interference in its affairs because of its location near one of the Straits Settlements. In the original deal that Raffles made to obtain Singapore, the island was administered by the temenggung of Johor, who handed over Singapore for a yearly payment. In order to give the agreement the necessary legal trappings, the EIC installed Prince Hussain as the sultan of Johor. He too received a yearly payment. Everyone, including the other Malay rulers, knew that Hussain was a sultan in name only.

When the temenggung died in 1825, his son Ibrahim assumed the office and was quite an able and ambitious man. He ingratiated himself with the British by assisting them in their efforts to eliminate piracy. This was not hard to do because he was an important backer of a group of Malay pirates. By withdrawing his financial and political support, he put the pirates out of business.

Ibrahim and his son, Abu Bakar, were forward-looking men and realized that their fortunes and those of their state could be best furthered by developing the commercial potential of something they had plenty of — inexpensive land. To this end, Ibrahim developed a system in which the Chinese from Singapore were given grants to lease land to develop pepper and gambier plantations in the interior of Johor.

The temenggung was careful to retain a significant degree of control over the Chinese ventures. Each plantation had a *kangchu,* or headman, who was responsible for his community. The contract to farm was renewable and was between the kangchu and the ruler. It could be withdrawn if the Chinese leader did not keep the peace. The Chinese involved were dominated by one dialect group — the Teochews — and only one secret society was allowed to operate. When Abu Bakar succeeded his father, he brought two Chinese into his advisory council, further cementing the cooperation that existed between the ruler and the immigrants. By 1870, there were about one hundred thousand Chinese living in Johor. This initiative was one of the reasons why Johor did not go through the painful nineteenth-century political adjustments that some of the other states did.

Ibrahim's economic good fortune soon drew the jealousy of Sultan Ali, the heir to Raffles' puppet prince, Hussain. Ali and his family had been living in Singapore, and for reasons ranging from high living to poor judgement, he had fallen into serious debt. The sultan viewed the newfound wealth being created in Johor as a solution to his problems. He asked the EIC government to recognize his position as sultan and give him a share of the state's wealth. The temenggung wanted nothing to do with this arrangement. In fact, he expelled Ali's supporters from the state.

The British were faced with a dilemma. Since the breakup of the Johor Empire, the temenggung, for all practical purposes, had become the ruler of Johor. This particular one, Ibrahim, was doing a good job, had many friends among the Singapore merchant community, and was willing to accept British advice. On the other hand, Sultan Ali was their creation. He had a legal right to rule according to the deal Raffles had struck in 1819. An open conflict between the two would threaten the stability of Johor.

The issue simmered for over a decade. Finally, in 1855, Governor Butterworth brokered a deal between Ali and Ibrahim. Ali was proclaimed sultan, given the district of Muar to rule, and paid a yearly stipend by the temenggung. In return, Ali gave up all rights to involve himself in the affairs of Johor and recognized the temenggung and his family as the legal rulers of the state. As a result of Abu Bakar's campaigning, the British government raised his status to royalty. In 1868, they conferred on him the title of maharaja. After the death of Sultan Ali in 1877 and Abu Bakar's agreement to a treaty of alliance with Britain in 1885, the British recognized him as the sultan.

Pahang Civil War

On occasion, commercial interests also caused the British to set aside their stated policy of non-intervention. A case in point was the Pahang Civil War that took place in the east coast states of Pahang and Trengganu between 1858 and 1863.

Trengganu had been part of the old Melaka/Johor Empire until the early eighteenth century when a member of the Johor royal family, Zainal Abidin, established an autonomous state. He proclaimed himself the first sultan of the state. The state prospered with an economy based on the export of pepper and gold, as well as the weaving of fine Malay textiles and boat building. In the late eighteenth century, Trengganu fell under the influence of Siam. Unlike Kedah, it experienced little interference in its affairs. While the Anglo-Siamese Treaty of 1826 viewed Kedah as an actual province of Siam, Trengganu and Kelantan to the north had a significant degree of independence.

Although it was a trading state, Trengganu did not suffer a dramatic upheaval when foreigners took over much of the trade in the area. This was because it actually produced something — textiles and ships. In fact, its textile industry grew as a result of the introduction of British manufactured textiles. The weavers of Trengganu made high quality cotton/ silk sarongs that were used by Malays for special occasions. Inexpensive British-manufactured cotton thread reduced the cost of the goods the weavers produced, making them available to a wider market in the archipelago. Major benefactors of the growth in the industry were the merchants of Singapore, who supplied the raw materials for the weaving and conducted a thriving trade with the eastern coast in general and Trengganu in particular.

By the middle of the nineteenth century, Trengganu was one of the most stable and prosperous Malay states. It did, however, face a constant problem and that was how to maintain its independence from Siam. The events stemming from the Pahang Civil War and subsequent British reaction assisted it in its endeavor.

When the Johor Empire crumbled in the early nineteenth century, Bendahara Ali took control in Pahang, just as the temenggung had in the state of Johor. Bendahara Ali ruled the state until 1857. While the state did not progress along the lines of Johor or Trengganu, it did establish close commercial ties with Singapore and its merchant community.

When Bendahara Ali died, his two sons, Tun Mutahir and Wan Ahmad disputed the intentions of their father's legacy. Before long, the dispute developed into a full-scale civil war. Tun Mutahir, the elder son, received the backing of the temenggung of Johor, who, because of his close ties with Singapore's business community, convinced many of them that Britain's commercial interests lay with Tun Mutahir. Wan Ahmad enlisted the support of Sultan Ali in Muar, who saw an opportunity for revenge against the Johor temenggung. Trengganu and Kelantan weighed in on the side of Wan Ahmad. Colonel Cavenagh, the governor of the Straits Settlements at the time, offered to mediate but was rejected by both sides. Wan Ahmad felt that Cavenagh was biased in favor of his older brother due to the influence of the temenggung and Singapore merchants. Tun Mutahir rejected the help because he was winning the war.

In 1861, Mutahir forced Wan Ahmad and many of his supporters to flee north to Trengganu. Wan Ahmad fled to Bangkok. At this point, the Siamese became involved. They saw the disorder as an opportunity to exercise greater control over their east coast tributary states and extend their influence farther south into Pahang.

Living in Bangkok at the time was another exile, Mahmud, a descendant of Sultan Abdul Rahman of Riau, whom Raffles had replaced as the ruler of Johor. Because of this, Mahmud claimed to be the rightful ruler of both Pahang and Johor. Mahmud, Wan Ahmad, Ali, and the Siamese struck a deal to turn the civil war in their favor. The plan was to use Trengganu as a staging area and, with Siamese military assistance, to invade Pahang. Upon victory, Mahmud would be made sultan, and, as the bendahara, Wan Ahmad would have control of the government. What Ali would get out of this one can only speculate — if they won, there would then be two claimants to the throne of Johor. Mahmud and Ahmad then proceeded to Trengganu with the Siamese navy.

The Siamese intervention caused great alarm in Johor and Singapore. The merchant community saw it as a threat to their economic interests not only in Pahang, where Siam had never had any influence, but also in Trengganu and Kelantan, where the presence of Siamese officials and troops was a threat to their independence and Singapore's trade with the area. Cavenagh demanded that Siam withdraw. The Siamese, believing that Cavenagh's hands were tied by the British policy of non-intervention, refused. In 1862, Cavenagh dispatched a British warship to blockade the coast off Trengganu. When the Siamese still failed to withdraw, he bombarded the fort at Kuala Trengganu. This got the attention of Bangkok, and it eventually acceded to his demands. Ironically, after all the intrigue, the civil war ended in favor of Wan Ahmad because the Pahang chieftains supported him and because Mahmud was dead.

Cavenagh was sharply criticized in London for exceeding his authority and drawing Britain into the disputes of local Malay rulers. His action, however, was effective. The Siamese were convinced that the British were going to protect their commercial interests on the eastern coast and to insist that Kelantan and Trengganu remain free of direct Siamese interference. The sultan of Trengganu benefited, although it was his fort that was attacked. As long as he paid his tribute every year, he could maintain his independence from Bangkok. The incident did point out the difficulties that Britain would have in continuing its policy of non-intervention. It was on the western coast, however, that events conspired against British policy, making it impossible to continue pursuing it.

Tin Mining and Chinese Immigration

The creation of the Straits Settlements and the demarcation of British and Dutch spheres of influence were already undermining the traditional Malay feudal state. In the mid-nineteenth century, two new factors further contributed to political instability in the peninsula — tin and Chinese immigration.

Malaya had been a source of tin for centuries. Tin was a key commodity in the peninsula's international trade, especially with China, but in the mid-nineteenth century, there was a significant change in the nature of the industry. Demand for tin had increased dramatically as manufacturers in England and the United States found new uses for it, such as canning food. Coinciding with this boom in demand was the discovery of large new deposits of tin in Malaya, especially in Perak and Selangor. The development of these tin fields required capital and labor far beyond the resources of the Malay inhabitants. To address this problem, local chieftains and leaders of the tin areas turned to Chinese businessmen in the Straits Settlements.

The main sources of capital that flowed into the interiors of these states on the western coast were from Chinese merchants and *kongsi*. The latter was an organization that was a combination of a company and a Chinese dialect association. Men of a similar clan or dialect group pooled resources, be it capital or labor, to form a cooperative business venture. Bound together by ties of family and culture, they shared the profits based on what they brought to the organization. The economic fortunes of these Chinese ventures were closely tied to the British merchant community in Penang and Singapore. The general prosperity of the colonies, business

127

connections between British and Chinese firms, and British interests in shipping meant that the Straits Settlements had a tremendous stake in the future of the tin mining industry, not only in mining tin but in selling it on the world market.

Equally important was its effect on the Malay political system. All of a sudden, local Malay leaders in the interior had huge sources of income, and many became wealthier than the sultans and officials in the coastal royal capitals. The underpinnings of the feudal Malay political system were being threatened as new leaders with revenue and purely local interests challenged the traditional power structure. In the absence of other factors, this might have been part of a healthy evolution from feudalism to a modern state, much like what took place in Japan and Europe. The problem was that at the very time that this change was taking place, the Malay states were faced with the influx of huge numbers of Chinese migrants who came to work the tin mines. The sultanates were in no position to cope with the instability and disorder caused by this population change.

Malaya had been home to immigrants for centuries. For example, the Bugis and the Minangkabau represented waves of immigrants who came to the peninsula and settled, eventually becoming part of the population. Earlier groups that had moved to Malaya were from the

A Chinese tin mine of the early twentieth century.

archipelago, and while they were different, they shared a common religion, similar languages, and a common tradition as part of the archipelago cultural area. This was not unlike succeeding waves of European immigrants to the United States. Each new group, be it Irish, Italian, or Polish, had enough in common with those already in the United States that by the second or third generation, they had assimilated to a large degree.

The wave of Chinese migrants in the nineteenth century was a totally new phenomenon because the Chinese did not assimilate into the local population. The Chinese had been in Malaya since the time of Melaka, but they had come in small numbers and had basically adapted. This time they came in large numbers. In Perak, Negri Sembilan, and Selangor, they eventually outnumbered the Malays and lived separately from the local inhabitants. Through their kongsi, secret societies, and dialect groups, they were self-sufficient and had little desire to interact with the Malays, except when feuds broke out between Malay chiefs, and the Chinese were forced to take sides.

The long-term consequences of their separateness are felt to this day and will be discussed in later chapters. In the short run, the problems they caused were similar to those of the Straits Settlements in the early years. The difference was that in the Malay states, their conflicts took place in areas where the political systems, for all practical purposes, had fallen apart. The repercussions of their rivalries on civil society eventually forced the British to reevaluate their policy of non-intervention and take control of the peninsula. The civil wars in Selangor and Perak were two cases in point.

Civil War in Selangor

Large deposits of tin had been discovered along the major rivers of Selangor, and by the time Sultan Abdul Samad assumed the throne in 1857, five minor princes were vying for the wealth and power of the state. The weak rule of the previous sultan and the revenue from tin had created fiefdoms, which were aggressively defended by those who held them and coveted by other members of the royal family. Sultan Abdul Samad wanted little to do with these rivalries and withdrew to his palace, where he apparently preferred his opium pipe to affairs of the state.

War broke out over control of the district of Kelang, a tin-producing area that controlled the mouth of the Kelang River, down which tin from the interior traveled. Control of the area had been given to Raja Abdullah by the previous sultan but was claimed by Raja Mahdi, whose father had governed it previously but lost it when his tin ventures went bankrupt. Mahdi attacked Kelang and drove out Abdullah and his backers.

Around this time, Sultan Abdul Samad married his daughter off to the brother of the sultan of Kedah, Tengku Kudin. The sultan created the position of viceroy for Kudin, effectively turning over the affairs of the state to him. Kudin tried to mediate between Mahdi and Abdullah's sons, who, after the death of their father, carried on the war under the leadership of Raja Ismail. Mahdi rebuffed the efforts of Kudin and drove him into Ismail's camp. Kudin imported fighters from Kedah, and the anti-Mahdi faction recaptured Kelang. The war escalated with both sides recruiting allies to strengthen their cause.

In the 1860s, large numbers of Chinese laborers In the interior of the state worked the newly discovered tin fields in Ampang, north of the junction of the Kelang and Gombak Rivers. They too were fighting among themselves. On one side there was the Hai San secret society, which was based around the newly established town of Kuala Lumpur and led by one of the famous early leaders of the Malayan Chinese community, Yap Ah Loy. On the other side were the Ghee Hin who mined the fields around Rawang in the hills north of Kuala Lumpur. The competing Chinese factions were drawn into the Malay civil war when Raja Mahdi, in an effort to recoup his fortunes after his defeat at Kelang, recruited the Ghee Hin as allies and attacked Kuala Lumpur. Yap Ah Loy had no choice but to throw in his lot with Tengku Kudin's forces. The Chinese had become embroiled in a Malay civil war.

The conflict could not help but spiral beyond the borders of Selangor and into the Straits Settlements. Both secret societies had significant followings in Penang and Singapore. In 1872, Mahdi and the Ghee Hin successfully captured Kuala Lumpur, but Yap Ah Loy managed to take it back in 1873 with the help of recruits from Pahang.

British and Chinese businessmen had significant investments in Selangor. The disorder made it difficult to obtain tin at a time when demand was rising. Both sides in the war had borrowed money from people in all the three Straits Settlements to conduct the war, and this added to the concern businessmen and leaders had in the eventual outcome. The government of the Straits Settlements eventually weighed in on the side of Tengku Kudin, in part because he was believed to be the legitimate authority, having been appointed by the sultan, and in part because Mahdi and some of his followers had attacked shipping in the straits.

Most importantly, the business community of Singapore felt that Kudin would maintain the stability needed to carry on trade. The colonial secretary, J.W.W. Birch, publicly voiced British support for Kudin and lent him a British warship to blockade Mahdi's base at Kuala Selangor. Governor Sir Harry Ord encouraged Pahang to send in fighters to support Kudin's cause. In 1873, the tide of victory turned in Kudin's favor, most probably

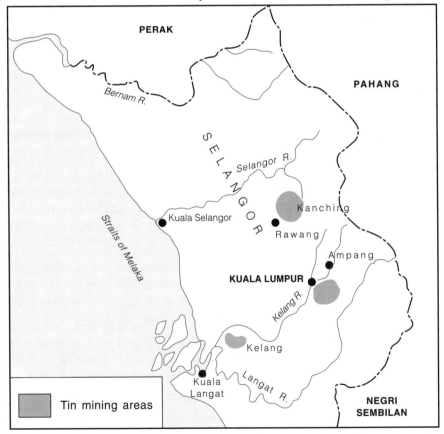

Tin mining areas in Selangor.

131

because of British intervention. Kudin's victory was a point well taken by other leaders in the peninsula. Kudin had won a Malay civil war with little Malay support. A traditional Malay power structure could survive if the British were on its side.

Perak

Perak suffered a fate similar to that of Selangor in which Chinese rivalries mixed with Malay politics and caused large-scale violence and civil disorder. Perak had traditionally been a source of tin, but in the 1840s, large deposits were discovered in the Larut district of the state, which was led by a local chieftain by the name of Long Ja'afar. Long Ja'afar invited Chinese merchants into the area to develop and work the tin mines. There was a "tin rush," and within two decades, over forty thousand Chinese were working the tin fields. This number was greater than the entire Malay population of the state.

Long Ja'afar died in 1857 an extremely wealthy man, and his son, Ngah Ibrahim, inherited his interests in Larut. He not only received his father's wealth but also the headaches that went with the Chinese migrant population and its secret societies. Initially, he solved the problem of Chinese rivalries by playing the two most prominent groups off against each other, the same two secret societies that had clashed in Selangor, the Hai San and the Ghee Hin. It was a game Ngah Ibrahim could not win.

In 1861, violence broke out between the two groups over a gambling dispute, but the real issue was control of the mines and the opium trade. Ngah Ibrahim realized the Hai San were the stronger of the two and sided with them despite the fact that they were the ones who had started the fight. As a result of the chieftain's actions and their inferior numbers, the Ghee Hin were driven out of their mines. Many of them fled to Penang.

Significant numbers of miners had originally come from the Straits Settlements or claimed they had, and as a result, they were viewed as British subjects. The Ghee Hin appealed to Governor Cavenagh for compensation and the return of their mines. Cavenagh agreed with their position and demanded that the sultan address their grievances. Sultan Ali, like many of his contemporaries in Malaya at the time, had limited control over the revenue from the state's resources and was weak politically. Local chieftains, such as Ngah Ibrahim, were wealthier than the sultan and could buy the support needed to defy him. The British then blockaded the coast to force a settlement. Ngah Ibrahim caved in, paid compensation, and returned the mines to the Ghee Hin. In return for his acquiescence, the sultan bestowed a new title on Ngah Ibrahim — *orang kaya menteri*, or elder minister — and gave him control over the Larut area. For a commoner, this was heady stuff, greatly increasing his power and prestige.

For a while, relative peace returned to the area, although both secret societies carried blood grudges against each other. These occasionally flared up. For instance, in 1867, open warfare between the two spilled into the streets of Penang. It took British authorities ten days to put down the fighting, and hundreds of people lost their lives.

Upon the death of Sultan Ali in 1871, these disputes between the Chinese factions became intertwined with Perak politics of succession. Raja Abdullah was the *raja muda*, or crown prince, and the traditional

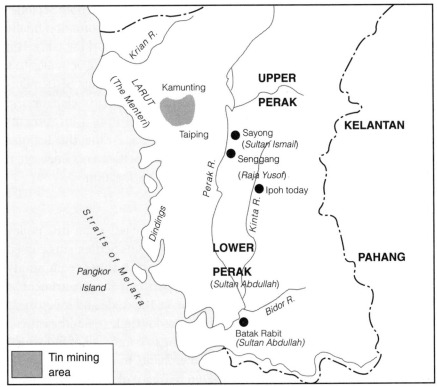

Perak during its civil war (1862–1873).

heir to the throne, but under Perak's laws of succession, this required the approval of the council of chiefs. Many of the chiefs in the interior, especially Ngah Ibrahim, felt Abdullah would be an unacceptable choice. Ngah Ibrahim felt Abdullah would bring the tin fields under the control of himself and his backers. Playing on the fears of all the chieftains of greater central control, he convinced the council of chiefs to install Bendahara Raja Ismail as the new sultan. His task was made easier by the prevalent view that Abdullah was a coward. Earlier, Abdullah's wife had run off with the brother of Raja Mahdi of Selangor, and he had done nothing to exact revenge for this treachery. His inaction was thought to be a sign of cowardice. This view was reinforced by Abdullah's non-attendance at the council of chiefs in the interior.

The state now had two claimants to the throne, Abdullah and Ismail. Abdullah turned to the Ghee Hin for support, and the Hai San, because of their ties to Ngah Ibrahim, supported Ismail in the ensuing civil war. In 1872, control of Larut changed hands a few times, with both societies bringing in more fighters from the Straits Settlements. A situation finally evolved in which the Hai San controlled the tin fields and the Ghee Hin organized a blockade of the coast, bringing the tin mining activities to a virtual standstill. Merchants and civil servants in the Straits Settlements clamored for a change in British policy. The disorder in Selangor and Perak seriously disrupted commercial activity, and British investments and Chinese interests were threatened. There was a fear that the disputes in the peninsula would spill over into the Straits Settlements once again unless something was done. The British finally took action.

Treaty of Pangkor

The British policy of non-intervention had originated as an EIC policy and continued when the administration of the Straits Settlements passed over to the British government. For some time, the business community in the Straits Settlements had been trying to persuade the government to change the policy. Besides the need to preserve the trade and investment they had in the peninsula, other opportunities for trade in Southeast Asia were being curtailed. The French were moving to control all of Indochina and were making it difficult for British merchants to do business there. The Dutch were ignoring the Anglo-Dutch Treaty of 1824 and placing restrictions on British trading in their part of the archipelago.

It seemed to businessmen in London and Singapore that the British needed to act in order to preserve the one area that had potential for increased trade, the Malay Peninsula. The British government itself was also going through a change in attitude toward the area. Apart from the aggressive expansion of the Dutch and the French, Germany was a rising power that was actively in search of areas for colonization. The fear was that one or all of these European powers would take advantage of the civil disorder in the peninsula to intervene and extend their influence.

The actual change in policy took place when the Conservative Party replaced the Liberal Party in the British government. The conservatives were amenable to imperial expansion and the acquisition of new territories as sources of raw materials for British industrial expansion. Thus, in 1873, when a new governor, Sir Andrew Clarke, was sent to the Straits Settlements, he was authorized to embark on limited interference in the affairs of the Malay states. His official orders called for the "preservation of peace and security, the suppression of piracy and the development of roads, schools and police, through the appointment of a political agent or resident in each state."

Clarke took the law into his own hands and acted swiftly to end the policy of non-intervention. Within two months of his arrival in Singapore, he summoned a meeting of the warring factions to end the Perak Civil War. The meeting took place aboard a British ship off Pangkor Island in January 1874. It was attended by Raja Abdullah, Ngah Ibrahim, the chiefs of lower Perak, and the leaders of the two Chinese secret societies.

This meeting produced two results. One was that the Ghee Hin and Hai San agreed to cease their warfare, disarm, and accept a British government commission to enforce the peace. By far the most significant agreement to come out of this meeting was the Treaty of Pangkor. This treaty signified the beginning of the creation of British Malaya. Under this treaty, Raja Abdullah was recognized as the rightful sultan, and he was to accept a British resident "whose advice must be asked and acted upon on all questions other than those touching Malay religion and custom." The resident was to take charge of the collection and control of all revenue, and the chiefs were to be given allowances. Ngah Ibrahim was to accept an assistant resident in Larut under the same conditions as those of the resident. This was the start of the system of so-called indirect rule, whereby the British planned to modernize and develop the Malay states.

Chapter 8

BRITISH INTERVENTION

The agreement between the British and some of the leadership of Perak at Pangkor signaled a significant moment in Britain's relationship with the Malay states. It marked a commitment on the part of the British to actively involve themselves in the maintenance of law and order; in the creation of modern government along more Western lines; and in the injection of their personnel into the day-to-day political life of the Malay states. It is highly unlikely that the men who signed the Treaty of Pangkor truly understood the ramifications of their actions, especially the Malays. It took time to determine the nature of the relationship between the Malay rulers and the British advisors they agreed to take on. Indirect rule presented a challenge in maintaining the traditional Malay royal courts while at the same time introducing Western political and economic models.

State-by-State Intervention

Perak and Selangor

Sir Andrew Clarke, who helped bring about this official change in British policy, appointed the colonial secretary to the Straits Settlements, J.W.W. Birch, resident advisor to the Perak sultan. Captain T. Speedy, a former Penang policeman who had been hired by Ngah Ibrahim to set up a police force, was made assistant resident of Larut.

Clarke then turned his attention to Selangor, which was just emerging from its civil war. In 1874, using pirate attacks off the Selangor coast on straits shipping as a pretext, he urged Sultan Abdul Samad to accept British advisors. The sultan agreed because British intervention would bring stability to the state and guarantee him a comfortable income to pursue a life of leisure without the pressures of the intrigues that had plagued his state and complicated his life. Frank Swettenham, a young Malay-speaking official who had helped mediate the end of the Chinese warfare at Larut, took up residence at the royal capital in 1875. Tengku Kudin in Selangor was also agreeable to British intervention as it would solidify his position. Further, the first official resident was going to be J.G. Davidson, Kudin's personal financial advisor who had been helping him reorganize the administration of Kelang.

Negri Sembilan

After dealing with Perak and Selangor, Clarke next intervened in the area directly south of Selangor, the Minangkabau confederation of Negri Sembilan. Settlers from the Minangkabau regions of Sumatra began arriving in this area in the mid-fifteenth century. Succeeding waves of immigrants as well as intermarriages with local Proto-Malays created a relatively homogeneous Minangkabau cultural region that included a significant area of the southwest peninsula. Under their traditional political system and ruled by clan chieftains, the Minangkabau had organized into *luaks,* or mini-states (Sungei Ujong, Jelebu, Johol, Rembau, Naning, Kelang, Jelai, Ulu Pahang, and Segamat). These states fell under the political control of Melaka and then the Johor Empire. Under both sultanates, Negri Sembilan enjoyed a significant degree of autonomy. The people, for the most part, depended on agriculture for a living but had also developed tin mining areas along the Linggi River.

With the weakening and eventual break-up of the Johor Empire in the eighteenth century, parts of Negri Sembilan began to be sliced off into other states in the competition to divide up what was left of the empire. The Bugis in Selangor took over Kelang; Naning was incorporated into Melaka with varying degrees of autonomy; Segamat became part of Johor; and Ulu Pahang and Jelai were incorporated into Pahang. In the latter part of the century, fear of the disappearance of any more independent Minangkabau states brought the remaining states together under the leadership of a *yang di-pertuan besar*, or head of state. The problem was that the alliance was based on outside threats, and, as its neighbors weakened through civil disorder and foreign intervention in the area, Negri Sembilan became a confederation in name only.

Two forces at work in this area drew the Minangkabau states into difficulties similar to those of the other Malay states. One was the intermarriages between the families of the chieftains and the minor royalty of Selangor and Johor. Without any central royal family, each Minangkabau state attempted to increase its power and prestige at the expense of the other. Tin and the revenue from it added to this competition and contributed to battles among the states. The difference between their problems and those of other states was that they came to a head at a time when the British were willing to intervene directly.

The most important of the Minangkabau states was Sungei Ujong, which controlled the upper reaches of the Linggi River. The river constituted the border with Melaka, along which a significant portion of the area's tin was transported. Like other areas on the western coast, the tin mines in the region had been developed by Chinese capital and labor, and in this case mainly by merchants from the British colony of Melaka. A dispute broke out between rival chiefs, Dato Kelana and Dato Bandar, for control of the tax revenue along the river. This effectively ended the export of tin from the interior. The merchants of Melaka, being British subjects, appealed to the governor of the Straits Settlements to intervene and protect their investments. In 1874, Sir Andrew Clarke recognized Dato Kelana as the leader of Sungei Ujong and vowed to keep the river open. In return, Dato Kelana agreed to accept a British resident.

The dispute did not quite end with this decision because the loser of the Selangor Civil War, Raja Mahdi, joined forces with Dato Bandar in the hope of reestablishing their political fortunes. A civil war broke out. The war was short-lived because British policy was now backed by British troops, which were dispatched to Sungei Ujong to end the fighting. Dato Bandar became one of a succession of Malay rulers who gained pensions and were exiled for their opposition to British wishes. In his case, he spent the rest of his days in Singapore.

The British had hoped that, for the time being, this would be the extent of their involvement in Negri Sembilan. They had commitments to the governments of Perak, Selangor, and Sungei Ujong and needed to sort out how these relationships would actually operate. This was not to be because of Dato Kelana and the maharaja of Johor, Abu Bakar. Dato Kelana, full of arrogance from his recent victory, refused to recognize the nominal authority of the yang di-pertuan besar of Negri Sembilan over his state, opening up old wounds and disputes with other luaks. The British saw

Maharaja Abu Bakar as a mediator, but it soon became apparent that he was taking advantage of the instability to exert his influence over these states, which were once part of the Johor Empire. The Minangkabau chiefs saw through his political schemes and turned to the British for a deal similar to the one Dato Kelana had received. Over the next two decades, the British signed agreements with each of the states. In 1895, Negri Sembilan became a united state under the leadership of the yang di-pertuan besar and a British resident.

Pahang and Johor

The unification of Negri Sembilan and its acceptance of a British advisor left two Malay states that did not have any connection with Siam and took no advice from the British — Pahang and Johor.

In many ways, Johor was a special case, and for a number of reasons, the British refrained from intervening in its affairs officially. Under the leadership of Temenggung Ibrahim and his son Maharaja Abu Bakar, there was a period of relative stability in the state. While there had been an earlier struggle with Sultan Ali for control of the government, it was minor compared to what had transpired in Perak, Selangor, and Pahang. Secondly, both father and son made great efforts to modernize the government and put the state finances in a responsible position. The method employed by the rulers to absorb Chinese capital and immigrants worked well. Much of this progress took place during the reign of Maharaja Abu Bakar, who ascended the throne in 1862 on the death of his father. Abu Bakar is seen by many as the father of modern Johor.

With advice from British merchants in Singapore, the Johor government was reorganized on a Western model. Government departments were established with specific responsibilities and run by a well-educated civil service. Government services were expanded and new ones added. An administrative system developed with departments of health, public works, the treasury, land, and marine. A centralized court and police system was also established. Johor was the first state to produce a written constitution, which was promulgated in 1895.

The population and economy boomed during Abu Bakar's reign. In 1846, the population of Johor was only a few thousand spread out along its rivers. By 1868, it had increased to 78,000 and by 1895 to somewhere

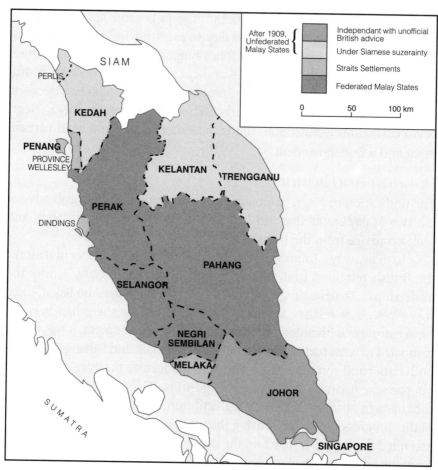

	After 1909, Unfederated Malay States {	Independant with unofficial British advice
		Under Siamese suzerainty
		Straits Settlements
		Federated Malay States

0   50   100 km

Malaya in 1895.

between 200,000 and 300,000. This increase was the result of the large numbers of Chinese and Malays who came to the state to take advantage of the economic opportunities. Johor's exports grew dramatically, and by the end of the nineteenth century, it was the world's largest producer of pepper. Johor also exported timber, cocoa, gambier, sago, and gutta-percha, a wild form of rubber. This growth was reflected in revenue to the government, which increased from $100,000 in 1855 to $2 million in 1894.

These changes created close political and commercial ties with Singapore. The island provided Johor with a port to export its goods and with the capital from British and Chinese sources to expand its economy.

140

These ties created a situation in which Johor rulers were on good terms with Singapore merchants and government officials. Thus, Johor's open economy and political stability gave the British little cause to meddle in its day-to-day affairs.

Pahang was a different story altogether. Sultan Ahmad, emerging from Pahang's civil war, did not have much control over the interior of his state. In order to win the war he had depended heavily on support from the chiefs of the interior. When it ended, they were not inclined to turn power over to a central government. Desperate for revenue, Sultan Ahmad decided to emulate Johor's model by leasing concessions for land in the interior to foreign interests, mainly the British and Chinese, in the Straits Settlements. The difference between Pahang and Johor was that most of the leaders in the interior did not think it was Sultan Ahmad's land to sell or lease, and he did it without their advice or consent.

By the 1880s, huge sections of Pahang were in the hands of foreigners with land claims that the sultan had no power to enforce. Many investors in the Straits Settlements began demanding that the British intervene to protect their investments. This, coupled with a British fear that some country, such as Germany or France, might step in and take advantage of Sultan Ahmad's greed and fiscal irresponsibility, made them insist he take on their advisors. At first, Sultan Ahmad resisted, but in 1888, with the encouragement of Sultan Abu Bakar, he finally accepted a British resident on the same terms as those in Perak, Selangor, and Negri Sembilan.

The Residential System

The British were moving into uncharted waters in their agreements with these Malay states. The sultans had accepted British residents and pledged to accept their "advice." What did this really mean? What would happen if the sultan did not accept the advice of the British resident? What could the resident do about it? Would he call in British troops whenever there was a disagreement? Against the backdrop of decentralization in the nineteenth-century peninsula, which brought about British intervention, even if the sultan agreed with a resident's decision, could he and the resident then enforce it without a large-scale British occupation of the state? There were definitely going to be some initial problems in this system of indirect rule, and much of its success rested on the shoulders of those who held power as residents.

The residents and British policy were in general operating under an assumption that was in itself a contradiction. They were charged with establishing a modern system of law and order and creating a central authority for the collection of state revenue to develop the infrastructures of the states. At the same time, they were to preserve the traditions and customs of the Malays. They had to modernize and preserve at the same time.

In one sense, the British were turning back the clock. Local chieftains, many of whom were not of royal blood, had grown wealthy and powerful in the nineteenth century, while the coastal royalty had weakened. The royal courts were feudal institutions that seemed destined for irrelevancy. The British restored the sultans' thrones and positions. On paper at least the sultans controlled the purse strings of the state. They ruled lands with defined borders, and they had the power of British backing to ensure the stability of their rule.

Trouble in Perak

These problems were manifested in the first state to accept an advisor — Perak. There was a time lag of about nine months between the signing of the Treaty of Pangkor and the arrival of J.W.W. Birch, the first resident. During this time, Sultan Abdullah, now that he had his hands on the reins of power, ran the state treasury into the ground to support his high living, gambling, and opium addiction. When he ran out of money, he sold off his right to collect taxes in part of the state to a Chinese supporter and sold the land in another district without consulting the local chief. The state had no revenue to pay off Abdullah's debts.

Birch faced a host of problems besides the ones Abdullah had created since taking power. The first was that Abdullah had only signed the Pangkor pact because it recognized him as the sultan of Perak. He had no intention of being told what to do by this stern, overbearing Englishman who did not even speak Malay. When it became apparent that British advice meant that the state was now going to collect and receive all taxes, the local chiefs who had not signed the treaty as well as those who did sign refused to go along with the proposed changes because their agreement would signal the end of their independent power and prestige.

Another problem Birch faced was that "modern" law and order flew in the face of Malay custom. For example, Malay tradition accepted that if

142

a person was unable to pay his debts, he and his family would become slaves to the lender for the rest of their lives. Nineteenth-century Englishmen opposed any form of slavery, and Birch attempted to abolish debt slavery. To the nineteenth-century Malay, this was part of their way of life, and ending it would wipe out the assets of the lenders.

The final problem Birch faced was his own temperament. His experience was as an administrator in the British colonies of Ceylon and Singapore, where the British ruled directly. There was no need to discuss, convince, or educate. In his experience, the government told people what to do, and they did it.

These problems created a shaky situation in Perak. Birch finally threatened to remove Abdullah as sultan unless he went along with the proposed reforms to centralize revenue collection and to end debt slavery. In July 1875, Abdullah gave in and signed the necessary proclamations but, at the same time, began plotting with his former civil war enemies to get rid of Birch — permanently.

Meanwhile, a new British governor of the Straits Settlements, Sir William Jervois, arrived in 1875 to replace Sir Andrew Clarke. Jervois felt that the solution to the situation in Perak was direct rule — British officials to collect the taxes, British judges to determine the law, and British police to maintain order. In other words, rule in the sultan's name; do not just advise him. In the long run, this was pretty much what the British did. This solution, however, was too quick and too dramatic to be accepted without a fight.

In November, when Birch went to lower Perak to proclaim the reforms, he was murdered. Jervois, who saw this as the start of a peninsular-wide uprising, called in British troops from India, Hong Kong, and the Straits Settlements. Perak was placed under military administration, and four of the murder conspirators were hanged. Sultan Abdullah and some of the major chiefs were exiled to an island off the east coast of Africa, while Sultan Ismail and a number of other chiefs were exiled to Johor. Yusuf, another claimant to the throne, was made sultan as a reward for his noninvolvement in the murder and also because of his general support for the British.

There is little doubt that Jervois had overreacted. The murder was done by a small group of the elite, and the ordinary Malays were not involved. On the other hand, his reaction taught an important lesson — the British had the power to ensure that the Malay leadership would go along with the policies they determined.

Pahang Chieftains Resist the British

There was a similar situation in Pahang where chieftains in the interior did not like the central state authority proposed by the British. A few chiefs refused to give up the independence and power they possessed, and this resistance led to a four-year war (1891–1895).

The British plan was to collect revenue from taxes and licenses and pay the traditional chieftains a salary. For most, this resulted in a reduction of income because they no longer received the income from the concessions to Chinese and European businesses in the interior. The most vocal and well-known chief was Dato Bahaman of Semantan. He refused to turn over the revenue from his area and encouraged others to do the same. The British increased the police presence in the interior with Indian policemen and attempted to arrest Dato Bahaman. Dato Bahaman and his large following of Malays and Orang Asli fought the invaders with hit-and-run attacks on police posts. For a while, central authority ceased to exist in some areas of the interior. Eventually, reinforcements were brought in from other states, and the rebels were forced into the jungle. The war simmered on until 1895 when forces led by Hugh Clifford finally forced Dato Bahaman across the border into Kelantan.

For many Malay nationalists, the Pahang War was one of opposition to British rule and evidence that the Malays did not accept colonialism quietly. There are many Malay stories of great bravery in the face of foreign invasion, and a popular folk hero, Mat Kilau, became a legend during this war.

Compromise and Stability

The residential system eventually succeeded in meeting many of the goals the British were trying to achieve by intervening in the Malay states. One reason for British success was the presence of a group of capable and knowledgeable residents and administrators. After the disastrous results of Birch's tenure, there appeared on the scene a different type of British advisor. Men such as Hugh Low in Perak, Frank Swettenham in Selangor and Perak, Martin Lister in Negri Sembilan, and Hugh Clifford in Pahang

144

represented a group of British administrators who developed an affection for Malaya and its people. They knew the language and customs of the Malay people. Most had spent a significant portion of their lives involved in the governing and study of the Malayan region. They realized that the Malay rulers had to be given deference and respect. Change would work if it developed slowly and if the Malay leadership was convinced that the change was in its own interests. For example, Low defused the issue of debt slavery in Perak by ending new slavery and phasing out the old over a period of time.

Through the efforts of these British leaders, a stable system of government emerged. Based in part on the model developed by Low in Perak, with some local variations, the leaders came up with a common structure of government. The idea was to incorporate as much of the existing Malay system of political leadership as possible. Under the old system, the sultans ruled through a network of chieftains, whose responsibility it was to collect revenue, administer justice, and maintain order in their areas. The districts controlled by these chiefs were further divided into subdistricts and headed by a penghulu who had similar responsibilities, usually for a group of villages. Below the penghulu was the *ketua kampung*, or the leader at the village level. The British divided the states into districts, with British district officers assuming the positions previously held by the chiefs but maintaining the system of penghulu and ketua kampung. Thus, at the "rice roots" level, the system did not change significantly.

Initially, these officers worked with the former chiefs, who were given allowances to replace their lost income, but as the chiefs grew old, the district officers became the actual administrators. These district officers reported to the resident, who in theory advised the sultan on what policies to adopt. There were also British officials responsible for specialized departments, such as the post and telegraph, mines, roads, surveys, and the treasury. At the top of the structure, in whose name the government was administered, was the sultan. Each state also had a state council, which acted as a consultative body to the ruler. It consisted of the sultan, the major chiefs, a couple of Chinese leaders, and the resident. The residents controlled the agenda but maintained the appearance of consulting with the Malays.

Another reason the residential system succeeded was its general acceptance by the Malay ruling class. The example of Perak taught the rulers the realities of life in the new order, and they made the best of it. Minor royalty accepted places on state councils and appointments to advisory boards and later legislative assemblies. Salaries, pensions, and allowances offered them reasonably comfortable lifestyles and some degree of continued status. Sultans and their courts had the security of tenure and income for themselves and their heirs. If a ruler went along with the British, he would have a beautiful palace, be accorded great respect, receive a generous salary, and be free of back-stabbing intrigue and general disorder, qualities that were characteristic of much of nineteenth-century Malay political life.

While indirect rule was in many ways a facade for British control of the government, the significance of the sultans should not be discounted. Their continued control over matters of religion and Malay custom made them strong symbols of Malay unity. As Chinese and Indian immigrants poured into the peninsula, the sultans stood as a reminder that these were Malay states and that, in the long run, the political future of the country was to remain in Malay hands. In the twentieth century, this became a major force in deciding what an independent Malaya and subsequently Malaysia would be politically.

The residential system had little impact on the everyday lives of a significant majority of the Malays. Their village leadership remained intact; the sultan was a distant figure and venerated as God's representative. The farmer and the fisherman had little contact with central authority prior to the intervention by the British, and the same was true afterward. Most Malays never laid eyes on an Englishman in their entire lives. The establishment of law and order, an end to debt slavery, improvements in public health, and more secure titles to their land did affect people in the village but did not significantly alter their traditional way of life.

Federated Malay States

By the 1890s, it became clear that the residential system was making great strides in achieving the primary motivation for intervention: the creation of conditions necessary for the economic development of the Malay states. For the most part, peace and order characterized the areas

146

under British influence. Investors no longer feared the disorder created by Chinese and Malay rivalries, as well as the uncertainties caused by the whims of local chieftains. Revenue collected from the states was used to build roads, railroads, and telegraph systems, making it easier to obtain and market resources, such as tin, while at the same time opening up new land for the cultivation of sugar, coffee, pepper, and later rubber. The creation of more consistent and enforced laws and regulations spurred further British and Chinese investments.

As time went on, it became apparent that the weaknesses within the system were retarding the potential of the area. One of these was the growing power and independence of the individual residents. In theory, each resident was answerable to the governor of the Straits Settlements, but in practice, they went their own ways. Communication with Singapore was poor, and the governor's primary concern was the administration of Penang, Melaka, and Singapore. Thus, the residents operated with little supervision from anyone. Differing codes of law and administration were evolving in the four states, and if the trend continued, these states would no longer operate as one. Infrastructure, such as roads, railroads, and communication, could only be developed efficiently through intrastate cooperation. There was a need for some kind of central coordination and control to ensure that the development of the four states as a group took precedence over what a particular resident saw as the needs of his state.

Another problem was unequal rates of development. Perak, Selangor, and, to a lesser extent, Negri Sembilan were progressing at a much faster rate than Pahang. The Pahang War had drained the state treasury, forcing it to assume a large debt. The resources of the state were more difficult to develop because of the inaccessibility of areas in the interior and the lack of revenue to build the roads to get to them. The northeast monsoon and the central mountain range also isolated Pahang and thereby retarded its growth. On the other hand, Perak and Selangor were doing quite well as a result of the revenue they received from their huge tin deposits. An example of the discrepancies was that in 1895, Perak had fifteen hospitals, Selangor fourteen, and Pahang only two.

The ramifications of these problems led to the call for some kind of centralized governmental control, which would create greater uniformity of law, rein in the power of the individual residents, and allow the use of the revenue of the more developed areas to help those that were lagging behind. Some, such as William Maxwell, the colonial secretary in Singapore, wanted to merge the protected Malay states with the Straits Settlements, while others, such as Frank Swettenham, then resident of Perak, thought centralization should be limited to the four states the British controlled. What finally emerged was close to Swettenham's model and became known as the Federated Malay States (FMS).

The plan called for the establishment of a federal capital at Kuala Lumpur and the creation of a new position of resident general. The latter would supervise the residents of the states and coordinate policy for the four states.

The sultans and the British approached the concept of this new government from opposite directions. The sultans saw it as an opportunity to put limits on the powers of their state residents. Part of the proposal called for conferences with the rulers and a federal council. The sultans believed that if they stood together they would bring greater influence to bear and increase their individual powers. Frank Swettenham, who was responsible for selling the idea to the sultans, played this angle to the hilt, although he shared the British view that the new system would actually improve British ability to control the political and economic life of the Malay states.

The British never intended to give any real power to the Malay rulers through the conferences or the federal council. Their plan was to create an efficient and effective government with the British in charge. Swettenham was appointed the first resident general and proceeded to demonstrate how the power of a centralized bureaucracy could usurp local power.

A federal civil service was established to coordinate policy among the main departments of state government — justice, finance, communication, and public works. The heads of these departments were answerable to the resident general. What this meant was that British heads of specialized agencies no longer reported to the resident in their state but to a department head in Kuala Lumpur. Residents, rather than being advisors to the sultans, now answered to the resident general.

When the federal council was established in 1909, the sultans soon realized that they had miscalculated. Rather than giving the sultans the opportunity to share a common front, the council further reduced their

Installation of Sultan Idris of Perak in 1886, with British officials Frank Swettenham and W. H. Treacher on either side of the throne. The sultan led his fellow sultans into the Federation agreement of 1895 but soon became critical of it. He deplored the lack of Malays in the growing civil service and was upset by the amount of control that the central government had over the states.

power and influence. The council was made up of the state residents, representatives of Chinese and British business interests, and the resident general. It was chaired by the governor of Singapore. The Malay members of the council became only four voices of many in the more centralized system.

In terms of the economic and governmental development of the Malay states, the new system was an important step forward. Roads and railroads were linked from state to state, and a common telegraph system was established. A commissioner of justice ensured that the legal systems and laws of the various states were consistent and established a court of appeals beyond the state courts. A commissioner of finance improved the collection of taxes and revenue, making money available to develop public services. All these changes made the FMS a more attractive place in which to invest. The export economy grew by leaps and bounds.

The new arrangement meant greater British control and more direct rule, but it was also the beginning of greater unity for the Malay states. The first rulers' conference in 1897 brought together in peace more than two sultans for the first time in history. Although the sultans did not have great power, the conference was one of the first steps in developing the attitude that there was a larger Malay identity beyond their individual states.

Another important trend was the creation of common institutions that transcended states. For example, the railroad belonged to the four states collectively and brought them closer together. Yet another example was the federal civil service. While it was dominated by the British, as time went on, it provided a structure for the Malays to participate in a government of Malaya rather than just in the governing of their individual states. The FMS was a model of greater unity, and ultimately it was the model for the establishment of the federations of Malaya and Malaysia.

Kuala Lumpur, the Capital

The choice of Kuala Lumpur (literally "muddy estuary") as the capital of the new federation was indicative of the changes that took place in Malaya. Originally, it was a town similar to many Western towns in the United States, which popped up as boom towns with the discovery of gold or silver. Kuala Lumpur was a result of the "tin rush" of the 1860s and 1870s; it was a small village prior to 1850.

Kuala Lumpur's survival was also due to the determination and force of personality of a Hakka immigrant: Yap Ah Loy. In many ways, Yap was representative of a group of Chinese immigrants who migrated to Malaysia and made significant fortunes. He came to the area at the age of seventeen to work as a coolie in the tin mines. He joined a secret society and served time as one of the gang's enforcers. Yap tried his hand at being a cook and a small businessman before he moved to Kuala Lumpur in 1862, where he built his fortune by developing interests in property and tin mines. By 1868, he was recognized as the Captain China, the leader of the Chinese community in the eyes of the Malay rulers. It is estimated that by 1880 he owned half the town.

The Selangor Civil War and a concurrent drop in tin prices devastated the town. Yap stepped in and virtually rebuilt it. In his efforts to revive Kuala Lumpur, he spent his entire fortune and went deep into debt. His gamble almost failed when the entire town burned down in 1881, but

Yap built it again. His efforts were rewarded when Kuala Lumpur became the capital in 1880 and later the capital of the FMS. Since he owned a significant part of the city, Yap quickly rebuilt his fortune. He was apparently unable to pass his abilities on to his family. His heirs squandered his entire fortune.

The creation of this federal capital was significant for two reasons. It signified the end of the traditional capitals of the Malay states, which were situated on the coast where major rivers met the sea, and it established the fact that the British were, henceforth, going to determine where the administrative capitals of the Malay states were going to be.

When Frank Swettenham established the administration of the FMS in Kuala Lumpur in 1896, the old adage in Malaya that "the land divided and the sea united" became obsolete. Kuala Lumpur had a central position because of the efforts of the British to unite the land through the building of roads and railroads. The Malay world of river villages and traveling by water became part of a bygone era. By the 1890s, people could travel by road from Melaka to Butterworth, the town opposite Penang on the mainland, and a road was opened up over the central range to Pahang, thereby ending its isolation. By the early twentieth century, people could travel by rail north-south from Butterworth to Johor, and Kuala Lumpur became the hub of this new rail system. The economic and political centers of the peninsula were moving away from Malay towns to new urban areas created by tin and rubber, populated by Chinese, and run by the British.

Unfederated Malay States

As the century drew to a close, administrators in the FMS and the Straits Settlements were increasingly eager for British intervention in the Malay states still under the influence of Siam. The states were Perlis, Kedah, Kelantan, Patani, and Trengganu. During the nineteenth century, the British government had rejected the pleas for intervention from these states because of British policies toward Siam. The latter played an important role as a buffer zone between the French in Indochina and British interests in the peninsula. A strong, friendly Siam was more important to the British than the potential benefits of controlling the northern Malay states. British trade and relations with Siam had improved tremendously in the second half of the century, and London did not want to rock the boat by threatening

Siam's interests to the south of its country. In the early twentieth century, this policy toward northern Malaya changed.

For the last three or four decades of the nineteenth century, the four northern states enjoyed a period of relative peace, stability, and independence. Part of the reason for this was the active presence of the British in the area. The intervention of the British in the southern states meant that their neighbors' civil conflicts and intrigues no longer spilled over the borders into the northern states. Disputes within the northern states were also relatively short-lived because of the absence of allies in the peninsula, who had prolonged and escalated their internal problems in the past. Apart from this, their lack of significant natural resources made it possible to avoid the destabilizing influence of the large numbers of Chinese, which had plagued their southern neighbors. While nominally under control of Siam, they enjoyed a considerable degree of independence because of a Siamese fear that efforts to directly control the northern states would give the British an excuse for intervention as had happened in Trengganu in the early 1860s.

Given the growing British economic and political interests in the peninsula, it was inevitable that their relations with Siam and the northern states would change. One factor that contributed to this change was the rise of Germany as a world power. Germany's massive military buildup, coupled with a desire to establish an empire to service its growing economy, drove the French and British into a common cause to counter this growing German threat. In 1896, the British and French committed themselves to maintaining an independent Siamese state, and in 1904, they agreed to respect each other's territories and spheres of influence — France in Indochina and Britain in the peninsula. These Anglo-French agreements eliminated Britain's need for Siam as a barrier to the French and thus lessened the need to please Siam by not interfering in the northern states. They, however, did not eliminate Britain's fear of German meddling.

In 1899, the Germans tried to convince the Siamese government to cede them the island of Langkawi off the coast of Kedah. While the Siamese eventually turned them down, these negotiations made the British nervous. Rebuffed in this attempt to gain a foothold in the archipelago, the Germans began looking into the feasibility of building a commercial canal across the Isthmus of Kra. The effects of such a venture to British control of the sea lanes and the economic success of the Straits Settlements would be disastrous. The Siamese did not appear to look favorably on this venture, but local conditions could potentially change their minds. Patani and Kelantan were looking for allies to sever their relationship with Bangkok. In the 1890s, they approached the British several times to ask for treaties of protection. The British, not wanting to offend the Siamese, turned them down, but the possibility that the states might turn to the Germans for help in their drive for independence was a British nightmare.

The chronic fiscal problems of the northern Malay states also contributed to British apprehension. Their lack of natural resources and therefore revenue made them perennial debtors and targets for European schemers. Kelantan, in an attempt to raise revenue, sold off about a third of the state to a former British police officer from Pahang named Duff, who bought the land for $20,000, quite a bargain indeed. His plan was to raise money through the sale of stock to develop the area he had acquired. This alarmed the British government. They did not want mini-states to be established in the peninsula, especially if Duff turned to non-British sources for capital.

All four states maintained the pomp and pageantry of their courts in spite of their poverty. For example, in Kedah, a succession of five lavish royal weddings virtually bankrupted the state. The British government feared that their inability to pay off their debts would invite foreign intervention to force payment or restitution in the form of territory. It was to meet this problem that the Siamese and the British signed a treaty in 1902. Under the treaty, the Siamese government appointed British nationals as financial advisors to these states.

A final factor that contributed to the change in Britain's relationship with the northern states was Siam's desire to change the nature of its relationship with Britain. In 1855, the Siamese had signed a treaty with the British, granting extraterritoriality to British subjects. This meant that British subjects were not liable for prosecution under the laws of Siam, somewhat similar to having diplomatic immunity. This was an affront to Siamese national pride. It seemed that any Chinese who had ever set foot in the Straits Settlements claimed to be British, and given the lack of travel documentation, it was difficult to prove otherwise. Thus, there were in Siam large numbers of Chinese who were not subject to its legal system.

The northern states became a bargaining chip in ending this situation.

All these considerations worked together to create the climate that produced the Treaty of Bangkok in 1909. Under this treaty, Britain agreed to pay off the debts of the four states, give up its extraterritorial rights in Siam, and lend the Siamese government four million pounds to build a railroad in the south of Siam. It also agreed not to interfere in the affairs of Siam or any areas under its control. In return, the Siamese transferred Perlis, Kedah, Trengganu, and Kelantan to British control and agreed not to let any foreign power build a canal across the Isthmus of Kra. With this treaty the northern border of modern Malaya was finalized.

The Treaty of Bangkok had an impact on the Malay world similar to that of the Anglo-Dutch Treaty of 1824. It arbitrarily divided the Malay community. Diplomats in Bangkok decided that the Malay state of Patani was to be permanently incorporated into the kingdom of Siam. The state had always experienced greater control from Siam because of its natural resources and strategic importance, but its people were Malay — they spoke Malay and were Muslim.

The intention of the British was to set up a relationship with the northern states similar to the one they had with Perak, Selangor, Negri Sembilan, and Pahang and to later bring them into an expanded FMS. The problem was that no one had asked the rulers of these states if that was what they wanted. The treaty had been negotiated without consulting the sultans and presented to them after the fact. Sultan Abdul Hamid of Kedah purportedly said at the time that "we have been bought and sold like a buffalo."

Kelantan, which had the most severe financial problems and was the most underdeveloped of the four states, readily accepted a British resident and the model of indirect rule, but the other states balked at the idea. Kedah, Perlis, and Trengganu initially accepted British protection but rejected British residents. They had seen what indirect rule meant in the FMS, and they had not spent a century or so trying to maintain their independence from Siam only to turn it over to British administrators and their so-called advisors.

Eventually, they were coerced into accepting British advisors, although these advisors did not have as much power as the residents in the FMS. Beyond this, they refused to budge and became collectively known as the unfederated Malay states. All four states had much greater Malay participation in the running of their state governments, and the ruling families enjoyed much greater independence from the "advice" of the British than the rulers of the FMS.

Johor

The remaining Malay state without an official British presence was Johor. The only formal tie between Johor and the British was a treaty signed in 1885. This gave Britain control of Johor's foreign affairs and elevated Abu Bakar from maharaja to sultan.

When Abu Bakar died in 1895, his son Ibrahim took the throne, and the British began to pressure him to accept a British advisor and take British specialists into his civil service. The British felt that coordinating Johor's policies with those of the Straits Settlements and FMS was essential. Johor's economy was closely tied to that of Singapore, and large amounts of capital from Singapore were invested in the state. Singapore served as the port for Johor's exports, and there were close ties of history, family, and race among the Chinese and Malay communities.

The economies of Johor, the FMS, and the Straits Settlements were increasingly intertwined, as was the infrastructure of the three areas. The exports and imports of the FMS primarily flowed through Singapore, and as their economies grew, Johor's independence was seen as an impediment to growth. For example, when the British wanted to push the railroad farther south through Johor to Singapore, Sultan Ibrahim wanted the Johor section under his control. The prospect of separate governments running separate systems went against the main thrust of British policy — integration and centralization. British commercial interests wanted common legal systems in the area. Modern communication, such as the telephone, required coordination. These instances of pressure finally persuaded Sultan Ibrahim to accept a formal British advisor in 1914.

While Johor was part of the physical and economic infrastructure that connected the FMS and Singapore, it maintained a certain degree of independence. Unlike any other state, Johor was able to preserve much of its Malay character, retain more control over its own administration, and provide wider opportunities for its Malay subjects.

Thus, until the Japanese invasion of 1941, Malaya was under three forms of government. There were the Straits Settlements of Singapore,

Melaka, and Penang. The FMS of Perak, Selangor, Negri Sembilan, and Pahang were in theory ruled indirectly but, for all practical purposes, run by a central government at Kuala Lumpur. The unfederated Malay states of Johor, Kedah, Perlis, Kelantan, and Trengganu followed the original indirect rule model of the British with Malay rulers and British advisors.

Chapter 9

THE BRITISH IN BORNEO

The island of Borneo today is divided among three countries. The Malaysian states of Sarawak and Sabah, along with the Islamic sultanate of Brunei, are on the northwestern coast, and the Indonesian portion, Kalimantan, is southeast of the central mountain range of the island. The northwestern part is of interest not only because it is part of Malaysia today but also because, historically, it had a far greater role in the Malay Mediterranean.

The first Malay contacts with the island took place later than those with the peninsula. Around the eighth or ninth century, Malay settlements began to appear around the river mouths on the northwestern coast of Borneo. These original settlements became part of the Sri Vijaya trading system. As time passed, Borneo's location near the Spice Islands of the

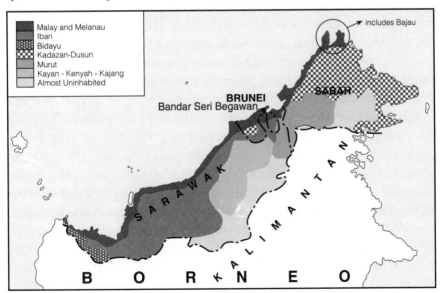

Major ethnic groups of northern Borneo in 1990.

157

Moluccas and Bandas and between the Straits of Melaka and China gave it the opportunity to develop as an entrepôt in its own right.

Brunei Sultanate

The first significant state to develop in the area was Brunei, which probably appeared as an independent entity in the early fifteenth century. By the end of the century, Brunei controlled most of the northwestern coast of the island. Its fortunes rose dramatically with the fall of Melaka to the Portuguese in 1511 because it drew many of the Muslim traders who fled Melaka. At around the same time, the Brunei royal family and subjects converted to Islam, further enhancing its appeal as part of the East-West trading system.

In the sixteenth century, Brunei was a relatively peaceful place to trade compared to the Straits of Melaka. It became an important distribution center for Indian textiles in the South China Sea and eastern archipelago; a source of jungle produce, such as rattan and bird's nest for China; and an entrepôt for spices, such as nutmeg, cloves, and pepper, from the neighboring islands. Unlike the other Muslim states, the leaders of the sultanate did not feel animosity toward the Portuguese and traded with them as well. At the height of its power and influence, Brunei stretched into significant portions of what is now the Philippines and boasted a thriving, wealthy capital city of some twenty to forty thousand people.

In some ways, the Brunei sultanate was quite similar to the Malay entrepôt states of Melaka and Johor. Its power came from control of the river mouths along the coast and the allegiance of the leaders of those settlements. Like Melaka, it drew its wealth and prestige from the trade that passed through its port and modeled its government after its Malay predecessor. In the sixteenth and seventeenth centuries, the sultanate prospered and was able to avoid the dislocations that took place in the peninsula after the arrival of the Europeans. Brunei was far away from the fiercely contested straits and was useful enough to all that it was left alone.

While its beginnings were similar to those of Melaka and Johor, the area originally controlled and influenced by Brunei evolved in a different manner. In the peninsula, there was a constant flow of Malay immigrants into the country. While this was happening, new lands were opened up, and the indigenous people were pushed farther into the interior. What developed were Malay agricultural communities away from the courts, which eventually formed the backbone of the Malay states.

The Malays who arrived in Borneo were confronted with indigenous people in far greater numbers. The rivers of the interior of Borneo were dangerous places that isolated the Malays along the coast, a minority of the resident population. While the Malays were the only group in the peninsula to whom the British felt any political obligation, on the island of Borneo, the Malays were one of many.

The indigenous people numbered more than those in the peninsula and were also much more aggressive in standing their ground. Headhunting and the enslaving of vanquished foes were part and parcel of their way of life. The primary goal of battle was to kill and then decapitate the enemy. The head was brought home, where it was smoked, dried, and hung from the roof beams of the longhouse, or community house. They believed that the warrior captured the spirit of his enemy, thereby enhancing his own power. Bidayuh women would not marry until their betrothed produced the head of a member of a rival tribe. There was probably a defensive dimension to headhunting as well. In an area where intertribal warfare was rampant, it made sense to be proactive. Warriors could send a message to potential enemies by taking a few heads first — a deterrent weapon so to speak.

THE LONGHOUSE

Most of the tribes of Borneo share a common style of architecture known as the longhouse, which is literally an entire village in one building. Like many semi-nomadic people of the area, they practise slash-and-burn agriculture, in which food production is a communal endeavor. In the past, the primary purpose of living together under one roof was for security in a hostile environment. For all practical purposes, the longhouse is a fortress. Most are built close to Borneo's highways, the rivers. Raised some 12 feet (3.6 m) off the ground, they were too high for the spears and poison-tipped darts of their enemies.

The longhouse is the home of the entire community, and the larger the number of inhabitants, the greater the security. Some are as long as 1,200 feet (365 m) and contain as many as one hundred families. Against one wall are rooms for each family. The length of the other long wall is a common area, a combination village lane and community center. Unmarried males live in the common area, while unmarried females live in a loft. A common practice among some tribes allows unmarried people to cohabit with multiple partners until they find a compatible mate.

A Sarawak longhouse.

In the eighteenth century, Brunei's control over its empire began to decline and continued to do so until it almost disappeared as a political entity in the nineteenth century. One of the reasons for this was the loss of its position as an important trading center. The rise in power of the sultanate of Sulu in the eighteenth century diverted a lot of Brunei's spice trade to the southern Philippines as well as weakened its influence over the northeastern part of Borneo. In the second half of the nineteenth century, Brunei's usefulness to the trading patterns of the area was further reduced by the growing Dutch and British control of trade and the sea lanes. With the loss of revenue from trade, the sultan's control over the other parts of the Brunei Empire began to decline. The result was that the minor royalty who controlled many of the river mouth settlements turned to the tried and tested backup in hard times — piracy.

Borneo was sufficiently far away from Dutch and British sea power for pirates not to worry about the consequences of their actions. Apart from this, Borneo had plenty of rivers with shallow mouths such that even if the pirates were pursued, they could escape the larger European ships. Arab traders in Brunei whose trading fortunes had declined bankrolled pirate expeditions and then helped dispose of the booty. Finally, there were indigenous groups whose warlike nature provided willing participants in the pirate trade. The Ibans were primarily a riverine people, whose agricultural methods quickly depleted the soil. Over time, this pushed them farther down the rivers to the coast. This migration eventually brought them into contact with coastal Arabs and Malays who offered them alternative work that suited their skills. These factors, together with the fact that most of the China trade passed through the South China Sea, made it open season for plunder.

By the early nineteenth century, due to a reduction in legitimate trade and a rise in piracy, the hold the sultan of Brunei had over the area had become tenuous. The sultan had control only over the coastal areas; he never had any over the interior. During this period, minor royalty were establishing their independence, and the political situation was chaotic.

Raffles, when he was lieutenant governor of Java from 1811–1816, wanted to intervene and establish British influence over the area. He sent representatives to show the flag and attempted to establish British trading ports. However, when the British withdrew from Java after the Napoleonic Wars, they lost interest in the area. Raffles continued to lobby for British action, but it fell on deaf ears. The Dutch were not interested in northwestern Borneo because they did not feel the returns would be worth the time, effort, and expense it would take to suppress the pirates. This left the way open for enterprising adventurers to take advantage of the instability on their own. One such person was an Englishman by the name of James Brooke.

Sarawak and Brooke

In many ways, Brooke was a disciple of Stamford Raffles. The latter believed that the advancement of British economic and political interests could coexist with a better life for the people of the areas they colonized. Through benevolent leadership, the people of the archipelago would benefit from

British rule and values. The abolition of slavery and the end to piracy, along with stability and justice, would raise them from the decay and cruelty of their lives. He never tired of preaching a mixture of British expansion and what would later be called "the white man's burden."

In the case of James Brooke, Raffles' message did not fall on deaf ears. Brooke, like his father, worked for the EIC but was forced to retire when he was wounded in action in 1825. After leaving the EIC, he travelled extensively across Southeast Asia and became convinced that Britain should extend its power and influence in the area. When his father died in 1835, Brooke took his inheritance and bought a ship, the Royalist, and sailed to the East. His original plans were for a voyage of exploration and scientific discovery in Borneo and the eastern archipelago. What he actually achieved was the establishment of a kingdom in Sarawak that lasted a hundred years.

When Brooke first sailed up the Sarawak River to the capital of Kuching in 1839, a civil war was in progress. Since 1837, a curious alliance of Malay chiefs and upriver Bidayuhs had been in open rebellion against

the sultan's governor, Makota. The Malay chiefs were not natural allies of the Bidayuhs, as their relationship in the past was marred by exploitation and cruelty on the part of the Malays. Makota had little regard for the local Malays, and in his attempt to obtain maximum financial gain, he usurped their traditional privileges. This forced the Malay chiefs into common cause with the Bidayuhs of the interior.

Raja Hassim, the uncle of the sultan of Brunei and heir to the throne, was sent to the area to quash the revolt but met with little

A Land Dayak warrior of the early twentieth century. Dayaks are now called Bidayuhs and number around one hundred thousand.

162

success. He even appealed to the government of the Straits Settlements for help. This was of no avail due to the existing policy of non-intervention.

During this first visit, Brooke traveled upriver and visited a number of Bidayuh settlements. His experiences at this time reinforced his belief that rule by the British could benefit the indigenous inhabitants of Sarawak. He was appalled by the evidence of headhunting but also developed a deep sympathy for the plight of the Bidayuhs vis-à-vis the coastal groups.

Brooke left Sarawak to complete the rest of his planned journey and did not return until about a year later. When he arrived in Kuching, the rebellion was still in full swing. A desperate Raja Hassim welcomed Brooke with open arms and offered him the governorship of Sarawak provided he helped put down the rebellion. Brooke seized the opportunity to do something about the problems he perceived in Sarawak.

It is quite amazing that Brooke was able to bring peace to the area, but there were forces working in his favor. The Bidayuhs were perfectly willing to accept outside intervention. The second largest of the indigenous groups, they were constantly being attacked by the numerically larger and more warlike Ibans. Perhaps a foreigner who was neutral could bring an end to this and to the poor treatment they received from Malay leaders.

Further, Brooke's ship and cannons contributed to a willingness on the part of the antagonists to talk peace. There was a wide technological gap between the weapons he possessed and those of the locals. Apparently, Brooke's personality also contributed to his success. A skilled negotiator, he was able to convince the various parties that a Sarawak under his leadership could offer a better future for all involved. Some had second thoughts later, but initially, he charmed and cajoled them into accepting peace. This placed Raja Hassim in a quandary. Brooke had fulfilled his half of the bargain, but Hassim did not have the power to give away part of the sultan's land. Hassim's hand was forced when Makota, who was the official governor, botched an attempt to poison Brooke's interpreter, and Brooke threatened to lead another revolt. Hassim proclaimed Brooke raja of Sarawak in November 1841. Thus began the succession of the three white kings of Sarawak, which ended when Vyner Brooke, James' great nephew, ceded Sarawak to the British in 1946.

Brooke now had a vast area in which to implement his version of enlightened British rule. Initially, his goal was to bring peace and order to the area. This entailed three objectives: to end piracy, to stop the Ibans from persecuting the Bidayuhs, and to end the practice of headhunting. The road to these initial aims did not look promising. He did not have the official sanction or support of the British government so he did not have access to its military, financial, or political resources. The state itself was virtually bankrupt, and its government had ceased to function as a result of four years of civil war.

The key to peace in the area was to pacify the Ibans and convince them to cease wrecking havoc in the interior and on the high seas. It was, however, difficult to differentiate between what constituted Iban piracy and what was Iban intertribal warfare. Brooke used them both to his advantage. He built forts manned by Europeans near river mouths to isolate the Ibans of the interior from the sea and the Malays who recruited them. He then turned to the British Royal Navy, whose responsibility it was to eliminate piracy in the area. Brooke persuaded Captain Henry Keppel and other British officers to attack the coastal pirate camps, many of which contained large numbers of Ibans, to rid the scourge of piracy in the South China Sea. The British steamships convinced many of the Ibans that there was a better way to make a living. These efforts and Brooke's ability to manipulate the conflicts within the Iban community eventually created Iban support for the rule of the White Raja. In fact, the Ibans became some of his greatest supporters.

The actions to subdue the Ibans also helped Brooke expand the area he controlled. Brooke had little respect for the ruling family of Brunei and felt that the sooner the areas it controlled were pried from its grasp, the better off the people would be. As he moved northward along the coast from one river mouth to another, he managed to coerce the sultan of Brunei into ceding him more and more territory in return for his efforts to control piracy as well as for yearly payments to the sultan. The latter, seeing the support of the Royal Navy for Brooke's actions, probably saw an official hand behind him and went along with his idea. The extent of the role of the Royal Navy cannot be underestimated. Brooke and officers, such as Keppel, convinced the British government that they needed a base in the area to suppress piracy. In 1846, Brunei ceded the island of

Labuan off the northern coast to the British, and the pirate menace was reduced.

As the 1840s wore on, Brooke became firmly entrenched as the ruler of Sarawak. There was a large degree of peace in the state. Brooke's achievements made him the talk of London and Singapore. In 1848, he visited London and was rewarded for his efforts with a knighthood. He was made the first governor of the new colony of Labuan.

Brooke's success was heady stuff and blurred the reality of Brooke's and Sarawak's true status. The British government had serious misgivings about becoming too actively involved in the area and feared that Brooke would draw them into ventures beyond their only interests in Borneo — the suppression of piracy and the protection of the China shipping lanes. They did not want to get involved in the local politics. Local leaders saw the position of the British in a different light. To them Brooke's governorship of Labuan and the occasional support he received from the Royal Navy meant that he had official approval from London. This worked to Brooke's advantage in his dealings with Brunei and other states in the area, and as a result, he did little to dispel it.

There was, however, occasional local resistance to Brooke's expanding influence. In Brunei, the sultan's inability to stand up to Brooke's dismemberment of the sultanate, coupled with his promise to cede the island of Labuan to the British, played into the hands of dissidents at the royal court. In 1846, Raja Muda Hassim and most of his family were murdered. This was done to prevent his possible accession to the throne and also because he was seen as an accomplice to British designs on Brunei. In 1847, Brooke and the British navy attacked the capital and forced the sultan to sign over Labuan to British control.

At times, the Malays and Ibans joined forces to defy Brooke. In 1849, a Malay known as the Laksamana assumed the leadership of the Saribas River Ibans. He challenged Brooke's authority by attacking villages along the coast and river mouths. Backed by the British navy, Brooke exacted his revenge. In the ensuing battle and its aftermath, over one thousand Ibans were killed and numerous villages put to the torch. Many historians see the campaign as one against Borneo pirates, but modern Iban historians, such as Empiang Jabu, see it as an example of Iban resistance to a foreign interloper.

From 1859 to 1861, while Brooke was out of the country, rumors spread that the White Raja had fallen out of favor with Queen Victoria. Sherip Masahor, a local Malay notable, took advantage of this situation to instigate a widespread uprising against Brooke's rule, making common cause with Malay chieftains and many Bidayuhs. The revolt spread to the west and across the border into Dutch Borneo. Charles Brooke, who had been left in charge, fought desperately to maintain control. At one point, the only area that remained loyal was around the capital of Kuching. Brooke returned in 1861 to rally support among the local population and to lead the fight. The Royal Navy once again pitched in as part of its war on piracy. Finally, the very nature of Sarawak's diverse population contributed to the end of the revolt. The traditional animosities and shifting loyalties of the various groups made any kind of sustained rebellion impossible.

Benevolent Rule

His initial goals achieved, Brooke faced the reality of actually running this area. The dream planted by Raffles of British benevolent rule created a dilemma for Brooke. Like many of the British who came to work in Malaya, Brooke developed an affection for the people and their traditional way of life. His dream was to eliminate the crueler aspects of their way of life, such as slavery and headhunting, through British guidance. At the same time, he would preserve the core of their culture in its traditional setting, the rivers and jungles of Borneo. To achieve these goals required an expanded and more modern governmental structure. Brooke had meagre financial resources, and any potential income could only come from the lands of the indigenous people. To cut down the jungle, dig for minerals, and plant cash crops would destroy the environment necessary to support the traditions and culture of the people. James Brooke and his nephew who succeeded him to the throne met the challenge in three ways: through the system of government administration that was established, through an economy structured along racial lines, and through tightly restricted economic development.

The state was divided into districts with British administrators in charge of them. Below the district officer were subdistricts responsible for groups of longhouses and villages and presided over by government appointed British and Malay officials. The key roles of the state government officials were to act as judges and police to ensure headhunting was wiped out and to serve as arbitrators to settle disputes that broke out between rival tribes and groups. In other words, to keep the peace. For the indigenous groups, such as the Ibans, Bidayuhs, Melanaus, Kenyahs, and Kayans, the traditional forms of community leadership were left intact, and thus at the lowest levels, life went on the same way as before.

The system provided a connection between people in the interior and the larger state ruled by the raja, but at the same time, the groups were highly autonomous as long as they accepted some curbs on the perceived excesses of their former lifestyle. At the top of this governmental structure was the raja whose rule was absolute but who accepted the advice of the Council Negri, or state council. The state council consisted of the raja, district officers, Malays, Bidayuhs, Iban chiefs, and eventually representatives of the Chinese community. The system of indirect rule set up by Hugh Low in Perak reflected his having spent time in Sarawak.

A further tool used by Brooke in his attempts to find a balance between development and preservation was the organization of the government and economy along racial lines. Chinese immigrants were invited into the state to provide the impetus for economic growth. Most of them settled in the towns along the coast and rivers, and they provided the retail trade, developed most of the export crops, and manned the mines. There was some indigenous participation in the economy as well. Ibans and Bidayuhs provided jungle produce for the world market, and the Melanaus grew sago, but the Chinese were key middlemen in the marketing of these products. By having the Chinese develop the economy, it was hoped that the indigenous people would be insulated from the effects of a modern capitalist economy. At the same time, the economic activities of the Chinese would provide the revenue to run the government.

The Malays were drawn into the state administrative service. In their roles as civil servants and policemen, they maintained some of their status as the former rulers of the state. This is not to say that was all the Malays did, as many found work in agricultural pursuits. They were, however, the primary local group that was invited into the day-to-day running of the government.

The Ibans made up the majority of the state military. This had a duel role — one was to draw on their warrior traditions but steer their loyalties to the raja, and the other was to create a source of unity for a divided community. Ibans from various areas, many of whom had fought each other for years, now served together and had a stake in the future of Sarawak.

The people of the interior carried on as they had for centuries, living a nomadic life of subsistence agriculture. They were involved in the larger economy only through the collection of jungle products, which provided them with enough money for tools, clothes, and ceremonies. That the system worked and was preferred to those in other parts of Borneo is evidenced by the immigration to Sarawak of not only the Chinese but also of large numbers of the indigenous people from Brunei and Dutch-controlled Borneo. They wanted to take advantage of the relative peace and stability in the state, and in the first decade of Brooke's rule, the population more than quadrupled.

Brooke decided that any economic development of the state was going to be on a limited scale. Foreign investment would be tightly monitored and controlled, and he confined increased economic development to the coastal plains. The interior, for the most part, was off limits.

This outlook toward development made powerful enemies for James Brooke. Merchants and investors in Singapore and London had anticipated an open-door policy on the exploitation of Borneo's resources. When it became evident that Brooke had no intention of allowing uncontrolled development, the very men who had lauded him for bringing British civilization to Borneo turned against him. Interventionists joined in common cause with non-interventionists and accused Brooke of using the Royal Navy for his own expansionist purposes and glory. In order to serve his own selfish ends, he was said to have attacked peace-loving locals, whom he labeled pirates.

There is much truth in these accusations as he did manipulate the navy, but to talk about peace-loving Ibans at this time is an oxymoron. No doubt Brooke was an empire builder, but neither he nor his heirs ever derived great wealth from their endeavors in Borneo. Brooke exhausted virtually all his own resources in pursuit of his dreams. In his later years, the only way he kept the state afloat was through periodic loans from a wealthy English heiress who sympathized with his objectives.

In 1854, a naval commission convened in Singapore to investigate the charges against Brooke and exonerated him completely. The attack on Brooke turned out to be counterproductive to those who wanted to increase the development of Sarawak because some in the Chinese community interpreted the criticism and subsequent naval investigation as signs of Brooke's weakness. This coincided with a general rise in anti-British sentiment among the Chinese because Britain was at war with China. At the same time, there were rumors circulating in Sarawak's Chinese community that the Chinese government was offering £25 for every Englishman killed. In 1857, hundreds of Chinese miners attacked and occupied Kuching, forcing Brooke to flee for his life. The Chinese rebellion was short-lived as Brooke returned with the support of the Ibans and Malays to exact what he felt was a just revenge. One thousand Chinese were killed and 2,500 fled the territory. The Chinese uprising, which slowed down economic development, convinced Brooke to put severe restrictions on Chinese immigration.

The Chinese who stayed continued to play a key role in the state's economy. This was exemplified by men such as Ong Ewe Hai, who built a great fortune as a merchant. Later generations built on this and became prominent economic and political leaders of Sarawak. Ong's great grandson organized the Sarawak United People's Party (1959) and later became a minister in the Malaysian government.

James Brooke died in 1868 and was succeeded by Charles Brooke, who ruled Sarawak for nearly fifty years. Charles spent ten years as an administrative officer upriver in the Bidayuh and Iban communities and shared his uncle's views about the future of the state. While James was in some respects a dreamer, Charles was what the state needed — a practical administrator. He inherited a state that was heavily in debt and had been ruled in a very personal way by his uncle.

Charles' contribution to the history of Sarawak was to place the state on a firm financial footing by paying off Sarawak's debts and ensuring that government expenditure remained within its income. In the later years of his reign, he began to reverse James' anti-Chinese policy and encourage Chinese immigration, which boosted the economy and government revenue and created a more stable and orderly community than those in the peninsula at that time.

The government was actively involved in the movement of the immigrants into the territory. It was monitored closely with financial assistance; land was offered to many of the Chinese. In 1870, the Chinese population was about five thousand. By the early twentieth century, this grew to some forty-five thousand settlers. A unique dimension of these immigrants was the inclusion of a large number of Christian Chinese families, who had fled persecution in China and were actively recruited by the Brooke government. The city of Sibu owes much of its existence to this wave of immigrants. In order to provide the people with educational and social services, Charles also opened the door to greater missionary penetration of the state. Sarawak's high percentage of Christians today reflects that policy. By and large, the basic goals and intentions of James Brooke's rule of Sarawak were kept intact by his nephew.

British North Borneo

By the last third of the nineteenth century, the sultan of Brunei, desperate for revenue and with little real influence outside his capital city, was willing to give his approval to almost any scheme that would produce income for his court. This was already the case in the area Brunei had controlled south of its capital. James Brooke had gradually incorporated large sections of Brunei into Sarawak in return for increased yearly payments to the sultan. In the area north of his capital, a similar process was taking place in the area now known as the Malaysian state of Sabah.

The northern end of Borneo east of Marudu Bay was long associated with Brunei. This was so until the latter part of the eighteenth century when the sultan of Brunei ceded his rights to the Sultan of Sulu. Although the land no longer belonged to Brunei, the reigning sultan saw nothing wrong in selling it again in his search for increased income. Brooke's success in Sarawak encouraged a number of European adventurers to attempt similar ventures, albeit for more commercial reasons.

Charles Moses, an American, was the first to show direct interest in North Borneo. He arrived in Brunei in the 1860s and convinced the sultan to cede him the land that had already been ceded to the sultan of Sulu in return for an annual payment. Moses, who carried the documentation of an American consul to the royal court of Brunei, gave some hope to the

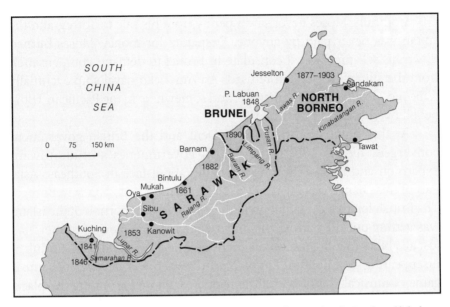

Sarawak, Brunei, and North Borneo (1841–1903) and dates indicating when the British established control in each area.

sultan that perhaps the Americans could act as a counterweight to the British and Brooke's growing dismemberment of his sultanate.

Moses was a poor choice. His claim as American consul was highly dubious considering he had been dishonorably discharged from the American navy. Also, few people in Washington, D.C. had ever heard of him. He quickly turned around and sold his rights to another American named Joseph Torrey. The latter was proclaimed raja of Ambong by the sultan of Brunei, and he established an American presence in North Borneo under the auspices of his American Trading Company. If Torrey had been a better businessman, the history of Sabah might have been radically different. His venture, however, failed. He sold his interests to the Austrian consul-general to Hong Kong, Baron von Overbeck, who entered into a partnership with a British businessman, Alfred Dent, to develop the resources of North Borneo. Overbeck negotiated treaties with both the sultan of Sulu and the sultan of Brunei in order to solidify his and Dent's claims to the area. In 1881, Dent bought out Overbeck, and as a result, the rights to North Borneo were held by his company, Dent Brothers.

Ironically, Moses never saw a penny from his sale to Torrey, and the sultan was never paid by anyone. Desperate for money, Moses burned down his self-proclaimed consulate in Brunei to demand compensation from the sultan. The sultan refused. An American naval ship eventually removed Moses from the sultanate, and somewhere in the Pacific in 1867, he fell overboard and drowned.

At this point, the interests of Dent and the British government converged. By the 1880s, the British government's attitude toward expansion and intervention had done an about-face in Southeast Asia. Part of this change was the result of a reevaluation of its policy in Borneo. The British felt that the situation in the northwestern portion of the island was getting out of control. The only organized local power, Brunei, had lost all ability to influence events in the area and appeared on the brink of disappearing as a political entity. North Borneo had degenerated into a game of musical chairs, with little regard to who was running the place. Sarawak had become a law unto itself, viewed as British by many in the area but with no control on its actions from London.

The instability created a fear on the part of the British that another European power might take advantage of the situation to extend its influence in the area. To prevent the intervention of another power, in 1888, North Borneo, Brunei, and Sarawak were made British protectorates, and all three accepted British control over their foreign relations. In 1905, Brunei entered into an agreement much like those in the peninsula. A British resident was appointed to the sultanate, and British indirect rule was established. Brunei's existence as a state was thus saved. Sarawak received the security and control of British protection, and the stage was set for a larger British presence in North Borneo.

In many ways, the British takeover of North Borneo was colonialism on the cheap. Alfred Dent was given the go-ahead to establish the British North Borneo Company,* which in turn was given the right to administer and develop the resources of the area. This seemed to be a return to the situation that existed under the old East India Company, and in some respects, this was true. The future of the land and people was entrusted to those whose main loyalty was to directors and shareholders in London.

---

* *Because it was granted a royal charter by parliament in 1881, the company was often referred to as the Chartered Company.*

There were a few differences in that the British government had more control than in the areas previously administered by the EIC. The Royal Navy was stationed in the area, the governors were approved by the British government, and the actions of the company were subject to parliamentary review, giving London a great deal of leeway to interfere if it so wished.

In fact, compared to Sarawak or the peninsular states, North Borneo was poorly administered for the first few decades of company rule. Many of the problems faced by the Straits Settlements under company rule resurfaced in North Borneo. Company officials had little or no knowledge of the country, people, or languages. An attempt was made to copy Sarawak's system of governing the interior but with little success. Hugh Clifford, a British official and governor, is said to have remarked in 1896 that not one of the district or subdistrict officers spoke a word of the language of the people for whom they were responsible. Decisions were made in London by directors whose sole interest was the corporate bottom line. As a result, policy was short-sighted and ill-informed. Government influence and control was usually coastal in nature. To most tribes in the interior, British rule did not represent any kind of improvement in their lives. Change came, although slowly, only in the twentieth century with the exploitation of timber and the introduction of rubber.

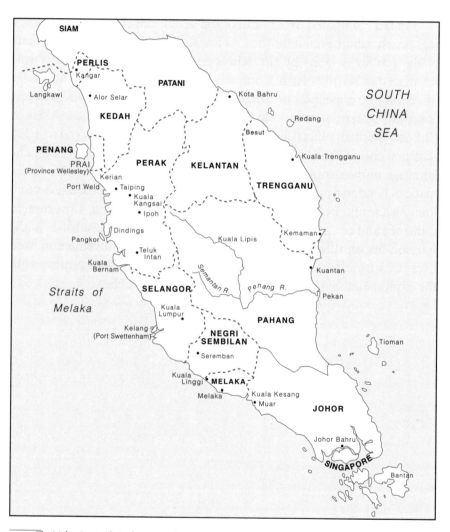

The Malay Peninsula in the twentieth century.

Chapter 10

IMPACT OF BRITISH RULE ON MALAYA

The establishment of British rule in Malaya had tremendous consequences for the peninsula. In the short run, the development of modern government along a Western model created the climate for rapid economic growth. This in turn generated the revenue necessary to sustain that growth. Modern government also established conditions that were conducive to the sizable population growth, which provided the labor needed to create great wealth for British and other non-Malay investors. In the long run, British rule created a multiracial society with serious economic and political inequalities, which the government of Malaysia grapples with to this day.

The British employed a variety of rationalizations to justify their intervention and control of the area known today as Malaysia and Singapore — to secure shipping lanes; ensure free trade; end piracy; deliver the local inhabitants from corrupt and incompetent leaders; bring peace and order; end abuses, such as slavery and headhunting; preserve the traditions of societies threatened by foreign immigrants; and create the conditions necessary for economic development. All these reasons were true but were secondary to the primary British motivation for its rule of Malaya in the twentieth century — to create the necessary environment for British investors to profit from the development of Malaya's natural resources, especially in the FMS. And profit they did. Economically, British Malaya became one of Britain's most successful colonial ventures.

In the nineteenth century, the focus of Malaya's role in the world economy changed from that of an entrepôt with limited amounts of local resources for sale to that of a major producer of raw materials. With the seizure of the entrepôt by the British, economic growth in Malaya could only come about by developing its natural resources. Most of this initial

175

growth, whether in tin mines in Perak or pepper plantations in Johor, was achieved by Chinese capital and labor. The nature of the Chinese business organization, be it the family or the kongsi, and the availability of inexpensive coolie labor lent themselves to the high risk situations that existed in the peninsula, which were brought about by its political instability and civil disorder. Chinese investments were labor intensive, the risks were shared, and the businesses incurred little loss by using cheap coolie labor. An example of their success is that at the turn of the century the Chinese controlled virtually all the tin mining areas in Malaya.

In the twentieth century, British investments poured into Malaya, and the British replaced the Chinese as the major producers of the peninsula's export products. By 1930, British-owned concerns controlled about two-thirds of Malaya's tin production. The value and amount of tin produced increased dramatically under the British. In the period 1898 to 1903, Malaya produced $30 million worth of tin; by 1924 to 1928, this had more than doubled to $78 million. At the outbreak of the Great Depression in 1929, Malaya was producing over a third of the world's tin.

When the change from Chinese to British control of the export economy took place, the Malayan economy registered a phenomenal growth rate. In 1895, total trade of the FMS stood at $18 million; by 1925, it had risen tenfold to $182 million. The Chinese had a share in this growth, and many continued to prosper, but most of the twentieth-century growth was the result of British commercial expansion, especially in the product that truly built Malaya's colonial economy — rubber.

Rubber

In the twentieth century, a combination of visionary British officials, technological change, and British policy caused a rubber bonanza in British Malaya. A form of poor quality wild rubber called gutta-percha had been exploited in Malaya for some time and was exported on a small scale with other jungle products. Its usefulness, however, was limited. In the 1870s, the domesticated trees, *Hevea brasiliensis*, which became the mainstay of Malaya's economic growth, were brought from Brazil to the Kew Gardens in London. Seeds from these trees were sent to Ceylon and Malaya, but British plantation investors were not interested in the product. Many of them thought that the most promising plantation crop for Malaya would be coffee and planted thousands of acres of it. They also wanted quick returns on their investments, and rubber trees took six to eight years before they could be tapped for latex.

An early rubber plantation.

The active encouragement of two far-sighted British officials helped to change the attitude of the planters. Sir Hugh Low brought seeds from Singapore and planted them on the grounds of his home in Perak where he was the British resident. As these trees gave up seeds, he passed them out to local coffee planters, attempting to sell them on the idea of an alternative crop. His efforts, however, met with skepticism.

More important to the introduction of rubber as a cash crop was the head of the Botanical Gardens in Singapore, H. N. Ridley. His experiments with rubber at the gardens produced hardier trees, efficient methods of tapping the trees, and ways to turn the sap from the trees, latex, into rubber sheets that could be easily collected and exported. Although he is viewed as a genius today, at the turn of the century, he was seen as an eccentric who toured the country with rubber seeds, trying to convince sugar and coffee planters that rubber was the wave of the future. Among the Europeans, he was known as "Mad Ridley" or "Rubber Ridley."

In 1839, Charles Goodyear, an American, discovered the process of vulcanization, which made rubber products sturdier and less malodorous. The popularization of bicycles using rubber tires and the invention of the automobile added greatly to the demand for rubber, especially with the invention of the inflatable tire by Charles Dunlop in 1888. When Henry Ford began to mass produce cars and make them available to the average person, rubber's future was guaranteed. The worldwide market for natural rubber created one of the most important growth industries in the early twentieth century.

The British colonial administration in Malaya provided a third impetus for a successful rubber industry in Malaya. When it became obvious that coffee was not going to be a successful export crop and that rubber was the crop to develop, the government of the FMS offered plots of 1,000 acres at inexpensive prices to investors who would plant rubber. They further encouraged rubber planting by waiving land taxes and taxing the exported rubber at low rates.

The combination of all these factors brought about a tremendous rubber boom in Malaya led by British investors. Rubber was first planted in Melaka in 1895 by Tan Chay Yan for commercial purposes. By 1902, there were 16,000 acres under cultivation. From there, it took off like a rocket. Within twenty years, more than two million acres of land in Malaya were under rubber cultivation, constituting about half the world's total rubber, a phenomenal expansion. In 1927, the world produced 604 million tons of rubber, out of which 344 million tons came from the British Empire, primarily Malaya.

It is important to note who took advantage of this boom and who benefited from these British policies. By 1938, in the three jurisdictions that made up British Malaya, over two million acres were under cultivation. Out of this, Europeans (most of whom were British) owned 1.5 million acres, Chinese 300,000, Indians 87,000, and Malays 91,000. There were

585 plantations with a size of 1,000 acres or more in British Malaya. The larger the plantation, the more efficient and cost-effective it was. Of these 585 large estates, 514 were in the hands of the British with a few owned by Americans and other Europeans. The Asian entrepreneurs had much smaller estates and lacked the sophisticated and expensive machinery to produce good quality latex.

Many Malays planted trees on their agricultural land to supplement their income, but their trees were small and produced low quality rubber. British officials feared that the Malays would shift from growing needed food crops to cash crops, such as rubber, and banned the growth of rubber in some designated Malay-reserved land, further obstructing the entry of the Malays into this industry.

Modern Administration

There are a number of other reasons why this incredible growth based on British investment took place. One important consideration was that the British administration, especially in the FMS, created the necessary conditions for investor confidence. British companies had to be convinced that Malaya was a secure place in which to invest.

By the early twentieth century, the British had brought the power of the central government to all but the most remote areas. This was more pronounced in the FMS but slowly evolved in the unfederated states as well. The creation of a professional police force whose loyalty was to the state meant that the lawlessness of the nineteenth century was a thing of the past. There were occasional anti-government uprisings, but British businessmen could rest easy that their ventures would not be disrupted.

British confidence was further enhanced by the legal and administrative systems that were established. To do business, investors must be convinced that the legal system in a country is transparent and consistent. In Malaya, this was true, and the system was familiar. Commercial and property laws were built on a British model. Claims to property and profit were no longer determined by the whim of the local ruler.

One of the most important functions of the early British administrators was the proper surveying of land in order to secure clear title to a property. Not only did foreign groups developing the land benefit, but it was one of the few policies that reached down to the average Malay. Due to the mobility of the Malay agricultural community and nineteenth-century upheavals, few Malays had secure ownership of the land they tilled. The British surveys and consistent property laws gave them title to their land.

A modern administrative system along British lines was essential to providing another key prerequisite for economic development, a modern infrastructure. The building of roads and railroads and the establishment of communication systems, such as post offices and telegraphs, were necessary foundations for developing Malaya.

The British administration attacked the problem of infrastructure with a vengeance. In 1896, the FMS spent nearly half their total revenue on road and railway construction and other public works. By 1900, $23 million had already been invested in railway construction, and 360 miles (579 km) of track had been laid. From 1900 to 1912, more than half the annual expenditure was spent on public works, buildings, roads, bridges, and railways. Railway mileage increased to 1,014 miles (1,632 km) in 1920. By 1928, there were paved roads from Johor Bahru to the Siamese border. Bridges were built, port facilities were developed, and rivers were dredged, all in the name of providing the necessary conditions for Western capital to develop Malaya's economy.

The pattern of this construction was indicative of British economic interests. The first railways were built from the Perak mining areas to the coast, but as industry grew and expanded to other areas of British influence, the railways were developed North-South to provide access to the ports and the tin smelting facilities in Penang and Singapore. The vast majority of investment in the transportation system was along the western coast in general and among the FMS in particular, which had the lion's share of British investments. Transportation was a key factor for the rubber industry as well, as it was able to export rubber through Singapore and Penang.

A Multiracial Society

The availability of a pool of cheap labor was important in the economic development of the areas under British influence. The most logical source of labor would have been the indigenous Malay population. For a variety of reasons, however, they played a minor role in providing the labor needed to develop Malaya's rapidly growing economy. Instead, the British actively encouraged the importation of labor from China and the Indian subcontinent. This was especially true in the Straits Settlements and the

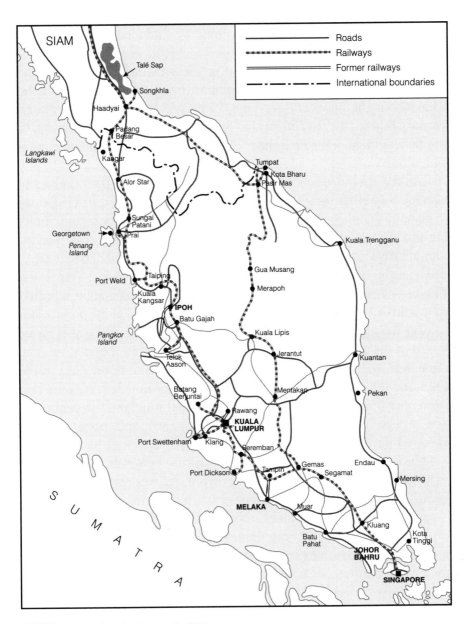

Malayan roads and railways in the 1920s.

FMS. The consequences of this decision were major factors that molded modern Malaysia. The next chapter discusses in more detail why the Malays were either unwilling, unable, unqualified, or excluded from this period of economic growth.

By far the greatest contribution to the growth of Malaya and the Malayan economy by migrant labor and immigrants came from the Chinese. In the nineteenth century, Chinese immigration had created virtual Chinese cities in Penang and Singapore. The Chinese were vital to the development of the tin industry in Perak and Selangor and plantation agriculture in Johor, Melaka, Penang, and Province Wellesley.

In the first three decades of the twentieth century, the numbers of Chinese as well as their roles expanded dramatically. Unrestricted entry to migratory Chinese not only increased the size of the Chinese community but also brought about a diversification in their economic roles that reached into all areas of the FMS and to a lesser degree the unfederated states. Between the turn of the century and the outbreak of World War II, the Chinese population in British Malaya tripled from some eight hundred thousand in 1900, when they made up less than a third of the population, to over 2.5 million in 1941, when they had become the largest racial group in the area, constituting close to half of Malaya's population. The same year, the Chinese made up the majority of the population in the FMS, and it was only their smaller numbers in the unfederated states that prevented the Chinese from being a majority throughout the peninsula. The Malays had become a minority in their own land, accounting for about 41 percent of the population.

Just as significant as their growth in numbers was the incredible variety of economic roles the Chinese played that were essential to British plans for development. Many Chinese, when they first arrived, provided cheap coolie labor in tin mines, rubber estates, and ports. As time went on, they began to act as middlemen and retailers. The British were interested in large-scale capital investment that could produce profits for their shareholders back home and in developing a market for their manufactured goods. This left a host of economic activities that the Malays were either unable or unwilling to undertake. Small-scale enterprises, such as trucking firms, ice factories, coastal shipping, buses, food processing, pawn shops, entertainment centers, and rice milling, were

RACIAL POPULATION OF MALAYA

	Population in thousands				Percentage of total population		
	1911	1921	1931	1941	1921	1931	1941
Europeans	11.1	15.0	17.8	31.4	0.4	0.4	0.6
Eurasians	10.9	12.6	16.0	19.3	0.4	0.4	0.4
Malays	1,437.7	1,651	1,962	2,278.6	49.2	44.7	41.0
Chinese	916.6	1,174.8	1,709.4	2,379.2	35.0	39.0	43.0
Indians	267.2	471.7	624.0	744.2	14.0	14.2	14.0
Others	29.3	33.0	56.1	58.1	1.0	1.3	1.0
Total	**2,672.8**	**3,358.1**	**4,385.3**	**5,511.1**	**100**	**100**	**100**

areas of the economy that Chinese immigrants gladly stepped into and eventually dominated. The Chinese also filled key areas of skilled labor as welders, mechanics, carpenters, and bricklayers, areas essential to a growing economy.

In the same vein, while the British wanted to sell the goods coming out of their factories at home, they had no desire to run the shops that actually sold these goods to the general population. As Malaya's population grew and developed a taste for manufactured goods, the Chinese stepped in to dominate the retail trade of the peninsula. The Chinese shop house with the family living upstairs and conducting business downstairs has become one of the most enduring images of Malaysian life and has fed the stereotype of the Chinese as a race of shopkeepers and businessmen.

This movement of the Chinese from migrant laborers to a group that played a variety of economic roles was reinforced by the fact that more and more Chinese began to view Malaya as their home and sink roots into their communities. For example, in 1911, only 8 percent of the Chinese population in the FMS was native born. By 1931, this had increased to 29 percent. These numbers climbed with each passing year.

This trend toward a more settled Chinese community was given a boost by the migration of increasing numbers of women to Malaya. The Chinese were moving away from a community of migrant laborers to a community of permanent immigrants, which also reinforced their growing economic position.

Among the many countries that have grown and prospered in the last hundred years, a common ingredient has been the existence of a large immigrant population. Canada, the United States, Australia, New Zealand, South Africa, Singapore, Hong Kong, and Argentina have large numbers of people with immigrant mentalities. Immigrants, by their very nature, carry with them the qualities needed for economic success. They are the risk takers, the ones that look at poor conditions in their home countries and are willing to strike out on their own to strange lands to seek new opportunities. They are unwilling to accept what fate has dealt them and want to build new and better lives. They are adaptable and willing to accept new ideas and new ways of doing things. Beyond this, once they leave, there is no turning back. They have to make it or starve. They have cut off ties with their friends, families, and villages; if they fail, there is no one to turn to for help. They are thus willing to work long hours at any job to lay the foundation for future economic success. These factors are important reasons why the United States has become the world's leading economic superpower. They also explain why Chinese communities all over Southeast Asia have prospered to this very day.

Another aspect of the Chinese community worth noting is where they lived. For the most part, they were urban dwellers and lived mainly on the western coast. As Malaya's new cities — Ipoh, Kuala Lumpur, Penang, Singapore, and Johor Bahru — grew, a common factor was the presence of large numbers of Chinese. At the time of independence in 1957, half the Chinese lived in the cities and towns, and about two-thirds of the populations of Malaya's cities were Chinese. The British controlled the production and export of raw materials; the Malays, by law and custom, controlled most of the staple agricultural food production; and as the country prospered, the Chinese lived where the economic action was — in the cities and towns.

The Chinese community also provided the market for what would prove to be Malaya's most important source of government revenue. Throughout British Malaya in the first few decades of the twentieth century, much of the money needed to build roads and railways came from the sale of opium. The various governments of British Malaya made money from opium in two ways: through import duties on opium when it entered the country and through licenses sold to those who in turn sold opium to the addicts.

The importance of opium to the finances of the Straits Settlements, where as late as 1928 it still made up a third of government revenue, has already been pointed out. Using opium as a source of income might have been understandable in Singapore and Penang as they were free ports and had few sources of income. In the peninsula, however, the growth of export industries, such as tin and rubber, offered tremendous potential sources of government income. Despite this, in the period 1900 to 1930, close to a quarter of government revenue in the FMS was generated by opium. The figure was 43 percent for Johor in 1913, and in 1922, it was 29 percent. Similar statistics existed for Kedah, Kelantan, and Trengganu.

It is quite clear that British authorities were perfectly happy to benefit from the addiction of Chinese coolies, many of whom spent 40–50 percent of their wages on opium. This made it possible to keep taxes on tin and rubber, which were dominated by British commercial interests, at very low levels. It could be argued that the low taxes were necessary to encourage investments and economic growth, but the opium trade was not one of Britain's finest moments in its stewardship of the area.

The Indians

Although they never made up the numbers of the Chinese, Indians played a key role in the modernization and development of twentieth-century British Malaya. While the Indian community grew in numbers in the first few decades of the twentieth century, as a percentage of the overall population, it remained quite stable. In 1901, the Indian population of the FMS was around 60,000; by 1921, it had increased to around 300,000. It continued to grow but was always about 10 percent of the total population.

Like most of the early Chinese migrant laborers, the Indians planned to be in Malaya only long enough to improve their economic lot and then return home. This plan was more of a reality than in the Chinese community and tended to create a transient Indian population. Much of the reason lay in India being part of the British Empire. As a result, labor recruitment and contracts were better organized and enforced. The nature of what most Indians did and their impermanence consigned them to minor economic and political roles in Malaya.

The term "Indian" in Malaya's population figures described all Indians from the subcontinent, be they Hindus from India, Muslims from India, or Buddhists from Ceylon. Although most Indians came as laborers, especially to work in the plantation industries, there was an economic diversity in the community. In 1931, over one half of the Indian population in the FMS lived on plantations, and the Indians made up two-thirds of the labor force in those areas. However, coming from an area that had a history of dealing with the British and access to the English language resulted in many Indians filling positions as clerks in the government and private industry. Because of their experience with the Indian railways, there was heavy Indian representation in both the running and building of railroads. The same was true of the police force. As time went on and professions became more open to Asians, there was a representation of Indians beyond their percentage of the population in areas such as medicine and law.

As a group, the Indian community that settled in Malaya did not prosper as much as the Chinese. By the 1950s, the per capita income of the Indians was a third less than that of the Chinese. To this very day, large numbers of Indians are still over-represented in low paid occupations in manual and menial labor. It would seem that the "immigrant mentality" would have driven them as it did their Chinese counterparts. The reason for this lies in the fact that a majority of the Indians in the peninsula did not have an immigrant experience in its classic sense. Their opportunities for social and economic mobility were held back by the plantation system. Being British subjects with close ties to British India, the Malayan government took a deeper interest in the terms and conditions of their employment. They were given housing on the plantations with education for their children and access to health care, as well as food and clothing. There they lived in a secure and isolated society that was vastly different from the more dynamic sink-or-swim experiences of the immigrants who went to Malaya on their own.

This is not to say that the Indians lived in some kind of paternalistic workers' paradise. Conditions on the plantations varied from place to place. Generally, pay was low and the amenities basic. Opportunities outside the plantation were limited. Because of the need to maintain a pool of inexpensive rubber tappers, educational opportunities were deliberately kept at a minimum. Education on the plantations was conducted in Tamil and stopped after the primary level. Over half the

PRINCIPAL OCCUPATIONS OF RACES (1932)					
Occupation	Europeans	Malay	Archipelago Immigrants	Chinese	Indians
Fishermen		5,715	307	7,291	56
Rice Planters		78,009	11,113	1,038	1,892
Rubber Estate Owners, Managers, etc.	1,121	1,803	910	1,514	58
Others in Rubber Cultivation		27,618	20,825	100,789	131,099
Coconut Estate Owners, Managers, etc.	11	744	66	23	9
Others in Coconut Cultivation		4,262	5,982	1,256	8,010
Unclassified and Multifarious Agriculture	23	18,168	7,381	16,115	9,883
Tin Mine Owners, Managers, etc.	48	8		214	
Others in Tin Mining	282	543	465	70,704	4,622
Proprietors and Managers of Businesses	246	475	574	16,894	4,428
Salesmen, Shop Assistants, etc.	144	541	105	16,576	3,790

Indian community in Malaya was cut off from the economic boom and had little opportunity or ability to participate in it other than as laborers. This contrasted with the lifestyle of the Indian community in Singapore, which had access to English-language schools. The Indians there truly lived the immigrant experience and subsequently benefited from it. The same development and prosperity were true of many Indians who migrated to the cities and towns of Malaya.

Health Care and Education

Another problem the British had to overcome was that Malaya was not a particularly healthy place to live. Development could not realistically proceed until some attempt was made to deal with the malaria, dysentery, cholera, and smallpox that flourished. Public health problems were further complicated by the growing cities and the consequent large numbers of people living in close proximity. In 1910 alone, malaria claimed sixty lives out of every thousand people in British Malaya. The building of Port Swettenham (now Port Kelang) near Kuala Lumpur was almost abandoned because of the number of workers who were dying from tropical diseases. In the Straits Settlements, it was estimated that one in five indentured coolies died, in part because of low public health standards. Improvements in public health standards had to be an important priority.

The most successful of British efforts to improve health standards were their fights against malaria and beriberi. In the late nineteenth century, British and Italian researchers discovered that the Anopheles mosquito was the carrier of malaria. This discovery gave a British government medical officer in Malaya, Malcolm Watson, the key to fighting the disease. His pioneering methods of attacking the breeding grounds of the mosquito later earned him a knighthood. The draining of swamps and the oiling of streams and drains proved there were ways to control malaria. In the first two decades of the twentieth century, a mosquito advisory board was established to coordinate the efforts of mosquito destruction. On the western coast of Malaya, the death rate from malaria was cut by over two-thirds. Watson estimated that over a hundred thousand lives were saved through government efforts.

In 1896 alone, over two thousand Chinese died from beriberi. W.L. Brandon discovered that the disease was caused by a vitamin deficiency. The Chinese especially preferred to eat polished rice from which all the nutrients had been scrubbed. Once their diet was adjusted, the disease was virtually eliminated.

The move to improve public health was most successful in the federated states because of the existence of a centralized health bureaucracy that could bring to bear modern medical practices. It should be noted that this was an important consideration in the economic development of the area because of the need for a healthier workforce. Significant amounts of government revenue were directed toward the building of hospitals, the establishment of sanitary boards with health inspectors, improvements in water supplies, and the setting up of infant welfare centers. A further indication of the importance of this problem to the British was that the first few opportunities for Asians to enter the professions were in the area of medicine. In 1905, the King Edward VII College of Medicine was established in Singapore to train local doctors for service in British Malaya.

Health services in the unfederated states tended to lag behind those in the federated states due to lack of revenue and distrust of Western medicine. Even in the federated states, there were significant inequities between health services provided in the towns and plantations and other rural areas. This problem reflected a combination of Malay custom and British priorities. On the whole, however, British Malaya was probably the healthiest place to live in Southeast Asia before the start of World War II.

The growth of government and the variety of services it provided, along with the tremendous expansion of the economy, brought about the need for a modern educational system. British policy on public education was a host of conflicting attitudes, contradictions, and objectives that reflected the multiracial society they had created to develop the economy. The policy also reflected the ambiguities of the system of indirect rule. British Malaya did not have an educational system as such. It had a variety of systems operating simultaneously and based on race, language, and class.

British educational policy toward the Malay community reflected the facade of indirect rule and attempted to preserve Malay life and culture. Two educational policies evolved: one for the Malay aristocrats in whose name the British ruled and one for the common rural Malays whose culture they were "preserving."

With the expansion of the size and role of government, British advisors were faced with the need to staff the system with at least some officers who knew and understood the Malay people. To train and recruit sufficient British personnel to do this would be difficult and expensive. Also, they were faced with a generation of the Malay ruling class that had little role or purpose in the new order. To deal with these problems, they provided English education to the sons of the Malay elite and then brought them into the civil service, albeit at the lowest levels. The most successful example of this goal was the establishment of the Malay College at Kuala Kangsar in 1905. There the sons of the ruling class were brought together at the "Eton of the East." Malays of high birth were treated to the curriculum, sports, and rules of the English private schools, although they also studied

Islam and Malay. Other members of the Malay ruling class were offered scholarships to English-language schools in Ipoh and Kuala Lumpur, as well as in the Straits Settlements. With English education, these men could assume positions in the civil service or royal courts.

The impact was twofold. The education tended to further isolate the ruling class from the common Malays, and it reinforced the position that Asian participation in government was to be dominated by the Malays.

The educational policy for the average rural Malay was four years free primary education in the Malay language. The British believed that the expectations of the Malays should not be unduly raised and that they were best suited to agricultural occupations. Initially, in the late nineteenth and early twentieth centuries, even these basic government schools were not popular with the rural Malay communities. Traditionally, education among rural Malays had revolved around the study of Islam, and many parents and religious leaders were highly suspicious of these new secular schools. To Muslim teachers, they were a threat to their positions in the community. To parents, they represented government intrusion into a rural value system as well as the loss of necessary labor on the farm.

Those who attended government schools had poorly educated and trained teachers, but this situation changed in the 1920s and 1930s. One of the contributing factors was the establishment of the Sultan Indris Training College (SITC) in 1922. The aim of the college was to train Malay-language teachers and thereby improve the quality of rural schools. It also offered an avenue for the creation of a modern Malay identity. Malays of common background were drawn from all over the peninsula, and the college quickly became a center for the study of the Malay language and a clearing house of ideas and opinions about the challenges facing ordinary Malays.

The graduates of SITC, along with the efforts of Richard Windstedt, the director of education, breathed new life into the Malay-language schools. The curriculum failed to provide the rural Malays with the necessary tools to compete in a modern economy, but the study of the Malay language and literature did help define more clearly what it meant to be a Malay.

The educational policy toward the Chinese reflected the government's overall view of the scheme of things in Malaya. In the eyes of the government, the Chinese were a transient labor force, and thus there was no need to provide education for them. Up until the 1930s, education was purely a private affair. A proliferation of schools in the Chinese language were established by clan groups, dialect groups, kongsi, wealthy Chinese, and itinerant teachers. The quality of these schools differed significantly throughout British Malaya. Some in the urban areas that enjoyed generous, private funding were quite good, but most were inadequate. Large numbers of Chinese schools were run by teachers whose only qualifications were that they could read and write.

In the 1920s and 1930s, the government took a greater interest in the Chinese schools but for political rather than educational reasons. Some teachers in the Chinese schools were recent arrivals from China. These teachers carried with them the turmoil that had engulfed China after the fall of imperial China in 1911. There was a civil war between the noncommunist Kuomintang (KMT) and the Chinese Communist Party (CCP) to decide who would replace the Ch'ing dynasty as the next ruler of China. This ideological battle was brought to the Chinese schools in Malaya by teachers and supporters from the two sides. The schools were used as sources of propaganda and as vehicles to raise money for the competing factions.

Both sides in the Chinese civil war were deeply nationalistic and wanted China free of foreign control. They foresaw a new and powerful China free to establish its role in Asia. This view easily translated into Chinese chauvinism* and anti-British agitation, which caused concern among British officials. To counter this development, a Chinese inspectorate of schools was established in the 1920s to monitor the curriculum. In the 1930s, the government began giving financial aid to the schools. These two actions were meant to give the government control over what was taught in the schools. The effectiveness of these measures was limited because there were budgetary constraints during the Great Depression, and the British were unable to observe and understand all

---

Excessive, almost blind patriotism or racial pride.

that was going on. Little was done to improve the quality of instruction, and the schools continued to be taught only in the Chinese language.

By stepping in to oversee Chinese education, the British began to acknowledge that many of these Chinese intended to stay in Malaya permanently. They, however, still failed to realize the need for schools to promote a Malayan outlook, that is, to foster among Chinese youth a feeling that Malaya was their home. The continuation of the curriculum in the Chinese language reinforced the separateness of the races and reflected the roles the government foresaw for the different races. To many British policy makers, the Malays were to remain as fishermen and farmers, the Chinese were to work for other Chinese as laborers or retail traders, and the Indians were to remain clerks, plantation workers, and laborers.

The three races did intermingle in many of the English-language schools. The British view that the races should be educated in their own native tongues was qualified by the need of the government and economy for English-educated Malayans. The government already offered opportunities to English-educated Malays, but as the economy grew, it began to offer opportunities to the English-educated among all the races. The language of commerce was English. As the population expanded and the country modernized, opportunities in the professions widened. The country needed doctors, lawyers, engineers, and architects, and it was impossible and impractical for them all to be British. The road to participation in any of these areas was only through the English-language schools.

The English-language schools were primarily in the urban areas, and they were established through a mixture of public and private efforts. The government established Raffles Institution in Singapore and later other schools, such as Victoria Institution in Kuala Lumpur, the Penang Free School, The Malay College in Kuala Kangsar, and King Edward VII in Taiping. These schools, however, were not for everyone. The government felt that English education should be limited to small numbers of Asians so as to avoid creating a surplus of highly educated people who could not find jobs. The colonial government was also hesitant to allocate large sums of money for education, a limited view given the rapidly expanding economy. However, before criticizing government inadequacies in public education in Malaya, it must be borne in mind that government-funded education only began in Britain in the late nineteenth century, and the concept of public education was new to the British.

Much of the demand for English education was absorbed by the establishment of mission schools. Some of the finest schools in Malaysia and Singapore today started as mission schools. The Methodists established an extensive school system, setting up Anglo-Chinese schools and Methodist boys and girls schools. Schools, such as St Francis Xavier in Penang, St John's in Kuala Lumpur, St Paul's in Negri Sembilan, and St Joseph's in Singapore, were established by the Catholic Church. The success of the mission schools helped convince the Malayan government that it had miscalculated the need for English education. It subsequently began to support expanded English education.

What the English-language schools achieved besides offering a quality education was the creation of a new multiracial elite. English gave students access to government and commercial positions. It also gave them access to higher education in English in Malaya and abroad, which the local language schools could not fulfill. Studying a Western curriculum, having a common language — English — and having good prospects for the future gave these multiracial groups more in common with one another than with their own racial groups. In the 1930s, the breakdown of the racial composition in these English schools in the FMS was 49 percent Chinese, 27 percent Indian, and 15 percent Malay, with a few others. The leaders who brought Malaya and Singapore to independence were primarily the products of these schools.

Legacy of British Rule

The legacy of British rule up to World War II was a booming economy that made huge profits for British investors while offering some opportunities to immigrants and the Malays. The British built a modern centralized government with specialized services in areas such as health care and education. They created the modern infrastructure needed to spark off economic growth. They established the rule of law. All these accomplishments have been extolled by British ex-civil servants, British historians, and British authorities.

While the British could point to solid achievements in Malaya, there were some serious flaws in the economy and society they had created. The economic health of the country was basically tied to only two commodities — rubber and tin. Good times and bad times were determined by the world market prices for these two products.

The reality of depending on only two commodities was brought home by the Great Depression. When the world demand for these products dropped, the economic fortunes of most of the immigrants fell with them. Tens of thousands of Chinese were forced to the fringes of the jungle, where they found unused land and became subsistence farmers in order to survive. Many Indians were forced to return home to a country that could not absorb their labor. The Malays were a little better off than the immigrant races because they had little contact with the modern economy and were already subsistence farmers. This in itself was indicative of the society that had evolved in British Malaya. The poorest faced the least dislocation because they had little stake in the new economy. Serious inequalities of wealth had been created both among the races and within the races.

Chapter 11

IMPACT OF BRITISH RULE
ON THE MALAYS

One of the most important effects of British control of the Malay Peninsula was the relegation of the Malay population to the bottom rung of the economic ladder. As the area grew and prospered, the Malays benefited very little from that progress. In 1957, when Malaya gained independence from Britain, the average annual income of the respective races in the country was Chinese $3,223, Indians $2,013, and Malays $1,463. These numbers include the value of what the Malays grew and consumed themselves. In 1970, after thirteen years of concerted effort by the government to raise the economic level of the Malays, the annual income of Chinese households was $4,644, Indians $3,720, and Malays $2,148. The Malays were outstripped economically in their own country by immigrant races. In the words of Lennox Mills, "when the British came, the Malay was a poor man in a poor country; when they left he was a poor man in a rich country." British attitudes and policies, what the Malays did for a living, the strengths of the immigrants, and the nature of the Malay value system all contributed to their backward economic position.

The British had a paternalistic attitude toward Malays that reflected a liking and sympathy for them. British policies were meant to preserve the Malay way of life, which they did, but these policies also consigned the Malays to the lowest strata of economic life. As one historian aptly put it, "The British liked the Malay but didn't respect him." A stereotype was accepted by many colonial administrators, which portrayed the Malays as lazy, fun loving, and lacking in the ability to be successful businessmen or wage earners.

The British helped perpetuate this myth both in word and action. While it was true that some sons of Malays of high birth became "acceptable" as a result of an English education and could consequently participate in the running of the government, on the whole, the British view was that the Malays should limit their horizons to pursuits such as agriculture and fishing. The history of British policy in the peninsula is one of keeping the Malay population "on the farm." In the Selangor Annual Report of 1902, the then British resident said:

> "it is a matter of history that it is a superhuman task to persuade a Malay to take up with interest work to which his personal inclination does not take him."

This view of the Malays was reinforced by the famous colonial administrator, Sir Frank Swettenham, who spent thirty-two years in various positions of authority in Malaya. He did not feel the Malays had a role in modern economy. He believed that only the English and perhaps the Chinese possessed the necessary traits to succeed in Malaya's modern economy. Swettenham wrote numerous books and articles on Malaya and was considered one of the foremost experts on the subject. Long after his retirement from Malaya, his views continued to influence British policy. They were the conventional wisdom.

These views about the inadequacies of the Malays were manifested in government policies, especially in education. Free primary education was offered to all male Malays, but this education was strictly limited. According to Swettenham:

> "[it was to make the children] better farmers rather than offer them any wider views of life. The longer the Malay is kept away from the influence of civilization the better it will be for him."

The curriculum, taught in the Malay language, was restricted to simple reading, a little mathematics, and religious teaching. Malay education was not geared toward the changing needs of Malaya and had the effect of tying the Malays to their traditional agricultural pursuits. It did not train them for a more active role in the development of their country.

In the 1920s and 1930s, reforms were made in the Malay educational system to make it more compatible with the modern world. One of these reforms was the establishment of SITC. The aim of the college was to prepare talented rural Malays to be teachers in the Malay-language schools. The college was instrumental in providing a respectable profession for Malays from humble backgrounds. It was the first institution to bring together non-aristocratic Malays from all parts of British Malaya. Malays of similar social standing from the FMS, the unfederated states, and the Straits Settlements lived and studied together and began to recognize the common economic and political problems they faced in colonial Malaya. While SITC provided better trained teachers for the Malay schools, it also produced political and intellectual leaders who saw the need to strengthen Malay educational and cultural institutions to confront a twentieth-century, multiracial society.

The Great Depression actually helped some Malays find employment. In an attempt to reduce spending at that time, the government cut back the number of British civil servants and hired less expensive Malays. The drawback was that the government jobs available to Malays were only in the administrative areas. The high-paying, specialized functions of government that required doctors, engineers, architects, and accountants were closed to most Malays because of their lack of knowledge of English. In the private and commercial sectors of the economy, decades of isolation left the Malays unable to compete with the Chinese and Indians even if they wanted to succeed in those areas. Thus, when increasing numbers of Malays woke up to their economic predicament, the racial roles in the economy had already been firmly established. The educational system, racial stereotypes, and non-Malay control of the modern economy had placed what seemed to be insurmountable barriers in the Malays' path.

The Malays would have been better off economically if they had produced more, of greater variety, and of more value, from the land. Some colonial administrators, such as Sir Hugh Clifford, felt that the goal of preserving the culture of the Malays was not at odds with improving their economic position. Clifford argued that the answer was to make the Malays better and more efficient farmers. Clifford's view that the standard of living of the Malays could be raised while they remained primarily rural was not reflected in administrative policies. There was little serious effort to improve and modernize the Malay agricultural sector of the economy. During the years 1910–1940, not once did any state spend more than 5 percent of its budget on the agricultural sector. Even in Kelantan, which is 90 percent

Malay and predominantly agricultural, this fact held true. For many years, more money was spent supporting royal households than on agriculture in the unfederated states.

The Malays had problems becoming more productive farmers. Islamic inheritance laws contributed to rural inefficiency by breaking the land into smaller, less-productive units and dividing it among all the heirs. Most rice farmers grew only one crop a year and had little knowledge of advanced methods of fertilization or irrigation or access to new strains of high quality seeds. Another factor that contributed to low productivity was that a significant portion of Malay farmers were tenants. Because of indebtedness or recent immigration from Indonesia, nearly half of the Malay farmers worked someone else's land. Where was the motivation to increase production when it was benefiting an absentee landlord?

British land policy also had an impact on the Malays' role and position in the economy. In the first two decades of the twentieth century, British and Malay leaders became concerned that the booming economy would strip the Malays of the one asset they had — land. The fear was that the booming land prices would encourage the Malays to sell their land to foreign and immigrant interests. To stop this from happening, laws creating Malay reserve land were passed.

Beginning with the Malay Reservation Enactment of 1913 and strengthened by subsequent revisions, significant portions of each state were set aside for ownership only by the Malays. The laws went a step further than to simply protect Malay land ownership. They also stipulated what the land could be used for — agriculture. As the Malays began to plant rubber and other commercial crops, the authorities, fearing a drop in food production, created new legislation that made it illegal to use rice land for other agricultural purposes.

Although many found ways to skirt these laws, the message was that the Malays were not only to remain rural but also to produce their traditional crops. The irony is that although the British wanted the Malays to produce the nation's staple food supply, the lack of serious commitment to increasing their productivity meant that in the decades prior to World War I, Malaya imported about half its supply of food. There were other ramifications of this land policy. One was that the land, and therefore the country, belonged to the Malays, and second that the immigrant races were effectively barred from agriculture, thus reinforcing the urban/rural population patterns of the races. By 1921, only about 6 percent of the Malay population lived in towns, with populations of over a thousand people.

Where the Malays lived did not merely block their access to jobs and English education but also helped determine their income level. Two-thirds of the Malay population lived in the most economically backward and undeveloped states of Perlis, Kelantan, Trengganu, Kedah, and parts of Pahang. The economic development, the wealth, and the markets were in the Straits Settlements, the FMS, and Johor. To take advantage of that growth meant severing strong ties with the kampungs and becoming virtual immigrants in their own country.

Where the Malays lived also affected their access to markets. The infrastructure of railroads and roads was built with the needs of the export sectors in mind. For the most part, they were along the western coast, connecting the mines and plantations to the new cities, such as Ipoh and Kuala Lumpur, and to the ports of Penang and Singapore. Little attention was paid to the food producing areas or the eastern coast. The only predominantly Malay state that had a somewhat higher standard of living was Kedah, and that was mainly because of its proximity and access to Penang.

The Malays' ability to raise their income level was also constrained by their lack of understanding of markets and a monetary economy. The complexities of market prices, transportation costs, distribution systems, and interest rates were lost on the Malays. To them, money itself was a relatively new and rare commodity. Their lack of knowledge and access to markets left the Malays in the hands of middlemen, mostly Chinese, who provided the link between the Malays and the ultimate consumer of their produce. The distribution and sale of rice and other agricultural products were dominated by Chinese commercial interests, and the transportation system, from remote and rural areas to the towns and cities, was controlled mainly by Chinese private interests.

The Malays' lack of understanding of market prices and interest rates placed them at a disadvantage when dealing with their closest source of credit — the local Chinese merchants. Like farmers everywhere, once they went beyond feeding their families and produced for a larger market, credit was necessary to take them from harvest to harvest. Imagine a situation in which the borrower thinks in terms of pounds of rice, while the lender thinks in terms of dollars, interest rates, and what the price of rice will be when the loan is due. Leon Comber cites an example in the late 1960s of Chinese shops that gave Malay farmers RM40 to RM50 credit against their future rice crop. The credit was to be repaid with a quantity of rice bearing a market value of about RM80, resulting in a profit of at least 60 percent. Suffice it to say the Malay farmers rarely saw anywhere near the full value of their crops unless they lived near an urban center, and even then this is doubtful.

Criticism of British rule in Malaya is often based on a condemnation of British policies that contributed to a classification of economic roles along racial lines. An interesting question is this: what would have been the consequences had the British pursued a policy of creating wage earners, businessmen, and artisans, that is, brought the Malays into the modern economy? Swettenham's probable answer would have been that landless, dispossessed people with no roots in their traditional culture would have been the result. British policies were a result of such stereotyping of the Malays, but the latter's ability to compete with the other races at this particular point in time warrants a closer look.

The question is this: when the British decided to allow unrestricted immigration to Malaya, did that seal the fate of the Malays? Historically, the Malays were not just farmers and aristocrats. They were traders, seafarers, scholars, and artisans. They had participated in the world's commerce for centuries. While it was true that the European seizure of their trade forced many into rural pursuits, there was still a sizable group of Malay skilled workers, such as carpenters and iron mongers, in the royal capitals of the sultanates. These towns also had a number of traders, merchants, and shopkeepers who were Malay. Once large-scale immigration took place, these urban Malays were unable to stand up to the onslaught of immigrant competition.

Those Malays who wanted to participate in the modern commercial economy had to compete with those who had immigrant mentalities as well as with the realities of twentieth-century Malaya. The newcomers had left their homes to seek their fortunes. Like immigrants everywhere, they did not like their old lives and were trying to start anew. They were determined and resourceful as they had nothing to fall back on. The Malays involved in nonagricultural pursuits did not have a chance. Before long, the immigrants had replaced the Malays as small traders and in most areas of skilled and semi-skilled labor. Whatever the Malays could do, the Chinese could do more quickly and less expensively.

The towns changed in character. The small Malay shops could not stand up to the competition of the Chinese. In the early part of the century, many Malays were willing to work for a wage. In 1911, 10 percent of the wage earners in the FMS were Malays; in 1931, only one half of one percent of the wage earners were Malays. By the 1930s, those Malays who did want to participate in the modern economy were forced back to the land.

Around the same time, many Malays began to recognize the potential dangers of their economic position. It is, however, not clear what they could have done to change or turn the process around. The export of raw materials and the importation of manufactured goods was, for the most part, controlled by British firms. The transportation, distribution, and sale of imported goods were largely controlled by the Chinese. The Chinese not only provided the retail arm for the profitable functioning of British import-export businesses, but given their numbers and relative wealth, they also became good customers of the British. The power of this symbiotic relationship was almost impossible to penetrate. Beyond this, the professions and skilled labor were controlled by the British and immigrants who had access to educational opportunities in English in the urban areas.

Once the Chinese gained control of a particular service, skill, or market, they were not about to give it up easily. They were determined to survive in their new country. Richard Winstedt cites numerous examples of this determination. A Malay once tried to deal in rice in a state that was predominantly Malay, but the only motor transport system was owned by a Chinese firm, and it gave the Chinese rice dealers cheap rates until the Malay interloper was driven out. A Malay cooperative society arranged to sell its rubber directly to a British firm in Singapore; this affronted the Chinese middlemen who had previously handled the sale, and the British firm's large Chinese clientele threatened to withdraw their business unless the arrangement was cancelled. When the government gave loans to Perak fishermen to sell their catch directly to the market and cut out the middlemen, Chinese manufacturers refused to sell ice to the fishermen until the old arrangements were restored. When a government-sponsored cooperative on the eastern coast tried to sell its copra directly to Singapore, the Chinese coastal steamer left its produce sitting on the docks.

From the 1930s to 1950s, as the economic backwardness of the Malays became a more important issue, some began to see the problem as one that went much deeper than merely a fight over a piece of the economic pie. Whether it be the native Hawaiians in Hawaii, the Maoris in New Zealand, the Fijians in Fiji, or the Malays in Malaya, all these groups took an economic back seat in their own countries as a result of a clash between their traditional ways of life and the driving forces of immigrants. Some believed that the Malays' economic situation reflected a Malay way of life that was ill-equipped to compete and prosper in the modern capitalist economy of that time.

The Malays' values and way of life were not just rural but were distinctly Malay, with roots in adat law, village life, and Islam. What the Malays thought was important in life made them poor competitors in a modern market economy. In the Malay kampung, status, or the measure of a man, was not necessarily how rich he was but rather how he got along with fellow villagers. The depth of his Islamic faith was more important than that of his pocketbook. Malay society stressed manners and form; confrontation and aggression were frowned on. Relationships, be they economic or personal, were rarely dealt with directly for fear of causing offense or placing unreasonable demands on fellow villagers or family. The attributes that promoted cooperation were the most important guides to action. The value system of the Malays was incompatible with the traits needed to survive in a modern economy, where competition, aggressive behavior, greed, and individual achievement are the keys to success.

Other analysts go a step further and claim that the values and world view of the Malays prevented them from effectively addressing the problems of inequality even when they assumed the levers of government after World War II. These observers believe Malay values of compromise, tolerance, and lack of aggression allowed the immigrants to continue following their own customs, languages, and traditions without insisting on the assimilation one would have expected from a host country. The Malays' desire to live and let live kept them from demanding a larger share of the economic pie.

This clash of cultures between immigrant Asians and Malays is interesting to note in the light of contemporary discussions of Asian versus Western values. There are those today who claim that an important ingredient in Asia's economic success is the willingness of the Asian individual to give up personal needs or desires for the good of the group, which in turn lays the groundwork for a more stable and prosperous society.

This theory does not hold true for Malaysia. In the case of British Malaya, those who failed economically did so because the British attempted to preserve their traditional "Asian" values, and those who succeeded were in many ways rejecting many of the values of the Confucian society they had left behind. Traditional Confucian society did not offer much hope for upward mobility. Chinese society was run by a privileged gentry, whose power was based on rote acceptance of the Confucian classics. Occupations in commerce and trade had low status in China's stratified social system, and acceptance of one's position in the social order was considered a key condition for stability in society. Singapore philosopher Martin Lu has argued that the Confucian contempt for money making was an impediment to economic development and the entrepreneurial spirit. The Chinese who came to Malaya rejected the stratified Confucian value system and adopted values necessary to compete in a capitalist society.

When they handed power back to Malayans, the British had left behind a society with serious inequalities. Between the urban and rural areas — one was mainly immigrant, tied to a modern economy, and prospering and the other was Malay, traditional, and cut off from the peninsula's increasing wealth. Between the eastern and western coasts — one had a modern infrastructure that spurred economic activity, and the other was underdeveloped and backward. Within the races themselves, there were divisions in the Malay community between the royal elite and the masses; in the Indian community between the plantations and urban areas; and in the Chinese community between traders and laborers. All these divisions would manifest themselves as challenges to those who led Malaya to independence and those who ran the country afterward.

Chapter 12

SINGAPORE UNTIL 1942

In the three decades prior to World War II, Singapore continued to grow in importance as a port and trading center. Then as now Singapore was strategically placed to take advantage of the economic development around it. The booms in tin and rubber in Malaya and the discovery of oil in Borneo and the Dutch East Indies (Indonesia) provided many opportunities for Singapore's dynamic population to grow and prosper.

Trading and Financial Center

By the turn of the twentieth century, Singapore was the most important port in Southeast Asia and the seventh largest port in the world. As the production of raw materials in the area around it grew, Singapore had the geographical advantage as well as the services necessary to facilitate the expansion of trade and commerce. Financial and commercial services were required to make this growth possible, and the island was able to provide them. Even though large amounts of capital were raised from outside the area, the need for credit and banking facilities in Malaya boosted Singapore's financial community significantly. The money necessary to expand production, buy machinery, and finance trade brought increased profits to established banks and drew new banks from the United States, France, the Netherlands, and the Middle East. The need to insure cargoes to and from the area resulted in the setting up of an insurance market in Singapore. These developments rapidly established Singapore as an important financial center as well as a thriving port city.

Many companies that owned rubber estates and tin mines were in London and did not have the personnel or expertise necessary to facilitate their production. As such, many well-established companies in Singapore stepped in to take advantage of the rubber and tin booms. Guthries, Sime

Darby, Bousteads, and others acted as agents in purchasing supplies and equipment, providing labor and management services, and facilitating the shipment of raw materials to the rest of the world. These agencies also acted as distributors of imported products to meet the growing demand for Western manufactured goods.

WORLD WAR I AND THE INDIAN MUTINY

Although most Singaporeans were unaffected by the international conflict that took place between 1914 and 1918, World War I did leave its imprint on the country's history. Economically, Singapore benefited from the rise in demand and prices of raw materials from Malaya and the archipelago. Property and businesses owned by Germans were seized and turned over to British subjects. Regular British armed forces were transferred out of Singapore, and the defense of the country was the responsibility of British Indian troops. It was from the Indian soldiers that the most notable incident of the war resulted — the Mutiny of 1915.

Muslim troops serving in the British Indian army had mixed loyalties during World War I. Turkey was allied with Germany, and the idea of fighting fellow Muslims upset many of these men, especially since the sultan of Turkey was considered the *caliph*, or leader of the Islamic kingdom. Furthermore, many of the troops believed a story spread by Turkish agents that the Kaiser had converted to Islam. At the mosque near the Singapore Indian barracks, the *imam*, or the person who presides over prayers, inflamed the troops with anti-British propaganda, telling them that it would be sinful to aid the enemies of the Turks.

Executions of mutinous Indian soldiers in Singapore in 1915.

205

On February 15, 1915, Muslim troops mutinied, killing many of their officers and then going on a rampage, murdering British civilians. Initially, most people on the island did not take much notice of what was going on because it was Chinese New Year, and the gunfire was mistaken for firecrackers. There were few British troops on the island, and the forces put together to oppose the Muslim Indians were a disparate group. The sultan of Johor led his state's army to join the authorities. Men were called in from ships in the harbor; European and Japanese civilians were enlisted and armed. Eventually, the mutiny was put down when regular troops from Burma and warships from the Allied powers arrived. Over forty people had been killed by the Muslim troops.

When peace was restored, the leaders of the mutiny were court-martialed and executed in public. In the end forty-seven ringleaders died in front of firing squads, drawing huge crowds. The entire episode was one of the darker chapters in the history of the British Indian army.

While most of these agencies were owned by Europeans, many Chinese prospered along with them and in spite of them. These Asian entrepreneurs provided the link between the small producers of tin, rubber, and straits produce and the agencies who were the prime exporters. Chinese businessmen also distributed a large portion of the imported goods at the consumer level, and their financial and commercial institutions grew alongside the European concerns. Through contacts with other immigrant Chinese, the commerce of small ports and less important products, such as copra and spices, was dominated by Chinese merchants mainly based in Singapore.

An indication of Singapore's growth as a trading center is that in 1895 its total trade amounted to about $250 million; by 1923, it had increased to almost a billion dollars. The Great Depression hit hard, but on the eve of World War II, it had rebounded to close to the levels of 1927.

Singapore's role and services were not confined to the Malayan hinterland. Trade from Borneo and the Dutch East Indies also flowed through Singapore. Although the Dutch tried to prevent it, much of Indonesia's raw materials passed through Singapore because of its superior port and trading facilities. The Dutch tried to establish free port entrepôts, such as Riau, in competition with Singapore, but these were not as successful as Singapore.

An example of the bow to Singapore's position was the assumption of a role it plays to this very day — being the most important oil bunkering facility in Asia. The discovery of oil in Borneo, Sumatra, and East Java and the increased use of petroleum products for fuel created the need for a central facility for its storage and ready availability. Singapore became the clearing house for kerosene and, later, other oil products. The first plant was set up on Pulau Bukom in 1905 by the forerunners of Shell, and it remains one of Shell's most important facilities almost a hundred years later.

Singapore's economic lifeblood depended not only on its geographical position but also on its ability to offer a good infrastructure for trade. To this end, significant progress was made toward improving Singapore's capacity for a smooth flow of trade. A key concern at the turn of the century was the island's ability to expand and improve its harbor and dock facilities to meet the increase in trade. The docks of Singapore were all privately owned, the majority by the New Harbor Company. This company was owned primarily by London investors who were receiving healthy returns on their investment and were not willing to spend millions on expansion and improvements. In 1905, Governor Sir John Anderson decided that the government would buy out the company and take over the docks and harbor.

In 1913, the administration of the port was turned over to a newly formed government agency — the Singapore Harbor Board, which administers it to this day. A large expansion of the port took place, culminating with the opening of the Empire Dock in 1917. This was the largest dry dock in the area. Without government intervention, Singapore's port would probably have choked on its own success.

The causeway that linked the island of Singapore with the peninsula was opened to rail traffic in 1923. This meant Singapore was connected directly to the rail and highway systems of Malaya. The latter's exports could be delivered directly to the dock area. Electric tram lines were built, new roads laid down, and reservoirs dug to service the growing port and city.

In 1937, Kallang air and sea plane port were opened. This marked the beginning of a new role for Singapore as a hub for air travel. As early as the 1930s, KLM Royal Dutch Airlines, Pan American Airlines, Qantas,

The causeway linking Singapore and Malaysia was opened in 1923 by Governor Laurence Guillemard of Singapore (cutting ribbon) and Sultan Ibrahim of Johor.

and Imperial Air Ways (later British Air) used Singapore as their central destination in Southeast Asia. Although the airstrip crossed roads and barriers had to be dropped when planes landed, it was the beginning of Singapore's fame as an international airport.

Strategic Defense Center

Singapore's importance as a port grew dramatically in the decades before World War II, as did its strategic and military importance. Since its victory over Russia in 1904 and its alliance with Britain afterward, Japan had continued to increase its naval power and influence in Asia. Prior to and during World War I, Britain was content with Japan's growing role as it freed Britain to meet the German challenge in other parts of the world. By the time the war was over, Japan had moved from the position of a convenient ally to that of a military and commercial threat to British interests in Asia.

World War I had exacted an expensive price for British victory. Many of the best and brightest of a generation had died in the trenches of France. Britain also paid a huge financial price to fight the war, draining its reserves and putting itself in debt to American banks for billions of dollars. When the war was over, Britain had neither the will nor the resources to reestablish its traditional naval role in Asia.

Originally, the problem of Japan's rising power was thought to have been solved at the Washington Conference of 1921, during which Britain, the United States, and Japan agreed on a ratio of 5:5:3, respectively, in capital ships, and Britain and the United States agreed not to build any bases within striking distance of Japan. The treaty was easy to circumvent, and it was soon evident that Japan was building a navy that could dominate the Pacific. Britain faced a dilemma. It could not afford to build a second fleet to meet Japan's challenge in the Pacific, nor could it move the fleet that defended its home waters to the Pacific. The solution was to build a base capable of accommodating the home fleet in an emergency. The navy would not be stationed in Asia but could sail there quickly if required.

Singapore was chosen as the site for the new base. At the same time, the United States built up Pearl Harbor in Hawaii as a deterrent to Japanese naval power. The decision to build the base in Singapore was announced in 1923, but it took over fifteen years to complete it. The base became a "political football" as governments changed in Britain, but its building took on new urgency when Japanese intentions became evident with their invasion of Manchuria in 1932. By the time the base was completed in 1939, it had cost the British taxpayers close to $500 million. It was an impressive facility, boasting the largest dry dock in the world. It was touted by Sir Winston Churchill as the Gibraltar of the East, "Fortress Singapore."

The problem was that there was no fleet to occupy the base, and when the time came for one, Britain's fleet was too busy fighting Germany. Regardless of Britain's inability to use the base properly, Singapore had taken on new significance as the British military headquarters in the Far East. The jobs provided by the building of the facilities and by the increased military presence were a boon to Singapore's economy.

In the 1930s, Singapore and British Malaya were of great importance to Britain and the United States. As Britain geared for war and the United States began to rearm, Malaya and Singapore provided the rubber, tin, and oil essential to war industries. The area was a key source of desperately needed income for the British who needed dollars to purchase war materials from the United States. In 1937, Singapore's trade was over a billion dollars, and half that trade was with the United States. As the United States bought raw materials from Southeast Asia through Singapore, those dollars made their way back to London for use in the war. Prior to World War II, some called British Malaya "Britain's dollar arsenal."

Emergence of an Immigrant Society

Singapore's growth in economic and strategic importance was impressive between the two world wars. The problem was that its strengths were also its weaknesses. The island's prosperity was tied to trade and its ability to facilitate the production and sale of the area's raw materials. As a result, the Great Depression hit Singapore hard.

As factories in the West closed, the demand for tin and rubber fell and with it the income Singapore derived from them. As economies collapsed and countries scrambled to put up trade barriers to protect their markets, Singapore suffered from the drop in world trade that resulted. For many people in the countries near Singapore, falling back on the land to survive was always an alternative. Urban Chinese who fled the cities in Malaya and the rural Malays could survive, but for most people in Singapore, this was not an option on an island that was 26 miles by 13 miles (42 km by 21 km) and highly urbanized. There was massive unemployment and economic hardship.

For Singapore, the Great Depression not only marked economic bad times but also a turning point in the nature of the community. Economic fortunes improved with time, but the social ramifications were dramatic and long lasting.

The most important impact of the Great Depression was a fundamental change in the nature of Singapore's Chinese community brought about by changes in British immigration policy. Already facing high unemployment in Singapore, the government feared an influx of immigrants fleeing hard times in China. As a result, the British established the first immigration restrictions on Chinese entering British Malaya. A quota system reduced to a trickle the number of Chinese men who were allowed to enter Singapore.

In 1930, 158,000 Chinese males arrived in Singapore; by 1933, this had been reduced to 14,000. At the same time, the government offered to pay the passage of anyone who wanted to return to China. For the first time, there were actually more people leaving the colony than entering it. Significant to this quota system was that the government did not restrict the entry of women and children. Families in China sent thousands of what they saw as unneeded daughters away from the hardship of war, depression, and famine. In 1921, there were more than two males to every female in Singapore; by the end of the 1940s, the ratio was almost one to one.

It is difficult to overstate the ramifications of this female immigration. The women who came to Singapore in the 1930s have been called by some "the mothers of Singapore." Prior to this huge influx of women, the majority of the Chinese community in Singapore consisted of male migrant workers. These males had no ties to the community, provided cheap labor, and contributed to many of the social ills of Singapore, such as drug taking, prostitution, and gambling. As the male/female ratio began to balance out in the 1930s and 1940s, more and more Chinese began to accept Singapore as their home. In 1931, 38 percent of the Chinese community in Singapore was locally born; by 1947, this rose to about two-thirds. The majority of Chinese citizens in Singapore today only dates its ties to the country from this time, a time when Singapore ceased being a migrant society and became a true immigrant one.

Prior to the 1930s and 1940s, much of government policy in Singapore had been based on a view that, because most Chinese were transient, it had little obligation for their welfare. As long as many of the social problems were confined to single, male transients, there was little urgency in dealing with them. The transformation of Singapore's population in the 1930s made those government views obsolete.

Take, for example, the problem of opium. Worldwide pressure had been building against Britain's legal drug dealing. In the colonies, British administrators were less than eager to give up this important source of government revenue. Their initial response was to take control of the market to end the crime and the excesses that existed. The government took over the direct sale of opium and in the 1920s required all addicts to register themselves. As long as the government could portray the problem as primarily a coolie labor one, there was not sufficient public pressure to end the sale and consumption of opium. Some colonials even argued that, given the drudgery of a coolie's life, opium was not an altogether bad antidote for backbreaking labor.

As the nature of the population changed, the government's position no longer became defensible. In 1934, no new addicts were to be registered, and the authorities were committed to ending government-sanctioned drug use. World War II interrupted some of this progress, but between 1920 and 1935, the amount of opium imported into Singapore was cut by over 60 percent. When the British returned in 1945, opium sale was no longer legal.

Up until this time, Singapore had a reputation as "sin city." It was a port with a predominantly male population and was famous for its vices. As increasing numbers of Chinese began to sink roots in Singapore and raise families, the social problems and crime could no longer be overlooked. The Asian population began to demand that the British address the problems of law and order in the various communities. The police force expanded to some four thousand men, and numerous new police stations were set up across the island. While Singapore was hardly crime free, crime rates, after peaking in the 1920s, went down. The rise in the number of police officers, the inclusion of more Chinese into the force, and the upgrading of police training programs also made Singapore a safer place to live.

The stabilization of the Chinese population in the 1930s presented challenges that the authorities had earlier downplayed or ignored. One of the most important issues was housing. Before 1930, a significant portion of the population could be housed dormitory-style with little provision for privacy, sanitation, or comfort. The male laborers were viewed as temporary residents who could endure temporary accommodations. A majority of immigrants in the 1930s lived in substandard housing with little access to services such as a proper sewerage system. Singapore's Chinatown, for instance, was one of the most congested areas in the world. Thousands became squatters, living in kampungs in undeveloped areas of the island, such as Toa Payoh and Tampines. In some ways, they were better off than those in the downtown districts because they had space and community, but they had little access to basic amenities, such as water and electricity. When these new families started having children, this further contributed to the congested conditions.

The change from a society of transients to a resident society was so quick and dramatic that there was no way to cope. Within a decade,

Singapore had to provide homes for tens of thousands of new families and their children. An attempt was made to deal with the problem with the establishment of the Singapore Improvement Trust (SIT), which was the forerunner of the Housing and Development Board (HDB). This body was meant to clear slum areas and provide new housing, but the Depression and World War II hindered its progress, and nothing much was achieved until the late 1940s and 1950s.

Pre-War Politics

More and more Chinese were settling down and calling Singapore their home, but only a minority viewed the political affairs of Malaya and Singapore with much interest. The Chinese were a divided community with few common causes or interests. Apart from traditional divisions in the Chinese community along dialect, clan, and family lines, the Chinese were also divided between those with roots in the area — the Straits Chinese — and those who were more recent arrivals.

The Straits Chinese were a minority whose political outlook was directed toward their adopted home, Malaya. They were mostly educated in English and had a higher standard of living than their immigrant counterparts. The vast majority, because of their longevity in the area, were British subjects. Their lifestyle, dress, and social activities tended to resemble those of the West and Britain more than those of the Chinese newcomers. The Straits Chinese wanted the focus of Chinese political activities to be on British Malaya, their home and their future. Lim Cheng Ean, a prominent Penang lawyer, speaking in 1931, reflected this view:

> Who is to say this is a Malay country? When Captain Light (or in the case of Singapore, Raffles) came here did he find Malays or Malay villages? Our fore-fathers came here and worked as hard as coolies — weren't ashamed to become coolies — and they didn't send their money back to China. They married and spent their money here and in this way the government was able to open up the country from jungle to civilization. We've become inseparable from this country. This is ours, our country ...

While most Malays would take issue with this view, many Straits Chinese, having lived in the area for generations, saw no reason why the civil service in the Straits Settlements and membership in the legislative council should not be opened up to greater numbers of Asians, especially to non-Malays who were British subjects. Organizing themselves through the Straits Chinese British Association (SCBA), they formed one of the first legal political organizations of Asians in British Malaya. Led by Tan Cheng Lock, they lobbied and fought for Straits-born British subjects to have expanded representation in the government. There were a few accomplishments prior to World War II that reflected their agenda. In the Straits Settlements, the civil service began to accept and recruit qualified Asians, that is, English-educated Asians, and more Asian members were appointed to the legislative councils of the colonies, although not as many as the SCBA had requested.

Except for this elite minority, most Chinese showed scant interest in the political affairs of the place in which they lived. They were too busy trying to make a living and survive to concern themselves with much else. What little political activity that did exist among these more recent immigrants was concerned with what was happening in China. Singapore had always been fertile ground for the raising of finances to support political activities in China. Dr. Sun Yat Sen, the leader of the 1911 revolution in China, visited the area a number of times to raise money and support. After 1911, Dr. Sun's party, the Kuomintang (KMT), continued to court the overseas Chinese, especially Singapore Chinese. The importance of the immigrant communities was evidenced by the fact that the Chinese republican government declared that all overseas Chinese were citizens of China unless they publicly and legally renounced their citizenship.

A branch of the KMT was organized in Singapore in the early 1920s, and much of its activities revolved around the promotion of Chinese education based on a curriculum formulated in China. As in Malaya, KMT activities in the Chinese schools drew the ire of the British authorities because of their chauvinistic and anti-British flavor. Under the governorship of Sir Cecil Clementi (1930–1934), many of their activities were curtailed, and on occasion their leaders were jailed for threatening the peace of the community. In the 1920s and 1930s, the numbers of the KMT were not large — there were only a few thousand active members.

In China, the Nationalist movement up until 1927 had included both the KMT and the communists. This had given the communists an opening to infiltrate the KMT in Malaya and Singapore. Using the KMT as legal cover, they competed with the noncommunist KMT activists for support among Chinese students and laborers.

In 1927, Chiang Kai-shek expelled the communists from the United Front in China, and this in turn brought about a purge in Singapore. Forced underground, the communists regrouped, and in 1930, they formed the Malayan Communist Party (MCP). In the 1930s, the MCP's activities revolved around organizing Chinese workers, especially in the factories, on the docks, and at the naval base. Strikes called by the communists, although rarely successful, had a disruptive effect on the economy and drew repressive measures from the authorities. By the mid-1930s, the MCP in Singapore probably numbered some five thousand committed members and had some success in influencing the trade union movement. However, like the KMT, it was only able to mobilize a small portion of the recent immigrant population.

The one issue that did capture the interest and emotion of most Chinese in Singapore was the Japanese invasion of China in 1937. The MCP and the KMT in Singapore once again joined in common cause to form the National Salvation Movement. These two organizations were joined by groups such as the Hot Blooded Corps, the Traitors Elimination Corps, the Dare-to-Die Corps, and the Anti-Enemy Backing Up Society. There was even a group of prostitutes, the Fragrance of Chrysanthemum Sisters, which sold flowers to raise money for the anti-Japanese cause. Led by the prominent businessman and philanthropist Tan Kah Kee, successful boycotts of Japanese goods were organized, demonstrations held, money raised for China, and campaigns set up to promote Chinese unity.

As time went on, even these activities ran out of steam. Some Chinese objected to the anti-British rhetoric, and there were inherent divisions within the Chinese community. Ultimately, the KMT and MCP were more interested in furthering the interests of their separate parties than in uniting to oppose the Japanese.

For the Malays in Singapore, the 1920s and 1930s marked a period of increasing political awareness and a change in the community's leadership. This reflected the high level of literacy among the Malays. Some two-thirds or more of the Malay heads of household were literate at least in their own language. This was close to twice the number for the Chinese. As a result, the Malays were more susceptible to involvement in civil affairs. Their traditional links with the area also gave them greater motivation to take an interest in the political decisions of the British that affected their lives.

The Malay population tended to be lumped together by the authorities as a Muslim community rather than as a Malay one. The Malay community had traditionally been led by wealthy Arab and Arab/Malay families. Many of these Arab families played key roles in Singapore's economic and social affairs. The Alsagoffs, the Aljunieds, and the Alkaffs have streets and buildings named after them.

In the 1920s, many Malays wanted to replace Arab leadership of the Muslim community with Malay leaders. To this end, they fought for a Malay seat on the legislative council as opposed to a Muslim one. Their efforts paid off in 1924 when the British expanded the Asian representation on the legislative council and appointed Mohammed Eunos bin Abdullah, a prominent Malay journalist and civic leader, to the council.

Eunos had been editor of *Utusan Melayu*, which emphasized local, urban Malay news and commentary on public issues. The newspaper was known for urging Malays to improve themselves and was not afraid to advocate awkward Malay causes when necessary. At the same time, the newspaper was impartial and balanced in its criticism and responsive to the government line. Eunos had also been an informal advisor to the government on Malay affairs, and his influence within his own community was great. He was active in social and welfare organizations and was a member of the Muslim Advisory Board. He was appointed justice of the peace, then municipal commissioner, and finally the first Malay member of the Straits Settlements Legislative Council.

Among the leadership of the Malay community it was felt that Eunos needed a Malay organization behind him to give his views credibility and weight. In 1926, the Singapore Malay Union (SMU) was founded to further Malay interests. Indicative of the split in the Muslim community, it barred membership to Arab and Indian Muslims. This was the first Malay political organization formed in British Malaya. Led by English-educated journalists, civil servants, and merchants, it provided an interesting contrast to the political leadership of Malaya. While both groups were mostly English-educated, Singapore's Malay leadership was non-aristocratic, reflecting the urban, immigrant nature of its Malays. It showed that Malays were perfectly capable of pushing for a political role in government without the assistance and participation of the traditional ruling elite.

The SMU expanded its activities in the 1930s when it set up branches in Penang and Melaka. In many ways, it was a model for and forerunner of similar groups in the peninsula before World War II — conservative, willing to cooperate with the British, and concerned with furthering Malay educational and economic interests. The SMU's example and inspiration led to a congress of Malay associations in Kuala Lumpur in 1939, which could be characterized as the beginning of what would become the primary Malay nationalist organization after the war — the United Malays National Organization (UMNO).

The next chapter looks again at this progressive Malay community and analyzes its economic position in pre-independent Singapore. These developments reinforce the view of Singapore as an intellectual, political, and religious center for Malay culture.

Singapore and its inhabitants were changing, but it took World War II to convince them that they should take a greater interest in their political, economic, and social destinies.

Chapter 13

WORLD WAR II AND BRITISH MALAYA

The successful Japanese invasion of British Malaya from December 1941 to February 1942 and the subsequent three-and-a-half-year occupation were dramatic turning points in the history of the area. The humbling military defeat of the British Empire and the experiences of the people of Malaya during the Japanese occupation were death knells for colonialism in British Malaya.

The Rise of Japan

In the second half of the nineteenth century, Japan embarked on an impressive program of modernization and industrialization. It transformed itself from an isolated, feudal, agrarian society into a world power. At the same time, Japan's greatest weakness was that it was an island nation with few natural resources. Its economic survival as an industrial power depended on trade and access to raw materials. Japan's initial moves to secure sources of raw materials and gain access to markets came at the expense of the Chinese and the Russians.

In the nineteenth century, the European powers had taken advantage of the weaknesses and ineptitude of the dying decades of imperial China, which had been sliced up into spheres of influence by Britain, France, Germany, and Russia. Japan fought China in 1895, obtaining Taiwan as a result, and Russia in 1904, when it obtained Korea and Russia's sphere of influence in Manchuria. The latter was especially important to Japan's goals because of its large deposits of coal and iron.

The imperial government of China fell in 1912, but the republic that replaced it was far too weak and divided to prevent foreign control of parts of the country. By the late 1920s, it began to appear as if Chiang Kai-shek and the Kuomintang had developed the ability to truly govern China, and fear of losing their sources of raw materials caused the Japanese to act. In 1931, the Japanese took physical control of Manchuria and set up a puppet state known as Manchukuo.

The Great Depression hit Japan hard. Japan was a trading nation, and as country after country put up barriers to trade to protect their contracting economies, Japan suffered. For example, by 1930 Japan had replaced Britain as the largest supplier of textiles to the Malayan market. In good times this may not have been a problem, but when the Depression hit, the British put quotas on Japanese imports, effectively cutting the trade to Malaya to half.

The hardship and suffering caused by the Depression had a tremendous impact on some of the leadership of Japan, especially on the officer class of the military. This group formed a core of leaders who wanted to make sure that Japan would never again be dependent on the economic policies of other powers. The answer was to secure sources of raw materials and markets for their exports. To this end, Japan attempted to expand its control of northeastern Asia by going to war with China in 1937.

For some time, the British had recognized that the Japanese represented a potential threat to their interests in Asia. The money and resources spent on the construction of the naval base in Singapore were ample evidence of this. But into the late 1930s, the threat was not seen as especially menacing. Even if the Japanese controlled China, they were so far away that an attempt to attack Malaya would be apparent well in advance to head it off. The Japanese would have to cover 2,500 miles (4,023 km) before they reached Malaya.

Apart from sheer distance, the British felt they could count on other deterrents to Japanese expansion in the Pacific and Southeast Asia. The Americans would never allow the Japanese to dominate the Pacific, and their impressive fleet stationed at Pearl Harbor in Hawaii represented a strong counterweight to Japanese ambitions. The French in Indochina would also shield any threat to British Malaya by acting as a buffer to Japanese moves south. Added to this were the Dutch in Indonesia who would provide a useful ally in case of an attack.

German aggression and the outbreak of World War II in Europe turned the British defense strategy on its ear. By 1941, German actions in Europe and the North Atlantic had changed the entire basis of British planning. Germany had conquered France and Holland, thus Britain could expect no help from them in defending Southeast Asia from Japan. More importantly, the administration of Indochina was now controlled by Japan, an ally of Germany. The Germans had established a puppet government in France, known as the Vichy government. This pro-German French government continued to rule Indochina and allowed the Japanese to build air fields and military staging depots in what is now southern Vietnam. In theory, Vichy France and Japan were allies. The Japanese were no longer 2,500 miles away. They were just a flight across the South China Sea.

Fall of Malaya

Britain fought on alone but was wounded badly and fighting for survival. It was under constant attack by German submarines in keeping open its lifeline with the United States for food and war materials. At one point, the Germans were sinking British ships faster than they could build them. At the same time, the Royal Air Force was busy trying to establish air superiority over the German Air Force to prevent an invasion of Britain itself. Britain's lone hope for help in the Pacific was the United States, which had not yet entered the war.

While the war in Europe was unfolding, Japan's war in China was bogged down. Japan controlled the coast and most of the major cities, but the Kuomintang and the communists continued to deny victory to the Japanese. Both Britain and the United States supported the Chinese government with war supplies and denied the Japanese the raw materials — rubber and tin from Malaya and oil and scrap iron from the United States — for their war machine. The need for raw materials to fuel its industry and war machines, together with the weakened state of European control, made the colonies of Southeast Asia too tempting for Japan to pass up.

In December 1941, unable to gain American acceptance of its control of China, Japan expanded its area of conquest beyond China. At the same time that Japanese planes decimated the American fleet in Hawaii, Japan attacked Hong Kong and the Philippines and landed troops at Kota Bahru in Kelantan, Malaya. Within months, the Japanese controlled an area that stretched from Burma to the Philippines, from Indochina to Indonesia and as far away as New Guinea, and began threatening Australia.

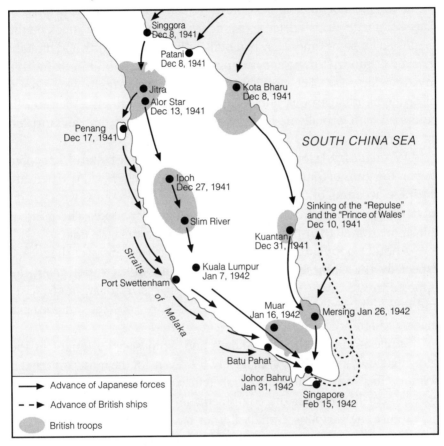

Japanese invasion of Malaya leading up to the fall of Fortress Singapore.

The Japanese conquest of British Malaya and Borneo took about ten weeks to complete. The speed with which the Japanese were able to defeat 130,000 British troops shocked Britain and the United States. The British had invested hundreds of millions of dollars to establish an impregnable bastion in Southeast Asia. The British public had been led to believe this fortress could hold out against all odds. No one could understand how it could have fallen so quickly.

There are a lot of popular myths about the fall of Malaya in general and Fortress Singapore in particular. One is that when the British built the defenses in Singapore, the massive guns that protected the base and island were pointed out to sea to defend against a naval attack and that the British had not taken into consideration an attack down the peninsula. This is not true. British defense planners had considered an attack on the peninsula for some time. They had built air fields in the north and brought in over a hundred thousand troops, which actually outnumbered the invading Japanese. The problem was that many of them were poorly motivated Indian troops and inexperienced Australians. All were ill-equipped with virtually no tanks or anti-tank capability and an outdated air defense.

When the battle for the peninsula was over and the battle of Singapore began, the guns of Singapore could fire north, which they did. There are Japanese accounts of the destruction and havoc these guns wreaked on advancing Japanese troops, but by then it was too late. The guns of Singapore, for all their power and cost, could not turn the tide.

Another popular criticism of the British is that many of the locals, especially the Chinese, were willing to fight but were not given the opportunity to do so. Had the British been less "arrogant and racist" and willing to arm these tens of thousands of people, they might have made a difference.

While it is true that the Malays and Chinese who fought in the campaign fought effectively and bravely, they were for the most part trained soldiers. To arm and train the general civilian population was absurd. The government had neither the equipment nor the men to teach civilians how to use the weapons. Britain did not have enough resources to fully equip its own army let alone thousands of raw recruits. Evidence of this can be found in the British retreat from continental Europe in 1940. Many of the 350,000 British troops that were evacuated from the beaches of Dunkirk in France still had not fully replaced the gear they left behind.

Some have blamed the British military and political leadership in Malaya for bungling the defense once the Japanese landed, that generals such as Percival were indecisive and fatally underestimated the ability of the Japanese. While there is some truth in this, even if they had been flawless in their judgement and unflinching in their courage, it would have made no difference. The Japanese had absolute control of the sea and air. As the defenders fought bravely to blunt the Japanese advance down the peninsula, the Japanese landed new troops along the coast to the rear of the defenders. Time and again the defenders fought hard and held their ground only to be forced to retreat to avoid being cut off from the rear.

It is interesting that many of the popular explanations as to the fall of Singapore and Malaya have focused on British mistakes and omissions rather than Japanese strengths. It is almost a racist form of denial — that the Japanese would not have won if not for British mishandling of the situation.

The Japanese won because they had a well-equipped, highly motivated, well-trained, and well-led attacking force. Historically, these are good reasons for military victory. One of their foremost advantages was control of the air. The Japanese air force quickly dispatched the units of the Royal Air Force that were committed to the defense of the area, catching many of them on the ground. Most of the planes committed to Singapore's defense were outdated and slow, but even if the British had been willing to send their best planes and pilots to Malaya, it is doubtful they would have changed events. The Japanese fighter planes were the finest in the skies at this time and had better speed and maneuverability than even the best British plane. Many British actually believed a stereotype that Japanese had poor eyesight — because many wore glasses and had "small, squinty eyes" — and would therefore be unable to produce quality pilots. On the ground, the Japanese troops that hit the beaches in Malaya were seasoned veterans of the China campaign. Usually, an attacking force must outnumber the defenders to ensure victory. In this case, the Japanese were outnumbered two to one, but their experience and deeply held devotion to duty carried them through. In the end, the question is moot because there was no way the British were going to divert resources that were needed to defend the United Kingdom to Malaya.

The Japanese battle plan was well-executed and backed by excellent intelligence, but even they were surprised by the swiftness of their victory. When the British surrendered on February 15, 1942 in Singapore, Japanese commanders at the time said that their greatest fear was that the British would counterattack. The campaign had been so swift that the Japanese had outrun their lines of supply, and most troops were down to their last few rounds of ammunition. In this respect, the Japanese had overestimated the British. The strategy of the British had been to hold on until reinforcements reached Singapore. When the battleship Prince of Wales and cruiser Repulse were sunk by Japanese dive bombers on the second day of the fighting, which gave the Japanese control of the sea as well as the air, the war was over. No naval or air reinforcements were coming, and it would have made no difference even if they had because the British were in no position to halt the Japanese advance.

British women and children fleeing Singapore as the Japanese advance down the peninsula.

The significance of the fall of Singapore goes far beyond the history of Malaysia and Singapore. After World War I, Britain was an empire in decline but not in the eyes of most of the people of Africa and Asia. Singapore, the greatest base of the greatest empire, had fallen, not to another European power but to an Asian one. The Japanese victory was symbolic in the eyes of millions as the end of European invincibility. When the Union Jack came down on February 15, 1942, it was a moment of great historical significance in Malaya.

The Occupation

For the people of Malaya and Singapore, the Japanese occupation may have had as important an impact on their futures as their experience of the defeat of imperial Britain. The Japanese arrived in British Malaya and Borneo offering a vision of a new era of peace and prosperity. It was to be "Asia for the Asians" as part of the Greater East Asia Co-prosperity Sphere. The Japanese had freed them from Western rule and would help them develop as part of a massive Asian market. Most of this was eyewash as what the Japanese had in mind was little different from what the British wanted — sources of raw materials for Japanese industry and markets for Japanese manufactured goods.

The methods the Japanese employed to achieve their goals were a far different matter altogether. Malaya, and especially the immigrant communities, went through three-and-a-half years of purgatory. Times were so bad that in 1945 thousands lined the streets seriously cheering the return of the British colonial power. As C.V. Devan Nair, Singapore's third president put it, "when the Japanese attacked some of us were anti-British and pro-Japanese; in three years we were all anti-Japanese."

The Japanese occupation brought tremendous economic hardship to the area. It was brutal in its methods and incompetent in its administration. The co-prosperity sphere turned into a co-poverty sphere. While not everyone was physically abused by the Japanese, everyone suffered economically.

There were many reasons why the Japanese were unable to benefit from the economic success of British Malaya. Foremost was that after its initial successes in 1941 and 1942, Japan lost control of the sea lanes. When the Japanese attacked the American fleet at Pearl Harbor in December 1941, they dealt the Americans a heavy blow, but they failed to knock out American aircraft carrier capabilities. This came back to haunt them in 1942 when the Americans won two key naval battles that blunted Japanese advances. In the battle of the Coral Sea and the battle of Midway late in May and June 1942, the American navy turned the tide of the war and dealt the Japanese navy a blow from which it did not recover. These two sea battles were also significant in the history of naval warfare. Because of advances in naval gunnery, naval air support, and radar, these were the first two battles in history in which the opposing ships never even saw their enemy.

Allied submarines were able to harass Japanese shipping within the co-prosperity sphere to the point of crippling Japan's maritime trade. In Malaya, export industries dried up and imported goods became scarce. Life in the urban areas became miserable with tremendous food shortages. Prior to the war, Malaya had imported half the food it consumed, and Japanese inability to keep the sea lanes open made many imports inaccessible. Those in the rural areas who grew food were not affected too badly because they could still eat, but rural Malays who grew cash crops, such as rubber and copra, saw a dramatic drop in their living standards. Singapore, being the most urban of the British territories, had the hardest time. People were growing food in their backyards, along the roadsides, anything, anywhere in order to survive. Trade was Singapore's lifeblood, and it was virtually dead.

The problems of the economy were made worse by the disappearance of much of the infrastructure that had made British Malaya work. The internment of the Europeans meant that the people who knew how to operate the mines and plantations were no longer available. The agency houses that were important to the smooth running of the system were closed. The people who ran the key government departments were behind barbed wire. The Chinese, who were essential to the retail and distribution system, were frightened and uncooperative because of ill treatment by the Japanese. Also, most of the machinery needed to run the export end of the economy, such as tin dredges, had been destroyed by the retreating British.

Into this vacuum were injected incompetent administrators. Many were military personnel or Japanese residents of the area who knew little about running a modern government. Prior to World War II, a sizeable Japanese community had sprung up in the area, especially in Penang and Singapore. They had fled Japan because of bad times caused by the Great Depression and made their living in Malaya as barbers, photographers, fishermen, and brothel operators. These Japanese were hardly the pool from which to draw the administrators for the *New Malai*, or Malaya, and *Syonan-to*, or the "Light of the South" — Singapore.

226

The worst economic problem caused by the Japanese was inflation. Shortages due to a drop in imports alone would have driven up prices, but the Japanese aggravated the inflation by producing worthless currency. With the disruption of the economy by the war and invasion, there was little revenue available to run the government. The Japanese answer was to print money that had nothing to back it. As prices rose, the Japanese merely printed more money, and the territory became caught up in a terrible cycle of runaway inflation. Called "banana money" by Malayans because of the pictures on the bills, the money originally had serial numbers. As time went on, these numbers were dropped because no one really knew how much was being printed. The following table gives an example of the situation caused by the unbridled printing presses:

Items	Dec 1941	Dec 1943	Dec 1944	Aug 1945
Rice (500 grams)	6 cents	$2.50	$8.20	$75.00
Pork (500 grams)	48 cents	$4.00	$22.00	$280.00
Sugar (500 grams)	8 cents	$3.80	$18.00	$120.00
One egg	3 cents	28 cents	$1.25	$35.00

People were forced to sell their possessions to survive, and those dependant on fixed incomes became destitute. No one was spared the economic dislocation caused by the worthless currency circulated.

The Japanese administration not only contributed to the economic misery but used methods to control Malaya and enforce its will that are still remembered with anger by older Malaysians and Singaporeans. Any semblance of justice disappeared and was replaced by summary military punishment and a police force run by the *Kempeitai*, or the Japanese secret police. Torture and brutality became common, and the punishment for any suspicion of anti-Japanese feelings or activity was swift and fatal.

The Chinese were singled out for the worst treatment. China and Japan had been enemies for years, and the Chinese community in British Malaya had been a generous supporter of the Chinese government in their fight against the Japanese invaders. Many of the Japanese troops were veterans of the war in China and viewed all Chinese as enemies. The communists were especially despised by the Japanese because of their spirited defense in China and their participation in anti-Japanese resistance

Executions of civilians by Japanese soldiers.

movements in the conquered territories. People were beaten for failing to perform the required bow to Japanese soldiers. Accused criminals were beheaded in the public streets. In the early period of Japanese occupation of Singapore, thousands of Chinese were rounded up for being communist or anti-Japanese and were never seen again. The estimates of the number of political executions that took place during Japanese rule run between 20,000 and 120,000, and the vast majority of them were Chinese. This policy was eased somewhat as time went on because the Japanese desperately needed the Chinese to keep the economy going, but for most Chinese, the occupation represented three-and-a-half years of fear and suffering.

Malayan Resistance

It should come as no surprise then that the lion's share of the armed resistance to the Japanese came from the Chinese in general and the communists in particular. During the Japanese purge of communists and anti-Japanese in Malaya, thousands of Chinese fled to the jungle to fight as guerrillas. A number of groups sprung up in opposition to the occupation. The largest and best organized was called the Malayan People's

Anti-Japanese Army (MPAJA). Building up to some six or seven thousand recruits by the end of the war, this group was mainly led by the Malayan Communist Party, which itself was predominantly Chinese.

The British set up a special operations task force called Force 136 to gather intelligence and support these resistance groups. Supplied with new arms and resources by British air drops and in some cases trained by British officers, members of the MPAJA were heroes to many in the Chinese community. They had a natural source of support in the hundreds of thousands of Chinese who had fled the urban areas during the Great Depression and Japanese occupation to live on the fringes of the jungle. These communities provided the backbone of what was called the Anti-Japanese Union (AJU), which provided the guerrillas with supplies and recruits.

One such hero was Lim Bo Seng, a wealthy trader and brick supplier from Singapore. When the Japanese forces arrived, Lim fled to India where he was recruited by Force 136. He in turn recruited other Chinese, and they returned to Malaya to establish contacts with the MPAJA. There he set up an intelligence organization, worked undercover, and raised funds from his many business contacts. Nine members of his family in Singapore were arrested and never seen again. In 1943, Lim was captured and tortured by the Japanese. He died in prison the following year.

How much damage these groups did to the Japanese war effort is debatable, but they represented a new phenomenon — Chinese who were fighting for the future of Malaya. Although their vision was for a communist government, the MPAJA and the AJU represented the first major Chinese political drive to help determine the future of what they now saw as their country.

Apart from the communists, there were other significant resistance groups. In Perak and Pahang, there were sizable Malay groups who fought the Japanese bravely. Tun Abdul Razak, who later became prime minister of Malaya, was an officer in the Pahang force, Wataniah. There was a group of Chinese fighters around the border with Thailand that was linked to the Kuomintang. Then there were anti-Japanese groups who were nothing more than bandits taking advantage of the chaotic situation. Except for the bandits, all these groups were symptoms of forces that would appear in greater strength after the war — the forces of Malayan nationalism.

Japanese treatment of the Malays was somewhat better than their treatment of the Chinese. When the Japanese took control, they appeared to offer the Malays a privileged position in their new order. The Japanese proposed that Malaya would be a Japanese protectorate and Singapore a colony. They led the Malays to believe that they would run their own country. Malays kept their government positions, and new opportunities were opened up to them. This was especially true in the police and security forces. Malay fears of Chinese political assertion were used to organize Malay security forces to attack the mainly Chinese resistance groups.

In the 1930s, groups of non-aristocratic Malays had begun to assert themselves beyond their traditional roles as farmers. To many Malay-educated Malays, the Japanese offered an opportunity to assert Malay political and economic power. The old colonial barrier had been torn down by the Japanese, and groups such as the Kesatuan Melayu Muda (KMM), or Young Malay Union, were establishing ties with Indonesian groups and speaking of pan-Malayan unity and independence.

These Malays made up only a minority of the educated population, and as the occupation wore on, fewer Malays had positive feelings toward the Japanese. The promise of self-rule was a sham; Malaya was actually under military rule. Its function was to provide raw materials for the Japanese war effort. When forced labor was required, the Malays were not exempt from impressment. When Japanese troops needed food, Malay supplies were usually treated no differently from Chinese supplies. Apart from this, most Malays were far removed from issues of pan-Malayan solidarity, nationalism, and self-rule. They were struggling desperately to survive the economic nightmare of Japanese rule. Few had a Malayan perspective. Their interests were local — their family, their kampung, and, on a stretch, their sultan and state. The Japanese created further animosity among some Malays by handing back the northern states to Siam as its reward for allying with the Japanese.

The Indian community was viewed as a potential ally in the Japanese war effort. The Japanese army had conquered much of Burma and was close to its ultimate goal of invading India. To this end, it planned to draw on anti-British and pro-independence feelings in the Indian community. S.C. Bose, an Indian nationalist leader, was brought to Singapore by the Japanese to head an Indian government in exile. They promised to give India independence once the British were defeated. Bose was instrumental in organizing the Indian National Army (INA) among the Indian community and Indian prisoners of war. They were to fight alongside the Japanese in their final push from Burma into India. When Malaya fell, 55,000 Indian troops under British leadership were taken captive by the Japanese. Of these 40,000 agreed to pledge their allegiance to Bose's government and join the INA.

Disillusionment with these Japanese promises was quick to set in among many Indians. As large-scale unemployment grew among the plantation workers, thousands of Tamil Indians were drafted to help build the railroad into Burma from Thailand. Malnutrition, disease, and outright mistreatment killed the vast majority of these workers. When the INA joined the Japanese in their advance into Burma, it took horrific casualties. Poorly led, ill-equipped, and untrained for jungle warfare, they probably wished they had taken their chances in the POW camps. Suffice it to say the Japanese contribution to Indian dreams of nationhood was a nightmare.

After the war, the members of the INA were hailed as courageous freedom fighters by the leaders of the Indian independence movement. When some of the officers of the INA were charged with treason and murder by the British, their trial in India became a rallying cry for anti-British agitation. When they were convicted, the British commuted their sentences because of large-scale public opposition in India.

Impact of the War

When the British returned in 1945, they were greeted as conquering heroes by most in British Malaya. The dark days of 1942 to 1945 were over, and there seemed for the first time in years some hope for the future. But the future as perceived in 1945 was vastly different from the future that had been envisaged before the Japanese invasion.

Although the people of Malaya were glad to see them return, the British had lost the moral authority to rule. For almost a hundred and fifty years there had been in Malaya an aura of British political and military invincibility — the Royal Navy ruled the waves, British industry was supreme, and fair-minded British administrators dispensed justice. The Japanese invasion had ended that perception once and for all. The British had failed in one of their primary functions as a governing power — to provide for peace, order, and security. The Japanese had continued to humiliate the British throughout the occupation, and the sight of half-starved British prisoners of war doing menial tasks further eroded the British imperial image. Thus, there was little doubt that the days of British Malaya were numbered. The war had changed the views of both the Malays and the immigrant races as to what the new political order should be.

PRISONERS OF THE EMPIRE OF JAPAN

When the emperor of Japan conducted a state visit to Britain in 1998, hundreds of World War II British veterans lined the streets. As the emperor's motorcade went by, they turned their backs on him, symbolizing the bitter memories that still lingered after more than fifty years. For the allied troops that were imprisoned after the fall of Singapore, life was three-and-a-half years of living hell.

To the Japanese soldier, surrender was an act of cowardice. True military men were expected to fight to death in the Japanese code of honor. The treatment they meted out to their captives reflected the utter scorn they held for men whom they saw as dishonorable. It is estimated that close to a third of the British Commonwealth troops who were prisoners of war in Southeast Asia died from malnutrition, disease, poor medical care, forced labor, beatings, and executions. In contrast, the number of allied prisoners who died in German POW camps amounted to about 5 percent.

Perhaps the most dramatic example of the experiences of these POWs was the construction of the Burma Railroad, or Death Railroad, as it has been called. In order to avoid the allied naval blockade, the Japanese decided to build a rail link from Thailand through Burma to invade India. The railroad would stretch some 450 miles (724 km) through jungle and over mountains. It was to be built in a little over a year, primarily by forced manual labor.

The cost in lives among the POWs and Asian laborers was horrendous. Over fifty thousand POWs worked on the railroad, and only about thirty thousand survived. Of the 270,000 Asian civilians it is estimated that one in three died. A commander of one of the POW work camps describes the conditions as follows:

"No lighting was ever provided, even surgical operations were performed in the open by moonlight or the light of a campfire. The hours of work continued long — so much so that the majority of the men never saw their camp by daylight. It was monsoon season and it rained almost incessantly. No facilities existed, and no opportunities were given, for drying of clothes, cleansing of bodies, or resting, and it is not surprising that with this combination of infamous conditions, disease should be rampant. Malaria, dysentery, beri-beri, and above all, what the Japanese resourcefully described as 'Post Dysenteric Inanition' on death certificates, but what was actually starvation — stalked through the camps."

In Malaya, the occupation was both divisive and unifying. It was divisive in that racial tensions were heightened. Organized Chinese groups began to campaign for an independent Malaya. Prior to the war, although the British called most of the shots, colonial officials ruled in the name of the Malay sultans, who in turn ruled the Malay states. A political role for the Chinese was almost unthinkable. They were migrant workers who were supposed to make their money and return to China. The war brought home to many Malays that not only did large numbers of Chinese view Malaya as their home, they also wanted a say in the future of the country. The Chinese communists wanted an even stronger say — they wanted to dictate the future. The assertiveness of the Chinese frightened many Malays, and the Japanese encouraged their fear by using them in security operations against the MPAJA. Some in the Chinese community felt that many Malays were collaborators and deserved punishment, which they proceeded to mete out in the closing days of the war and early days of peace.

The fear of the communists was unifying in the sense that, for many Malays and non-communist Chinese, it called for some kind of counter action. Among the English-educated elite of the three races there was a growing realization that they had to work together and find common ground to keep the country from falling apart. The British had acted as a somewhat neutral referee among the races prior to the war, but they were planning to end colonial rule. New political arrangements had to be put in place to replace them. Many Malay leaders realized that the fact that half their population were immigrants had to be addressed, and many immigrant leaders were aware that the Malays were afraid that they would be displaced politically by immigrants. The specter of armed Chinese extremists forced the English-educated elite to pull together to chart a democratic future.

For Singapore, the occupation was a significant force in the creation of a Singaporean identity. The Chinese community had stabilized in the 1930s to the point where a majority of the population was born on the island. For most of these Chinese, the occupation was a common experience that transcended dialect, class, and education. They spent three-and-a-half years finding ways to survive in the face of a hostile occupying force. It is the shared experiences of history that are the building blocks of nationalism, and the most powerful of shared experiences are war, hardship, and suffering, all of which were abundant among the Chinese in Singapore.

It was also *their* experience. The British had failed them. It was obvious where British priorities were — in Europe. The Singapore that had been willing to work, prosper, and grow under British direction no longer existed. Most of them were born in Singapore. They had survived against all odds, and the island would never really be British again. In their minds, Singapore was theirs, and they wanted a say in its future.

The group the occupation probably affected most was the Straits Chinese. Prior to the war, they had taken pride in their British nationality and their English education — they were the "King's Chinese." The war changed this, and they began to see themselves as Malayans rather than as British. It was from this group that leaders emerged to take Singapore to self-rule — men such as Lee Kuan Yew and Goh Keng Swee. British rule was reestablished in 1945, but because of the war, that rule only turned out to be a transition to rule by the people who lived there.

Chapter 14

MALAYA AFTER THE WAR

An observer of Malaya in the 1930s remarked that it was "a country without politics." For the most part, this was true prior to the Japanese occupation. The immigrant races seemed more interested in the politics of their home countries, and the average rural Malay had little interest in the affairs of state. The Malay aristocracy was secure in its role as the symbol of Malay rule. Unlike countries such as India, Indonesia, and Vietnam, there was no significant nationalist or independence movement in Malaya. The Japanese occupation changed this. When the British returned in 1945, the peninsula had become intensely political. The changing population, the war, and British plans for the future of Malaya worked together to create interest in the political future of all who called Malaya home.

The war and the Japanese occupation had fundamentally changed some of the basic premises of Malay political life. One of these was the idea that immigrant races were to be excluded from politics and government. Prior to the war, Malays had been assured of their right to rule through the sultans and of a "Malay only" policy for entry into the government administrative services. The immigrant races were considered transients who were not to participate in the workings of government.

A growing number of native-born Chinese and Indians challenged this belief, especially after the MPAJA had fought for Malaya by resisting the Japanese. The vast majority of those who fought the Japanese were Chinese who were not just interested in defeating the occupiers. Dominated by communists, their message was also about a post-war communist Malaya. Their activities politicized not only the Chinese but also the Malays. For the first time, Chinese political leaders in Malaya were talking about their plans for their country. This was a direct threat to the Malays' view of Malaya as their country and their land, as well as their government.

Another belief — that the British were the protectors of *Tanah Melayu*, or land of the Malays — was destroyed. The belief that the British could be trusted to preserve the states as Malay states was rapidly fading. The British had lost Malaya to the Japanese, and when they returned, their plans for the political future of Malaya were viewed as destructive to Malay interests.

POPULATION OF MALAYA AND SINGAPORE, 1950		
Racial Groups	Singapore	Malaya
Chinese	789,160	2,011,072
Malays	123,624	2,579,914
Indians	72,467	564,454
Europeans	11,504	
Eurasians	10,093	
Others	8,605	71,109*
Total	1,015,453	5,226,549

Figure includes both Europeans and Eurasians.

Malay Political Unity

During the war, the colonial office in London had formulated a blueprint for post-war Malaya. Although it accepted little input from the Malays, it recognized Malaya's fundamental political dilemma — balancing the desires of native-born immigrant races for citizenship and political participation with the Malay view that political control should remain in Malay hands. This problem was further accentuated by the fact that the Malays had become a minority, albeit the largest, in British Malaya by the end of the war. British planners realized that the days of the empire were numbered. Malaya, like the rest of its colonies, was inevitably moving toward self-rule. At the same time, the British had huge investments in Malaya and wanted to protect their economic interests in the area. This required a friendly, stable government that would allow British commercial ventures to continue to prosper. To achieve these goals required greater Malayan unity and more resources for development. To these ends, they proposed the creation of the Malayan Union.

The Malayan Union represented a fundamental change in the nature and organization of the way Malaya was governed. Under the union plan, the FMS, unfederated states, Penang, and Melaka would be joined together to form a unitary state ruled from Kuala Lumpur. The individual sultans were to be persuaded to give up their sovereignty to a governor who would rule in the name of the British crown. There would be legislative and executive councils that would be responsible for law making on a national basis. There would still be sultans, but they would have less power, basically over religion and Malay custom, and the states would not be governed in their names.

The British plan was revolutionary. Citizenship would be bestowed on all who were born in Malaya or had lived there for ten of the previous fifteen years. All others in Malaya could obtain citizenship through a future residency requirement of five years. There were to be equal rights for all in the political life of the new state. Government administrative posts were to be opened up to the immigrant races. After a transitional period, this new arrangement would lead to a democratic, self-governing Malaya independent of the British crown.

Singapore was to be spun off as a separate colony because its large Chinese population was seen as a political threat to the Malays and also because of its strategic and military importance to Britain. The plan was meant to be a way to offer the immigrants a future, unite the country, and provide the means to help the less developed parts of the country. What it turned out to be was a total disaster, especially in the eyes of the Malays.

Initial British moves to institute union had met with success. They had quietly convinced the sultans to acquiesce to the Malayan Union. The sultans went along with British plans for two reasons. The most important was that British officials put pressure on those sultans who had refused to leave when the Japanese arrived. They even removed two who had ruled during the occupation. What had seemed sensible in 1942 was now open to accusations of collaboration with the enemy. Another reason was that the British fast-talked the sultans and played down the ramifications to the Malay community. Whatever the reasons, the sultans failed as a first line of defense for Malay political rights.

To most Malays, the Malayan Union was a sellout that would make them second class citizens in their own country. The assumption had always been that the immigrants could participate in the economic life of the area, but the political life was to be dominated by the Malays. The sultans were powerful symbols of the fact that the states of the peninsula were Malay and would always be under Malay sovereignty. Even though indirect rule had been a facade in most areas, colonial office planners misjudged its importance in the eyes of the Malays.

The special position and privileges of the Malays, backed by British guarantees, did not exist under the Malayan Union. In a democratic unitary state with liberal citizenship laws, it would only be a matter of time before the immigrant races controlled the political as well as economic power of the country. In five of the wealthiest states, the Malays were already in the minority, and the symbols of Malay power, such as the sultans, were the only political links they had with their own country.

The Malayan Union brought to the fore the concerns about the size and economic power of the non-Malay immigrants, which Malays educated in the Malay language had begun expressing in the 1930s. As long as the British could be depended on to maintain Malay sovereignty, these concerns were relatively low key, but the war and the Malayan Union no longer made them so. The average Malay was relatively apolitical, but there were groups that were trying to make the Malay public aware of the economic and political threats posed by the immigrants.

Attempts to mobilize the Malay community in the new world of the 1930s and 1940s and the creation of a Malay political and national consciousness revolved around three schools of thought. One response was religious in nature. In the early twentieth century, there was greater contact between the Malay community and the Middle East. In part, this came about because increased prosperity and inexpensive travel had made it possible for greater numbers of pilgrims to visit Mecca and participate in the Haj. It also took place because rising numbers of Malays were going to the Middle East for religious training and higher education. Many of these students returned fired up with the spirit of Islamic reform, which was popular in the Middle East at that time. They felt the answers to the problems of the Malays could be found by returning to a purer form of Islam. They believed that Islam in Malaya had been corrupted by adat law and local custom, making it unable to stand up to the cultural and economic threats of the West and the immigrants. With allegiance to the true teachings of Islam, the Malay community could preserve its position and values.

A second group of Malay leaders that arose at this time came from the Malay-educated intelligentsia, made up mainly of Malay-language school teachers, minor government officials, and journalists. Most of these people had their roots in rural Malaya. Their awareness of the problems facing the Malay community had been heightened by access to schools, such as the Sultan Idris Training College, where they had been exposed to the ideas and literature of the larger Malay-speaking world, including the anti-colonial nationalism coming out of Indonesia at this time.

One of the first Malay political organizations came from this group — the KMM, or Young Malay Union, led by Ibrahim Yaacob. Pan Malayanism as a bulwark against the immigrant races had great appeal to this group. During the war, the KMM was encouraged by the Japanese to assert itself and develop its contacts with Indonesian nationalist groups. They saw race and language spanning across into Sumatra and other Malay-language areas to create a greater Malay nation strong enough to stand up to the challenge of the immigrants.

The third and most successful of the groups competing for leadership of the Malay community came from the traditional ruling elite. British rule had been good to the Malay aristocracy. Their thrones and positions had been stabilized and guaranteed by British intervention in the civil disorder of the nineteenth century. Access to English education at schools, such as the Malay College and Victoria Institution, had led to positions in the government. Because of their English education, many had gone on to further their education in Britain and as a result moved easily in British political and commercial circles. It was in the name of these elite families that the British ruled Malaya, and these families felt they had the traditional right to rule. Men such as Tunku Abdul Rahman, Tun Abdul Razak, and Dato Hussein Onn, Malaysia's first prime ministers, were all from this group.

A democratic Malaya with equal political rights for the immigrant races was not only a threat to Malay political dominance but was also a threat to the traditional elite. What would be their position in a democratic country with a majority population of immigrants? In their eyes, the only answer to Malaya's future was some kind of accommodation between the political desires of the immigrants and the Malays' right to rule. They realized that the immigrant races were not just going to go away and were essential for the economic future of all in Malaya. These aristocratic leaders believed strongly in the special position of the Malays but saw negotiation and compromise with the other communities as the path to follow in creating a post-British political arrangement.

The leadership of the post-war Malay community fell to the traditional elite quite easily. The religious option appealed to some, especially those in the former unfederated states, but it had many opponents because these reformers were a threat to the existing religious establishment. During British rule, the sultans had retained control over Islamic affairs and had established a strong link between the palace and the mosque. Throughout the states, the religious bureaucracies were firm supporters of the status quo. Acceptance of Islamic laws and customs from the Middle East was also a threat to the role of adat law in the community. One of the draws of Islam in Malaya had been its tolerance and accommodation of existing beliefs, laws, and customs. These twentieth-century reformers were asking rural Malays to give up an important part of their traditional village culture. Thus, many members of the religious establishment were vocal opponents of the reforms offered by such groups as the Pan Malayan Islamic Party, known today as the Parti Islam Se-Melayu/Malaysia (PAS)

Pan Malayanism also had limited popular support. While it appealed to Malay-educated Malays, for the ordinary Malays, grand schemes of unity in the archipelago fell on deaf ears. The world of the rural Malays was quite small and did not reach much beyond the villages. Few Malays at this time had any concept of Malaya, let alone countries beyond its borders. Their political loyalties were to their traditional leaders — the village headman and the sultan. In addition, the concept of Pan Malayan unity required a reevaluation of the role of the traditional rulers and was couched in criticism of the traditional aristocracy. Because of this, many Malays turned against the Pan Malayan leaders even though they had come from their own rural ranks.

That the Malay community rejected the ideas of the reformers and embraced leadership by their traditional elite was in itself an impact of

British rule. The British had preserved the link between the Malay aristocracy and the Malay peasantry in its traditional form. The intricacies of indirect rule meant little to the rural Malays. The British had maintained the trappings of the old feudal society and through their policies had maintained not only the concept of Malay rule but rule by the families of the rulers with whom they had made their initial nineteenth-century arrangements. The royal courts' continued responsibility for Islam and Malay custom had perpetuated the connection between the court and the kampung. The traditional concept of daulat still existed in the minds of most Malays and reinforced the view that the elite of the Malay states were their rightful leaders.

The Malay reaction to the Malayan Union was widespread and vocal. It was the first time that large numbers of Malays throughout the peninsula made common cause with one another. That the movement in opposition to Malayan Union was national in nature proved that the English-educated Malay elite could work together as a group and mobilize Malay public opinion.

To lead the battle against the Malayan Union and its threat to the Malays' position, the first major Malay political party was organized in 1946 — the United Malay National Organization (UMNO). Led by Dato Onn bin Jaafar, chief minister of Johor, UMNO organized large public demonstrations against the union and coordinated a policy of noncooperation. Malays refused to sit on any of the committees or councils that were set up under the union. The sultans refused to attend state functions and boycotted any consultations or meetings with the British. Without the support or participation of the Malay political leaders, the Malayan Union was dead.

The ability of the Malay political leadership through UMNO to mobilize Malay public opinion caught the British by surprise. A people who only a decade earlier had seemed docile and apathetic were suddenly making their views known through mass demonstrations. The strength and emotion of the Malay reaction convinced the British that they had miscalculated.

Both the dominant Malay leadership and the British realized that some kind of national entity had to be created for Malaya to move toward independence. Both also realized that the conflict between immigrant rights

241

and Malay rights had to be solved for any viable country to emerge. The British sat down with the Malay political leadership to come up with an alternative to the Malayan Union.

Through 1946 and 1947, British officials and representatives of the Malay rulers and UMNO hammered out a new arrangement, which resulted in the creation of the Federation of Malaya in 1948. The federation was to be an interim arrangement whereby the British would rule during a period in which greater local participation would take place in government, and the final constitution and structure of an independent Malaya would be decided.

As opposed to the union proposal, instead of a British governor, there would be a British high commissioner to the states of Malaya who would act as the head of the central government. The sovereignty of the states and the positions of the sultans would be maintained as per pre-war arrangements. Governmental powers were to be divided between the states and the federal government. For example, land laws and policies would be retained at the state level.

The special position of the Malays was guaranteed, and the sultans and high commissioner were the guarantors. Citizenship laws for immigrants were stricter than those of the union proposal, and final arrangements in this area were to be negotiated for an independent Malaya. Legislative councils for the states and the federation were established, but the majority of Malayan participation in those councils was to be Malay. What the agreement meant was that in the period of time that Malaya moved toward independence, the Malays would control the levers of government. Singapore was still to be spun off as a separate colony. Most in UMNO viewed this with relief as it reduced the number of Chinese in what had been British Malaya.

The Emergency and the Communist Threat

The post-war Malay political goals and leadership were determined with a large degree of unity, but the battle to determine the agenda and leadership of the Chinese community was slow and bloody. The Chinese were a diverse community whose political interests, if they had them, had revolved around the power struggle in China. There was no "traditional" leadership in their community, and when the war was over, the direction of the community was up for grabs.

At the end of World War II, the Chinese in Malaya were the wealthiest of the three races. Their superior average income and control of the retail trade, however, disguised sections of their community that had serious economic grievances and were threatened by the new order. Being wealthier on the average did not mean that all Chinese were well off. Over 500,000 Chinese, about a quarter of the Chinese population, were squatters who had fled the towns and cities as a result of hard times caused by the Great Depression and the Japanese occupation. Living on the fringes of the jungle, they had no title to their land and were isolated from government influence and services. If educated at all, it was poorly and in Chinese. For the most part, they survived off the proceeds of small rubber and vegetable holdings. Very few of these Chinese were native born, and under new citizenship laws it would be a long time before they had any access to political power. As the British and Malays negotiated the political future of the country, their needs and interests were being ignored.

The majority of the Chinese who lived in the cities made their living from relatively low paid jobs as factory workers, laborers, or hawkers. They were urban dwellers and educated in Chinese. Their concerns about education, housing, and working conditions would no doubt be low on the list of a Malay government with a rural Malay political base. A fundamental priority of any elected Malay government had to be the economic improvement of the Malays vis à vis the other races. Any attempt to move Malays into the modern economy would impact on the Chinese the most because their manual and semi-skilled jobs were the ones that would initially draw Malay competition.

For over a half of the Chinese community, immigration to Malaya had not resulted in great fortunes but in low incomes and hard labor. China-born or the children of China-born, few had citizenship or any kind of legal or political standing, and yet, they planned to stay. That they stayed in Malaya was probably more a testament to poor conditions in China than to good times in Malaya. The battle for leadership of the Chinese community was dependent on these two groups, the squatters and the workers.

At the end of the war, there was a significant shift in the leadership of the Chinese community. Prior to the war, the dominant political group had been the nationalist KMT due to its association with the ruling party of China and support from Chinese business interests backed by secret societies. By 1945, the communists had significantly increased their stature and position among the Chinese in British Malaya. There had been communist activity in the Chinese community for some time, reflecting the divisions and politics within China itself. Communist agents had been active in the Kuomintang organizations and in the labor unions. By the time of the Japanese invasion, it is estimated that there were 37,000 active communists in Malaya and Singapore, the vast majority of whom were Chinese. With the Japanese victory, thousands of these communists fled to the jungle, not just to survive and fight the Japanese but to prepare for the establishment of an independent, communist Malaya.

When the MPAJA emerged from the jungle after the war, they were viewed as heroes by many in the Chinese community. They participated in the victory parades and were given medals and cash awards by the British for their anti-Japanese efforts.

The communists were also the best-organized political group in the Chinese community. In the first couple of years after the war, the Malayan Communist Party (MCP) openly joined the political process, establishing branches in most of the major towns and concentrating on labor activities. The new Labor Party government in Britain was sympathetic to the activities of labor unions, and the communists took advantage of this. Organizing the Pan Malayan General Labor Union in 1946, their plan was to cause serious disruption to the economy through strikes and labor agitation and then ride the tide of discontent to power.

Chinese schools also provided fertile ground for recruitment and agitation by the communists. The British abandonment of the Malayan Union had convinced many young Chinese that the Malay leadership planned to relegate Chinese to permanent second class status. Their future seemed bleak, and the communists offered hope.

There is no doubt that the post-war recovery was slowed by the MCP's activities, but by 1947, it was apparent that their tactics were not generating the mass support necessary to take power. Many workers had become disgruntled by the political nature of the labor movement. In

1947, a general strike was called as well as hundreds of other strikes. The strike pay was insufficient, and most participants were feeling economic hardship with few concrete results for their protests. Apart from this, the party was split between its leader, Lai Teck, who wanted to continue using open and legal means to gain power, and much of the rank and file of the party, who felt this strategy was futile.

Lai Teck himself was facing serious problems of credibility. There were rumors that he was a double agent for the British and communists and most probably also had worked for the Japanese during the war. The basis for these rumors was the charmed life he seemed to lead. He had appeared in Singapore in 1934, having escaped a general crackdown on communists in Hong Kong and Shanghai. Some believe it was at this time that he was recruited by British Intelligence in return for his freedom. During the war, Lai Teck lived openly in Singapore and escaped two Japanese raids on meetings of the MCP leadership, fueling the suspicion that he was in league with the Japanese. After the war, his commitment to open constitutional means in the face of large-scale opposition from his comrades fed the belief that he was in cahoots with the British.

In 1947, a meeting of the central committee was called to confront Lai Teck and determine the course of the movement. Lai Teck failed to show up and disappeared, along with funds belonging to the party. He was never heard of again. It was at this time that the twenty-six-year-old Chin Peng assumed leadership, and it was decided that the MCP would undertake a "war of national liberation" against the government of Malaya.

What ensued was the Emergency, a twelve-year guerrilla war between communist insurgents and the Malayan government backed by British Commonwealth troops. The conflict drew its name from the fact that the civil government of Malaya had declared a state of emergency in order to assume extraordinary powers to fight the communists. Perhaps more importantly, by calling it an emergency and not a war, it was possible for businessmen to collect for damage to property from insurance companies. The fight against the MCP was directed by civilian authorities with the support of the military and thus was a "police action." To the thousands of British, Australian, New Zealand, Fijian, and African troops stationed in Malaya, the semantics meant nothing. They fought and died to prevent the communists from taking over Malaya.

Malayan troops on jungle patrol during the Emergency.

Once the decision was made to fight, the MCP drifted back into the jungle and dug up the arms they had hidden at the end of the war with this eventuality in mind. The irony is that many of the weapons the communists used against the Malayan government had been supplied to them by the British during World War II to fight the Japanese. The communists proclaimed that their fight was anti-colonial and that their goals were to end British rule and create a democratic, socialist Malaya. Calling themselves the Malayan Races Liberation Army (MRLA), they put 6,000 to 8,000 regular fighters on the battlefield, many of them veterans of the fight against the Japanese.

The MRLA had a natural base among the Chinese squatter community and was able to reestablish its World War II support system. Previously called the Anti-Japanese Union but now known as the Min Yuen (Organization of the Masses), this group of active followers numbered in the tens of thousands and provided money, food, and recruits to keep the fight going.

The first few years of this conflict were bleak for Malaya's British administration. The MRLA's activities devastated the economy and administration. It followed a two-pronged attack that in the years 1948 to 1950 seemed to be successful. One was to destroy the export economy

246

owned by the British. Much of its activity was directed at the large rubber plantations and tin mines. Rubber estates became dangerous places to live. European estate managers and their families were attacked frequently, and their homes became armed camps. About one in ten British managers were killed, about 10 percent of the rubber trees in Malaya were destroyed, tin dredges were blown up, and roads and railroads were unsafe unless under military protection. In the first years of the war, the MRLA's success stretched the British forces to their limits just trying to protect these areas from communist attack, let alone going on any kind of counteroffensive.

The other main area of communist activity was to undermine government credibility and eliminate opposition to their leadership in the Chinese community. By 1950, over a hundred British and Malayan civilians were being killed every month. The MRLA hoped that the loss of leadership would create vacuums into which it could step and declare "liberated" areas of the country. The high point of communist activity took place in early 1951 when a unit of the MRLA ambushed and killed British High Commissioner Sir Henry Gurney on the road to Fraser's Hill, which was about 62 miles (100 km) from Kuala Lumpur. If the highest British official in Malaya was not safe from attack, who was?

Although the assassination of Gurney was a serious psychological blow to the country, by 1951, the British had discovered the right formula of actions that would eventually result in victory. The British realized the battle was political as well as military, and both had to be won in order to defeat the MRLA.

On the military side, Britain was a major world power with modern air and ground capabilities and was able to commit the military resources to seriously outnumber the guerrillas. In order to free the military to fight and not merely defend, the police force was expanded from about nine thousand in 1948 to about sixty thousand in 1952. The great majority of this increase in the number of police officers came from the Malay community, which had little sympathy for the MRLA cause. Most Malays saw the MRLA activities as a Chinese attempt to gain power and were thus highly motivated in their defense of the government. Also atheistic communism had little appeal for the Muslim Malays.

Politically, the key strategy was to separate the MRLA from its main base of support, the squatters, by offering these Chinese reasons to support the government. The main vehicle to this end was called the "Briggs Plan," named after the head of military operations in 1949, General Sir Harold Briggs. The idea was to relocate the half million Chinese squatters into "new villages" away from the isolation of the jungle fringes. The plan had two goals — one was to move these people into new towns that were under the control of security forces, which could protect them from the MRLA. This would dry up the supply routes and sources of recruits for the insurgents. Much more than that though, the government could provide services never before available to this group of Chinese. Millions were invested in providing new housing, schools, and clinics. For the first time, they had running water, electricity, sewage, and other modern utilities. Thus, on one hand, the government was attacking the supply lines of the MRLA and on the other was winning the loyalty of the people the communists depended on to continue their struggle.

By increasing the number of security forces and cutting off support for the guerrillas, the military was freed to move into the jungle to attack the camps and communication lines of the MRLA. Long range jungle patrols supplied by air drove the MRLA deeper and deeper into the jungle, effectively taking away its offensive capacity, and by 1954, it was no longer a serious military threat. Britain's elite Special Air Services (SAS) made their initial reputation during the Emergency. Small groups of fighters spent weeks in the jungle beating the MRLA at its own game and on its own turf, taking away the advantage that irregular guerilla forces usually have against conventional armies.

A key ingredient in British success was the police intelligence arm, known as the Special Branch. Well-trained and highly professional, the men of the Special Branch were responsible for intelligence gathering and covert anti-communist operations. All major operations by British forces against the communists had to be cleared through the Special Branch. Much of its success was attributed to the large numbers of Chinese members. The Malayan police and army were dominated by the Malays, while the guerillas were mainly Chinese. Without the Special Branch, the government would have had few eyes or ears in the Chinese community. The ability to identify who were the enemies and what their plans were contributed greatly to winning the war. It is said by some that many Chinese fortunes were made in the Special Branch, which literally bought off many of the communists by offering substantial rewards to members who either deserted the communist cause, acted as double agents, or provided information. The reward for the capture of one communist was the equivalent to ten years of wages for the average Chinese worker. The reward rose with the rank of the person captured and the amount of military equipment seized. A platoon commander of some ten fully armed men who sold out to the British could retire from the cause a wealthy man.

The fact that the Emergency was directed by the police and civilians had important ramifications for post-independence Malaya and Singapore. Police primacy reduced the role of the army and established the principle that the military was subservient to civilian authority. In Southeast Asia today, it is only in Malaysia and Singapore that the army has never played a significant political role. This is a legacy of the anti-communist effort.

With the Briggs Plan, increased military capabilities, and an excellent intelligence network, the British had found the right ingredients to win the war, but it took inspired leadership to make the plan effective. In 1952, General Sir Gerald Templer was given control of the civil administration as high commissioner and was made director of military operations. By combining civil and military commands, Templer was able to follow a carrot-and-stick strategy. The country was color coded black, grey, and white, depending on the amount of MRLA activity and support. If the area was black, which meant a high degree of communist activity, the authorities could make life miserable for those living there through curfews, food rationing, and searches. Control of the new villages meant the government could virtually shut down normal life. On the other hand, areas that contributed information toward capturing guerrillas and cooperated with the authorities were classified as white and received overwhelming government support.

Templer made the choices real by his hands-on approach, constantly traveling across the country to show the flag and demonstrate to the people that the government took a sincere interest in their problems and future. This approach rubbed off on his key advisors who also spent much time outside Kuala Lumpur and as a result had a real feel for what was happening in the countryside. In his two-year term as high commissioner, the numbers of active fighters in the MRLA was reduced dramatically, and the majority of the country lived in peace. The people of independent Malaya named a national park after Templer in recognition of his contribution to winning the war.

The impact of the war on Malaya went far beyond the military conflict that took place. It heightened racial tensions in the country at a time when leaders were searching for a way to create a united multiracial society. The fact that the MRLA was predominantly Chinese and the police and army predominantly Malay gave the conflict significant racial overtones. Many Malays resented the amount of money spent to resettle the Chinese in the new villages. It seemed ridiculous to spend millions to improve the lives of immigrants who were potential enemies, especially when many Malays lived without the services that were being lavished on the squatter Chinese community. On the whole, the conflict increased the mistrust in the Malay community of the loyalties and objectives of the Chinese. This mistrust took decades to overcome.

The Emergency brought a large portion of the Chinese community into the mainstream of political and economic life. A fifth of the Chinese community was resettled, making it even more urban than it had been previously and giving this group access to the modern economy. More than this, the Chinese community was forced to become part of the political community of the country. The Chinese could no longer exist apart from government control and influence. It was their country, their government, and their future too. As Malaya moved toward independence, the Chinese community had to decide how it would deal with post-British Malaya.

Independence

Defeating the communists militarily was important, but for the country to move forward, the Chinese community needed a political alternative to the MCP. There were large numbers of Chinese who opposed the MCP, but they were slow in coming together to meet the communist threat. In 1948, when the federation was being negotiated with the Malay leadership, the lack of Chinese input was as much due to Chinese diversity and apathy as it was to Malay indifference to Chinese needs. British officials expressed frustration at obtaining Chinese views of the federation agreement because there was no group with a significant following or interest besides the communists.

The one group that did make its voice known was the Straits Chinese. This group was very vocal in its support for the rights of Malayan-born immigrants. Because Malaya was also their country, the Straits Chinese saw no reason why they should not have rights similar to those of the Malays. Their problem was that they were an English-speaking elite of the Chinese community (about 10 to 15 percent of this group), with few ties to the more recently arrived Chinese-speaking community.

There were two other main sources of noncommunist support in the Chinese community: the thousands of Chinese who ran family retail businesses and the Chinese-speaking merchants. Neither group had much interest in politics nor had any kind of political organization to make their opinions known. The merchants had access to leaders but skirted political controversy in the interests of business. Among the three groups, there was a growing awareness of the need for a Chinese mass organization that could be a mouthpiece for their needs. Negotiations were taking place to determine the future of the country, and they were standing on the sidelines.

The Malayan Chinese Association (MCA) was founded in 1949 as a noncommunist Chinese political voice. Although its leadership was dominated by the English-educated, it represented diverse noncommunist interests. Its first president was Sir Tan Cheng Lock, and it came into existence at the urging of the British who desperately wanted a moderate Chinese voice in politics. The MCA did represent a group of Chinese who wanted to create a political role for the Chinese community as it moved toward independence. Many of its early activities were directed at the new villages, running social welfare programs, and helping with the problems faced by people who had been resettled. This was an important role for the MCA because these people not only needed better lives but also to be brought into the noncommunist political life of the country.

By the early 1950s, the MCA was a full-fledged political party whose views were sought and respected. It represented a significant portion of Chinese opinion. Lack of any other Chinese voice of importance other than the communists gave it the lead role in representing the Chinese community.

In post-war Malaya, the Indian community was in a weak political position. As the British began to hand back power to the inhabitants of the peninsula, the Indians did not have much influence on the nature and structure of politics. There were many reasons for the weakness of the Indian bargaining position. The Indians made up only 7 or 8 percent of the population, but the Indian community's inability to play an important political role after the war went deeper than just its low numbers.

The Indian community, like the Chinese, was divided. About half were Tamil-educated plantation workers who were isolated from the urban half of the community. Some urban Indians had taken advantage of access to English education and had created an English-speaking, white-collar elite whose lives were far different from the Indians who provided much of the manual labor in the cities. The three groups did not have much contact with one another, and unlike the Chinese, they did not have the clan, dialect, and trade associations to bring them together.

Like the Chinese prior to World War II, the Indian community had little interest in the politics of Malaya. Their political attention had been directed toward the anti-British struggle in India. Evidence of this can be seen in the success of Bose in recruiting Indians from Malaya to join the INA during the war. They enlisted with the idea that they were going to participate in the liberation of India from British rule. Even after the war, the more transitory nature of the Indian community contributed to their political apathy. Only a little more than half were born in Malaya, and thus, many did not see the country as their home. Although this changed with time, in the decade after the war, there was not much political fire coming from the Indian direction.

While the Chinese could use their economic power to obtain concessions for their community, most Indians did not have this leverage. The concentration of Chinese in the cities, where they made up the majority of the population in 23 of the country's 25 largest towns and cities, meant that in a democratic system there would be a Chinese majority in these areas. The Indians were a dispersed and divided community, and nowhere in the peninsula would they make up a majority of the voters. They would have to ride the coattails of the Chinese to defend the rights of the immigrant races.

The first major Indian political group was the Malayan Indian Congress (MIC), which was formed under the leadership of John Thivy in 1946. In the 1940s, the MIC did not represent a significant portion of Indian public opinion. Its non-Tamil, English-educated leadership adopted a non-communal approach to politics and joined together with other radical groups in opposition to the federation proposal. In its early years, its ties to the largely laboring class of Indians were weak at best, and this proved to be its greatest weakness. Thus, aside from their small numbers, the Indian community had no political leadership that could articulate their needs and aspirations.

The Malayan Constitution

When Sir Gerald Templer arrived in Malaya in 1952, he made it clear that Malaya was being prepared for independence. That was the British commitment to the Malayan people, but the politicians knew that independence would come only when some kind of system was devised that provided for multiracial participation and cooperation in the political life of the country. Given the needs and demands of the different races, it was going to be difficult to reconcile democracy with interracial cooperation.

The Malay community was highly suspicious of any move that increased immigrant political rights. The reality of the census figures and the experience of the Malayan Union and the Emergency had made it unlikely that any Malay leader would accept one man/one vote democracy with liberal citizenship requirements. For the Malays, control of the government went beyond questions of Malay control of their lands. The Malays saw government as a means to rectify the economic inequities in the country. A Malay-controlled government would be an active force in setting up programs to lift the Malay economic position. Malay political prominence and Malay economic improvement were the bedrock of the Malay leaders' agenda and were non-negotiable.

On the other hand, the immigrant communities had legitimate concerns about their future in the country. Some of the immigrants had lived in Malaya for generations — far longer, for example, than some of the Sumatran immigrants, who were classified as Malay and were therefore part of the group with special rights. They had helped build the economy

253

and the country and saw no reason why they should settle for second class citizenship. Hundreds of thousands of more recent immigrants had no citizenship. As China had by now become a communist country, the Chinese did not want to return there. Many had prospered in Malaya and wanted guarantees that their wealth and prosperity would be secure from a Malay government intent on raising Malay economic levels. Were these groups to be excluded from the political process?

Many issues had racially charged overtones. Take, for example, the questions of language and education. Many Malays saw them as vehicles for national unity. They believed that the immigrant races should accept Malay as the national language, that is, learn and use the language of their adopted country. To this end, a national educational curriculum had to be implemented so all the races learned in the same language.

This idea was reasonable. Chinese moving into the United States accepted that they had to learn English. But to the Chinese in Malaya, a national Malay language was a threat to their own cultural heritage. Perhaps if this demand had been placed on them when they first arrived, they would not have objected. British policies of separate school systems, racial economic roles, and indirect rule had isolated communities, and there had been little interaction across racial lines. The Chinese and Indians had been able to preserve much of their language, traditions, and culture, and these were threatened by the Malay proposals.

The different communities had to find some common ground. In their dealings with the Malays and UMNO, the British had been clear — they would not hand over rule to a government consisting of only Malays. It had to be a Malayan government. The British felt that any attempt by the Malays and UMNO to rule alone would result in social disorder and instability. Progress toward solving the difficult conflicts of interest among the races was made possible by the evolution of the Alliance Party, made up of UMNO, the MCA, and the MIC.

The beginnings of cooperation and dialogue between UMNO and the MCA came about in part because of a split in UMNO's leadership. Dato Onn bin Jaafar, the founding president, felt that the organization should be a party for all Malayans. His proposals to admit non-Malays did not go down well with the rest of the organization, and as a consequence, he left the party to form a new multiracial party known as the Independence of Malaya Party (IMP). Dato Onn was replaced as leader of UMNO by Tunku Abdul Rahman, a British-educated lawyer who was the brother of the sultan of Kedah.

In the early 1950s, the British initiated some first steps toward democratic self-rule with elections for town and municipal councils. In Selangor, fearing the multiracial IMP in a state with large numbers of non-Malays, UMNO entered into a pact with the MCA to win the elections. The strategy proved successful as the two swept the elections and was the start of what would become a more formal relationship. With the inclusion of the MIC in 1954, the Alliance Party was created under the leadership of Tunku Abdul Rahman. While each of the three parties maintained its separate identity and structure, they came together with a common party platform and candidates at election time.

By this time, the MIC had virtually reinvented itself. With the advent of representative democracy, the sheer numbers of Tamils in the Indian community forced the MIC to change its leadership and outlook. Tamils took over the key positions in the party, and the MIC began to vocalize the needs of the ordinary Indian worker. The party dropped its non-communal outlook and was able to find some political voice for the community as part of the Alliance.

The creation and success of a party that represented the three major racial groups were received by the British with relief, and they agreed to speed up measures toward self-rule. In 1955, elections were called for the federal legislative council, in which for the first time a majority of the members were democratically elected by the people of Malaya. The Alliance won 80 percent of the vote, 51 of the 52 seats available, and as a result the Tunku (as he was known to most Malayans) became the first chief minister of Malaya.

The election set the tone for the future of political parties in the peninsula. Dato Onn's multiracial party was annihilated, and to this very day, political parties have found success only by appealing to single racial communities. The British legacy of the separation of the races had found its way into the electoral process.

The popularity of the Alliance, coupled with the winding down of the communist threat, convinced the British that Malaya was ready for complete independence. Before *merdeka*, or independence, could occur, there was hard bargaining that had to take place among the leaders of the races as to the nature of the new country's constitution. The elections of 1955 were evidence of the need for adjustment. Under the citizenship laws in place at the time of the election, only half the adult Chinese and Indian populations were eligible to vote.

Thorny issues of citizenship, language, Malay rights, and representation all revolved around issues of race, and it is to the credit of the leaders of the Alliance that they were able, at least in the short run, to find sufficient compromise and accommodation to move forward. A British Commonwealth commission was set up to write a new constitution for independent Malaya, but for the most part, it relied on the recommendations that came from negotiations between UMNO and the MCA.

That the two parties were able to find common ground spoke volumes about the shared outlook and temperament of the elite of the racial communities who led these parties. While people such as the Tunku and Tan Cheng Lock fought hard for the interests of their communities, they probably had more in common with each other than they did with their own racial constituents.

Under British rule, the different communities had developed separately with little interaction among the races. Differences of race, religion, language, and custom, as well as economic and geographic distinctions, had acted as serious barriers to cooperation. This was generally not the case for the elite. For the most part, they were educated in English. Many of the MCA and UMNO leaders had gone to school together in Malaya and Great Britain. They were more Westernized than most of their compatriots and had respect for many British institutions, such as parliamentary democracy, rule of the law, a free enterprise economy, and basic human rights. By nature, they also had a Malayan outlook. Many of the Malay leaders had been or were civil servants and knew the benefits of central government services to promote development. Many of the Chinese were businessmen who were aware of the potential and benefits of a national market. They all agreed that they had to create a structure that would develop a Malayan identity. This, however, would be easier said than done.

The task of the leaders of the Alliance Party was to reconcile the differences among the races. By 1956, UMNO and the MCA had come to agreement on a number of formal and informal measures. This made it possible for the constitution to be written. The "deal" that was struck represented compromises on the part of both the Malay and immigrant leaders.

Any progress toward a democratic multiracial, independent Malaya could only be achieved by the recognition of the "special position"* of the Malays, for whom this recognition was non-negotiable. What did this special position mean? In general, it meant that the constitution should recognize that Malays were the indigenous people of the peninsula and that government and society had a responsibility to protect their political power and improve their economic standing.

This special position was accepted by the Chinese leaders and was reflected both formally in the constitution and in informal agreements between UMNO, the MCA, and the MIC. There were a number of provisions written into the constitution. The country was to be a constitutional monarchy with its king elected from the nine sultans, meaning the head of state would always be a Malay. The king was given the responsibility of safeguarding the special position of the Malays. The monarchy created was unlike any in the world. The king of Malaya, later Malaysia, was to serve for a term of five years. When his term was up, the sultans would select another of their peers to serve the next term. There was also a second in command to reign when the king was unavailable. The custom was and still is that the states take turns to provide the country's monarch.

Second, the state religion would be Islam. Other religions could be practiced but were barred from converting Malays who were by birth Muslim. Thus, Islam would be maintained with government sanction as a unifying force for Malays.

Third, Malay would be the official and national language. English was accepted as an official language of the government and the courts for a transitional period of ten years, but after this period, the business of government was to be conducted in Malay.

---

*The term used in Malay for the people who enjoy special status is Bumiputera, which literally means "son of the soil." Today, it includes the Orang Asli, the Malays, and the indigenous people of Borneo.

Fourth, the formal recognition of the special position of the Malays was written into the constitution. This special position translated into reality in a number of ways. Large areas of land that had been reserved for the Malays were maintained as they had been under the British. There were quotas for admission into the civil service that guaranteed Malay dominance of the bureaucracy. In 1952, an agreement had been reached to allow non-Malays into public service but at a ratio of four Malays to every one non-Malay, and this was continued. There were also quotas in the issuing of licenses for the operation of certain businesses and services, such as taxi licenses, fishing boat permits, timber concessions, and preferences in government contracts. Malays were also to receive preference in educational opportunities, including quotas for scholarships, and preference in entering institutions of higher learning.

Informally, UMNO and the immigrant parties agreed that electoral boundaries would be drawn and Alliance Party candidates selected in such a way that a Malay majority in parliament would always be guaranteed, and thus, the prime minister would also be a Malay. Evidence of this is still seen decades later. For example, in the 1982 election, the Petaling constituency in Selangor, which was urban and had a Chinese majority, had a total voting roll of 114,704, while Kuala Krai, which was Malay and rural, contained 24,445 voters, yet each had one member of parliament. In the 1986 and 1995 elections, 70 percent of the seats in parliament represented Malay majority constituencies, ensuring Malay parliamentary dominance.

UMNO and the other parties also agreed that the police and army would continue to be largely Malay as they had been to this time. Finally, it was agreed that a concerted effort would be made to raise the economic position of the Malays.

In return for going along with the safeguards for the Malay position, what did the Chinese receive? Citizenship laws would be written whereby it would be possible for virtually all the immigrants to become citizens immediately and in the future. By the 1959 election, the Malay percentage of the electorate had dropped from 80 percent to about 58 percent as many immigrants had become citizens under the new laws.

A second concession was the right of immigrant races to maintain educational institutions in their mother tongue. It was agreed that at the primary school level, the Chinese and Indians could study in Chinese- and Tamil-language schools. This concession and a guarantee of religious freedom were key to assuring the immigrant races that they could continue to maintain and pass on their own unique cultures.

Informally, it was agreed that the immigrants would be allowed to continue prospering, and there would be no large-scale attempt by the government to redistribute wealth. Private property would be respected and, not withstanding the government's affirmative action programs, free enterprise would continue. Attempts to uplift the Malays economically at the expense of the Chinese and Indians would be avoided. In the eyes of many Chinese leaders, their economic role was ensured.

In a nutshell, the leaders of UMNO, the MCA, and the MIC had traded Malay political domination and special rights for immigrant citizenship, a role in the political process, and the right to practice their cultures. The Malay elite had retained the right to rule and lead their community to higher living standards, while the Chinese elite had protected their residency and the vested interest they had in the economic future of Malaya.

The Tunku declares independence on August 31, 1957.

Many voices in the three communities, however, were not heard when this deal was struck. Many of the ordinary people in Malaya felt they had been sold out by their leaders. Many Malays felt that the Chinese had been granted too large a political and economic voice, while many Chinese felt they had been granted second class citizenship. When they made their voices heard later on, the fabric of the original agreement would unravel, but for the moment, enough had been done to ensure the transfer of power from the British to the Malayans in a stable, optimistic environment.

On August 31, 1957, the Union Jack was lowered for the last time in Kuala Lumpur, and Tunku Abdul Rahman took the oath of office as the first prime minister of an independent Malaya.

The British legacy was mixed. The British left behind a prosperous country with tremendous potential. A modern, Western-style democracy was in place with an infrastructure unmatched in the region. There was order and stability in the country, and the races seemed to be cooperating to lay the foundations for independence. Most saw a bright future for the new Federation of Malaya. On the other hand, there were forces at work beneath the surface that were also Britain's legacy. Economic and political inequalities among the races were time bombs waiting to go off.

〜

Chapter 15

SINGAPORE: THE ROAD TO SELF-RULE

Thousands of cheering Singaporeans lined the streets waving the Union Jack when British troops reoccupied Singapore in September 1945. But behind the relief and joy of the end of Japanese occupation was a society that had changed vastly from the one the British had presided over in the 1930s. The clock could not be turned back to the days of imperial rule when British officials could govern without question. In many ways, the British realized this, but it took time for Singaporeans and the British to find a new course and leaders for the island.

For over a century, Singapore had been the administrative center for the Straits Settlements and later British Malaya. The Malayan Union and the Federation of Malaya that replaced it absorbed Penang and Melaka

Singapore welcomes the return of the British.

261

but excluded Singapore. The Malayan administrative center had shifted to Kuala Lumpur, and Singapore remained a British colony. Many Singaporeans objected to this move because they saw themselves as an important part of what had been British Malaya. For the next fifteen years, most Singapore politicians were committed to finding a future for Singapore as part of Malaya.

Political attitudes had changed. Singaporeans were happy to have the British return but viewed themselves and the future in a different light than they had three-and-a-half years earlier. While there were serious disagreements and divisions about what kind of political future they wanted, Singaporeans were in agreement about what they did not want — outsiders telling them how to run their lives and society.

An important element in any country's national identity is what its citizens have in common. This might be language, race, or religion, as well as shared experiences. The more dramatic the shared experiences, the more they bind people together. Of all national experiences, war and occupation are the most telling.

Being predominantly Chinese, the people of Singapore had suffered more at the hands of the Japanese than had the people of Malaya. As a group, Singaporeans had found ways to carry on and survive in the face of Japanese domination and cruelty. These shared experiences brought them together and instilled in them a belief that this was their land. They had fought for it, and they had carried on in spite of and without the British.

While many British had shared the suffering from behind the barbed wire of internment camps, the sight of British civilians fleeing Singapore in the face of the Japanese onslaught in 1941 was still fresh in the minds of many. Singaporeans could not and did not leave. There was nowhere to go; this was their home through good times and bad. This shared experience was reinforced by the settling down and sinking of roots by the Chinese community. After the war, the English-educated vocalized these changed attitudes first, but within a few years, the Chinese-educated made themselves heard, too.

Singapore was changing in sheer numbers as well. In the fifteen years between 1930 and the end of the war, the population of Singapore doubled to a million people. For the first time in Singapore's history the population was growing not so much from immigration but rather from resident families having children. In the 1940s and 1950s, the island had one of the highest birth rates in the world. By the 1950s, half the population of Singapore was under the age of fifteen. Population growth and the economic and social problems it caused were key factors in shaping the political course of the island.

There was thus a new assertiveness on the part of Singaporeans to determine their own destiny. The political course that resulted in an independent sovereign Singapore in 1965 went through a number of stages. From 1945 to 1948, political discourse was dominated by relatively radical English-educated Singaporeans. In the following five years, the political agenda on the island was determined by a conservative middle class leadership. This swing to the right during the years 1948 to 1953 was a result of British suppression of communists and their sympathizers during the Emergency. From 1954 to 1959, the political pendulum swung back to the left as politicians scrambled to gain the support of the Chinese-speaking community by addressing their grievances. The final stage was self-rule, which included an attempt to gain independence through merger with Malaya and a battle between moderates and extremists for control of the ruling PAP.

As in Malaya, when the British returned to Singapore, they intended to chart a path to some form of self-rule. Singapore's future was complicated by its economic and strategic importance to Britain's post-war aims in the area. Its future therefore had to be weighed carefully. The island was key to reestablishing and expanding Britain's economic dominance of the straits. The port and Singapore's financial community were to operate as a launching pad to help rebuild Britain's export economy, which was shattered by the war.

In addition, Singapore's military importance to the British was enhanced by the post-war confrontation between the communists and the free world, the Cold War. The outbreak of the Emergency in Malaya, the communist victory in China in 1949, and the Korean War of 1950–1953 contributed to the belief that Singapore was a key outpost for Britain and its allies. Singapore's political future had to be viewed in a global context.

Looking at Singapore today, it is easy to forget how significant its position was as a British garrison and naval base. Close to a fifth of Singapore's total area was controlled by the British for military purposes. In the first two decades after World War II, most of Seletar, Sembawang, Changi, Tengah, Nee Soon, and Alexandria were occupied by British military bases. Some forty thousand Singaporeans depended directly on the British military for their livelihoods, and thousands of others benefited indirectly from British military spending. Thus, because of its economic and military importance, the speed with which the British were willing to relinquish political power was slower than the desires of Singapore's Asian leaders.

Post-War Politics

In the first stage of Singapore's post-war development, from 1945 to 1948, the political leadership was dominated by a group of English-educated leftists and communists. Attempts by these leaders to set the political agenda included the formation of Singapore's first broad-based political party, the Malayan Democratic Union (MDU). Founded in 1945 under the leadership of Gerald de Cruz, John Eber, Lim Hong Bee, Lim Kean Chye, and Philip Hoalim, the MDU brought a number of groups together in its quest for self-rule. Apart from this leadership and like-minded individuals, the party also included members of the MCP and other communist-dominated groups.

That the English-educated would lead the way through much of Singapore's post-war political development was not surprising. Most of them had stronger ties to Singapore and Malaya than to their Chinese-speaking counterparts. Given the low levels of literacy and initial political apathy among the Chinese-speaking group, the English-educated saw it as their natural role to assume political leadership.

The leaders of the MDU had a Malayan outlook and were at the forefront of what opposition there was to the Federation of Malaya proposal. They saw it as undemocratic and discriminatory to the immigrant races and were determinedly opposed to Singapore's exclusion from Malaya. They were able to generate some support in Singapore and among the Straits Chinese and communists from Malaya against the federation proposal. To most of the Malays in the peninsula, the MDU's view and the non-Malay composition of its leadership were seen as threats to Malay political dominance. In Singapore, the MDU brought together widely diverse groups with their anti-colonial rhetoric and "one big tent" philosophy — that communists, noncommunists, and anti-communists could work together to end British rule in Singapore and Malaya. After that, they could fight over who would run the government.

The MDU agitated for more than self-rule. It wanted a new educational system that was national in nature rather than community based. It fought for the creation of the University of Malaya and the expansion of educational opportunities. It also wanted the government to take over basic industries and services that were owned by the British and put them in local hands. It wanted an elected majority in the legislative council by 1948. It wanted income redistributed through the establishment of a progressive income tax. The proposal the British found most appealing was the income tax and were happy to institute it, but for revenue purposes rather than for any idea of equality.

The communist thrust after the war was directed toward the labor union movement. Taking advantage of the slow economy immediately after the war, the MCP resuscitated the Pan-Malayan General Labor Union under a new name, the Singapore Federation of Trade Unions (SFTU). By 1947, the SFTU controlled some two-thirds of the unions in Singapore and had a union membership of over fifty thousand workers. One of the reasons for its success in organizing workers was that, initially, it produced results. Between 1945 and 1947, the unions it controlled called 119 strikes, and about 75 percent were successful in attaining better pay and working conditions for members. It is interesting that the leadership of much of this union activity came from the English-educated elite, considering that many of the people it was trying to organize spoke Chinese. Many labor leaders who were jailed by the British as communists, such as Sandra Woodhull, Devan Nair, and J.J. Puthucheary, belonged to this elite.

While the MCP had a common cause with the MDU in achieving labor victories, the party was seriously divided on the goals of the MDU. The MCP branch in Singapore, like the branches in Malaya, was split between those who wanted to follow legal, constitutional methods and those who believed that the only way to power was through armed insurrection and civil disorder. When the leadership of the MCP fell to the latter, Singapore's communists went to jail, went underground, or went abroad.

The British response to this new political situation was to go slow and offer limited local participation. In 1948, they called for a reorganization of the legislative council in which thirteen members of the council would be mostly Asian unofficials (non-government members), and nine would be officials. Of the thirteen, four would be appointed by the governor, three selected by the three major chambers of commerce, and six popularly elected by an electorate of British subjects.

The MDU labeled the election a sham because only six of twenty-five seats would be chosen by the electorate, an electorate that was severely limited because the majority of Singaporeans were not British subjects as they were recent immigrants. Unless a majority of the seats were elected and elected from all residents of the colony, the MDU refused to participate. They called for a boycott, and as a result, only 23,000 people registered to vote, and three of those six seats went to a newly formed conservative party, the Singapore Progressive Party (SPP).

Three months after the election, the British declared a state of emergency because of the armed insurrection in Malaya. This proved to be the death blow to the MDU as many of its noncommunist members no longer wanted to be associated with the MCP now that it was part of the insurrection. In 1948, the MDU disbanded voluntarily, and the next few years of Singapore politics were dominated by right wing parties such as the SPP.

The outbreak of armed rebellion in the peninsula caused great concern among the British officials in Singapore. The large Chinese community, its established communist infrastructure, and the recent left wing labor agitation made Singapore ripe for manipulation by the radicals and the MCP. Emergency laws restricting political activity were rushed through the legislature. Public meetings for political purposes were banned except at election time. The police were given wide ranging powers of arrest and detention, and the definitions of subversive activities were broadened considerably. Many of these powers remain on the books to this day, such as the Internal Security Act (ISA), which allows detention without trial in cases of threats to Singapore's peace and order.

In the years 1948 to 1953, the authorities in Singapore made it clear how a small country could maintain peace and stability through the good political intelligence gathering of the Special Branch of the police. Communists, labor leaders, and anyone suspected of communist sympathies were either arrested or silenced. This created a political vacuum that the more conservative and cooperative political groups filled.

The SPP was ideally suited to play a leading role at this time. Its leaders, C. C. Tan, J. Laycock, N. Mallal, A. P. Rajah, and Thio Chan Bee, reflected the makeup and goals of the party. The products of English education in Singapore and British universities, they led a rank and file that was primarily made up of conservative middle and upper class members. They felt that Singapore was not ready for full self-rule and should move slowly in that direction until the population was more literate and politically experienced. Francis Thomas, a leading educator who was a political activist in the 1950s, labeled them "something between government stooges and the protectors of wealth."

Due to the repressive political climate and an electorate limited to British subjects, when an election was called in 1951 to expand the elected representatives in the legislative council from six to nine, the SPP won six of the seats. In this election, the registered voters increased to 48,155, but only 24,578 bothered to vote.

Accepted by the British as the elected political voice of the people, the SPP was able to influence policy. A champion of English education, it was successful in its push for expansion. The number of students enrolling in English schools more than doubled in the decade after the war. By 1956, for the first time in the history of Singapore, more students were starting their primary education in English than in Chinese. This took place at the expense of Chinese education and was resented by much of the Chinese-speaking population.

With their prodding, important strides were taken toward the Malayanization of government jobs. (In this context, Malayanization meant Asians who were citizens and residents of British Malaya.) This terminology reflected the view that Singapore should still be part of Malaya. The SPP was also able to convince the British that locals in the civil service should be paid salaries equal to those of their expatriate British counterparts.

The Malayanization of the civil service was an important reform but only benefited those with an English education. Perhaps the greatest legacy of the SPP was the establishment of the Central Provident Fund (CPF), a savings and retirement scheme. The SPP's narrow base of support and limited goals contributed to its lack of success when the political franchise was expanded to greater numbers of Singaporeans in the mid-1950s.

CENTRAL PROVIDENT FUND

In the 1950s, Singapore instituted a savings plan for workers, known as the Central Provident Fund, or CPF. (Malaysia has a similar program known as the Employees Provident Fund, or EPF.) Originally meant as a forced retirement savings program for low income workers, it has taken an increasingly important role in the lives of most Singaporeans.

Each month, a percentage of the salaries of Singaporeans is deducted from their pay and placed in an individual account. The employer also deposits a corresponding amount in the employee's account. The contributions of both parties are tax deductible, and the interest earned is also exempt from taxes. The basic premise is that workers contribute to the fund throughout their working lives and then withdraw the total amount, plus interest, when they retire.

At its inception in 1955, the percentages paid by worker and employer were relatively small, 5 percent by employer and 5 percent by employee. The percentages peaked in 1984 at 25 percent for both employer and employee. In the early 1990s, the figures were 20 percent for both.

In the late 1960s, the program went beyond its original aim by allowing contributors to use their savings to buy residential properties. This corresponded with the government's intention to move public housing in the direction of a home ownership program. It is highly unlikely that Singapore could have achieved the high percentage of home ownership it enjoys today without this program of compulsory savings. Singaporeans could use balances in their accounts to meet the down payment on a home loan and their monthly CPF contributions to meet the mortgage payments.

By the 1980s and 1990s, contributors were allowed to buy approved shares of companies and health insurance and use their CPF savings to pay for medical expenses. Under present guidelines, 15 percent of the contributions are set aside in a Medisave account, which is meant to be used for medical expenses.

Apart from the social security, medical, and housing dimensions of the program, CPF has provided Singapore with a large pool of domestic savings, which can be tapped by the government for major infrastructure projects. At the end of 1989, total assets amounted to some 37 billion Singapore dollars, 89 percent of which was invested in government bonds, which in turn made it possible to implement major improvements, such as the expansion of Changi International Airport and the Mass Rapid Transit (MRT) system.

Political Change in the 1950s

In 1953, the political tide in Singapore began to change as the needs and aspirations of the Chinese-speaking community began to make themselves known. The Chinese-educated/speaking community was the sleeping giant of Singapore politics. Singapore was 75 percent Chinese, and out of this figure, two-thirds were educated in Chinese and spoke the language. As Singapore edged toward democratic rule, by sheer numbers, they determined the direction of Singapore's political future.

There are a number of reasons why the Chinese-speaking community of Singapore began to flex its political muscles and demand a greater role in Singapore's future in the 1950s. The Chinese had a host of social and economic grievances that British authorities had failed to handle effectively. While opportunities for English-educated Singaporeans had expanded after the war, the massive population boom had brought about conditions that were lowering the standard of living and quality of life for the majority of the Chinese-speaking population. Problems that had been shunted aside because of the war and the Emergency now moved to center stage and had to be addressed.

The population explosion had generated a housing shortage of epidemic proportions. The working class Chinese, who were crammed into the city center, were the hardest hit. Studies of the Chinatown area in the 1950s show abysmal conditions. Small shophouses gave shelter to as many as a hundred people. The average living space was 9 feet by 9 feet (3 m by 3 m), about the size of a prison cell. Many lived in dark, dingy cubicles with no windows or access to fresh air. Public services, such as sewage disposal, water, and electricity, had been built for a community a third of the size of the existing one.

The physical condition of much of the existing housing was dismal. An important reason for this was the Rent Control Act of 1946. This was a well-intentioned effort by the authorities to prevent landlords from raising rents to take advantage of the housing shortage. The act controlled the rents, but since owners could not increase their returns, they neither maintained nor carried out repairs on their properties. The end result was worse housing and ingenious methods of circumventing the laws through under-the-table payments such as key money.

Many Chinese did not live in the crowded downtown areas. Twenty-five percent were squatters on the fringes of the urban areas. They lived in Chinese kampungs constructed of wood, tin, and thatch and made their living from agricultural pursuits and part-time labor. The extent of their labors was evidenced by the fact that Singapore was virtually self-sufficient in the production of poultry, eggs, green vegetables, and pork products. The Chinese farmer tending his vegetable patch was as much part of the Singapore landscape as its teeming urban areas.

As the population grew, there was no way Singapore's economy could grow fast enough to provide sufficient jobs. About a quarter of the Chinese-

Crowded housing in Chinatown in the 1950s.

speaking households lived below the government's definition of the poverty line. The high rates of unemployment and poverty were not just due to the population expansion. Chinese who attended Chinese-language schools had limited opportunities for jobs in government and commerce because of their lack of English-language skills. Their Chinese education not only caused job discrimination but was in itself substandard because of government neglect, lack of funds, and poorly trained and educated teachers. When the Chinese-educated entered the labor force, they were at a serious disadvantage. Although wages rose during the boom years of the Korean War, when demand for tin and rubber rose dramatically, the surplus of workers chasing low and semi-skilled jobs depressed wages and further contributed to the low standard of living. These conditions created a conducive environment for leaders who could articulate the needs and aspirations of the Chinese-speaking community.

From about 1953 onward, political activity and participation began to increase dramatically. One reason was that the British had turned the corner in their fight against the Malayan Races Liberation Army (MRLA) in Malaya and began to ease up on the restrictions on political activity in Singapore. Between 1948 and 1953, around 1,200 people had been arrested for communist and anti-British activities. As the authorities began to release them, many ex-detainees became spearheads of agitation for political and economic change. There was a natural constituency for the communists and radicals among Chinese-language students and workers, whose grievances only needed leadership to make them known.

The students in Chinese-language schools had legitimate concerns of discrimination that alone would motivate them to political action, but there were other factors that would determine the radical path they would follow. One was the communist victory in China. The unification of China under one government and its ability to stand up to the United States and the West in the Korean War instilled in many young Chinese a new pride in their race. The communist party's attempts to form a more just and equal society held great appeal and were relevant to their own expectations.

The Chinese-language schools had always been highly politicized, and now that the communists had emerged victorious in China, their influence in the Singapore schools increased accordingly. Government attempts to control political activities in the Chinese schools were portrayed

Neighbors chat outside their tiny rooms in Chinatown.

as attacks on Chinese culture and identity. This radicalization of the students was given a further boost by the presence of large numbers of overaged students. Some were in school because the war had interrupted their education; others were virtually professional student agitators. Notable among them was Lim Chin Siong who was instrumental in organizing Chinese student unions whose primary functions were political and anti-government in nature. Schools such as Chinese High School and Chung Cheng High School became hotbeds of communist and Chinese chauvinistic activity.

On the other side of the political spectrum, the Singapore Chinese Chamber of Commerce also played an important role in raising the political consciousness of the Chinese-speaking population. In 1954, this conservative business group led a campaign to demand action on Chinese grievances. It fought hard and vocally for the Chinese language to be given equal status with English in public affairs and for the creation of Singapore citizenship that encompassed all the residents of the island and not just those who had accepted British nationality and protection. Thus, from the right and the left, the Chinese speakers were being prodded into greater political activity.

The easing of the Emergency restrictions and the release of detainees led to the resurgence of militant trade unions. In the immediate post-war era, the trade union movement was dominated by English-educated leaders, and much of its success was among white collar workers, such as teachers and civil servants. This changed in the 1950s. The old line leaders were still around, but they were eclipsed by younger Chinese-educated leaders.

272

Through the Singapore Factory and Shop Workers Union (SFSWU), men such as Lim Chin Siong and Fong Swee Suan began to organize the low paid, low skilled workers. Their Chinese-educated roots and success in achieving better wages for their followers brought them widespread support. Within a couple of years of its inception in 1954, the SFSWU had grown to an organization that represented thirty unions and some thirty thousand workers. Its agenda was not just working conditions — many of the strikes it called were political in nature and were meant to ferment unrest against the government and to meet the political needs of Chinese speakers and communists.

Post-War Malay Community

It is natural to dwell on the Chinese community of Singapore because of its dominance in terms of numbers, but the Malay community of the 1950s bears close scrutiny because it was at odds with the conventional wisdom of the time — that it was impossible for the Malays to compete with immigrant Chinese because they were only equipped to pursue rural occupations and that they did not want to compete for urban employment. The Malay community in Singapore did not fit this stereotype, but the stereotype hid the economic reality of the community.

Perhaps because Malays tended to live together in kampungs outside the urban areas, they appeared to be following traditional occupations, but the kampung was a social phenomenon, not an economic one. Malays preferred to live close to those who shared their religious and cultural values. They wanted to preserve their traditional cooperative values in the face of an overwhelming alien population.

Dr. Goh Keng Swee, who later served as minister of finance, did an exhaustive study of the incomes and occupations of Singaporeans in the early 1950s. In terms of per capita income, the Malays of the 1950s held an economic position on par with that of the Chinese. The locally born Malay had a monthly income almost equal to that of the locally born Chinese and a third higher than the immigrant Chinese. His monthly income was twice that of the Malay in Malaya. Only a small percentage of Malays in Singapore were involved in agriculture and fishing. The vast majority were wage earners.

The point is that the Malays could adapt and survive in an urban wage earning situation. The Malays' backward economic position vis à vis the other races in Singapore did not take place until after self-rule and independence. .

In the political and social arena, Singapore's overwhelmingly Chinese majority would determine the leadership of Singapore, but the Malays were a large enough minority that their views and sensitivities could not be ignored. This was especially true when viewed in the larger context of communal politics in British Malaya.

Malay political influence in Singapore was dramatically exemplified by riots that took place in 1950 as a result of a court case involving a young woman by the name of Maria Hertogh, a Eurasian whose father had served in the Dutch army in Indonesia. Facing internment at the time of the Japanese occupation, her mother left the four-year-old in the care of a Malay friend, who raised the child as her own daughter. When the war was over, Hertogh's parents were repatriated to the Netherlands and lost contact with their daughter and their friend, Aminah binte Mohammad, who had moved to the eastern coast of Malaya. It was not until 1949 that Hertogh's parents found her, a twelve-year-old Muslim girl with a Malay name. The Dutch authorities went to court to have the girl returned to her natural parents. In the ensuing legal battle, emotions ran high in the Malay Muslim community. The courts first turned Hertogh over to the custody of the Social Welfare Department. On appeal, she was given back to her foster mother, who arranged for Hertogh's marriage to a local Malay. The appeal was then overturned, the marriage annulled on the grounds that Hertogh was only thirteen, and custody given to her natural parents.

Throughout the entire legal tussle, the press had a field day. The Malay press depicted Hertogh as a Muslim who was forced back into Christianity and away from the only mother she knew. For the English press, it was a human interest story of a mother finding her long-lost daughter and returning her to her culture and religion. Extremist Malay politicians seized on the issue and inflamed the passions of the Malay community in Singapore. They decried the injustice of a system that would take a Muslim child away from the mother she loved and her new husband and turn her over to Christians who had abandoned her.

Eventually, the issue boiled over into the streets, and Malay crowds attacked Europeans and Eurasians indiscriminately. For three days, the British army and Singapore police battled furious Malay mobs. The city was placed under a week-long curfew, and when the smoke cleared, eighteen people were dead, hundreds injured, and hundreds arrested. For Singapore, it was a painful reminder of how race and religion were issues that could at any time explode into civil disorder.

The 1955 Election

British constitutional reform also contributed to the level of political participation. The 1951 election and subsequent municipal elections had been failures in terms of voter turnout. The problem of low participation, coupled with the need to map out Singapore's constitutional future, led to the creation of a commission under the leadership of Sir George Rendel in 1953. The Rendel Commission's report, which was published in 1954, proposed that a new constitution establish a legislative assembly in which twenty-five of the thirty-two members would be popularly elected. The executive council would be replaced by a council of ministers under the leadership of a chief minister who represented the party with the greatest number of seats in the assembly. British officials would retain control over defense, internal security, foreign affairs, and finance.

While it proposed only limited self-government, the new constitution did mean that a significant portion of government responsibility would be turned over to the elected representatives of the people of Singapore. By the automatic registration of voters, the electorate was increased from 75,000 to around 300,000. This set the stage for Singapore's first meaningful election both in terms of representation and participation.

There are some who say that the constitution of 1955 was tailor-made for an SPP victory. The SPP's desire to move slowly toward self-rule and cooperate with the British would probably have made the changeover smoother than it was. However, it is hard to believe that the British truly expected to bring about an SPP victory, especially given the quality of their political intelligence through the Special Branch. When the election was over, the SPP had taken a drubbing, winning only four seats, and most of its leaders had been defeated. This was a natural result of the enlarged electorate that had moved the political agenda markedly to the left.

After the election, no one party had a majority of the seats in the new assembly. The Labor Front won the most number of seats — ten. This was a left-of-center party organized in 1954 and led by David Marshall and Lim Yew Hock. It drew much of its support from the more moderate trade unions and also had significant middle class backing. Another new party, the PAP, had won three of the four seats it had contested. Led by Lee Kuan Yew, the PAP had a large following among the Chinese-educated community and the more militant communist influenced labor unions.

The Labor Front formed an alliance with the Singapore version of the Alliance Party of Malaya, which had won three seats. When the governor used two of his appointed seats to place Labor Front supporters in the assembly, Marshall had a majority and became chief minister of Singapore's first elected government.

David Marshall and the Labor Front

Marshall was a Jew from the Middle East whose family had lived in Singapore for close to a century. A brilliant lawyer and indefatigable orator, his flamboyant style gave a rousing start to limited self-rule. The Labor Front had never really expected to be in the position of forming a government. Like the PAP, it had planned to sit in opposition until full self-government came into effect at a later date. Thrust into power, the chief minister and his party faced a sea of troubles.

Marshall presided over a weak government, and his job was made even more difficult by those who wanted to see him fail. His government and party had problems from the outset because they did not have a popular mandate. Many of Marshall's ideas were widely accepted — full self-rule, merger with Malaya, and educational reform — but his party had not won a majority of seats, which is important in a parliamentary system. The party was new and encompassed a coalition of liberals, socialists, trade unionists, and political newcomers. As a result, it did not have the cohesion of a more established, experienced political party.

In parliament and the streets, Marshall and the Labor Front were under constant attack from opponents on the left and the right of the political arena. In the legislative assembly, the PAP, led by Lee Kuan Yew, portrayed Marshall and his government as tools of the British who were standing in the way of the wishes of the masses. Debates between Marshall and Lee were articulate and entertaining but unproductive. The PAP was more concerned with its image in the Chinese-educated community and future elections than with the smooth running of Singapore's first elected government. The SPP and the conservatives saw Marshall as a radical who was a threat to the position and power of the English-educated. Marshall and his colleagues were caught in the middle and could not please anyone.

In the streets, the militant trade unions and Chinese students were determined to discredit the Labor Front government through strikes and demonstrations. The communists and their sympathizers used the grievances of workers and students to destabilize the city and lay the groundwork for their assumption of power. Within a month after the Labor Front took power, a strike at the Hock Lee bus company by union extremists escalated into a full blown political riot. Before the strike was settled, two policemen died, an American reporter was killed by a mob, and property worth millions of dollars was destroyed. In 1955 alone, over three hundred strikes were called by unions controlled by men whose goals were far more political than economic.

British skepticism made Marshall's problems worse. While leaders in London were willing to move toward greater self-rule, the British officials in Singapore made the transition difficult. Many British were having a hard time coming to grips with the end of the empire. Their reluctance to give up their power and special privileges to elected Singaporeans made the Labor Front's attempts to meet the demands of the people a Herculean task. In the eyes of British administrators, the civil disorder was proof that Singapore was not ready to rule itself. Singapore's military and economic importance to Britain was being threatened by communists, riots, and a government unable to rule effectively. In many ways, the hesitancy of the administrators helped make the failure self-fulfilling.

The conservative British business interests and many in the middle class wanted Marshall to crack down on the left and establish law and order. If he did so, Lee Kuan Yew and his allies would accuse Marshall of being in the pocket of the British. Marshall's personality and strong convictions made his dilemma worse. A man of deeply ingrained principles, he was committed to social justice, democracy, and civil liberties. Marshall sympathized with many of the grievances of the lower end of Singapore society, and this made the use of police power against them an agonizing decision. In the Hock Lee riots, his attempt to find non-autocratic solutions was interpreted as weakness by his opponents. When he was finally forced to bring in security forces to put down the disorder, Marshall was portrayed as a British puppet.

A further problem was that, like many men of deep conviction, Marshall found compromise difficult. While this trait is an asset for a trial lawyer, it is not necessarily good in a politician. Marshall's dramatic and uncompromising stands were useful in his dealings with hide-bound British civil servants in Singapore but not when negotiating Singapore's future in London. At home, his insistence that the British authorities respect the elected government and let it handle its own business was probably one of his greatest legacies. After the 1955 election, there were Singaporeans in charge of most of the government services that affected the daily lives of people. When the British failed to provide adequate office space for him and his colleagues after they took office in 1955, he set up his desk under a tree outside City Hall until space was found. Twice he threatened to resign unless the local British authorities went along with what he wanted — when the governor tried to block the appointment of four assistant ministers and when Marshall and Governor Sir Robert Black disagreed over the powers the governor held. Black felt he had virtual veto power over the wishes of the assembly. Marshall insisted Black had to "act on the advice of the chief minister and the assembly," except on issues of defense and internal security. The issue went all the way to administrators in London, who agreed with Marshall.

When Marshall went to London in 1956 to negotiate for complete self-rule, his uncompromising style brought him down. Before leaving Singapore, Marshall declared that he was going to obtain full self-rule, except for defense and foreign affairs, or resign. After seeing the civil disorder and the growth of communist influence, the British were not about to give up control of internal security. Singapore was too important to them militarily and economically to back off. Marshall refused to compromise and returned home empty handed. Although his party did not ask for it, he felt duty bound to resign as chief minister. After a little more than a year in power, Marshall was replaced by his deputy, Lim Yew Hock.

Lim Yew Hock

Lim Yew Hock was an English-educated Straits Chinese who had been active in the trade union movement. His organization, the Singapore Trade Union Congress, was a moderate alternative to the unions that had fallen under the influence of communists and other leftists. He was staunchly anti-communist and, unlike Marshall, was willing to use the powers at his disposal to block communist control of the unions and Chinese student organizations.

In 1956, his government put forward a proposal to bar student groups from political activities. The reaction was swift: militant Chinese students seized control of six Chinese-language schools and barricaded themselves inside them. Lim retaliated by sending in the police to clear the schools. The students took to the streets and almost two weeks of rioting ensued in which fifteen people died and hundreds were injured. The streets of Singapore became a battlefield between security forces and Chinese radicals. Numerous arrests were made under the ISA, culminating in the 1957 detention of many leading extremist members of the PAP, including Lim Chin Siong, Fong Swee Suan, and Devan Nair.

Lim's determination to maintain law and order paved the way for new talks with the British in 1957 about the political future of Singapore. He was willing to find a compromise that would allay British fears while achieving control of the government by Singaporeans. The deal was much like the one that had been offered to Marshall. A State of Singapore would be created, with a democratically elected assembly of fifty-one members. Singapore would have a prime minister and cabinet in control of all functions of government except defense and foreign affairs. In foreign affairs, Singapore would have control of commercial relations with other countries. Singapore would have its own flag, citizenship, and national anthem. The British governor would be replaced with the *yang di pertuan negara*, or local head of state, chosen by the assembly.

An internal security council was set up. It consisted of three British officials, three Singapore ministers, and a chairman who would represent the Federation of Malaya and cast the tie-breaking vote. This was acceptable to the British because they knew any representative sent by the Alliance government in Malaya would be as anti-communist as the British. The deal was acceptable to the majority of Singapore politicians because the council would have a majority of Asians. In any case, most Singaporeans felt there would be some kind of merger with Malaya in the future. These compromises set the stage for a general election in 1959 to establish the new government.

The four years of Labor Front rule were years of turmoil, but they did result in some important legacies. Whoever won power in 1959 would inherit a civil service that for the most part had been Malayanized, an important building block for any future government's plans. In 1957, a citizenship ordinance had been passed that added another two hundred thousand people to the electoral rolls. The vast majority of those living on the island now had full citizenship rights. A further reform that was instituted was the Education Ordinance of 1957. It created equality in education in all four language streams in the schools and set the stage for a common curriculum.

The Labor Front had created the conditions necessary for self-rule but gained little political benefit from its efforts. Throughout its four years in power, the party had been unable to generate much mass support. Lim had produced some positive results but could not translate them into any passion for his party. Many of the Chinese-educated were alienated by what they saw as anti-Chinese and heavy-handed efforts to maintain law and order. Added to Lim's problems was the discovery toward the end of his tenure that his minister of education had received $700,000 to further democracy from American sources (some say the CIA) and then diverted the money to his own ends. In the eyes of many people, not only was Lim's government on the American payroll, it was also corrupt.

Finally, Lim's hold on power was tenuous because his most capable opponent, the PAP, had laid the groundwork for a convincing victory in 1959. The PAP had significant support among the Chinese-speaking and thus — with masterful manipulation of charges of corruption, anti-Chinese bias, and elitism on the part of the Labor Front — was able to sweep to victory.

The Rise of the People's Action Party

When we speak of the PAP today it is hard to separate the man, Lee Kuan Yew, from the party. Throughout its forty-five-year history, Lee has endured as the prominent public symbol of this incredibly successful party. Looking back, it is difficult to imagine how tenuous his hold was on the leadership of the party in its early years. The history of the PAP's first decade of existence is a fascinating study of Lee's political skills, determination, and survival instincts.

The roots of Lee's political career and the PAP can be traced to London in the immediate years following World War II. Lee Kuan Yew, like many of the best and brightest English-educated Singaporeans of his generation, went to Britain to continue the education that had been interrupted by the war. For young students from all parts of the empire, these were heady days to be in Britain. The Labor Party that had been elected in 1945 was sending clear signals that the days of empire were drawing to a close. Students from the British colonies rubbed shoulders with the Asians and Africans who were destined to be the first leaders of newly independent nations. Fired with a spirit of nationalism, they were heavily influenced by the agenda of the Labor Party. The socialist policy of the British leaders, with its goals of social justice and equality, was very attractive to those, such as Lee, who saw them as applicable to their own societies. British government policies in the areas of health, housing, education, and income that were geared to break down class barriers in Britain seemed the road to follow in places such as Singapore, which faced serious inequalities of wealth and services.

During his student days in London, Lee came into contact with other Malayans who shared his dreams and goals. An organization known as the Malayan Forum, organized by Goh Keng Swee and Abdul Razak, brought them together to discuss the kind of society and government that would replace British Malaya. The men in the forum had a common background. They were members of an English-educated elite who felt it was their destiny, being the educated and talented, to provide the leadership for an independent Malaya. It is here that Lee began to have a common cause with two other prominent future leaders of the PAP and Singapore — Toh Chin Chye and Goh Keng Swee. Together, these three men provided the driving force behind the success of the PAP.

Lee returned from Britain in 1950 with a law degree and full of ambitious plans to free Singapore from colonial rule. The initial steps to this end were made by drawing together Toh, Goh, and other like-minded English-educated anti-colonials, such as S. Rajaratnam, to form the Council of Joint Action. The council was mainly a discussion group of men who planned their version of the future of Singapore's political system. The strategies and goals of the PAP had their origins in the discourse of this group.

Lee realized that any path to real power in Singapore had to go through the Chinese-educated. In many ways, this group was alien to Lee. Culturally, they came from different worlds. He was Straits Chinese; they were recent immigrants. Lee spoke English, Malay, and some dialect; their leaders were Chinese-educated. Lee was a moderate socialist; most of the Chinese-educated leaders were much more radical.

Lee's brilliance as a lawyer and politician made it possible for him to bridge these differences with leaders of the Chinese-speaking community. Much of the political support for the Chinese-educated leaders came from the labor unions and student organizations. For these groups to be successful, they needed someone who could speak the language of the commercial and governmental power structure of Singapore. The unions needed to be able to negotiate and deliver results. Lee became the legal council for numerous unions and emerged as a prominent defender of workers' rights. Both the unions and student organizations constantly ran afoul of the authorities because of their aggressive methods, and Lee was the one who defended them in court. In a short period of time, his activities as a lawyer gave him a reputation as a defender of those who felt that Singapore's commercial and government leaders discriminated against them.

In 1954, Lee, Toh, and Rajaratnam were key players in the organization of a new political party, the PAP. The party was an odd alliance of noncommunists, English-educated professionals on one side and left-leaning trade unionists and Chinese chauvinists, such as Lim Chin Siong, on the other. In many ways, the two groups planned to use each other to gain political power. They had the common goals of freeing Singapore from colonial rule and creating a more equitable society, but both knew that once one obtained power, the other would have to be destroyed because they disagreed over too much else.

Lim Chin Siong, the most popular leader of the Chinese-educated faction, was very different from Lee. While Lee was in Britain studying law, Lim was in the Chinese-language schools organizing students against the British. When Lee returned to follow a professional career, Lim had been expelled from Chinese High School for his political activities. He worked as a bus conductor and was very good at organizing workers. Lee was Straits Chinese; Lim was of recent immigrant stock. Lee was from the middle class; Lim from mere humble origins. They were bound for a showdown.

The PAP had made its first impact on the political scene in the 1955 election when it had won three of the four seats it contested. Contesting only four seats was a calculated decision on the part of the PAP leadership because it gave them a forum for their views but placed them in the opposition. At a time of political and social unrest, it gave them the opportunity to criticize both the Labor Front and the British to score points in the Chinese community. They could portray their rivals, men such as Marshall and Lim Yew Hock, as oppressive and undemocratic when they attempted to maintain law and order. This the PAP did very successfully.

The English-educated PAP leaders, however, were walking a fine line. To maintain party unity and keep the support of the unions and students, they could not publicly attack the pro-communist riots and strikes that were meant to bring the communist faction in the PAP to power. On the other hand, men such as Lee and Toh were anti-communist and committed to constitutional and peaceful change. Reconciling these two positions was not an easy task.

The first serious clash between the two factions in the PAP took place in 1957. The Labor Front government had invoked the Internal Security Act and rounded up many of the radical union leaders as threats to public order. Ending these laws was a key tenet of the radical left as they felt the laws were the government's way to deny them power. For years, Lee had been vocal in opposing arrest under these laws, but when Lee accompanied Lim Yew Hock to London in 1957 to negotiate self-rule, the laws were accepted by the Singapore team. Many of the PAP radicals questioned Lee's motives for compromising on this issue. The continued existence of the Internal Security Council with British and Malayan representation was a direct threat to the left's future, given its confrontational methods.

The radical faction of the PAP feared that they were being sold out and at the party's annual conference in 1957 took control of the party's central committee. Lee and his colleagues resigned from their leadership positions, and it appeared that they had lost control of the party. The political future of the PAP moderates was saved at this point by an unlikely source — Lim Yew Hock. Using the internal security laws, Lim arrested five members of the new PAP central committee as communists and threats to public order. Lee Kuan Yew and his group quickly regained control.

The incident was a classic example of Lee's brilliance as a politician. Although Lim had saved his bacon, he attacked Lim for doing the bidding of the British. He accused him of using dictatorial methods and thus reestablished his credentials among many of the Chinese-educated. At the same time, the party structure was revamped. There were to be two kinds of members — cadre and ordinary. Only the cadre membership could determine who were to be the leaders of the party. These special members, about a thousand in all, would have to be approved by the party's central committee. With this rule change, Lee and the moderates could determine their own electors, thus guaranteeing future control of the party. From this moment, Lee chose the people who elected the party leaders.

It was one thing to control the party and another to win elections. Lee had no choice but to continue to court the favor of the left-leaning Chinese leadership if he was to gain power. He needed these people. In the lead-up to the 1959 election, the leaders of the PAP branded their more conservative English-educated opponents as corrupt pawns of the capitalists, defenders of privilege, and anti-Chinese. They vowed that if elected they would never serve until their "comrades" were released from detention. The support of radical labor unions, the backing of Chinese-speaking students, and a message of democratic socialism were the core of a successful strategy. The PAP swept to power with forty-three of the fifty-one contested seats. Many of the victories were close, and if the anti-PAP politicians had united, the results might have been even closer. At thirty six, nine years after his return to Singapore, Lee was sworn in as Singapore's first prime minister.

Chapter 16

⌒

MALAYANS TAKE CONTROL

Malaya from 1957

When Tunku Abdul Rahman, Malaya's first prime minister, declared independence, the country held tremendous promise but was beset with problems. Malaya had inherited an established administrative structure that included a capable, well-educated civil service. The peaceful transfer of power from the British to the Malayans had taken place smoothly, without the upheaval and recrimination that often take place when governments change leadership.

Many British civil servants stayed and ensured an orderly Malayanization of the government. For example, the last British chiefs of staff in the Malayan/Malaysian navy and air force did not retire until 1967, a full ten years after independence, and the last British judge did not step down until 1969. The country faced a relatively prosperous future with tin, rubber, and palm oil providing the foundation for export earnings and economic growth. While there were poor people in the country, it was not the abject poverty associated with much of the developing world at this time. There was a well-developed infrastructure of roads, railroads, and communications that would be key to economic growth. From an economic point of view, many predicted a rosy future for Malaya. Finally, there was for the most part peace and stability in the country. The communist threat was reduced to nuisance raids across the Thai border, and the government could ensure law and order — a far cry from many other emerging nations.

There were, however, some sensitive problems that faced the new government. There were serious economic inequalities in the country along racial and geographic lines and within the races themselves. This colonial legacy was a serious challenge.

The main priorities were to create national unity and a national identity. These goals were complicated by the need to improve the economic lot of the Malays. Could these goals be achieved by favoring one race over the others, as was the intention of the Alliance government? Race was the fundamental political and social issue of the country; every action on the part of the government was viewed through racial glasses. In the eyes of most Malayans, it was a zero-sum game. Help for one race was viewed as a loss for another and vice versa. Loyalty to the country would be difficult to nurture among the immigrant races if they felt they were second class citizens politically. Acceptance of the immigrants by the Malays would be hard since they felt they should be favored over the immigrants. Unity and equity — could they be reconciled? It has been said that "high tides raise all boats," and perhaps rapid economic growth could help solve the racial problems.

Another problem was that the fruits of economic growth were going to be difficult to pass out to the citizens of the country because large sections of the economy were owned by foreigners, especially the British. The latter may have hauled down the Union Jack, but their economic dominance was well-established. The most productive rubber and oil palm plantations were owned by British companies; the tin dredges and distribution system were dominated by British interests. The banking and commercial infrastructure was for the most part under British control. The Alliance government was committed to a free enterprise economy and did not want to walk down the ruinous path of nationalization by seizing foreign-owned business concerns, which countries such as Burma and Indonesia had followed. The economic welfare of the country was a dilemma that required patience to solve, and in a racially charged atmosphere, patience was in short supply.

The Alliance Government

The electoral symbol of the Alliance government was a Malay sailboat, an apt portrayal of the interests and nature of its leadership. The unspoken party slogan was "Don't rock the boat." Generally, the government was conservative, a party of the status quo. In many ways, it was a mirror image and a logical outgrowth of British policies. The three component parties — UMNO, MCA, and MIC — maintained their separate political identities. The Malay base was rural and agricultural, the Chinese commercial and urban, and the Indian divided and diverse.

286

The most prominent leaders were very much part of the British-supported establishment. Tunku Abdul Rahman, a prince from a Malay state, was a product of English schools in Malaya and was trained as a lawyer in Britain. In the first decade or so of independence, his leadership of the movement for freedom brought him tremendous popularity and prestige. Tun Abdul Razak, his second in command, came from a similar background and was in many ways the more capable planner, the nuts and bolts man so to speak.

The two had studied in London at around the same time, although the Tunku for longer. The Tunku was well-liked by all who met him; the British saw him as the epitome of what English education and influence could do for the Malay aristocracy. Malayan students in London saw him as an engaging visionary who could bring people together. He was welcome wherever he went, whether socially with British politicians or politically in discussion groups, such as the Malayan Forum.

Tun Razak was the more serious of the two. He had done better academically and was a master of action and details. During the war, Razak had gone into the jungle to fight the Japanese as an officer in the best-known Malay resistance group. After the war, he returned to Britain to finish his education and coached the Tunku through his law examination, which he had apparently failed several times. After the 1955 election, the Tunku was the charismatic leader pointing the way to *merdeka*, while Tun Razak planned the new educational system and rural development.

The best-known leaders of the MCA, Sir Tan Cheng Lock and his son Tun Tan Siew Sin, were English-educated Straits Chinese. Wealthy and Westernized, their role was to ensure that the MCA held the portfolio of the ministry of finance. It seemed almost stereotypical of the society the British had created — the Malays would run the government and act as custodians of their rural brethren, while the Chinese would control the finances and commerce.

Leading a country to independence is an altogether different proposition from ruling it, as has been discovered by many anti-colonial leaders in the past half century. The Alliance Party was committed to a democratic, multiracial Malaya. In the 1955 pre-independence election, the Alliance Party had buried its opponents, winning 81 percent of the vote and fifty-one of fifty-two seats in parliament. It would never have this dominance again because the lead-up to independence disguised weaknesses that all these parties had within their communities. UMNO was seen as the unquestioned protector of Malay rights and position by the vast majority of Malay voters. This position was evidenced by the huge majorities they piled up in the Malay seats, in most cases taking 80 percent of the vote. Given the citizenship laws of the time, only 11 percent of the electorate were Chinese, and most of them were Straits Chinese. Thus, between this and UMNO support, the MCA easily elected fifteen members of the Alliance Party to parliament, a much higher proportion of seats than the Chinese share of the electorate at the time. The MIC's two seats were mostly symbolic and barely represented 4 percent of the people who voted.

Once in power, the nature of the Alliance Party required compromise by the three component parties, especially UMNO and the MCA. In a multiracial society, this was essential, but given the realities of Malayan life, each compromise by the leadership to one race was seen as a sellout by the other races in their respective communities. Each time this happened, it opened the door for the political opponents within each community to garner support.

For UMNO the challenge came from the religious right. Many Malays felt the country should be an Islamic and Malay state and that the compromises made to the MCA in the original constitution had gone too far. The Chinese were guests who wanted to stay and thus had no business asking the owners of the house for any special concessions. The call for an Islamic state under Islamic law was picked up by the Pan Malayan Islamic Party (PMIP), later known as the Parti Islam Se Melayu/Malaysia (PAS). The PMIP drew a lot of support from the areas previously known as the unfederated states, which were predominantly Malay and rural. Until after World War I, these states had been ruled lightly by the British. Their customs and way of life were much less influenced by the modernization taking place in the rest of the country. Their contact with the Chinese, if any, had been as creditors and middlemen, hardly a relationship on which to base political accommodation.

The great weakness of the MCA was that it was out of touch with large segments of the Chinese community. The leadership and power of the party represented the interests of the Straits Chinese and of the Chinese-speaking business community. For the electorate of 1955, it was an appropriate voice but not for the newly emerging citizens among the Chinese-educated and urban working class. To many Chinese, the acceptance of English and not Chinese as an official language of government, the nature of citizenship rights, the Malay special position, and guarantees of free enterprise were indications that in the original "deal" the MCA leaders had only looked after their own interests. The lower middle class Chinese saw their position slipping. The Chinese-educated were products of a Chinese educational system that was highly politicized and chauvinistic. Given the special position of the Malays and the inadequacies of their educational backgrounds, the Chinese saw their economic future as bleak.

The MIC's position was especially tenuous. The Indian community had undergone changes in the last decade, and the MIC had not kept pace with these changes. Large numbers of Indians had moved off the plantations into the towns and cities. The base the MIC had built up among the rubber tappers was now responding to urban politicians and trade union leaders. In the eyes of many Indians, the leadership of the MIC was out of touch with their needs and the leaders' existence dependent on their marriage to the conservative Alliance Party.

The first election after independence reflected how different the body politic had become by 1959. After the euphoria of independence, the various communities had begun to take a more critical view of the original agreement on the constitution between UMNO and the MCA. Opposition politicians of all races had spent two years pointing out the inequities of the Alliance arrangement of government. The citizenship laws had created significant numbers of new immigrant voters. The Chinese electorate had grown from 11 percent to 35.6 percent of the total, and the Indians from 3.9 percent to 7.4 percent. The results of the 1959 election spoke volumes about the difficulty of reconciling the goals of a national identity, national unity, and economic equality.

The electoral boundaries for the election had been drawn in such a way that sixty-four out of the 104 constituencies were Malay majority seats. When the votes had been counted, it was apparent that UMNO's support among Malay voters had weakened. From its primary base in Kelantan and Trengganu, the PMIP had polled over a third of the Malay voters in the election, had captured the state governments of those two states, and had elected thirteen members to the federal parliament. There was now a competitive Malay political party in opposition that would scrutinize every decision the Alliance government made in the light of Islamic and Malay supremacy.

In the urban areas, the newly enfranchised immigrants also made a statement about who represented their political leadership. In states with heavy immigrant populations, the Socialist Front (SF) and the People's Progressive Party (PPP) made significant inroads into the Chinese and Indian votes. The SF won eight parliamentary seats in Penang and Selangor, while the PPP won four in Perak. Both these parties, although inter-communal in theory, had primarily Chinese and Indian leaders. Their messages of greater equality of opportunity had struck a chord among the working class immigrant races.

The Alliance as a whole saw its share of the vote shrink from 80 percent to just over 50 percent of the total electorate. In terms of parliamentary representation, it had gone from fifty-one of fifty-two seats to seventy-four of 104 seats, still a comfortable margin. In Malaya's parliamentary system, this was enough seats to amend the constitution if need be. But the fragmentation of the electorate within each race meant that meeting the economic problems of the country was going to be complicated by racially based opposition parties, the PMIP from the right and parties such as the SF and PPP from the left.

National Development

The path that the government's economic development plans took reflected the political realities of a democratic Malaya. The drawing of parliamentary electoral boundaries had ensured that rural Malays were the majority in almost two-thirds of the seats and would determine who ran the country. UMNO could only survive if it addressed the needs of the rural Malays. Thus, the fundamental priority of the Alliance government was to raise the economic position of this group. The name of the ministry that was to coordinate the development was in itself indicative of national priorities. Under the leadership of Tun Abdul Razak, it was called the Ministry of National and Rural Development, somehow indicating they were two different issues.

In the first two national development plans, huge resources were earmarked for improving the living standards of the Malay agricultural sector. In the second five-year plan (1961–1965), over 50 percent was to be spent on rural development. The main thrust was to raise income in the rural areas. One of the vehicles for this was FELDA (Federal Land Development Authority). Unused land and reclaimed land from the jungle would be given to thousands of landless peasants, and they would be given assistance with loans, seeds, etc.

The idea was to attack the problem of tenant farming by moving farmers to their own land to grow more profitable crops such as rubber. RISDA (Rubber Industry Smallholders Authority) was established to this end. In the same vein, MARA (in English, the Council of Trust for Indigenous People) was established to assist the development of rural industry and commerce. Government help was given in the setting up of batik factories as well as for retail trade, rubber processing, and construction. MARA subsidized bus and transport agencies and taught technical skills such as electronics and motor repair. Cooperatives were set up to increase the combined purchasing and selling power of farmers. Credit facilities through the soon-to-be-established Bank Pertanian (Agriculture Bank) would provide farmers with new sources of credit and were meant to break the Chinese grip on credit.

Ending the debtor relationship between the Malay and Chinese merchants was easier said than done. For many Malays, the old system of credit was familiar and convenient. Local Chinese merchants could dispense goods and services on credit as needed, and the system was tied to the cycle of rural crops and weather. Banks were alien institutions with unfathomable regulations. There was little or no paperwork or red tape involved with the local Chinese *towkay,* or boss.

At the same time, a massive mosque building program was undertaken. The new mosques were symbols of the government's commitment to Islam as the official religion of the federation and the ruling party's concern for the religious well-being of the Malays. The funds for mosques were also an investment in greater Malay unity.

Vast resources were also diverted to improve the quality of life in the rural areas. Better educational facilities were provided — between 1957 and 1963, 9,000 of the 13,000 new classrooms built were situated in rural areas. Access was given to better health care — in the 1957–1963 period, no new hospitals were built in the cities, but the system of rural clinics was expanded dramatically. Finally, much of the money spent on infrastructure was earmarked for rural areas. New roads into the kampungs gave greater mobility and access to markets, rural electrification saw a rapid expansion, and there were new jetties, public telephones, and so on. These efforts were evidence of the government's commitment to improving the lives of the average Malay.

The Alliance solution to the problem of the Malays was not much different from that of the British. There is no doubt there was a change in emphasis, given the massive resources directed at the rural Malays, but the message was the same — to help the Malays, make them better farmers. This reflected a paternalistic attitude on the part of the Malay elite. In essence, the aristocracy would continue to care for the kampung. There were also political benefits to be gained from the Malays remaining rural — it would guarantee the rule of the Malay elite. The Malays on the farm were homogeneous, traditional, and supportive of one another. Who knows what influences the modern economy and the city would have on their loyalties?

Although raising the standard of living of the Malays was the government's first priority, a second economic goal was to diversify Malaya's economy. Rubber and tin had brought wealth to Malaya, but they placed Malaya at the mercy of international market prices. An economy dependent on just two main commodities was vulnerable to the ups and downs of those two markets. This was coupled with the fact that much of this sector of the economy was controlled by foreigners.

The answer was to build up the country's manufacturing base. Most of Malaya's manufactured goods had been imported, reflecting its colonial relationship with Britain. Malaya did not have sufficient capital and expertise to move the economy in this direction, and the answer was to court foreign investors. Some foreign investors were drawn from Singapore when they moved their operations after the PAP victory in 1959. They felt threatened by the apparent communist influence in Singapore's ruling party. Others came because Malaya was offering tax holidays, tariff protection from competitors, financial assistance, and a well-developed infrastructure. The guarantee of a relatively free market within the country and political stability added to the package.

In the first decade after independence, the manufacturing, commercial, and construction sectors of the economy doubled as a percentage of Malaya's national income. The yearly growth in these areas was twice that of the agricultural sector, some 10 percent on average to agriculture's 5 to 6 percent. The majority of this growth was a result of foreign investment, but the Chinese community also participated to a significant degree. By 1970, foreigners owned 68.3 percent of the share capital of Malayan businesses, the Chinese owned 34.3 percent, and the Malays some 2 percent. While the foreigners ran much larger operations, about half of the new manufacturing and commercial concerns were owned by the Chinese. As the more modern sector of the economy grew, the economic action was once again in the urban areas where the Chinese were well situated to take advantage of this both in terms of where they lived and what they did.

In the period 1957 to 1970, household incomes more than doubled, but the relative position of the races remained the same across the country. Average Chinese incomes remained more than double those of the Malays. The number of people living in poverty had been cut in half, but 75 percent of the poor remained rural and Malay. There were still many poor Chinese, but there were fewer of them compared to the Malays. High tides may have raised all boats, but in the eyes of the Malays, they were in rowboats, while foreigners and immigrants sailed around in yachts and powerboats.

The reality of the situation was that, despite huge government efforts to change things, a decade after independence, little progress had been made to bring about greater economic equality. As long as the Malays remained primarily rural and agricultural, there was only so much the government could do. The real wealth was in the cities and towns. Some Malays had done well outside the rural sector of the economy. The expansion of government and government services had provided secure jobs for many educated Malays in the civil service. Members of the elite had found places in the private sector. Some Malays had taken advantage of government quotas favoring Malays in licenses and government projects to launch themselves into the urban, modern sector.

Many Chinese prospered and availed themselves of the labor opportunities in the cities, but there still remained a portion of the Chinese community, half or more, who felt things had become worse. In the eyes of the working class Chinese, the government only cared about the problems of the Malays. The cities faced acute shortages of housing and public services, such as a proper sewerage system and water. The average number of people per dwelling in the cities was higher than in the rural areas, although overpopulation was a serious problem in the rural areas. Calls for public housing programs or housing assistance fell on deaf ears. The quota system for such things as taxicabs, higher education, government contracts, and business licenses grated on the many poor, working class Chinese. Their opportunities were blocked by the indifference of the rich Chinese and the priorities of the Malay politicians.

This then was the Malayan political and economic situation that Lee Kuan Yew and the PAP faced when they campaigned for reunification. Singapore's 75 percent Chinese population was bound to add further complications to the racial and economic mix.

Singapore from 1959

The Constitution of 1959 had given much greater meaning to self-government in Singapore. Its residents were now the citizens of Singapore and not of the British Empire or stateless. The *yang di pertuan negara*, or head of state, was a Singaporean, not a British governor general. The PAP government held all the responsibilities of governing, except for defense and non-commercial foreign affairs, and had equal representation on the Internal Security Council. Singapore also had the symbols of independence — its own flag, stamps, national anthem, and prime minister.

The challenges facing this new government were enormous. The PAP had ridden to power promising to address Singapore's economic and social problems. Prior to this, the inequities and lack of progress could be blamed on the British. The new political leaders had to accept primary responsibility for improving the lives of people. Further, a national identity had to be created for a population of multiracial immigrants. The problem in this area was that the PAP's vision of a national future was tied to merger with Malaya, a country whose leadership was reluctant to accept Singapore's Chinese into its federation. These challenges were complicated by the fact that the PAP government was made up of two party factions that were bent on the political destruction of each other.

The outlines of how the PAP planned to attack the problems of unemployment, housing, communalism, and overpopulation began to take shape in the first three or four years of self-government. Most of the responsibility for dealing with Singapore's economic future was placed in the hands of Dr. Goh Keng Swee, Singapore's first minister of finance. The task was daunting. As Singapore's neighbors became independent, they wanted to steer their exports through their own ports, and as a result, Singapore's entrepôt trade stagnated. The trade problems were only a part of a much larger challenge. Singapore's booming population made it impossible for its traditional sources of employment to provide jobs to new workers entering the labor force.

Singapore had to diversify its economy. Given its small size and limited pool of capital, the only way to do this was to entice foreign investment into the island to create new sectors of the economy, such as manufacturing. This was a tall order. Many foreign businessmen had already left, fearing the radical rhetoric of the PAP during the election campaign. Singapore's history of labor unrest further added to the foreigners' lack of confidence in Singapore as a place to put their money. The government had to create the necessary conditions to change the international business community's perception of Singapore.

Economic Plans

In some ways, Goh built on Singapore's traditional advantages over its neighbors — its location, a hard working immigrant population, and a sophisticated financial and commercial infrastructure. In the past, British officials had seen only a limited role for government in Singapore's business affairs, and this had benefited Singapore's growth. This laissez-faire attitude had been key to Singapore's success as a port and commercial center but was less relevant to the Singapore of the 1960s. Goh faced a society that had grown from 500,000 mostly migrant residents in 1930 to 2 million in 1960, people who called Singapore home and were demanding jobs and economic opportunity. The answer to Singapore's problems was to use the full resources of the government to create an investor-friendly environment.

A primary goal was to create a more attractive workforce. To this end, education became a fundamental priority. At the time the PAP took power, Singapore had one of the highest literacy rates in the area, but this was not good enough. Scores of new schools were built in the first few years of self-rule. Teacher educational facilities expanded, and a common curriculum was established. During this period, the single largest budget item of the government was education. Emphasis was placed on the skills needed for an industrializing economy. Technical and vocational schools provided workers with the kinds of skills foreign investors wanted. The educational system that eventually evolved from PAP plans was one that reflected the economic realities of Singapore's future.

In order to diversify its economy, Singapore did not simply need educated workers but a labor force prepared to serve at all levels of the economy, from bus driver to corporate executive. The system that evolved was examination based and streamed as a result of those examinations. At ages ten, twelve, fourteen, sixteen, and eighteen, students in Singapore take examinations to determine where they will be placed in the next level of education. With each examination, those with the best results move toward higher education, while those who do not do as well are diverted into vocational training or the workforce. There are some second chances along the way, but not many.

The goals of the government were reinforced by the common sense of Singapore parents. By 1956, more students were entering English schools than Chinese ones. In the 1960s, this process escalated to the point that by 1968 more than twice as many students were attending English-language schools than Chinese-language ones. In the 1970s, schools that used Chinese as the primary language of instruction ceased to exist. Parents realized that the path to good jobs and prosperity was through the language of commerce — English. The government encouraged this trend as it could offer a hard working, well-educated, and English-speaking workforce to foreign capitalists. Another benefit of this trend was that English was racially neutral. The government could avoid the politically charged issue of which race's language would dominate in its multiracial society

Singapore has one of the best educational systems in the world. Its students consistently occupy the top spots in international standardized examinations in mathematics and science. The best of the relatively small pool of university graduates from the system become top-level civil servants, professionals, and business leaders. Along the way, the system of natural selection provides the appropriate level of education for the economic needs of the country. At the same time, the educational system contributes to goals of national unity, intermingling of races, and a common language for a society once driven by communalism.

Critics of the educational system say it drives parents and students to extraordinary lengths to ensure passing marks or distinctions. It is not uncommon for parents to employ tutors for their kindergarten children. Another criticism is that this system promotes rote learning and stifles creativity. Finally, there are those who say that it offers no hope for the late bloomers; students who hit their academic strides in high school or college would have already been weeded out in the Singapore educational system.

Images of strikes and radical action by workers would take longer to erase, but the first steps were taken in the early years of self-rule. A new umbrella organization for labor unions, known as the National Trades Union Congress (NTUC), was established. The government's objective was to have this organization form a partnership between organized labor and government. No strikes were to be called except with the approval of the NTUC and, by extension, the government. In the early 1960s, it had a competitor in the Singapore Association of Trade Unions (SATU), which was led by much more radical forces. Over time, a combination of job expansion and the arrests of many of the leaders of the SATU and its member unions gave the NTUC dominance over the labor union movement. The subsequent decline in strikes and confrontations added greatly to Singapore's draw among foreign businessmen.

The government also made large investments in creating a business-friendly infrastructure. Millions of dollars were poured into expanding the harbor and airport, developing the best communications network in Southeast Asia, building new roads, and expanding public services. At the same time as these physical changes took place, there was a big drive for an honest and efficient government. What graft and corruption there was had to be rooted out and capable and well-educated people brought into government. The

Public Services Commission did this job admirably. Evidence of the PAP's commitment to a well-run government is that since 1960 between 30 and 50 percent of the yearly graduates from Singapore's universities have been drawn into government service. In its efforts to develop the economy, the government was determined to nurture the best and brightest of its citizens. Singapore's message was this: "Things work in our country." When you deal with the government, you don't have to bribe anyone, and you don't have to wait an eternity to get things done. When you mail a letter, it will reach its destination; flights will leave on time; cargo will be cleared quickly and honestly.

The government actively courted foreign businessmen, offering them financial incentives. The Economic Development Board (EDB) was created as the lead vehicle in convincing foreigners to invest in Singapore. Through offices in cities such as New York, Tokyo, London, Frankfurt, and Houston, the EDB offered a virtual menu of attractive incentives — tax holidays for up to ten years, financial joint ventures to reduce risks, and help in promoting products outside Singapore. Industrial parks offered ready-to-use factories or land at inexpensive prices. There were tariffs if you wanted to produce for the local market. The combination of Singapore's workforce, infrastructure, and incentives was the foundation of three decades of incredible economic growth.

Urban Development

An equally impressive effort to solve Singapore's social and economic problems was its public housing program. High-rise, low-cost public housing had been introduced before 1959 under the aegis of the Singapore Improvement Trust (SIT), which hardly made a dent in the need for more modern housing, but the 20,000 plus units it built had introduced the concept of apartment living. The PAP took the idea, changed its name to the Housing and Development Board (HDB), and remade the face of Singapore. The millions spent and the number of apartments built in two decades were breathtaking. Entire new cities were built and communities created. By the 1980s, over 80 percent of Singaporeans lived in HDB apartments.

That it successfully housed a nation is one of the enduring legacies of the PAP, but the HDB program was much more than a housing project.

Singapore's public housing effort was probably one of the most impressive and successful feats of social engineering in modern times. The goals of the HDB went far beyond just putting roofs over people's heads. In the early years of the HDB, the primary objective had been to provide inexpensive rental apartments. The need to solve the problems of overcrowding and dismal living conditions was then a national priority, but as time went by, the HDB began to deal with the communal nature of Singapore. Racial quotas were established block by block and community by community. The people of Chinatown and the kampung were dispersed throughout the island in apartments that reflected the racial makeup of the overall society. The hope was that by breaking up the racial concentrations of the past and forcing one race to live next to another in HDB estates, the barriers between the races would be torn down. They were to see others as neighbors, not as Chinese or Malay or Indian. The mixing of races also ensured that politicians could not appeal to racial ghettos to get elected to parliament, effectively eliminating the race card from politics.

There were economic repercussions as well. The very scope and size of the millions that were spent on housing provided jobs for thousands of Singaporeans and business for construction companies and contractors. It is a measure of how far Singapore has come when you consider that new HDB apartments today are built by foreign workers because Singaporeans have moved on to higher paying jobs. Another economic spin-off was the creation of a strong work ethic. As the city redeveloped, less expensive housing alternatives to HDB housing disappeared. A person could no longer fall back on the family and kampung if out of work. Singaporeans had to work to keep and pay for their apartments.

The HDB program was also an important part of creating a national identity. By the mid-1960s, the most acute dimensions of the housing shortage had been tackled, and the emphasis shifted from providing rental apartments to selling them to the people. Home ownership was going to be a key ingredient in convincing people they had a stake in the country. If it had assets in Singapore, this immigrant society would feel a greater loyalty to its new country. It was also hoped that home ownership would lead to pride in the respective communities and a desire to maintain the security and value of homes. Some have contrasted this with the United

States, where they believe the rental nature of the country's public housing program has contributed to urban decline. It has been said that these Americans do not own their homes and as a result care little about their upkeep or their communities.

Merger with Malaya

As Singapore moved from a British colony to self-rule, a key question was what new identity it was to take on. To the government at the time, the vision was one of a Malayan identity. From their early days in politics, the leaders of the PAP had felt that Singapore's separation from Malaya in 1946 was an artificial and temporary measure. In their student days in London, in the original PAP manifesto, and as elected representatives in 1955 and 1959, there was one common thread — Singapore had to rejoin Malaya.

The arguments were compelling. Singapore was economically tied to Malaya. For a century, it had acted as Malaya's main port and gateway to the world. Singapore's commercial and financial institutions had close ties with and large investments in Malaya. If Singapore was to develop a manufacturing sector, Malaya offered an ideal hinterland to sell its goods. There were close racial and family ties between the two territories. It seemed as if everyone in Singapore had a relative "upcountry." The majority of Lee Kuan Yew's first cabinet had been born in Malaya. Goh Keng Swee was from Melaka and Toh Chin Chye from Perak. Both Singapore and Malaya had a common British heritage in terms of their legal, governmental, and educational systems and infrastructures. Leaders on both sides of the causeway had attended the same schools, knew one another well, and spoke the same language — English.

The early actions of the PAP leaders sent clear signals to the Malay leadership of their desire to merge and accept Malay political ascendancy. Singapore's first yang di-pertuan negara was Yusof bin Ishak, a Malay whose office had a Malay title. Malay was made Singapore's first national language and had been introduced into the schools as a compulsory language. The 1959 constitution recognized Malays as the original inhabitants of Singapore and acknowledged their special position. Even the words of the state's anthem, *Majulah Singapura* ("Let Singapore Flourish"), were in Malay.

YUSOF BIN ISHAK AL HAJ (1910–1970)

Yusof bin Ishak Al Haj became Singapore's first head of state in 1959. Six years later, when Singapore became a republic, parliament elected him as the first president, and he remained so until his death in 1970.

Originally from Taiping in Perak, Yusof was a self-made man. He was educated in Malay schools and at Raffles Institution but did not complete his education. He became interested in politics and publishing, joining the Kesatuan Melayu Singapura (Singapore Malay Union) and establishing the *Utusan Melayu*, a newspaper that was the voice of the Malay community.

As a Malay, Yusof represented a minority in Singapore and the majority in Malaysia. His position as head of state and head of the Malay community in Singapore helped to bring about the brief merger of the two countries from 1963 to 1965. He believed that "All races should be progressive, forward-looking, keen and prepared to take on challenges of the time."

Yusof bin Ishak inspects the guard of honor on January 1st, 1960.

After the 1959 election, Singapore leaders made a concerted effort to convince the Tunku, UMNO, and the Alliance to bring them on board. Initially, these overtures were spurned by the Malay leadership in the federation. The admission of Singapore and its two million plus Chinese would change the racial arithmetic of the country. A merger of Malaya and Singapore would make the Chinese the single largest racial group and, regardless of the gestures of Malay symbols, the leadership of UMNO was not very interested. The makeup of the PAP itself scared many Malay leaders, especially the extremists within the PAP such as Lim Chin Siong. After spending over a decade fighting Chinese communists in the jungle, UMNO did not want to let them in the back door to participate in Malayan affairs as members of the PAP. Their Chinese chauvinistic views of language and education also worried the Malay leaders.

In 1961, the Tunku did an about face and made a proposal for the creation of Malaysia, consisting of Malaya, Singapore, Sarawak, Brunei, and British North Borneo. One reason for his change of heart was that the British were pushing the idea. The concept of a federation of British possessions in the archipelago had surfaced a number of times in the nineteenth and twentieth centuries but had never gained much support. By the early 1960s, however, the British were looking for a way to withdraw politically from the area but leave behind a structure that would be friendly to their economic and strategic interests.

Whether it was a British idea or the Tunku's, the concept of a larger federation, not just the merger of Malaya and Singapore, appealed to the Tunku and a sufficient number of the UMNO leadership. Bringing in Brunei, North Borneo, and Sarawak, which had large Malay and indigenous populations, would offset Singapore's Chinese majority. The prospect of an independent Chinese island led by men such as Lim Chin Siong posed a threat of renewed political and racial disorder to the entire area. The Tunku felt that this situation could be more easily controlled if Singapore was a part of a larger federation run by the Malays. Lee Kuan Yew shared this view and never tired of using it in his dealings with Malaya. One also suspects that the prospect of a Malay government being responsible for a crackdown on the PAP's left wing opponents had great appeal to Lee and his colleagues as there would be less political fallout in Singapore.

The terms on which Singapore was to enter Malaysia still required some trade off and compromise. To allay the fears of many in UMNO, Singapore would be under-represented in the proposed Malaysian parliament. Although it was entitled to more seats by population numbers, it was agreed that Singapore would only get fifteen members, which helped the racial numbers game in the eyes of some of the Malay leadership. Because Malaya had stricter citizenship laws for immigrants, there would be an initial waiting period for some Singapore citizens to meet the residency requirements.

In return, Singapore was to retain control of its education and labor policies. For the PAP, these provisions were key to its survival. Although the schools were changing, Chinese language and education were hot issues in Singapore. To force Malayan policies on the Chinese schools in 1963 would have been political suicide. Labor policy was important because Malaya's labor union laws were considerably more liberal than the ones the PAP envisioned for Singapore, and the Malayan Trades Union Congress was independent of government influence. The PAP leaders felt that their role in and responsibility for unions were important to Singapore's economic success. Independent labor unions were not part of their plans for the future.

The unwritten agreements for Singapore to join Malaysia were somewhat ambiguous. The Malay leadership felt it had assurances from the PAP that it would buy into "the deal" arrived at between the MCA and UMNO, which constituted the basis of political life in the federation. Added to this was an undertaking by the PAP that they would abstain from active involvement in electoral politics in the peninsula. The problem was that both sides had differing perceptions of what this meant once the new country came into being.

Battle for the PAP

Progress was being made to provide jobs, diversify the economy, house the population, and create a sense of belonging, but the greatest challenge was probably in the political arena in general and in Singapore's ruling party in particular. The years 1959 to 1963 witnessed the inevitable conflicts between the two main factions of the PAP. The two sides had initially needed each other in the interest of political survival. Lee and the English-educated moderates needed Lim, the labor leaders, and the Chinese-educated extremists to gain power. Lim and the extremists needed the respectability of Lee and his followers to remain in power and avoid being jailed by the British.

Lee had campaigned for the release of political detainees, and eight of the most prominent leaders had been freed after the PAP victory in 1959. Lim Chin Siong, Fong Swee Suan, Sandra Woodhull, James Puthucheary, and Devan Nair were all subsequently given political appointments in the new government. It would not take long for the former detainees and their supporters in the PAP to try and set the political agenda.

The first publicly stated issue that divided the party was the question of detention without trial. While eight of the radicals had been released as fulfillment of Lee's election promise, dozens of labor activists, pro-communists, and Chinese student leaders remained behind bars. Lim Chin Siong wanted them released and the ISA abolished. As Lee had said before 1959, Lim felt the act was undemocratic and a relic of colonial authority. However, Lee's hold over the party was tenuous, and the Internal Security Ordinances were his backup.

Further divisions in the party appeared as the terms of merger with Malaya began to appear. Lim and the left branded the terms a sellout. The fact that many recent immigrants would not be citizens and the under-representation of Singapore were viewed as creating second class status for Singapore. Lee's insistence on keeping control of labor policy was ample evidence, along with the continued detention of the extremists, that his future plans did not include the leftists of the PAP and their supporters. They knew that Lee planned to use merger to destroy them.

In 1961, the cracks within the party spilled into public view during two by-elections. The first, oddly enough, had little to do with the clash between the two major factions but rather came from within Lee's moderate wing. At the time of PAP's election victory, Ong Eng Guan had challenged Lee for leadership of the party. A highly chauvinistic politician, Ong was English-educated but had the ability to reach out to the Chinese-speaking. From 1957 to 1959, Ong had served as mayor of Singapore on a short-lived elected city council. Ong had used the position to build his own power base. He had a flair for the dramatic, could communicate well in Hokkien, and had built up a considerable following in urban Singapore.

In 1959, the city council was abolished by the PAP, and Ong subsequently made a play for the party leadership. His ability to move the masses and cross between the two Chinese communities made him a considerable threat to Lee. Acrimonious charges were thrown back and forth between the two leaders, and eventually, Ong was expelled from the party. Ong resigned his seat in parliament, formed a new party, and forced a by-election in his Hong Lim constituency. In the ensuing election, the PAP leadership pulled out all the stops in an effort to maintain its credibility. Ong was accused of nepotism while in office as mayor, incompetence while a government minister, and his personal life was dragged through the mud. When the smoke cleared, Ong had won 75 percent of the vote — an ominous sign to Lee — and reinforced the Tunku's fears about the ability of the PAP leadership to control the party.

Later in 1961, a second by-election was called because of the death of the member for Anson. David Marshall used this opportunity to come storming back to the political scene he had left in 1957 when he resigned from parliament. Marshall had formed a new party, the Workers' Party, and presented Lee's foes in the PAP with an opportunity to discredit Lee's leadership. Marshall declared the Malaysia plan a sham. If Singapore could not join on equal terms, then it should become completely independent. Marshall campaigned for an end to the ISA and the end of the British military presence in Singapore.

The election was one of high drama. The flamboyant Marshall, with support from the labor unions and from Lim Chin Siong's faction, was pitted against the moderate wing of the PAP, which seemed to be placing the government's credibility on the line. In the end, Marshall won a narrow victory. Once again, the moderate leadership had been discredited. There were calls from Marshall and within the PAP for Lee's resignation, claiming Lee no longer had the authority to be prime minister. In a somewhat contrived scene, Lee offered his resignation, but Toh Chin Chye, as chairman of the party, refused to accept it. The two factions could no longer exist under the same roof; the party split.

Lim Chin Siong and his followers left the PAP to form a new party known as the Barisan Sosialis (Socialist Front). With him Lim took the heart of the coalition that had been responsible for the PAP's 1959 victory. The rank and file of the party were behind Lim. Out of the fifty-one PAP branches, thirty-five supported Lim and joined his new party; nineteen of the twenty-three paid political secretaries of the PAP also joined him; and thirteen PAP members of parliament crossed the floor and declared their support for the Barisan Sosialis.

The trade union movement also reflected the political turmoil. The Barisan organized the Singapore Association of Trade Unions to which some two-thirds of union members allied themselves. The threat to the future of Lee and the PAP was real. Lim had wide popularity among the working and lower classes of Singapore society. Most observers believed at that time that if there had been a general election in 1961, Lim and the Barisan would have won.

These were dark days for the PAP and its moderate leadership, but Lee Kuan Yew still had strong cards to play. The PAP controlled the government apparatus, and Lee had discovered that this was a far more valuable tool than a political organization. The government controlled the only broadcast medium at the time — radio — and used it effectively to get its message out. Rajaratnam, who controlled the Ministry of Culture, had large government printing and propaganda resources at his disposal and the ex-journalist used them well. The civil service was dominated by conservative, English-educated Singaporeans, and it proved to be a valuable ally to the PAP's cause, as the group feared the radicalism of the Barisan. Apart from this, Lee had extremely capable colleagues, such as Goh and Toh, men who could make programs work and deliver the goods to the voters.

Even with these resources, it was still an uphill task. By July 1962, the PAP had become a minority government, holding only twenty-five of the fifty-one seats in parliament. What saved it from falling were the divisions among its opponents. Four of its opponents in the assembly were the remnants of the old Labor Front government who had been elected in 1959. They had no sympathy for the goals and methods of the Barisan Sosialis, and without their support, the Barisan could not bring down the government in the assembly.

The political issue that the government embraced to rebuild its fortunes was merger with Malaya. It could only find safety in the arms of the anti-communist, conservative leadership that ruled Malaya. The PAP called a referendum on entry into Malaysia in September 1962. The stakes were high. Barisan and Marshall opposed the terms of merger and would fight tooth and nail, knowing that the credibility of the government was on the line. Any further defeats at the polls, especially on as important an issue as this, would mean the end of Lee and the PAP.

The choices presented to the voters in the referendum reflected the PAP's determination. A vote against merger was not possible. The voter could only choose between different terms of entry — the one negotiated by the PAP, entry as a state, such as Penang, with no conditions whatsoever on entry, or entry on the same terms as the Borneo states. The choices were somewhat disingenuous because the Malayan leadership was only going to offer entry under the terms negotiated.

For 345 days, the "battle over merger" raged in Singapore. The government machinery cranked out a daily barrage of propaganda extolling the rosy future Singapore would have as part of Malaysia. On billboards, on street corners, on the radio, and in the newspapers, the people of Singapore were bombarded with appeals by the PAP for their support in the way Singapore should join Malaysia. The Barisan and Marshall campaigned for people to cast blank votes as an act of protest for not being offered a clearer choice. The PAP prevailed, winning some 70 percent of the vote for the alternative they had negotiated. Only 25 percent of the electorate cast blank votes.

The results signified that the PAP still had the ability to fight back. The achievement of one of their primary goals, merger with Malaya, gave them new confidence. The playing field between Lee Kuan Yew and Lim Chin Siong seemed to be leveling.

With entry into Malaysia ensured, the government struck out against its opponents in February 1963. In a police action codenamed Operation Cold Store, over a hundred Barisan leaders, union officers, and "communist sympathizers" were arrested and detained under the ISA. Lee had convinced the Internal Security Council that these people were part of a communist threat to Singapore, Malaya, and the area's stability. In the assembly, the roles of 1956 were reversed — Marshall condemning Lee for authoritarian, undemocratic methods, and Lee defending arrests in the interests of public order and stability.

Many of those arrested protested long and hard that they were not communists and did not have any plans to destabilize the country. There is an interesting side note here in that some of these detainees, when they were released years later, went on to positions of responsibility in Malaysia. James Puthucheary and Sandra Woodhull became advisors to Malaysia's second prime minister, Tun Abdul Razak. Samad Ismail was the first editor of the *New Straits Times* when UMNO interests purchased it in 1972. Abdullah Majid became Razak's press secretary and later an UMNO member of parliament — strange jobs and causes for so-called communists in the bastion of anti-communism, UMNO and Malaysia.

A combination of factors would prompt the PAP to call for a general election in 1963. Economically and socially, some of the government's policies were taking root. The creation of new jobs and the success of the HDB were making strides in bringing the public around to the PAP's point of view. Politically, the success in the referendum and the jailing of many of his most effective opponents gave Lee the confidence to go to the voters.

In the ensuing election, the PAP won thirty-seven of the fifty-one seats in the assembly, Barisan Sosialis won thirteen, and Ong Eng Guan the remainder. The election was closer than the results indicated. In terms of the popular vote, the PAP only carried 47 percent of the electorate, and many of the individual contests were extremely close. Toh Chin Chye won his seat by a mere eighty-nine votes out of 11,000 cast. Rajaratnam won by only 220 in a district of the same size. A sidelight of the campaign was that it was the first time the government was able to use its newly established television service to deliver its message. The PAP had prevailed and was now ready to move its ambitions to a larger stage — Malaysia.

Borneo in the Twentieth Century

As Sarawak entered the twentieth century, it had been under the rule of Charles Brooke for close to thirty-five years. While he had been successful in placing the state on a sound financial basis, his style and objectives were not much different from those of his uncle. Charles presided over a government that flowed from him through a small group of some thirty to forty Europeans and a larger group of Malay administrators. Government and laws were highly informal and personal. Justice was dispensed on a case by case basis, and Charles was the final court of appeal. As for the indigenous people, a combination of the policies of the Brookes and geography had effectively isolated them from the modern world. The structure of the economy, society, and government along racial lines continued to be reinforced and perpetuated.

Charles had reversed earlier restrictions on Chinese immigration that had been established after their attack on Kuching in 1857. The Chinese who came were not migrant laborers but true immigrants. Most had left China permanently and brought their families with them. In the early twentieth century, much of the growth in the Chinese community came from children and the original settlers sending for their relatives in China. The stability of family and a high proportion of Christians meant that many of the social ills experienced by other Chinese migrant communities — opium, secret societies, and prostitution — were not nearly as prevalent among the Chinese of Sarawak.

Most historians regard Charles as a benevolent despot. He certainly seemed to want to protect the people from the pressures and changes of capitalism. A good example is when he discouraged Westerners from setting up rubber estates in the 1900s and encouraged Malays and indigenous smallholders to set them up instead. He truly respected the people as human beings, even if he was ruthless in crushing those who rebelled against him. He never made a large fortune and seemed in fact to hold Sarawak in trust for its people.

As the last years of Charles' rule wound down in the early twentieth century, his reign evoked strong emotion from many British and other outsiders. Some felt that he was a romantic, a benevolent peacemaker who was protecting the people of the interior from the ravages of modern civilization. They even went as far as implying that he was a well-meaning warden of a national park, protecting all within from hunters, poachers, and exploiters. Others saw him as an egotistical despot who kept order through his Iban Sarawak Rangers. They felt that rather than protecting these people, he was keeping them in fear and ignorance to further his own power and wealth.

Whichever way Charles is regarded, on his death in 1917 and after a rule of fifty years, the dynasty passed on to his son Vyner. The successor ascended the throne with extensive experience and knowledge about Sarawak. In 1899, at the age of twenty-six, Vyner had joined the Sarawak civil service and had served in the interior as a district officer. His father spent two to three months in England every year, and during that time, Vyner, for all practical purposes, had been the ruler of the state.

During his term in office as rajah, Vyner presided over dramatic changes in Sarawak. In the period between the two world wars, the nature of government began to change. Vyner encouraged a move away from the highly personalized rule of his father and granduncle to a more bureaucratic modern state. A more formal legal system was introduced with a written code modeled on the lines of the system used in India. Judges were appointed to replace the rajah and his advisors as the dispensers of justice. Instead of a generalist approach to government, the new rajah borrowed from the Malayan model, setting up specialized agencies that dealt with education, public works, and finance.

While the government became more specialized, Vyner did not move away from the stereotypical racial lines of Sarawak society. In educational and social policies, he still kept the indigenous people isolated from the modern sector of government and the economy. This was further reinforced by the sheer size of the area that he ruled and its scattered population. Any attempt to provide modern educational and social services to the people of the interior would have required financial resources far beyond those of his government. At the local level, the government continued to operate along tribal and clan lines and was protected from outside influences as much as possible. This was reflected in educational policy. The government had established schools for the Malays and Chinese but did not feel the need to educate the Ibans, Bidayuhs, and other indigenous people. The feeling was that modern education was counterproductive for these people; it would pollute their culture and give them skills and aspirations that were irrelevant to their lives.

Any educational facilities that were provided for the people of the interior came from foreign missionary endeavors. Mission schools made a great contribution to educating the children of Sarawak. The Methodists, Anglicans, and Roman Catholics did a lot with meager resources, but even they had most of their success in the towns and settled areas. Although they made up the majority of the population, in 1936, less than a thousand of Sarawak's school enrollment of 14,600 were indigenous people. Even with the help of the missions, literacy rates in Sarawak were far below those in the peninsula.

During Vyner's reign, Sarawak slowly began to be part of the world export economy. The Borneo Company had been the only foreign business venture allowed to operate in Sarawak. Its position and the size of Sarawak's economy at the turn of the century were exemplified by the company's role as the banker for the government — a result of the lack of formal banks in the state. This economic situation was to change between the two world wars. Before World War I, most of Sarawak's exports had been either pepper cultivated by the Chinese or produce that came up the rivers from the jungle. To modernize the government required revenue and revenue required economic activity. To this end, the country was somewhat opened up. Oil was discovered in the late nineteenth century near Miri, and in 1910, the Anglo Saxon Petroleum Company sank its first well. The oil fields were not large by world standards. At their peak in 1929, they produced 1 million barrels a year. Rubber was introduced in the early twentieth century but in a pattern much different from that in the peninsula. Most of the rubber cultivation was undertaken by Malay and Iban smallholders rather than by large estates. By World War II, some 200,000 acres (81,000 hectares) were planted with rubber. The isolation of Sarawak began to end as the state's economic health came to be determined increasingly by world market prices for rubber and oil.

As World War II and the 100th anniversary of the rule of the Brookes in Sarawak approached, it became clear to Vyner that the days of autocratic rule by white rajahs were coming to an end. The efforts by Vyner to change government were only minor steps compared with what had to be done as the country modernized. In 1937, the government's total revenue was $4 million. This was hardly enough to run a modern government and economy. As the world approached the mid-twentieth century, the methods that the Brookes had used to rule Sarawak were viewed as outdated. Vyner seemed to realize that Sarawak needed a more modern and centralized system of government, but a problem he faced was that his nephew and heir, Anthony, was determined to perpetuate the old system and would work behind the scenes against his uncle's plans for modernization.

In 1941, Vyner planned to introduce a new and written constitution for Sarawak. He foresaw the rajah taking a role much like that of the sultans in the FMS — a symbol more than a monarch. He planned to change the state council from an advisory body to one that was legislative in nature. The growth in the economy required a growth in infrastructure that only modern government could provide. The attitudes of the people toward government were changing, and Vyner anticipated the need for broader participation. His plans never came to fruition because of the Japanese invasion of Sarawak.

The Japanese occupation was swift and met with little resistance. In theory, Sarawak was a protectorate of Great Britain, but there were few troops to spare for this backwater state. The one brigade of Indian troops sent to defend Sarawak surrendered quickly but not before oil company and British officials were able to deny the Japanese the prime objective of their Borneo invasion — the oil fields. In retreat, the British destroyed the pumping and production facilities of most of Borneo's oil capacity. What little the Japanese were able to get working again was a fraction of the pre-war levels.

The war experiences of the people of Sarawak were not much different from those experienced in Malaya. Sarawak was a net importer of food, and as the war years progressed, less and less was available for the general population. For the people of the coastal areas, especially the Chinese, fear and hunger set in. The people of the interior were for the most part untouched by Japanese rule. One consequence of the war on this group was that, with the internment and escape of Sarawak's European officials, the incidence of headhunting grew again, especially against the Japanese who ventured upriver with few escorts.

None of the Brookes was resident in Sarawak when the Japanese took control. Vyner established a government in exile in Australia and during the war held extensive discussions with the British about the future of his fiefdom. Both realized that there was a need for drastic change. The modern economy that had grown between the wars was in shambles and would require significant funds to rebuild, money the old regime under the rajah could not generate. Although some changes had been made in the Sarawak government in the 1920s and 1930s, they were not enough for the post-World War II world. The funds and know-how required to build better educational and social services that Sarawak desperately needed were beyond the government's capabilities. When the war was over, Sarawak could not go back to the old system, and

Vyner realized this. They were living in the twentieth century with a nineteenth-century system.

In return for financial support for his family and himself, Vyner agreed to cede Sarawak to the British government. It was to become what James had initially planned, a British colony. There was opposition to Vyner's decision. Many Malays feared their special position in the government would be changed by British rule and were highly suspicious. Many of the Ibans and Bidayuhs had deep personal loyalties to the Brooke family, and these were not necessarily transferable to an anonymous British government. Anthony Brooke, the heir to the throne, believed that Vyner was selling his birthright and conspired with those in opposition to British rule in an attempt to block the move.

When the proposal was taken to the state council for approval, the vote was close, eighteen to sixteen. Britain had acquired its last colony. Opposition to direct British rule continued among the Malay community for some time, and in 1949, the British governor of Sarawak was assassinated by a Malay opposed to colonial status. The shock of the killing was instrumental in deflating the fervor of those opposed to British colonial rule, and eventually, even the Malays saw the benefits of their new government.

The resources available to the new colonial government went far beyond those the Brookes could have mustered. Impressive strides were made to rebuild and expand the economy and infrastructure. Between 1946 and 1955 alone, revenue from the oil industry increased from $51 million to $292 million. Efforts to encourage the search for offshore oil were made, and there were important new oil discoveries. The building of new roads and airports added impetus to economic growth as previously inaccessible areas were brought into the modern economy. New schools and teacher training facilities were built, and education offered to all groups. Growth in government and government-aided schools increased the number of school-going children dramatically. By 1962, the number of children attending school had quadrupled from pre-war levels. This was impressive, but literacy levels for Sarawak were still less than half of those for Malaya and Singapore.

Thus, the British made great efforts to develop Sarawak between the end of World War II and the early 1960s. However, when the Malaysia proposal was put forward, Sarawak was still backward compared with the infrastructures of the states in the Malay Peninsula.

North Borneo

The motivation and goals of British penetration of North Borneo were quite different from their intentions in Sarawak. What the North Borneo Company wanted from the area was a world apart from what the Brookes maintained they were trying to achieve. Given these differences, it is remarkable that their respective societies were so similar and that they developed economically and governmentally along somewhat parallel paths.

Demographically, North Borneo and Sarawak were quite similar. By World War I, North Borneo was home to a significant Chinese minority, and like Sarawak, it was immigrant in nature with stable family structures. The Chinese shared the coastal areas with a Malay community that had its roots in the early expansion of the Brunei sultanate. The percentage of the community that was ethnically Malay was (and still is) a little hazy because the government considered all Muslims Malay, including indigenous people who had converted to Islam. The majority of North Borneo's population was indigenous, living in the interior of the state and made up of Kadazan-Dusuns, who constituted about 30 percent of the total population, and significant numbers of Muruts and Bajaus. The role of most of these indigenous people in the economy consisted of collecting jungle produce.

As in Sarawak, these groups had little contact with the outside world. Their isolation in North Borneo came about for many of the same reasons as it had in Sarawak. Scattered communities were spread out over large areas of primary forest, and the governing authority had meager resources to develop any kind of infrastructure in the interior. They were able to maintain their traditional way of life because the government was ineffective, not because the government was trying to preserve their cultures. In Sarawak, the indigenous groups had a tie to the central government through their loyalty to the Brooke family. In North Borneo, they had little connection whatsoever to modern government.

About the time of World War I, economic and governmental changes came to North Borneo. The territory, while under company rule, was subject to parliamentary supervision. As a result, it was in the company's interest to avoid drawing the kind of attention that gross misrule would bring. The supervision motivated the company to establish a more professional administrative service. North Borneo began to operate more and more administratively like a colony. Many of the bureaucrats who ran the government departments were recruited from the Malayan civil service, and procedures followed in Malaya tended to take root in North Borneo. Increasingly in the 1920s and 1930s, policies and directives to the empire from the British Colonial Office were accepted and implemented in the territory. This added a greater degree of organization and structure to the government but little beyond that. As long as the funds to develop the area had to come from the company, there was not much hope for serious change.

The new breed of civil servants were an improvement on the older company officials but knew little of the language and culture of the indigenous people. Educational and social policies mirrored those of Sarawak. What education that was available was provided mainly by mission groups and was concentrated in the coastal areas. There were some Malay-language schools established by the government because of Muslim aversion to Christian missionary influence, but those few schools and the establishment of an education department were the extent of governmental involvement. At the outbreak of World War II, in a total population of about a quarter million people, there were about eleven thousand students attending school, and out of this figure, only a handful were Kadazan-Dusuns, Muruts, or Bajaus.

Between the world wars, there was a significant expansion of North Borneo's export economy. Prior to World War I, most of the economic activity revolved around company efforts to develop export crops, especially tobacco and pepper. Both had turned out to be disappointments. American tariffs effectively closed off the tobacco market, and the pepper trade suffered from a lack of capital and competition from other parts of the archipelago. In the first few decades of the twentieth century, the planting of rubber became North Borneo's most important economic activity — it was earning tens of millions of dollars in exports by the middle of the century.

Rubber's success in North Borneo was due to the efforts of William Cowie, who was the dominant force behind the company's success. Before moving to London in the 1890s, Cowie had spent twenty years trading in the South China Sea. One of the many colorful characters of this era, he had been a gun runner in Sulu, had managed a coal mine in Brunei, and had been deeply involved in the intrigues surrounding European control of North Borneo. While head of the Chartered Company, he had been instrumental in building the railroad along the northwestern coast of the territory, a venture that had caused the company serious financial problems. But in the end, it was Cowie who saw the future of rubber and was responsible for its growth as a vital part of North Borneo's economy. In 1905, he offered a guaranteed 4 percent return on any rubber investments in the territory and a fifty-year exemption from export taxes. A rubber boom followed. In 1907, there were 3,226 acres (1,307 hectares) under cultivation. By 1917, this had risen to 34,828 acres (14,105 hectares), much of this land along the railway line, which had originally been considered unusable. By 1928, North Borneo had almost 100,000 acres (40,500 hectares) under cultivation and exported 15 million pounds (7 million kg) of rubber.

Timber showed the most growth potential among the different sectors of the economy. British capital entered the territory on a large scale to exploit North Borneo's most important resource — its rain forest. The growth of rubber and timber as export commodities in the years between the world wars contributed to the establishment of two urban areas in North Borneo — Jesselton in the west (Kota Kinabalu today) and Sandakan in the east. The export of jungle timber grew at such a pace that by World War II North Borneo had become one of the world's most important sources of jungle hardwood. With over $100 million worth of timber sold annually, it had become the most important export item of the area by the 1950s. Over time, profits from timber created an ecological problem for North Borneo that exists to this day. The remoteness of logging concessions and the available profits quickly outstripped any efforts at conservation and created immense opportunities for corruption.

World War II saw a change in the British government's attitude toward North Borneo. The presence of an active resistance and extensive allied bombing had caused great destruction in North Borneo. Mainly Chinese, the extent of this resistance was exemplified in 1944 when the rebels, believing liberation was close, actually stormed and captured Jesselton. In addition, Australian forces had landed in North Borneo in an attempt to liberate the state. In the fighting that ensued, the North Borneo economy and towns were ruined. Jesselton only had one building left standing when the Japanese surrendered, Sandakan had been completely leveled, and 15 percent of the male population of the western coastal area had been executed by the Japanese.

During the war, the decision had been made that North Borneo, like Sarawak, needed a new governmental arrangement for development and reconstruction. Thus, company rule ended at the end of the war, and North Borneo became the crown colony of British North Borneo. The handover to the British government resulted in a commitment of funds and personnel similar to that in Sarawak. Educational facilities were expanded, the number of government schools increased from forty-eight at the end of the war to 146 by 1960, and government-aided mission schools tripled in number. There was a significant rise in literacy rates as education was made available to the indigenous people of the interior. Hundreds of miles of roads were built, linking the coastal areas and providing some access to the interior.

The Malaysia Proposal

Some political progress had been made in both territories under direct British rule. In Sarawak, plans were under way for an elected majority in the state legislative council, while in North Borneo, the legislative council now had a majority of unofficials, that is, locals. Progress, however, was slow due to the diversity of the societies and their lack of constitutional progress prior to World War II.

Political activity in the two Borneo territories accelerated dramatically with the proposed creation of Malaysia in 1961. The British were all for the incorporation of North Borneo and Sarawak into a larger federation. Sarawak had a population of 750,000 people and North Borneo 400,000.

Their small populations, underdeveloped economies, and lack of modern infrastructure meant that any kind of real self-rule was highly improbable. British support and guidance would be needed for a long time. Britain, however, was trying to divest itself of its colonial responsibilities. Britain in the 1960s could no longer afford its empire.

Reaction to the Malaysia proposal in the Borneo states was initially somewhat negative. There were many objections and questions. Were the people of Borneo going to trade rule by British colonial administrators for that of the Malays from the peninsula? If this was going to be the case, they wanted no part of it. Missionaries in both states had been highly successful among the indigenous and Chinese populations. The percentage of Christians in Borneo was much higher than in the peninsula, and they feared that Islam would remain the national religion under the new proposal. The Chinese in both territories had found stable lives for themselves and feared being relegated to the political position of their counterparts in Malaya. Both territories were economically and educationally backward and distrusted a Malay government whose developmental priority was to the rural Malay population in the peninsula.

The only group from which there was strong support for the Malaysia proposal was the Malay community. The benefits for them were obvious. They would be benefactors of the special position of the Malays in the federal constitution. Since they were a minority community in both Borneo states, the Malays felt that Malaysia was an avenue to more political and economic power.

Of the two, Sarawak was further ahead on the path to democratic participation and had several established political parties by 1961. The most prominent one was the Sarawak United People's Party (SUPP), which had a strong base in the Chinese community and in the urban areas. The SUPP and newly formed parties, such as the Sarawak National Party (SNAP) and Barisan Raykat Jati Sarawak (BARJASA), expressed opposition to the Malaysia plan. The only support from a political party in Sarawak came from Parti Negara Sarawak (PANAS), which was primarily a Malay party.

In North Borneo, the Malaysia plan gave impetus to the formation of new political parties mainly along communal lines. The largest and best organized was the United National Kadazan Organization (UNKO), which was led by a prominent journalist and half-Kadazan-Dusun, Donald

Stephens. After the Tunku's visit to Borneo in mid-1961 to sell his plan, Stephens and the leader of the SUPP, Ong Kee Hui, announced publicly their rejection of the proposal.

What followed was an intense period of politicking by the leaders of Singapore and Malaya to convince political leaders in Borneo of the benefits of Malaysia and to find the right formula to bring the Borneo territories on board. They were successful in convincing the major politicians to keep an open mind, and to this end, UNKO and SUPP led the way in establishing the Malaysia Solidarity Consultative Committee. This group represented political and governmental leaders from Borneo and political leaders from Singapore and Malaya, that is, the PAP and the Alliance. It was within this committee that the deal to bring the Borneo states into Malaysia was eventually negotiated.

What did it take to convince leaders such as Stephens and Ong that joining Malaysia was not detrimental to the interests of their states? The final arrangement offered to the Borneo states gave them a considerable degree of autonomy in many areas. They were given power over immigration to allay fears of being overpowered by migrants from other parts of the peninsula. This created an odd situation after the merger in which visitors to Malaysia had to get separate visas for East Malaysia (Borneo), and people moving from one part of the country to another, even between Sabah and Sarawak, had to get the approval of a state government.

The imposition of Malay as the single national language of government and education was delayed for ten years. English would hold equal footing with Malay, and any later changes would require approval by the Borneo states. These states would keep their own civil services for at least the immediate future and would have control over their own educational policies. To allay the fears of non-Muslims, it was agreed that Islam would not be the state religion, and in answer to apprehension about Malay dominance, both states were given over-representation in the new federal parliament. For example, North Borneo with a population of about half a million people had greater representation than Singapore with its two million people and other states in the peninsula with similar populations. In addition to this, the indigenous populations would be offered the same Bumiputera status as the Malays in Malaya with the same constitutional benefits. These concessions were sufficient to convince most leaders that Malaysia was going to be of benefit to North Borneo and Sarawak.

Federation of Malaysia

The new Federation of Malaysia came into existence on September 16, 1963 with Tunku Abdul Rahman as its first prime minister. The future was not quite as grand as had been originally envisaged — Brunei had decided not to join at the last minute. Internationally, the new country faced opposition from Indonesia and the Philippines, which challenged the legitimacy of the creation of Malaysia. From within, Malaysia faced the challenge of a more complicated racial makeup. It had to deal with the further fragmentation of its population with the inclusion of new groups from Borneo, as well as the challenge of absorbing Singapore's Chinese population.

There are a number of reasons why the sultan of Brunei decided Malaysia was not for him and his country. The first reason was financial in nature. In the 1920s and 1930s, large reserves of oil had been discovered in Brunei. With a population of less than a quarter million people, Brunei's economic future was bright. If it joined Malaysia, the sultan feared that significant amounts of Brunei's oil revenue would be diverted to the federal government in Kuala Lumpur in the form of taxes and revenue sharing. This was too much to give up. It is doubtful whether his son Hassanal Bolkiah, the present sultan of Brunei, would have become one of the world's richest men today if the country had entered Malaysia.

Joining Malaysia would also have brought about greater democratization of Brunei's political system since Malaysia was a democracy. Brunei's experience in limited democracy had not gone well. The leaders elected by the people had threatened the royal position and power and in 1962 had actually staged a short-lived rebellion. The sultan wanted no further significant participation by the common people in the political decision making process.

Also, the sultan of Brunei was not pleased with his place in the line to be a future king of Malaysia. Brunei was to be the tenth state whose sultan would be eligible to be king of the country, and the sultans of the peninsula had made it clear that Brunei would have to wait its turn. Not foreseeing the prestige of being king in his lifetime, added to his other concerns, prompted the sultan of Brunei to continue his relationship with Britain as a protectorate rather than join Malaysia. Brunei achieved full independence in 1984.

Regional Opposition to Malaysia

The Philippines opposed the creation of Malaysia on the grounds that the part of British North Borneo east of Marudu Bay belonged to it. Manila's claim was based on the assumption that when the North Borneo Company took over control of the area in the nineteenth century, that portion of North Borneo was part of the sultanate of Sulu, not Brunei. Manila maintained that the sultan of Sulu had merely leased it to Dent and his successors and thus, because Sulu was part of the modern Philippines, that area really belonged to the Philippines. Negotiations took place between the Tunku and the leaders in Manila to try solve the dispute, but the issue had become one of national pride in the Philippines, leaving no room for a compromise.

In the end, Malaysia and the British rejected Filipino claims, and North Borneo became the Malaysian state of Sabah. Politicians in the Philippines played up the perceived slight. Anti-Malaysia demonstrations were held, and the free-wheeling Filipino press trumpeted this injustice. As the years passed, the issue faded and lost its fervor in the face of more pressing domestic issues in the Philippines. Decades later, an interesting phenomenon is the rising Filipino influence in Sabah as a result of immigration. A problem faced by Sabah today is the hundreds of thousands of illegal immigrants from the Philippines who have slipped into the state to take advantage of the good economic prospects.

The origins of Indonesia's objections to Malaysia were more complex and revolved around the political problems and personality of the country's first leader, President Sukarno. In the early 1960s, Indonesia faced serious problems — gross mismanagement of the economy, nationalistic policies that alienated foreign investors, and corruption that brought the country to the edge of bankruptcy. All levels of society felt the hardships caused by runaway inflation and shortages of nearly everything from rice to nails.

Sukarno had maintained his position in power by the respect he received as the father of independent Indonesia, his rhetorical skills, and his ability to play his strongest challengers — the army and the communists

— off against each other. Sukarno had grand visions of a greater Indonesia, one that would rival the areas controlled by pre-colonial empires such as Majaphit. His message was that Indonesians were the heirs to past glories, and he would lead them to new heights of greatness.

A foreign scapegoat is a useful tool to distract the minds of the people from the realities at home. Malaysia was a neo-colonial plot, thundered Sukarno to the masses. Sabah and Sarawak should be part of an Indonesian Borneo, and Britain was denying them this opportunity by hooking them up with its puppets in Malaya. Sukarno vowed to "crush Malaysia" and sent troops to fight the new country. The conflict between Indonesia and Malaysia went on for three years.

At times this "Confrontation," as it was called, was almost comical, but there were real battles with real people dying. In the peninsula, the impact of the clashes was not great, and the odd commando raid caused little damage. For example, in September 1964, Indonesian special forces were to be parachuted into Johor. The Indonesians had been told that the Malaysian masses would welcome their Indonesian brothers with open arms and that it was only their leaders and the British who believed in Malaysia. What followed was a debacle. Four planeloads of troops were involved in the "liberation." One plane failed to get off the ground in Indonesia. A second plane crashed in the Straits of Melaka. A third dropped its troops in the wrong place. Stragglers from this plane flagged down a

Commonwealth soldiers in Sarawak stand guard while women wash their clothes during the Confrontation with Indonesia.

passing vehicle, and the Malaysian driver took his "liberators" to the nearest police station. The only commandos who were dropped on target were quickly rounded up by the Commonwealth troops.

In Singapore, most of the attacks were also failures, blowing up the odd sea wall or beach. There was, however, an occasion when the saboteurs managed to place a bomb in MacDonald House along Orchard Road, resulting in fatalities.

The conflict did have a dramatic effect on Singapore's economy. The loss of Indonesian trade brought Singapore's economic expansion to a standstill. The economic problems caused by Confrontation added to the political difficulties of the leaders who had to make adjustments as part of the federation.

In Borneo, the situation was somewhat different. A combination of the Indonesian army, Sarawak communists armed by the Indonesians, and Indonesian communists turned the remote border areas of Malaysia into battlefields. Troops from Malaysia, Britain, Australia, and New Zealand fought a jungle war in which many died. Their determination and courage acted as a strong deterrent to the Indonesian army's will to fight Sukarno's "war." Confrontation finally ended in 1966 with Sukarno's fall from power. The Indonesian army staged a coup that year in response to what it said was a communist attempt to take over power. The military takeover that established General Suharto as president of Indonesia restored friendly relations between Malaysia and Indonesia.

PAP's Entry Into Malaysian Politics

In many ways, Singapore's merger with Malaya was the triumph of hope over reality. The aggressive leaders of the PAP and Singapore's 75 percent Chinese population were bound to cause problems in a society obsessed with race. Although Singapore and the Borneo states had negotiated special arrangements to join Malaysia, most Malays assumed that the understanding between the MCA and UMNO that had established the original Federation of Malaya in 1957 was still in place. The new constitution of the Federation of Malaysia contained the same provisions and guarantees of Malay special status as had been in Malaya's previous constitution. Malay political leaders saw "the deal" as a fully functioning part of the new political situation. The acceptance of lower electoral

323

representation by Singapore and the gestures the PAP had made by adopting the Malay language, appointing a Malay head of state, and having a Malay-language state anthem were all assumed to be in agreement with the provisions of the 1957 arrangement. These actions and the speeches and statements made by Lee Kuan Yew and his colleagues in the run-up to Malaysia Day in 1963 seemed to make Malay political supremacy a given fact.

What was not a given was the political role of the PAP when it moved into the larger political world of Malaysia. The outlook of men such as Lee Kuan Yew, Goh Keng Swee, and Toh Chin Chye was Malayan in nature. To them Singapore's national identity was as part of Malaysia. As a result, they saw no reason why, once they joined Malaysia, they should not be major players in the larger political game. From the outset, Lee fought hard to be a part of the Alliance Party. The PAP leadership felt that the MCA represented only the wealthy Chinese community and that the PAP would be a much more effective and representative voice of the Chinese in Malaysia.

The PAP overtures for inclusion in the ruling party were rejected by the Alliance Party. Many in UMNO were suspicious of Lee's intentions and ambitions. The leaders of the Malay community in the peninsula were conservative defenders of the status quo in Malaysia and mistrusted the PAP agenda. UMNO had a good working relationship with the MCA. What they had seen and heard of the PAP's quest for "democratic socialism" over the years seemed too radical for their liking. The MCA did not want the PAP brought into the Alliance as they already represented the Chinese vote. Thus, when the federal parliament met, PAP representatives occupied positions as part of the opposition.

Differences between the PAP and the Alliance took on greater significance as time went on. Some of the problems revolved around economic issues. Singapore wanted the peninsula as a market for its growing manufacturing sector. Negotiations for a common market proceeded slowly because Malaysia feared the competition Singapore posed for its fledgling factories. Differences also surfaced over taxes and the amount of Singapore's contribution to the federal budget. These issues had not been defined well in the lead-up to merger, and conflicting perceptions were causing discord.

The relationship between the PAP and the ruling Alliance Party became worse with the PAP's entry into peninsular politics. When Malaysia was being formed, the Alliance thought it had an agreement that the PAP would stay out of politics in the peninsular area, at least in the near future. The Tunku, being sensitive to Malay politicians' fear of the Chinese from Singapore, felt that it was a political imperative for Lee and the PAP not to have a high profile in the Alliance's backyard.

In 1964, elections were held for the constituencies that represented the peninsula in the Malaysian parliament. The PAP saw the elections as its chance to discredit the MCA and proceeded to run nine candidates in Chinese-majority constituencies. It hoped that if it could show strength at the ballot box, UMNO would reconsider the PAP's position in government.

In Lee's view, this was only a limited move north, and besides, Malayan political leaders had voiced open support for the Singapore Alliance Party in Singapore's 1963 election. Some Malay leaders had gone so far as to brand Malays who voted for the PAP as traitors to their race. The results of both elections were similar. In 1963, many Malays in Singapore rejected UMNO's call to vote against the PAP, and in 1964, the Chinese electorate in Malaysia brought all but one of the PAP's candidates down to defeat. Devan Nair was the sole winner in a traditional stronghold of opposition in the Kuala Lumpur area. Perhaps if Lee had accepted his losses and laid low for a while, things would have turned out for the better, but this was not to be.

Lee's response to the 1964 electoral setback was to organize a coalition of opposition parties called the Malaysian Solidarity Convention (MSC). The main participants were the SUPP from Sarawak, the PAP, the PPP from Perak, and the United Democratic Party (UDP) from Penang. The UDP was a splinter group from the MCA led by Lim Chong Eu and included many supporters of the defunct Socialist Front.

The battle cry of the MSC was "Malaysian Malaysia." Holding rallies across the country and supported by the propaganda arm of the Singapore government, the new coalition called for equal rights for all Malaysians. Although not outwardly communal in nature, the MSC stirred the racial pot. The leaders were non-Malay, and the areas that supported the MSC were also mostly non-Malay. Their message of ending special privileges appealed to an urban-based, non-Malay electorate.

To many in UMNO, their worst fears for Malaysia were coming true. In the old Federation of Malaya, the Malay power structure had been in control, but this challenge was uncharted. A quick check of the racial mathematical tables told them that the PAP and the MSC were threatening the Malay special position and the arrangements of 1957. A coalition of the Borneo territories, which had been given over-representation; the Chinese of Singapore; and the non-Malay majorities of Penang, Selangor, Johor, Perak, and Negri Sembilan could add up to an electoral disaster for the Alliance.

There are some who claim that Lee and the MSC never meant to threaten UMNO's political primacy, simply that of the MCA and MIC. Their hope was that they could force different non-Malay partners on the ruling Malay party. The problem was that what Lee thought or hoped was not important. What was important was the perception of the Malay leadership in the peninsula. That perception was that Lee was rallying the non-Malays against the fundamental tenets of Malay political dogma, Malay rule, and the Malay special position. Equal rights and special rights could not coexist.

Racial sensitivities were further inflamed by race riots that broke out between the Malays and the Chinese in Singapore in 1964. The army was called in, and curfews were imposed to quell two episodes of violent disorder. In July and September that year, over five hundred people were injured in the inter-communal violence. Twenty-two people were killed. The political leadership of Singapore saw the riots as the result of agitation by the extreme wing of UMNO, which was determined to undermine the legitimacy of the PAP government. Malay political leaders blamed the riots on the PAP's use of sensitive racial issues to score political points. Some Malays saw it as a preview of potential disorder throughout the country if Lee continued to challenge the accepted racial accommodations. Many leaders in UMNO came to view the PAP as a direct threat to their right to rule. Some suggested that Lee leave the country as an ambassador to the United Nations to calm things down, but Lee would not agree to anything beyond a short stint. The more extreme Malays in UMNO wanted Lee and the other PAP leaders arrested under the ISA and for there to be

Riot police in Singapore during the racial riots of 1964.

direct rule from Kuala Lumpur until more amenable leaders could be found for Singapore.

For the third time, British support and intervention helped save Lee Kuan Yew's political career. In 1957, the British had supported Lim Yew Hock's arrest of the PAP radicals; in 1963, they had supported the arrest of Barisan Sosialis leaders in Operation Cold Store. This time British Prime Minister Harold Wilson made it clear that the British would oppose any move against Lee by the Malaysian government. Wilson had a strong bargaining chip in the form of Commonwealth troops that were defending Malaysia on the border in Borneo.

In the end, it was the Tunku who faced down those in his party who wanted Lee arrested and determined that the only alternative was for Singapore to leave the federation. The ties that had existed for centuries had to be severed once and for all. In August 1965, Singapore was ejected from Malaysia and became an independent nation. Singapore had to do what most said was impossible — it had to find a future on its own.

The causes of the failure of Singapore's short-lived experience with Malaysia would be debated for years to come. Viewed in the context of the

1960s, there is ample blame on both sides. In the larger picture, the experiment in merger was a casualty of the problems independent British Malaya faced in coming to grips with a multiracial society that had serious economic and political inequities. The failed merger is but one chapter in an ongoing saga of an area beset with the racial ramifications of British rule.

Kuala Lumpur in 1957 (top) and in the 1990s (bottom).

Chapter 17

MALAYSIA SINCE 1965

Singapore's exit from Malaysia lowered the percentage of Chinese in Malaysia but did little to change the underlying problems Lee Kuan Yew had stirred up. Over a decade after independence, Malaysia had not defined a common destiny for its diverse people. The PAP had touched a nerve in all the communities. The inequalities inherent in the 1957 arrangement would not and could not go away. Malay economic grievances and Chinese political frustrations were just below the surface, waiting to boil over.

The differences that stood in the way of national unity were not just among the races but also within the races. In the Malay community, there were many who saw little economic progress from the government that replaced the British. In the Chinese community, there was a serious division between the representatives in the ruling Alliance Party and the day-to-day lives of ordinary citizens. Geographically, the northeastern part of the peninsula and Borneo had societies far different from those in Kuala Lumpur and the western coast.

Status Quo Challenged

The disagreements of the 1950s had not been resolved. A new generation of Malays and Chinese in the peninsula had come of age, challenging the wisdom of the compromises made a decade earlier. The question of language had been postponed for ten years in the original constitution, and as the 1967 target date for the implementation of Malay as the sole national language approached, this became a highly emotional issue.

For the Chinese, the implications of this language change were both cultural and economic. Since government schools would be taught in Malay, there was a perception among many Chinese that this was a threat to one of the prime vehicles for preserving their heritage — their language. Losing English as an official language would benefit the native speakers of Malay in government, education, and business. For the majority of non-Malays, whose Malay-language skills were none to poor, English had provided a racially neutral language, and proximity to urban English schools had softened the fact that their languages were not officially recognized. In the modern commercial world, English was an avenue to economic advancement. For most Malays, the issue was straightforward: Malaysia was their country; Malay was the national language; and it was time for the immigrants to accept that fact.

The legislation enacted to implement the constitution's ten-year deadline, the National Language Act of 1967, pleased few people. It was a classic example of the dynamics of the Alliance Party. In an attempt at compromise, this legislation made Malay the sole national and official language but allowed the continued use of English in areas such as the courts, higher education, and specialized agencies. In government-aided schools, Chinese was to be phased out slowly, starting in secondary school and later spreading to primary schools. Private schools could continue to teach in Chinese. The extremists in both major races labeled the law a sellout to the other race.

Opposition parties exploited the language issue and other grievances in the run-up to the 1969 election. PAS labeled the leadership of UMNO tools of the Chinese and called for greater Malay domination of the economy and politics. Its message seemed to be that a truly Malay and Islamic government would lay down the law to the immigrants. Only the Malay language should be used in the land of the Malay. PAS felt that the continued poor economic position of the Malays was due to UMNO compromise with the MCA and that a truly Malay government would take immediate steps to address Malay economic grievances.

Non-Malay discontent was heard through two new political parties, the Democratic Action Party (DAP) and Gerakan Rakyat Malaysia (Malaysian People's Movement). The DAP originally consisted of the remnants of the PAP's foray into peninsular politics in 1964. It changed its name and symbols in 1966 but picked up the call for a Malaysian Malaysia. Although it professed to be multiracial and did have the odd Malay candidate, its message of equal rights for all and its urban power base made it primarily a Chinese party.

331

Gerakan was intended to be a multiracial party. Formed by a coalition of Malay and Chinese academics, professionals, and opposition leaders, it held forth an ideal that the races could cooperate in a single party and that social justice could create a less stratified Malaysia. Gerakan's problem was that its philosophy appealed primarily to urban and middle class voters, both of whom were mostly non-Malays.

The Alliance campaigned on a platform of its achievements — stability, economic progress for the nation, and interracial cooperation — and its position as the party that led Malaysia to independence.

When the results were tallied, the ruling Alliance political establishment received a rude jolt. In 1969, many Malaysian voters rejected the status quo and elected significant numbers of new opposition candidates. The Alliance's percentage of the votes for national parliament fell from 58 percent to 48 percent, and its percentage of votes for state legislatures dropped from 57 percent to 47 percent. For many Alliance leaders it was a debacle; for the opposition it was a great triumph.

The Alliance still had a majority in parliament, but there was a significant erosion of its support among the Malays to PAS and among the non-Malays to the DAP, PPP, and Gerakan. The MCA was discredited as the representative of the Chinese. Most of the seats it managed to keep were in Malay-majority constituencies or in areas with large Malay minorities. In the Chinese-majority constituencies, the MCA was wiped out. UMNO's numbers held better, but PAS made significant inroads into its power base as over one in three Malays had voted against UMNO. This presented a challenge to its previously unquestioned position as the defender of Malay rights. The two-thirds majority in parliament needed to amend the constitution now depended on the results in Borneo. It was a different world for the Tunku and the Alliance Party.

At the state level, the results were just as depressing for the Alliance. Gerakan secured a comfortable majority in the Penang state legislature, and PAS retained its control of Kelantan. In Perak, the PPP, the DAP, and Gerakan won half the seats and posed the possibility of a state government run by non-Malays. In Selangor, the state legislature was divided equally between the Alliance and an opposition made up of the DAP and Gerakan, creating an uncertain political situation.

The non-Malays had made their presence felt at the polls as never before. There was the possibility that Malay sultans would have to deal with non-Malay chief ministers in Perak and Selangor. Penang was two-thirds Chinese and had always been led by a Chinese chief minister, but Perak and Selangor were a different matter in the eyes of the Malays, especially Selangor where the nation's capital could end up in a state led by the opposition. The results struck at the very heart of Malay assumptions of Malay political dominance. UMNO and the Alliance had to come to terms with the reality that the legitimacy of the old arrangements had been rejected by large numbers of the electorate.

Race Riots and Emergency Rule

In the end, the future of the country was not decided in the ballot boxes but in the streets. Bloody racial riots erupted in the aftermath of the election. The outbreak of disorder on May 13, 1969 was the result of racial tensions that had been building for some time. In many ways, it was the culmination of the fears that had been expressed during the PAP's 1964 campaign for a Malaysian Malaysia. The actual disturbances were ignited by non-Malay victory celebrations and Malay reaction to the election results. Supporters of the victorious opposition parties marched through the streets of Kuala Lumpur heralding a new political day. During these demonstrations, many participants taunted Malay bystanders with "Death to the Malays!" and "Blood debts will be repaid with blood!" The thought of non-Malays controlling any level of government and the derisive attitude of the marchers touched off interracial fighting.

Matters were made worse by Selangor's chief minister, Datuk Harun Idris, who used his residence as a staging area for Malays who wanted to retaliate. Malays were bussed in from the rural areas, and this escalated the fighting. Old animosities and grudges resurfaced, and the facade of Malaysia's stability and multiracial cooperation was destroyed. Armed confrontation took place between roving gangs of Malays and Chinese; shops were looted and houses burned. In the words of Tunku Abdul Rahman, "Kuala Lumpur was a city on fire."

The tensions spread beyond Kuala Lumpur, and the Tunku asked the king to declare a state of national emergency. The newly elected parliament was suspended, and elections in the Borneo states were postponed indefinitely. The army was called in to occupy many cities and towns, and a twenty-four-hour curfew was declared on the western coast of the country. Hundreds were killed, hundreds more injured, and millions of dollars of property damaged. Thousands were made homeless, and the future of the country seemed to hang in the balance.

In the initial stages of emergency rule, UMNO took control of the government. The day-to-day running of the country was turned over to a newly created National Operations Council (NOC) led by Tun Abdul Razak. The NOC was organized in a manner similar to the government of the 1948–1960 communist Emergency. It consisted of UMNO politicians, senior civil servants, representatives from the military and police, and one representative each from the MCA and MIC. Thus, administration and security were coordinated from the same source. The difference between the NOC and the previous emergency government was that both the administration and security of the NOC were in the hands of Malay leaders. The suspension of parliamentary democracy and UMNO's takeover of the government sent strong messages to the country. One message was that the Malays held the levers of government, and the security forces supported them in this position. It also highlighted the point that the political success of the non-Malay opposition had been an aberration, and new political rules would be drawn up to make sure it did not happen again.

The riots of May 13 marked the end of the Tunku as Malaysia's leader. Although he carried on for a while as prime minister of the emergency cabinet, he had been discredited as a leader. In 1970, the Tunku resigned as prime minister and was succeeded by Tun Abdul Razak. The Tunku's dreams of moderation and a multiracial society had been shattered, and his party spent the emergency period of 1969–1971 trying to come up with an alternative arrangement among the races to the one made in the period 1956–1957.

The riots and their aftermath sparked off a furious debate within UMNO about the future of the country's political system. It was really a fight for the soul of the party. One group called for the creation of a Malay government. UMNO could go it alone and would be more effective in looking after Malay interests if it did not make compromises with other political organizations such as the MCA. This group consisted of old-line extremists such as Tan Sri Ja'afar Albar, who led the fight to arrest Lee Kuan Yew in 1965, and a new group of younger members led by Dr. Mahathir Mohamad of Kedah and Musa Hitam of Johor.

On the other side were moderates led by Tun Abdul Razak, who realized that more had to be done in cooperation with the other races. Their attitude reflected the words of the Tunku: "What are we to do? Throw the Chinese and Indians into the sea?" In the end, the moderates won the day. Mahathir was expelled from UMNO and Musa Hitam fired as assistant minister and sent on "study leave" to Britain, too far away to impact on local politics. A new political and economic arrangement emerged to replace the 1957 "deal." It was still favorable to the Malays, but the basic premise of a multiracial and multicultural country was preserved. The commitment to multiracialism was sincere, but security forces were increased in case racial confrontations recurred. Over the next decade, the size of the military more than doubled and its racial composition changed. In 1969, about 60 percent of the military was Malay; by 1981, this increased to about 80 percent. Law and order were to rest in the hands of the Malays.

New Economic Policy

To grasp the political and economic future that emerged from two years of emergency rule, what UMNO saw as the cause of the riots must be understood. The Malay leaders felt that the old system had unraveled for two basic reasons. One was the inability of the government to redress the economic imbalance among the races. Despite the money, attention, and effort channeled to Malay problems, Malays were still second class citizens economically, and until that problem was solved, there could never be true racial coexistence in the country. A second reason was the Chinese challenge to Malay rule. This had been the problem posed by Lee Kuan Yew and was continued by Chinese opposition leaders. Until the Chinese accepted the special position of the Malays unreservedly and until there was an uplift in the Malays' position economically, there would be no real racial peace in the country.

The Malay political leadership did not preclude the Chinese and Indians from maintaining their cultural identities. It did not preclude Chinese and Indian political participation, and it did not preclude the immigrants from prospering, but all these had to take place in the context of Malay goals.

The riots and the subsequent emergency rule brought about a new approach to the economic inequalities in the country. Prior to 1969, most of the government's efforts to improve the lot of the Malay had been within a rural context. During this period, the government had avoided any large-scale meddling in the export, retail, commercial, and manufacturing sectors of the economy, which were dominated by foreign and Chinese interests. After the riots, a New Economic Policy (NEP) was announced. The two primary goals of the NEP were to eliminate poverty and to integrate the economy. The implementation of these goals called for a radical restructuring of the Malaysian economy.

The goals of the ensuing Second Malaysia Plan (1971–1975) were as follows:

"The Plan incorporates a two-pronged New Economic Policy for development. The first prong is to reduce and eventually eradicate poverty by raising income levels and increasing employment opportunities for all Malaysians, irrespective of race. The second prong aims at accelerating the process of restructuring Malaysian society to correct economic imbalance, so as to reduce and eventually eliminate the identification of race with economic function. This process involves the modernization of rural life, a rapid and balanced growth of urban activities and the creation of a Malay commercial and industrial community in all categories and at all levels of operation, so that Malays and other indigenous people will become full partners in all respects of the economic life of the nation."

Tun Abdul Razak and his advisors had determined that there could never be national unity as long as the economy was organized along its traditional racial lines. As long as economic roles were determined by race, they felt the Malays would always play a secondary role. Thus, what the UMNO leadership meant by integrating the economy was a massive government effort to bring the Malays into the modern urban economy. The specific goals of the program were that by 1990 the occupations of Malaysians would reflect the racial composition of the country, and by the same year, 30 percent of the country's corporate share capital would be owned by the Bumiputera.

To move a traditional, rural people into the modern, urban economy in the numbers the government suggested was truly an ambitious goal. Apart from the mind-boggling logistics of this kind of affirmative action program, instilling in rural Malays the competitive values needed to survive in a world of commerce and industry would be a formidable task.

It should be noted that the government planned to make the percentages of occupations in the modern economy reflect the percentages of the races, but the reverse was not true for the agricultural sector — it would remain Malay. The connection between the Malays and the land was a strong symbol in Malaysia. The Bumiputera was the son of the soil, and his ownership of much of the land and control of food production went to the heart of who he was and whose country it was.

Malay Business Ventures

The primary vehicle for bringing the Malays into the modern economy was the creation of government corporations whose job it was to form new business ventures and offer these opportunities to the Malays. The National Corporation (PERNAS), set up in 1969, and other organizations offered start-up capital for all types of new companies. In transportation, insurance, finance, and manufacturing, the goal was to get these businesses going and then turn them over to Malay owners.

The government moved into ventures such as steel, shipping, and automobile industries with the same goal in mind — that once they were on their feet, the government could guarantee Malay direction and participation. An Urban Development Authority (UDA) was established in 1971 to provide an outlet for Malay participation in retail activities. Its goal was to build and buy shops and offices in predominantly Chinese areas in order to provide inexpensive entry for Malay small businessmen. MARA and Bank Bumiputera expanded their operations to include more urban, sophisticated facilities.

The goal of Malay ownership of a significant portion of the nation's corporations was limited by the lack of capital in the community. The National Equity Corporation (PNB) and National Trust Fund (ASN) were set up in 1978 and 1981, respectively, together with other large investment companies, to purchase ownership in the name of the Malay community.

Shares in these ventures were limited to Malays. The PNB and ASN transformed the nature of foreign ownership of parts of the Malaysian economy by buying out the British companies that controlled the mining and plantation sectors — companies such as Dunlop, Sime Darby, Guthries, Harrisons and Crossfields, and the London Tin Company. By buying at fair market value, the Malaysians did not scare off other investors.

In order to find the educated Malays who were needed to integrate the professions, entry requirements were eased and more places reserved for Malays in the country's universities and technical colleges. All institutions of higher learning were required to conduct most of their instruction in Malay, making it easier for Malays to succeed as well as fulfilling national language goals. By 1977, only 25 percent of the places in higher education were occupied by non-Malays. Quotas were placed on employment in new private business ventures to guarantee that Malays would be included at every level, from the factory floor to management positions. Companies that practiced aggressive Malay hiring were given preference for government contracts, licenses, and assistance. Companies were required to provide for Malay ownership participation, with quotas placed on percentages of Bumiputera share holdings. These new guidelines were placed on foreign as well as local investors.

There was irony in the quotas for institutions of higher learning, something the government would come to recognize in the 1980s and 1990s. While Malays were entering in larger numbers and studying in Malay, because of the quotas Chinese and Indian parents were forced to send their children abroad, mainly to the United States, Australia, and Britain. This meant that the non-Malays were receiving their higher education at more established schools and in English. As the economy grew and more foreign investment poured in, the Chinese were well-placed to take advantage of the globalization of Malaysia's economy.

These policies had far-reaching consequences. If these new laws were implemented at the expense of the other races, there was the potential for serious racial disorder and animosity. The only way this could be avoided was with sufficient economic growth so that Malay participation came about as a result of an ever-expanding economy.

In the 1970 to 1990 period, the Malaysian economy grew at a dramatic rate. This was aided in part by the injection of large-scale foreign investment, which came to take advantage of the relatively inexpensive, well-educated workforce and investor-friendly policies. The new government created industries, and foreign companies provided new "Malay" jobs without taking employment from the other racial groups, especially from the working class Chinese. The unemployment rate of the Chinese actually dropped during this period.

The discovery of new deposits of oil and gas along the eastern coast of the peninsula and offshore Sarawak also helped make economic growth possible. By 1980, Malaysia was exporting some $3.2 billion worth of petroleum products, 25 percent more than its rubber exports. These products provided a new sector of the economy for Malay participation through the National Oil Company (PETRONAS).

After Mahathir Mohamad became prime minister in 1981, there was a shift in the emphasis of government policy. Before, large-scale Malay participation in the corporate sector had been through government-owned businesses. Mahathir wanted to create a powerful group of capitalists in the private sector in the belief that Malay entrepreneurs would help the Malay community as a whole. As long as the state ran the business concerns, it was not creating businessmen but rather bureaucrats who ran businesses, hardly a way to groom a class of Malays who could compete with the non-Malay communities. To this end, three methods were used. One was the privatization of state-run corporations. Government-owned companies, such as the Malaysian International Shipping Corporation, Edaran Otomobil Nasional, Cement Industries of Malaysia, and Syarikat Telecom Malaysia, were sold to Malay businessmen. Second, infrastructure projects, such as new highways, water supply, sewerage systems, and mass transit projects, were turned over to Malay interests in the private sector. And third, licenses, such as those for new television stations, telecommunication services, and power, were granted to the private sector.

Efforts to create greater Malay participation in the private business sector met with mixed results. There is no doubt that Malays occupy a much more important position in private business than they did twenty years ago. Some of the giants of the corporate world in Malaysia today are Malays who seized the opportunities that came their way and built highly successful business conglomerates.

Economic inefficiency was one downside. Projects, contracts, and licenses were often dispensed without competitive bidding. This meant that political connections became important in obtaining the business. Often, Malay companies would obtain a government contract, then subcontract it out to non-Malays or foreign concerns. In 1987, a Malay company with a paid up capital of only RM2 won the contract to build a highway interchange in Kuala Lumpur and then paid a Japanese company to build it. The Malay company made a profit because it won the contract, not because it was a competitive builder. In 1993, another well-connected company won a 6 billion-ringgit sewerage contract that was then built by a British company. In neither case did the Malay company have any expertise in building the facilities. Both were what economists Jomo and Gomez call "political capitalists."

There were other areas of inefficiency. Malay ventures sometimes failed due to inexperience and lack of business knowledge. Inefficiency was also evident in Chinese and foreign efforts to skirt the spirit of the law. Overemployment resulted when Malays were hired for the sole purpose of meeting quotas. Profits were reduced by a bloated workforce that met government rather than market requirements. "Ali Baba" arrangements proliferated. These were business arrangements in which Malays (Ali) were given ownership and management positions in Chinese (Baba) ventures but were participants in name only. The Malays were paid, and the Chinese ran the companies.

Within the Malay community, there is a degree of dissatisfaction with this new business elite. Many younger Malays see the creation of a glass ceiling to their economic aspirations. They believe their paths to economic advancement are blocked by older Malays with longer or better political connections. It is a phenomenon not unlike the one faced by the Malay businessmen who supported Mahathir in his rise to power. This group saw their future held back by the traditional Malay aristocracy. Some in the present generation see the 1980s businessmen, who took advantage of Mahathir's policies of privatization and thus entrenched their positions of economic and political power, as a barrier to their advancement.

Another problem posed by these types of interventionist policies is that their success is highly dependent on continued economic growth. In the recession of the mid-1980s, racial tensions surfaced. The shrinking economic pie meant that there were racial economic winners and losers, due to affirmative action. Non-Malays and their political leaders, both within the ruling coalition and in the opposition, vocally expressed their dissatisfaction with the perceived unfairness of the system. In a crackdown on dissidence, scores of politicians were arrested under the ISA, accused of stirring up racial animosities. On the other hand, divisions appeared within UMNO itself. As government revenue shrank and economic activity slowed, there was greater competition among Malays for government-provided contracts and projects. This was one of the reasons for the split within UMNO and brought about a challenge to Mahathir's leadership in 1987.

As long as the government plays such an active role in the private commercial and industrial sectors of the economy, charges of political favoritism are open to credence. Also, until the Malays can truly compete on their own efforts and qualifications, the potential for racial discontent exists.

Political Change

A new political reality emerged from the difficulties of 1969 and emergency rule. A national ideology, which would frame the ground rules for the Malaysian political system, was proclaimed. Called *rukunegara*, which roughly translates as "the basic principles of the nation," it contained five basic principles that all were expected to accept:

- Belief in God
- Loyalty to King and Country
- Upholding the Constitution
- Rule of Law
- Good Behavior and Morality

When parliament reconvened in 1971 to end emergency rule, these principles were incorporated into legislation. The Sedition Act of 1948 was amended to make it illegal to bring up what were termed "sensitive issues." This meant that questions of the primacy of the Malay language, the Malay royalty, and the special position of the Malays were taken out of the political arena. Any challenge to these issues was treason. An unspoken assumption was that the Malays had to accept the participation of the non-Malays in the political life of the country, and this too was to be a "sensitive issue."

Out of the difficulties emerged a new political party system. Many of the leaders of the 1950s and 1960s were discredited, and a new political leadership took charge. Under the guidance of Tun Abdul Razak, a new elite gained power in UMNO. The old coalition of "court and kampung" based on deference and respect for traditional leaders soon disappeared. Government programs to uplift the position of the Malays produced a generation of professionals and civil servants whose leadership was based on patronage and access to the new economic system.

Tun Razak realized that the ruling coalition had to be broadened in the wake of the 1969 riots. The MCA and MIC no longer represented their respective communities. They were only two of many parties in the immigrant community. The Alliance Party was to be replaced with a new coalition, Barisan Nasional (National Front), which would be more representative of Malaysia's political realities. Gerakan, which had wide non-Malay support especially in Penang and Selangor, was brought into the ruling coalition, as was the PPP with its strong base in Perak. These two parties, along with the MCA and MIC, expanded the ruling party's influence among the non-Malays in the peninsula. For a brief period, PAS was also brought into the ruling coalition, creating a government of true national unity.

Borneo Politics

Politics in the Borneo states were somewhat more complicated than those in the peninsula. In Sabah and Sarawak, the ethnic communities were fragmented, and in neither state did any one community form a majority of the population. Sarawak was 32 percent Chinese, 31 percent Iban, 23 percent Malay/Melanau, and 8 percent Bidayuh. Sabah was 32 percent Kadazan-Dusun, 30 percent Muslim Bumiputera, and 23 percent Chinese. There was a religious dimension as well because Christian missionaries had been successful in both states, and the indigenous people were separated along Muslim and Christian lines. In Sabah, the Kadazan-Dusuns were predominantly Christian, and in Sarawak, there was heavy Christian representation among the Ibans and Bidayuhs. What this meant was that the chief ministers in these states would come from an ethnic and religious minority. It also meant that the Chinese would provide the swing vote in determining who would control the state government.

The Borneo states lagged behind the peninsula in terms of education, infrastructure, and income levels. This gave the federal government considerable leverage over state politics since aid from Kuala Lumpur was essential to economic development of the two states. Links between the Muslim-dominated central government in the peninsula and the Muslim Bumiputera politicians in Sabah and Sarawak added another dimension to state politics. The political situation in East Malaysia was influenced by what some have called "timber politics." Both Sabah and Sarawak had vast areas of untapped rain forest. The state governments' control of logging concessions offered those in power great resources to reward influential backers or punish them for their lack of support.

Tun Razak saw the need to bring political parties in Borneo into a more formal national coalition. National unity after the May 13 incident required a tightening of the ties between East and West Malaysia. Part of the motivation for greater unity came from the nature of the original Malaysia agreement. Although the Borneo states contained less than a fifth of the total population, they controlled over a quarter of the seats in parliament. Barisan Nasional needed two-thirds of those seats in order to amend the constitution, and this required the active support of the political parties in Borneo. Although parties in Sabah and Sarawak opposed one another at the state level, they often sat together at the federal level as members of the ruling coalition. Another reason for bringing Borneo into the peninsular political arena was for more control over it. The eastern states had a greater degree of autonomy and had a separate historical development, which tended to encourage independent politicians and even talk of secession.

Sabah

At the time of the formation of Barisan Nasional, the United Sabah National Party (USNO) was brought into the coalition. Led by Chief Minister

Mustapha Harun, USNO was dominated by Muslim Bumiputeras. Mustapha ruled the state in an alliance with the Sabah Chinese Association. By most accounts, Mustapha's rule in Sabah was both authoritarian and corrupt but was tolerated by the central government. This tolerance had its limits, though, and by the mid-1970s, his relations with Kuala Lumpur had soured considerably. Mustapha's support for the Muslim rebellion in the southern Philippines and reports that he was plotting secession led the federal government to encourage an alternative leadership in the state. Donald Stephens, who became Tun Mohammad Fuad, joined forces with Datuk Harris Salleh to form a new intercommunal party known as Berjaya (Sabah People's Union). Berjaya swept into power in the 1976 state election. For a while, both USNO and Berjaya were members of Barisan Nasional, but USNO was expelled in 1984 when it opposed the federal takeover of Labuan.

Mohammad Fuad was killed in an air crash just two months after taking office, and Harris Salleh became the chief minister. Berjaya had been brought to power by those who wanted reform and intercommunal power sharing. This was not to be. The mainly Christian Kadazan-Dusuns and the Chinese in the party became disillusioned with what they saw as pro-Muslim policies and widespread corruption. Joseph Pairin Kitingan, a leading Kadazan-Dusun politician, left Berjaya and, with significant Chinese support, formed Parti Bersatu Sabah (PBS, or Sabah United Party) in 1985. In the 1985 and 1986 elections, PBS took control of the state government. In 1986, PBS joined Barisan Nasional, but in 1990, it left Barisan Nasional and joined the opposition at the federal level.

The withdrawal of PBS from Barisan Nasional brought about a concerted effort by Barisan Nasional to regain political control of the state. UMNO established a branch in Sabah to provide leadership for the Muslim Bumiputera community. UMNO's considerable resources had an immediate impact on the political dynamics of the state. In the run-up to the 1994 state election, UMNO promised huge amounts of federal developmental aid (the sum total of the programs amounted to an estimated one billion ringgit) and a commitment to raise per capita income levels from RM3,500 to RM10,000 in five years. It was made clear that this largesse was dependent on Barisan Nasional wresting control of the state from PBS.

Funds were promised to the Chinese community to upgrade and expand Chinese-language education. This was added to the incentives many Chinese businessmen would receive from their participation in the proposed infrastructure projects. Barisan Nasional's efforts paid off when Yong Tock Lee led a number of the Chinese leaders out of PBS and established a new party, the Sabah Progressive Party (SAPP). This party was offered quick admission into Barisan Nasional.

At the same time, life was made difficult for PBS. Existing aid was cut back to weaken PBS's ability to provide for economic progress. From 1991 to 1994, the state received some of the lowest levels of per capita developmental aid, although it was one of the most backward economically. Pairin was charged and convicted of corruption, while his brother, Jeffrey, was arrested under the ISA for plotting secession. Many PBS leaders began to fear they might be next.

PBS won a narrow victory in the state election of 1994 by playing on ethnic loyalties and mistrust of the central government in Kuala Lumpur, but its days were numbered. UMNO had won nineteen of the forty-eight seats in the assembly, and SAPP had secured three. In the weeks after the election, there was a large defection from PBS. Three new parties were established, and all were admitted into Barisan Nasional. Adding insult to injury, Pairin's brother, who had been released from detention, also left PBS and joined Barisan Nasional. When the smoke cleared, Barisan Nasional ruled the state, and PBS was left with seven seats in the assembly.

Sarawak

After the 1969 political realignment in Malaysia, the government in Sarawak was led by Tun Abdul Rahman Yakub, the head of Parti Bumiputera (PB). This party represented the Malay/Melanau community and maintained power in part due to support from Kuala Lumpur. There was significant opposition in the state from SUPP, which was mainly Chinese with some Iban support, and the Sarawak National Party (SNAP), which was mainly Iban with some Chinese participation. The central government was able to exert enough pressure on PB and SUPP to form a coalition at the state level, which was basically a prototype of Barisan Nasional at the national level. In 1973, PB merged with a smaller non-

Muslim indigenous party, Pesaka, to form Parti Pesaka Bumiputera Bersatu (PBB). In 1976, SNAP was brought into the coalition, and the group of parties — PBB, SUPP, and SNAP — became popularly known as Barisan Tiga, which has remained in power to this day. In 1981, Abdul Taib Mahmud, who had represented PBB at the federal level, took over as chief minister from his uncle, Abdul Rahman Yakub.

In 1983, there was a split in SNAP when Leo Moggie led a group of younger Ibans out of the party to form Parti Bangsa Dayak Sarawak (PBDS). The Iban community felt that the ruling coalition was insensitive to the needs of the non-Muslim Bumiputeras. PBDS would be part of Barisan Nasional at the national level but in opposition at the state level.

The formation of PBDS reflected a view in the Iban community that the needs of the non-Muslim indigenous people were being neglected by Barisan Tiga. In their eyes, the bulk of the government's developmental programs were directed at the towns and coastal areas, where the Muslim Bumiputeras and the Chinese were best placed to benefit from them. Poverty levels among the Ibans and other interior ethnic groups were much higher than the state average. This was also reflected in lower literacy rates among the Ibans. PBDS felt a united "Dayak" community could do better outside the Barisan Nasional coalition. In state elections, PBDS polled well in the Iban community but could not crack Barisan Tiga's hold on power. In 1994, PBDS accepted the inevitable and returned to the Barisan Nasional fold.

Barisan Nasional

The first election contested by Barisan Nasional in 1974 was a smashing success. The party polled over 60 percent of the vote and won a two-thirds majority in the federal parliament. In the peninsula, it won 104 of the 114 possible seats. At the state level, it formed the governments in all the peninsular states with a two-thirds majority. In the election, the DAP emerged as the primary non-Malay opposition party, although its representation in parliament dropped from thirteen in 1969 to nine in 1974. It was a government of national unity, and Barisan Nasional would not have such results for another twenty years. Most of all, the election represented hope for the future of interracial cooperation within the Malaysian context.

Tun Abdul Razak played a key role in helping Malaysia recover from the trauma of the 1969 riots. He understood the frustrations of the newly emerging generation of Malays who wanted more economic opportunities for their race. By including younger voices from outside UMNO's traditional pool of leadership in the decision making process, Razak was able to act as a moderating influence on their views and actions. Over twenty years of experience in Malaysian politics had taught him valuable lessons in finding solutions based on compromise that reflected Malaysia's multiracial reality. The ability to reach out to diverse opinions was an important legacy during this emotionally charged era of Malaysian history.

The old guard of UMNO did not give up without a fight. When Tun Razak died in January 1976, the traditional leadership of the party pounced on Razak's protégés. Ghazali Shafie, the minister of home affairs, arrested a number of Razak's advisors, such as Abdul Samad Ismail and Abdullah Ahmad. Acting on the "advice" of Singapore's Special Branch, Ghazali accused these men of sympathizing with the communist cause and detained them under the ISA. It is amazing how quickly these men rehabilitated themselves when their leader, Mahathir, took over as prime minister in 1981. They were once again given responsible positions.

Dato Hussein Onn succeeded Tun Razak as prime minister and led a party that was divided. In many ways, Hussein was viewed as a caretaker leader, while the factions within the party fought for supremacy. As the son of Onn Bin Ja'afar, the original founder of UMNO, Hussein had impeccable credentials in the eyes of the old guard; among the newer leaders, he was acceptable because his poor health would mean a relatively short tenure. Hussein ruled in the moderate conciliatory style that was characteristic of Malaysia's first two prime ministers.

Hussein led Barisan Nasional into the 1978 election, and once again, the party showed its dominance of the Malaysian political process. Barisan Nasional won 131 of the 154 seats contested nationwide and 57 percent of the popular vote. Although this was marginally lower compared to the 1974 election, it was still impressive.

What also emerged from this election was the existence of two enduring opposition parties — PAS and the DAP. The former had entered the ruling coalition after the 1969–1971 emergency but was unable to coexist successfully in the Barisan Nasional fold. The need for compromise and moderation within Barisan Nasional sapped at its strength — an alternative voice in the Malay community. It left Barisan Nasional in 1977. The next year it won five seats in parliament and captured about a third of the total Malay vote. The DAP enhanced its status as the primary non-Malay voice of opposition in 1978 when it increased its representation in parliament to sixteen seats, polling close to half of the total non-Malay vote. In the past, opposition parties had risen and fallen — Socialist Front, Labor Front, Independence of Malaya Party, and PPP — but it appeared that these two were here to stay. Despite a number of stays in His Majesty's prison under the ISA, these leaders had come to play key roles in the evolution of Malaysian democracy.

The existence of two well-organized opposition parties with solid bases of support forced moderation and cooperation on the parties within Barisan Nasional. If regular elections were held, no amount of fiddling of electoral boundaries could change the challenge from the left — the DAP — and the right — PAS — when the party moved too far in any direction. If Barisan Nasional moved to allay the extreme voices in the Malay community, the DAP attacked its base among non-Malays, and if Barisan Nasional moved too far to accommodate non-Malay demands, PAS was waiting in the wings to grab the Malay vote. Neither party could ever challenge Barisan Nasional's control of the government individually, and the two parties could never cooperate to bring down Barisan Nasional. Their continued presence, however, acted as a check on Barisan Nasional, forcing the components within it to find common ground and take a moderate course.

The presence of PAS and the DAP is especially felt in Barisan Nasional's need to maintain a two-thirds majority in parliament. This majority gives the ruling party the ability to amend the constitution at will, and as long as this condition exists, parliament and the party controlling it have few checks on their power. Loss of this power would change the political dynamics of the country. For example, if the constitution were to become more of a set document and not open to constant tinkering, interpreting its meaning would move from parliament to the courts. Judicial review would take on greater importance, and the ruling party could no longer change the constitution to meet the political demands of the day.

Today, the presence of a competitive party system forces Barisan Nasional to be responsive to the needs and aspirations of Malaysia's multiracial electorate. This does not mean there is liberal democracy in the Western sense because there are serious limitations placed on the ability of the opposition to compete, while there are few checks and balances on the ruling party.

The media generally reflects the views of the ruling coalition. To the casual observer, a Malaysian newsstand may indicate a competitive newspaper industry with a variety of publications in the three major languages. If the observer looked close enough, she or he would discover that the printed media is owned by the parties within the ruling coalition or interests closely aligned to them. For example, the largest English, Malay, and Chinese newspapers in the country are owned by the Fleet Group, an investment arm of UMNO. The *Star*, the second largest English-language newspaper, is owned by business interests aligned with the MCA, and the Tamil press is controlled by supporters of the MIC. Criticism of the government by the printed media is a rare phenomenon. Every periodical must obtain a license yearly from the government to publish, and it will be revoked if the periodical "aggravates national sensitivities" or "fails to serve the national interests." At one time, the publication of the DAP, the *Rocket*, was circulated to the general public. Now, it can only be sold to registered party members. Censorship even goes so far as to include being on the wrong side of a conflict within the ruling coalition. For example, the *Star* was shut down for a while in 1987 because of a column written by the Tunku that was critical of Mahathir and his supporters.

There is regulation of the broadcast media as well. Radio and television speak for the government and spend a considerable amount of time covering the achievements of Barisan Nasional. The lead news stories on Malaysian television are always what Prime Minister Mahathir did and said that day. There is an independent station, TV3, but it is owned by the Fleet Group and thus also toes the party line.

The ISA and the Sedition Act further enhance the powers of the government to define the parameters of political debate in Malaysia. This was especially true in the aftermath of the 1969 riots and the decade or so following the disorders. Between 1960 and 1981, over three thousand people were detained without trial for "acting in any manner prejudicial to the security of Malaysia … or to the maintenance of essential services … or to the economic life thereof." Lim Kit Siang, the leader of the DAP, has seen the inside of Malaysia's jails three times under this law, as have other members of his party. The use of these laws has also extended to leaders of Muslim groups who are at odds with what the government deems acceptable Islamic doctrine and activities; to trade union leaders, such as the head of a union who led a strike against Malaysian Airlines; and even to members of the ruling coalition, such as in 1987 when UMNO and MCA activists were detained for stirring up racial sensitivities.

The first four decades of UMNO's existence point out an important dimension of Malaysian democracy — its diverse and participatory nature. Many of the safeguards of individual freedom that exist in the Western model of democracy are weak in Malaysia, but the nature of UMNO and the ruling coalition places checks on the political leaders and offers opportunities for Malay citizens to be part of a democratic dialogue. UMNO, like the other component parties of Barisan Nasional, is a grassroots party. It has a party membership of over two million people organized at the branch, division, state, and national levels. Delegates sent by grassroots branches have an important say in determining party leaders and the general direction of the party. The annual UMNO general assembly is not unlike American political party conventions. There are spirited and competitive contests for party leadership positions. Party policy is often debated openly and frankly. Like any party in a democracy, the amount of division and debate depends on the ability of the leadership to show direction and forge compromise. UMNO is not a top-down party like the PAP. It fosters the Malay citizen's meaningful participation in the process of governing.

Mahathir in Power

In the 1970s and 1980s, winds of change blew through UMNO, and no one represented this more than the man who took over after Dato Hussein Onn's resignation in 1981 — Dr. Mahathir Mohamad.

Mahathir was the first Malaysian prime minister to come from outside the traditional aristocratic leadership of the country. Although he had been in UMNO since 1946, and he was fifty-six when he took over, he was in tune with the younger generation of up and coming Malays. He was a commoner from Kedah, and his medical qualifications were from the University of Malaya, not from Britain.

He was in the vanguard of a group in UMNO that was fiercely critical of the style and methods of the generation that had led UMNO in its first thirty-five years. Mahathir's criticism of the Tunku after the May 1969 incident had resulted in his expulsion from the party. His tone and demeanor had offended the traditional power elite of the party, and his book, *The Malay Dilemma*, was banned at around the same time. The book, in many ways his manifesto, was a scathing attack on the British colonial legacy, Malay values, and the inability of the Malay leadership to do more for its people. To the older generation, Mahathir's confrontational style and impatience was almost "unMalay."

Many underestimated Mahathir. After an appropriate time in the political wilderness, Tun Abdul Razak brought Mahathir back into the fold and made him minister of education. From there his rise was meteoric. Within six years, he became prime minister.

Mahathir's rise was largely due to his ability to articulate the desires of a generation of Malays who had become much more assertive after the May 1969 events, as well as due to the success of the NEP. His outspoken manner reflected the view of many that the Malays had to discard the self-effacing, non-confrontational values that held them back in the modern world. Western leaders, the royalty in Malaysia, or Malay traditionalists were all fair game if they were at odds with Mahathir's world view. His "we're not going to take it anymore" attitude went down well with many Malays.

Much of the change in the Malay political community that brought Mahathir to power can be traced to the incredible growth of the government in the 1970s and 1980s as a result of the NEP. The size and scope of the programs introduced to benefit the Malay community had enlarged the government to the point where, by the mid-1980s, about a third of Malaysia's national income was generated by government spending.

Attempts to bring the Malays into the modern sector of the economy had virtually created a new class of Malaysians, a Malay middle class, many of whom were dependent on government funds and actions to secure their places in the economy. Some had prospered by the explosion of civil service jobs that came with all the new agencies and programs. Others were part of a growing Malay business community whose success was often tied to government funding and racial preference. What they had in common was that most had risen from humble rural backgrounds and did not belong to the traditional Malay economic and political elite.

Royal Power

A classic example of the political and economic changes Mahathir represented was his attempt to reduce the power and influence of Malay royalty. The sultans were powerful racial and political symbols in Malaysia. British indirect rule had preserved the respect and reverence accorded them by rural Malays. In the run-up to independence and the first couple of decades after, the sultans had been allies of UMNO, and their families had great influence within the party. They were the symbols of Malay rule in the face of an assertive immigrant population.

By the 1980s, Malay royalty began to lose the unquestioned loyalty of its subjects. Politically, in the eyes of the younger generation of UMNO leaders, royalty was seen as more of a hindrance than an ally. The ability of the sultans and the king to hold up legislation was a significant bargaining tool in thwarting or modifying the will of parliament and the state legislatures. On several occasions, the sultans angered UMNO by meddling in the appointment of elected officials or by supporting the opposition. They seemed to be anachronistic, feudal symbols in a modernizing world. As Malay numbers grew as a percentage of the overall population, the need for symbols decreased conversely. The mobility of the Malays from kampungs to cities and from state to state also weakened the ties between the palace and the people. Political loyalties were more to a party and an active government than to royalty.

Some saw the royal families as impediments to economic advancement. In the first decade after independence, much of the Malay business activity was controlled by members of the traditional aristocracy. The sons and daughters of royalty parlayed their race and political connections into choice business deals. A royal title such as tunku on the board of directors and a word in the right ear opened doors and facilitated government action. As a new class of businessmen from common backgrounds arose, the aristocracy blocked its access with its political connections and status. This group was more than happy to see the political power of royalty curtailed.

Mahathir made his first move in the period 1983–1984. He proposed a constitutional amendment that would end the power of the king and sultans to delay legislation or declare a state of emergency. Some objected to this because the power would then be transferred to the prime minister. For others, the move was too soon. Too many Malays still had close ties to and affection for their sultans. The Malays were too conservative at this time and could not understand royalty without power. Nothing was done to alter the powers of the sultans at the state level, but Mahathir did manage to end the king's right to hold up the legislative process.

At the end of the 1980s, the leadership of UMNO made a further assault on the power of royalty. A decade of change in the Malay community, coupled with a better plan of attack, brought about more success. This time the leadership of UMNO was prepared. In a well-orchestrated campaign in the early 1990s, politicians and the media began saying publicly what had previously only been mentioned in private — that the royal families abused their positions. Stories began to appear in the press of royal Christmas parties where the liquor flowed freely and of royal princes who committed crimes and were not punished. Tales of expensive cars and lavish lifestyles at public expense began to chip away at the credibility of the royal families. Government privileges were withdrawn from the sultans and legislation proposed to end their legal immunity.

The controversy over the role and powers of the sultans was and is confusing for the Malays. In the constitution, the sultans are identified as the protectors of the Malay special position. But how can they protect without any power? In theory, the sultans are sovereigns of their states, but what happens to the concept when royalty can be dragged into court like any other citizen? One suspects that the bottom line for the politicians who wanted change was that they believed UMNO to be the sole protector of the Malay special position, thus solidifying their political control of the Malay community. No other modern country has anything resembling this Malaysian system of nine royal families, and their somewhat awkward role is just another of the dilemmas facing Malaysia as it deals with the realities of economic growth and change.

There is an interesting role reversal that took place in battles over the power of royalty. The things that Mahathir and UMNO leaders were saying would have been considered treason if said by an opposition politician, especially if he was non-Malay. The rights and privileges of the sultans were one of the "sensitive issues" covered by the Sedition Act of 1971. On the other hand, there were non-Malay leaders who actually defended the powers of Malay royalty as necessary checks on the power of the elected executive.

The attack on royal privilege was only part of Mahathir's political agenda — the strengthening of central executive power in the hands of Barisan Nasional and the prime minister. In the late 1980s, he moved to clip the wings of the relatively independent judiciary. Mahathir felt that the judiciary was not meant to interpret the laws, merely to enforce them. Determining whether government actions and legislation were constitutional lay with parliament, not the courts. In parliament in 1987, Mahathir said that "if judicial review persists, the government is no longer the executive. Another group has taken over its role."

In 1986 and 1987, a series of court cases that went against the government and a crisis in the ruling party brought matters to a head. In 1986, the government revoked the work permits of two American journalists. On appeal, the supreme court overruled the government because the journalists had not been allowed to defend their cases, a violation of natural justice. In a second case, a supreme court justice overturned the internment under the ISA of an opposition politician, the DAP's Karpal Singh. In yet another case, the high court agreed to an injunction against the awarding of a contract to an UMNO-related company in an action brought by opposition politicians. These three cases served to harden Mahathir's view that the judiciary was thwarting the will of the executive.

A battle for the leadership of UMNO further drew the courts and the politicians into conflict. In April 1987, Tengku Razaleigh Hamzah, supported by Datuk Musa Hitam, challenged Mahathir for the presidency of UMNO, which in effect meant challenging him for the position of prime minister. In a hard-fought struggle, Mahathir barely held on. At the party's national conference, the vote went 761 to 718 in his favor. The fight then went to the courts. Razaleigh's faction sued, claiming that illegal party branches had voted. As a result, the court ruled that UMNO itself was an illegal organization. Mahathir's opponents appealed to the courts to call for new party elections without the illegal branches. The lord president of the supreme court, Tun Abas Salleh, scheduled the appeal to be heard by all nine supreme court judges, a unique occurrence in Malaysia. Mahathir's political fate was in the hands of the very men he had been criticizing. He struck back by prevailing on the king to suspend Salleh and to set up a tribunal to try him for misconduct. Salleh appealed to the supreme court on the grounds that the tribunal itself was illegal, and five members of the court issued a stay. All five were then suspended and a tribunal set up to investigate them. In the end, Salleh and two other judges were removed from the court, and the election results remained in Mahathir's favor. A strong message had been sent as to how independent the Malaysian judiciary could be.

Impact of the New Economic Policy

The New Economic Policy that emerged after the racial confrontations of 1969 and 1970 looked forward to the year 1990 and was meant to radically change Malaysian society and economy. There is no doubt that the Malaysia that emerged in the 1990s is very much different from the one that had produced the riots of 1969, but whether the economic base is solid enough for racial and national unity remains to be seen.

Huge foreign investments and massive government intervention in the 1970s and 1980s created a country that was recognized as one of Asia's emerging "tiger" economies. Malaysia changed fundamentally from an economy that reflected its colonial role as an exporter of raw materials and an importer of manufactured goods to one that was a much more diversified Newly Industrializing Country (NIC). The days of mentioning Malaysia and immediately thinking of rubber and tin were long gone.

The economy registered impressive growth. Between 1970 and 1990, the average growth of the Malaysian economy was close to 7 percent a year; in the 1990s, it increased to over 8 percent. While the economy as a whole grew by leaps and bounds, what Malaysia did to earn its national income also changed dramatically. During this period, manufacturing and commerce just about doubled and accounted for close to half of the nation's economy. By 1990, manufacturing alone made up 27 percent of the Malaysian economy, and even more indicative of the change, it made up

61 percent of the nation's exports. Even with the discovery of new deposits of oil, Malaysia was no longer dependent on the export of raw materials; it was more dependent on worldwide demand for computer chips, cellular telephones, and air conditioners than on oil, rubber, and tin.

The ownership of the economy also went through a transformation. By 1990, foreign ownership of corporate assets had fallen from around 60 percent to 25 percent. The Malay share of ownership had risen from some 2 percent to over 20 percent. Another 46 percent was in the hands of the immigrant races, mainly the Chinese. The increase for the Malays was truly impressive, although only two-thirds of Malay ownership was in the hands of individual Malays. The rest was held by government trusts and funds.

An irony here is that after twenty years of affirmative action and pro-Malay government policies, the Chinese had almost doubled their share of ownership. A case can be made that the inclusion of Malays as more active participants in the modern economy had not come at the expense of the immigrant communities. High tides had raised all the boats this time.

The economic growth led to higher incomes for most Malaysians. Household incomes during this twenty-year period increased threefold, and the number of 'people living on incomes below the poverty line dropped from 49 percent in 1970 to 15 percent in 1990. In the 1990s, with increased growth rates, these improved at an even faster rate. By the mid-1990s, unemployment and poverty had basically ceased to be problems of serious consequence to Malaysia's economic planners.

CLASS COMPOSITION OF COMMUNITIES IN MALAYSIA						
	% **Bumiputera**		% **Chinese**		% **Indian**	
	1970	1990	1970	1990	1970	1990
Upper & Middle Class	12.9	27.0	28.6	43.2	23.4	27.3
Working Class	18.0	23.2	41.6	33.8	24.7	34.8
Agriculture	62.3	37.4	21.2	13.5	41.0	23.4
Services	6.8	12.4	8.6	8.5	10.9	14.5

From the above figures, a number of generalizations can be made about the Malaysian population in 1990. There were significant changes in the racial stratification of Malaysia's population. The economic and geographic barriers that existed prior to 1970 had reduced significantly. For the Malays there was an important change from the stereotypical farmer/fisherman to occupations that were much more varied and open to economic opportunity. The new occupations meant that more Malays had moved out of the rural areas into the towns and cities to a point where a majority of them now live in urban areas. This is a far cry from the time of independence in 1957 when 75 percent of the Malay population was rural and involved in traditional pursuits.

These statistics should be qualified because farming is still very much a Malay occupation in most parts of Malaysia. In Kelantan, Trengganu, Kedah, and Perlis, the Malays are still primarily agricultural and rural and have a lower income than those in the rest of the country.

The Indian community also experienced changes. The agricultural pursuits they had followed were on rubber plantations, and the country's economic growth offered them opportunities outside their insular world. The view that the Indians were a race of rubber tappers and laborers changed somewhat during these two decades.

The Chinese too benefited from the growth of the modern sector of the Malaysian economy. As urban dwellers, they were already well-placed to take advantage of the growth. Their share of ownership of the economy increased. The preceding table shows a rise in the middle class and a reduction in the numbers of the working class. However, one-third of the Chinese population still draw relatively low wages compared to the rest in the community.

The implications of the growth of the Malay and Indian working class and the retention of a large group of Chinese workers are that all Malaysians are dependent on high economic growth. Relations among these three groups are highly vulnerable to an economic downturn, which will force them into competition for jobs in the industrial sector.

Social Changes

The economic transformation of Malaysia over the last quarter of the twentieth century has been phenomenal, especially for the Malays. As income levels rose and Malays became more urban and less involved in agriculture, the changes brought into question some of the underlying assumptions of Malaysian life. Chief among them is what it means to be a Malay.

A study of Malaysian history shows that the Malays are a mixture of people from all over the archipelago — Bugis, Achehnese, Minangkabau, Javanese, and others. When these people come together, what is it that gives them a common identity, both legally and socially, as Malay? A definition used by the government of Malaysia in the past is that a person is Malay if he or she habitually speaks Malay, is a Muslim, is born in the country, and follows Malay custom. Anyone can speak Malay and become a Muslim, thus the most important trait is to act like a Malay.

The problem for the Malays today is that the Malay value system and behavioral expectations have deep roots in the kampung and rural life. The move from the village to the city is a familiar one in history, whether it be in the United States, Japan, or Thailand. All who make this transition face serious challenges to their value systems. The problem in Malaysia is that the economy and political system are driven by racial considerations. There are legal and economic benefits that come from being Malay. The importance of racial definition goes far beyond one's view of oneself.

Traditional values bred in the kampung are not particularly conducive to success in the city. In the competitive atmosphere of a capitalist economy, values of cooperation and coexistence become increasingly irrelevant. The ability of the individual to compete becomes more important than relationships with neighbors. Status is determined by wealth and possessions rather than manners or seniority. The house you live in and the car you drive are determinants of the person as an individual and provide a status vastly different from the group-oriented values that determine stature in the kampung.

As the Malays became urbanized, they were exposed to diverse influences. The place they worked and where they lived were no longer homogeneous entities that provided the security of a community with shared values and expectations. The Chinese and Indians were now part of the Malay's community at work and at home. Their children went to the same schools. The urban areas and the modern economy also exposed the Malays to greater foreign influence. Movies, advertising, nightlife, videos, and shopping malls all bombarded the Malay with values geared to the individual. Consumption, self-satisfaction, and material success were all alien to traditional kampung values.

It is interesting that Malay values have been viewed as impediments to Malay economic success. From colonial administrators down to Prime Minister Mahathir himself, the Malays' poor economic position in the country was attributed to their lack of drive, avoidance of confrontation, deference to authority, and their live-and-let-live attitude. In the eyes of most observers, the immigrants outstripped the Malays because their values were more geared to a modern capitalist economy. Thus, for the Malays to prosper outside the traditional village context, they would have to give up many of the traditional Southeast Asian values and adopt new ones, another irony in the argument over Asian versus Western values that takes place today.

The implications of the movement of the Malays from the farm into the modern economy were great for individual Malays and the Malay community as a whole. The change was not evolutionary, as it was in many societies, but government driven and taking place in the space of one generation. What did the individual Malay find to fill the void left by the weakening of some of his core values? A car and a house are poor substitutes for a close-knit community. It was a strange new world for many young Malays moving from poor farms to universities and then to office buildings. To the Malay community as a whole, unity of purpose was key to their political dominance. The fundamental assumption of the Malaysian political system developed by the Alliance and Barisan Nasional was that people voted along communal lines. As people moved into the cities, they found they had much in common with their coworkers and neighbors that transcended race.

For many the answer to the void caused by change was commitment to and interest in Islam, which offered a familiar safe haven. On university campuses, Muslim renewal groups and youth organizations grew at an impressive rate. Organizations such as ABIM (Islamic Youth Movement of Malaysia), led by Anwar Ibrahim in the early 1970s, helped numerous young Malays make the transition into the modern economy by keeping one foot in the traditional. Groups such as these proliferated overseas. As the Malays went to universities in the United States and Britain, Muslim organizations were there to ease the culture shock.

Anyone who has lived in Malaysia for more than twenty years cannot help but notice the outward manifestations of a heightened interest in

Islam. The number of women who cover their heads has risen dramatically. There is increased importance and enforcement of fasting during Ramadan, or Puasa. Dietary regulations and attendance at mosques all point to a greater importance being placed on the faith.

This move is actively encouraged by the government, especially by Mahathir. In the 1990s, a host of government programs and activities has tried to make Islam a greater unifying force in the Malay community. Islamic civilization is taught in schools; the government actively encourages and supports those who wish to go on the Haj. An Islamic university was established. There is strong government support for Muslim youth and cultural groups, as well as government legislation that enforces Islamic laws against alcohol and unacceptable sexual relationships such as *khalwat*. (In essence, *khalwat*, or close proximity, refers to improper physical relationships between members of the opposite sex. Depending on how strictly it is defined, it may include everything from holding hands in public to adultery.)

There are political considerations to this new emphasis. At the back of many a politician's mind is the nagging question of whether the new urban Malays will need UMNO as much as the Malays of the 1960s to 1980s. In the eyes of many UMNO leaders, Islam is the glue that holds the Malay community together when dealing with economic and social changes. The mosque can help make up for the loss of the kampung as part of Malay life and values.

One dimension of this increased fervor for Islam is that it might veer toward fundamentalism and actually form a barrier to future growth and progress. Much of the inspiration for this religious revival comes from the Middle East, some of it forward looking and trying to define Islam as relevant to the twenty-first century. But there are also negative influences from this source, which are dangerous for a multiracial society. Religious fundamentalism can be backward looking, trying to defend or recapture perceived lost values. This is seen in Kelantan today, where PAS holds power in the state legislature. PAS wants to substitute Islamic law for the present Western-based law. It wants society-wide laws prohibiting alcohol consumption, the separation of sexes in public, and the enforcement of dress codes such as those in some Middle Eastern countries.

If the Islamic resurgence in Malaysia went in the PAS direction, foreign investors would find it a much less attractive place to put their money. The Western legal system and the openness of the society and economy have been two of Malaysia's important draws for foreigners. Above all, close to 40 percent of Malaysia's population is not Muslim, so imposing Islamic values and laws on the country as a whole could result in serious racial and social repercussions.

Thus, the government and UMNO walk a fine line. Islam eases social change and maintains Malay unity, but the more extreme religious zealots are a danger to the country. To this end, the government itself has become the arbitrator of what is and is not acceptable Muslim behavior and doctrine. A number of groups, such as Al Arqam, have been branded as deviationists and have been banned and/or their leaders arrested. Al Arqam practiced a version of Islam that appealed to many Malays in the new economic situation. It established urban communes and cooperative business ventures. The leader of the movement claimed he was arrested not for his religious views but because the growth of his movement posed a political threat to UMNO — it clashed with the UMNO view of how the new urban Malays should think and act.

One of Mahathir's strong points is the courage with which he has spoken out against the excesses and narrow-mindedness of fundamentalism and campaigned for Muslims to be more pragmatic, open-minded, and liberal in their understanding of Islam, as well as more tolerant of other faiths. He set up IKIM (Institute for the Propagation of Islamic Understanding), which examines current issues from an Islamic perspective and encourages dialogue with the organizations of other faiths.

Another effect of the social change is a serious drug problem in Malaysia. Islam has helped many deal with the social dislocation that takes place with changes, but for a minority, the answer has been in antisocial behavior, especially in abusing drugs. Estimates of the number of addicts in Malaysia run in the hundreds of thousands. These are big numbers for a country of twenty million people. They are especially striking in the face of the drug laws passed in the country over the last few decades. There are mandatory death penalties for trafficking or possessing relatively small quantities of drugs. Malaysia hangs more people per capita than almost any democracy in the world. Most of these executions are for drug offenses, and yet the problem continues to plague the country.

Further evidence of how social change has affected Malaysia's young is contained in a 1994 government survey of urban youth between the ages of thirteen and twenty-one. In the group interviewed, 71 percent smoked, 40 percent watched pornographic videos, 28 percent gambled, 25 percent drank alcohol, and 14 percent took hard drugs. In the United States, these numbers would not be quite as shocking, but in Malaysia, they are disturbing effects of urbanization.

Impact on the Chinese and Indians

The impact of the NEP on the immigrant communities has not been nearly as negative as feared by many at the time it was formulated. The economic environment for the Chinese and Indians has been quite favorable. Both have growing middle classes and have made impressive improvements in their living standards.

Even with this economic growth, there is discontent among both races. The middle class feels the pinch of the Malay-first quotas in many areas of life. Many have to make great sacrifices to send their children abroad because of quotas in higher education. Professionals and businessmen who deal with the government find themselves in a sea of red tape that goes with the affirmative action aspect of the NEP. Regulations pertaining to Malay ownership participation and Malay employment drive businessmen to distraction in their attempts to prosper and still meet NEP requirements.

In both immigrant communities, there is still a large urban working class that suffers from the competition caused by the Malay exodus from kampungs to cities. The level of working class discontent tends to rise and fall with the general economic health of the country. For example, the high point in the fortunes of the DAP took place in the 1986 election. The mid-1980s saw an economic downturn in Malaysia, and this was translated into twenty-four seats in parliament and over 21 percent of the popular vote for the DAP. Much of the DAP's success in this election reflected the frustration of working class Chinese and Indians facing Malay affirmative action when the economy was contracting.

It is quite striking how culturally unaffected the Chinese and Indians have been by the post-1969 changes. Chinese and Indians speak Malay much more widely than a couple of decades ago, and this reflects the reality of the country's educational and political life. Both communities, though, have managed to maintain their own languages and cultural institutions. In this respect Penang and Singapore offer interesting comparisons and contrasts.

In many ways, Penang and Singapore are alike, although one is a sovereign country and the other a state. They share a similar colonial history in the Straits Settlements, and at the time of independence, both were economically dependent on their ports and ties to Malaya's raw material production. The two cities share the problems of being Chinese islands in a Malay ocean and have been ruled by predominantly Chinese parties.

Their paths diverged in 1965 — Singapore going it alone because of its confrontation with the Malay leadership in Kuala Lumpur, while Penang's political leadership followed a path of accommodation by participating first in the Alliance and then as part of Barisan Nasional. Since 1965, both states have experienced rapid economic growth. In this respect, Singapore's experience has been much more impressive with personal income figures twice that of Penang. The latter, however, has not done badly for itself. It has diversified its economy into manufacturing and tourism and has full employment. In Malaysia, the people of Penang enjoy one of the highest standards of living in the country.

While Penang has not prospered as much as Singapore, it has managed to maintain its Chinese identity much more successfully. Chinese language and culture are alive and well in Penang. Chinese clan, dialect, and occupational organizations continue to play important roles in preserving traditional Chinese culture. The ceremonial core of what constitutes Chinese ideology is still an important part of life in the Penang community, but in Singapore, the physical redevelopment of the island has weakened it. There are academics who claim that if you want to see traditional Chinese culture in a modern context, Penang is the closest to this in the area.

How is it then that Penang, which had to deal with a Malay/Muslim central government, has been able to preserve so much? One reason is the existence of a relatively competitive democracy on the island. The political leaders of the state must stand up for Chinese rights or face problems at the polls. In the 1960s, when the MCA did not appear to be digging in hard enough to protect Chinese interests, Gerakan stepped in and defeated the MCA candidates. In the 1980s and 1990s, when the MCA and Gerakan joined Barisan Nasional, the DAP challenged Barisan Nasional to protect Chinese interests. In the 1986 and 1990 elections, the DAP posed a serious threat to Barisan Nasional power in the state, and Malay federal leaders had to step in to assure Penang voters that the central government planned to respect their language and culture.

A second probable reason is that, because of their minority position in the country politically and numerically, the Chinese in Penang held on tighter to their traditional ways. Language and culture became powerful symbols of unity in the face of perceived attempts by the Malay leadership to dilute the Chinese identity. Whether the immigrant races should cling to their separate way of life is a different issue altogether, but they have been successful so far.

A clash between the immigrant races and the Malays will probably never again be as bad as the debacle of 1969. The numbers over the last few decades have worked against them. In the 1940s and 1950s, the immigrant races constituted a majority of the population, but today, the numbers have changed. By 1990, Malays made up close to 58 percent of the population, with Chinese and Indians at 35 percent and 7 percent, respectively. This came about as a result of higher Malay birth rates, an influx of hundreds of thousands of Indonesian immigrants, and Chinese and Indian emigration to other countries.

The Malay community no longer has to fix the system to control it, and most in the immigrant races have accepted the inevitable. The real threat from the Chinese and Indian communities is not disorder. If the immigrant races face a future crisis of confidence about their roles in the country, many might just leave or their money would. For Malaysia, this would be a tragedy as its future prosperity would be damaged without the capital and skills of its immigrant races.

Chapter 18

INDEPENDENT SINGAPORE

Singapore's exit from Malaysia was a unique historical situation. It is hard to think of an example in history when a state was expelled from a larger country. More than this though, the separation was the end of a dream that the leaders of the PAP had carried with them since their student days. There was going to be a fundamental reevaluation for Singaporeans to decide who they were, where they were going, and what they were going to do to survive.

A new national identity had to be developed. After years of convincing Singaporeans that their national destiny was as partners with the Malays in the peninsula, they now had to view themselves as a separate nation. A new economic strategy had to be developed. Singapore had seen itself as the New York of Malaysia. It was going to be the commercial, financial, and manufacturing center of that country. It now had to look elsewhere for the source of its prosperity and find a new role in the area. It was no longer a Chinese state in a Malay nation but rather a Chinese nation between two Malay nations — Malaysia and Indonesia.

As if these challenges were not daunting enough, they were compounded by the British announcement in 1967 that Britain planned to withdraw all its forces from Singapore by 1972. On the heels of exit from Malaysia, this was devastating news for Singapore. The contribution of the British forces to Singapore's economy was significant — between 15 and 20 percent of its national income. Apart from this, the British decision meant that Singapore would have to defend itself, an unknown phenomenon for its people. A military establishment had to be built out of a people whose majority had no military tradition, experience, or national loyalty.

Stability and Purpose

The political leadership of Singapore faced two crises that no one had anticipated in 1959, when the original economic development policies began to be formulated. In order to meet these challenges, the PAP determined that the way Singapore was ruled and the rights and responsibilities of its citizens had to go through a basic restructuring. Lee Kuan Yew and his colleagues viewed Singapore as a society fighting for survival in a hostile world. They believed its small size and manpower base could not afford the luxury of a liberal democracy in the Western sense. Competing political factions would drain Singapore of the unity it needed to develop a national identity and reorder its economy. Its best and brightest were precious resources that would be squandered if they were divided by a competitive political party system.

Prime Minister Lee Kuan Yew celebrates the PAP's 1972 election victory in Tanjong Pagar.

With this in mind, a new social contract was articulated by the PAP. In essence, it said that if the people of Singapore were willing to accept more government control, give up some of their individual rights, and work hard, the PAP would create the environment that would deliver prosperity and a better quality of life.

The ramifications of the new social contract were felt first on the economic front. Singapore had found that good government, a developed infrastructure, and an attractive workforce were successful draws to foreign investment. With its exit from Malaysia, Singapore had to convince investors that this new country was a safe place to put their money and that it was stable socially and politically.

Given Singapore's recent past, stability was not necessarily an accepted fact. Singapore's prime resources were its location and people. While the labor force was well-educated, hardworking, and relatively inexpensive, union activity had given it a reputation for confrontation and disorder.

In the 1960s, the government had moved to curb the powers of organized labor and create a more attractive and less confrontational workforce. Some of the radicalism that existed within the trade union movement had been dampened by the arrests of many of its leaders between 1963 and 1966. Leaderless and under strong government pressure, the Barisan Sosialis union group, SATU, began to fall apart.

Weakening the power of the radicals in the union movement was only part of the government's strategy concerning organized labor. Their entire identity had to be recast. Two important pieces of legislation were passed in 1969 that would effectively end the adversarial role of unions in Singapore. The Industrial Relations Act curtailed the rights of unions to strike and placed the hiring and firing of workers outside the domain of union negotiations. The unions could collectively bargain, but if there was a dispute, it went to the Ministry of Labor or an arbitration court. The Employment Act defined the basic arrangements by which workers could be hired and fired, as well as detailed the number of working hours, overtime, holiday benefits, and compensation that workers were entitled to. The upshot of these two laws meant that unions were severely restricted in the issues they could bring up with management and the right to strike as a tool of labor power virtually disappeared.

During this same period, the role and power of the NTUC were redefined. The NTUC and its member units were to become partners with the government to pursue national interests. The leaders of the organization were to be approved and appointed by the government, and their objectives would reflect the government's national policies rather than those of the unions. In 1969, Devan Nair was appointed head of the NTUC to chart its new course.

These actions made Singapore's workforce very attractive to foreign investors. Industrial peace, defined working conditions, and weakened unions were significant incentives to doing business in Singapore. Workers had traded many of their union rights for the promise of economic growth and better jobs.

The government was also determined to instill a strong work ethic in the workforce. The social and economic safety nets that exist in many countries were not available to Singaporeans. There were no unemployment benefits if you lost your job; welfare benefits were meager and went only to the truly destitute. The only government assistance the citizens could count on was subsidized public housing, health care, and education. As time went on, even these areas required greater percentages of payments from the citizens. There was no free lunch in Singapore.

The British withdrawal, while a blow to Singapore's economy, offered opportunities as well. The land that had been used by British bases was now available for housing and industrial estates. Given the amount of land involved, this was of significant benefit to Singapore. For example, the British airfield and installations in Changi opened up an area that became the centerpiece of Singapore's regional hub in the aerospace industry, Changi International Airport. The British also left behind impressive facilities that were the foundations of new industries. The dry dock at the naval base became a key part of Singapore's growth as a center for ship repair and building. The aircraft repair and maintenance facilities at the three British air bases were converted to civilian use. Thus, although the British withdrawal cost jobs, it also created new ones.

The economic challenges caused by the exit from Malaysia and the British withdrawal also spurred greater active intervention on the part of the government to develop new industries. The Development Bank of Singapore (DBS) was established and funded to provide capital for joint ventures with foreign companies and develop new industries. Chartered Industries built up Singapore as a manufacturer of arms and defense-related products. The government set up Neptune Orient Lines as Singapore's national shipping company to free it from dependence on foreigners. The Sembawang Corporation came into existence to develop the old British naval base. These are all examples of a dual strategy on the part of the government — to attract and encourage foreign multinationals to invest in Singapore and develop new industries that took advantage of the country's location and the skills of its people.

Two events outside Singapore contributed to its ability to adjust the economy to independence and British withdrawal. Singapore became an important supply and logistics center for the American war effort in Vietnam. The Americans and their South Vietnamese allies needed everything from rope to soap and oil products to toothbrushes. Singapore acted as a middleman to procure what was not being sent from the United States. It has been estimated that the war added more than $100 million a year to Singapore's economy at a time when it needed it desperately.

The rise in oil prices as a result of the Arab actions in the 1970s gave great impetus to the offshore search for oil in Southeast Asia. Singapore was perfectly placed to become the center of this boom. While oil rigs were drilling in Indonesia, Malaysia, and other parts of the area, Singapore provided a logistics center, offering an efficient, comfortable place to set up corporate headquarters. The island's airports and ports became centers for supplying the rigs, and its new shipyards and industrial estates could build and repair the rigs themselves.

One Party, One Voice

In the political arena, the government embarked on a course of action to ensure that there was one dominant voice that spoke for the aspirations of Singaporeans — the PAP. This took place more easily than anticipated because of the ineptitude of Barisan Sosialis. It labeled Singapore's independence as "phony" and nothing more than a facade for Western economic and military influence in the area. The thirteen Barisan Sosialis members of parliament who had been elected in 1963 boycotted parliament, effectively leaving the political spotlight to the PAP. Their belief that they could mobilize public opinion outside parliament was not successful. Their problems were compounded in 1966 by a further round of arrests of radicals by the government under the ISA. With much of its leadership in prison or underground, the party floundered. When an election was called in 1968, Barisan Sosialis said it was a sham and refused to participate. As a result, the PAP swept the election, winning all the seats in parliament and about 75 percent of the vote.

The PAP monopoly in parliament would continue for thirteen years. It won all the seats in the 1972, 1976, and 1980 elections, and for all practical purposes, Singapore had become a one-party country. By the early 1970s, the Chinese-speaking community as a political force had been neutered. The radical political leaders were either in jail or discredited. The Chinese students were no longer a source of opposition because of the changing educational system and new economic opportunities. The labor unions were under the control of the government and no longer a source of political agitation.

In the late 1960s and early 1970s, students at Nanyang University and the University of Singapore occasionally showed signs of dissent. The odd demonstration in support of greater democracy, social justice, and academic freedom served as an irritant to the government and a potential source of political opposition. The government remembered the radicalism of the 1950s and 1960s on campuses and took steps to make sure it did not happen again. Political associations were not allowed on campus, and student unions were banned from political activities. Toh Chin Chye took over the administration of the University of Singapore, and students had to obtain "certificates of suitability." Each year, students received clearance for readmission depending on their political activities or rather lack of them. In a society with limited opportunity for higher education, this was a great motivator for students to hit the books rather than the streets.

The belief that Singapore could only afford one voice of the vision for the future was also reflected in the creation of a monopoly on the media and other sources of information. Rather than act as a check on the government and a channel for alternative views, as is the case in the West, the media was seen as a tool for creating a national identity and unity. In the eyes of the PAP, the media's job was not to criticize the government but rather to help it get out its message. Television and radio were owned and run by government agencies, and these were active participants in the PAP agenda.

Until the late 1960s, the newspapers of Singapore were relatively independent and competitive. In the 1970s, this changed. Editors and reporters of *Nanyang Siang Pau*, a leading Chinese newspaper, were arrested in 1971 for printing articles that were considered seditious and chauvinistic Chinese. *Utusan Melayu*, the conservative Malay paper pioneered by Yusof bin Ishak, was shut down in 1970 for stirring up sensitive racial issues. Reporters as a result became cautious in the way they treated important political issues. In 1971, an English-language newspaper, *The Eastern Sun*, was closed down because of reported ties to foreign and communist money. Many who had read the tabloid were surprised because it was such a tame, safe paper. If the communists were bankrolling it, they were not getting their money's worth. In the government's view, it was the paper's potential for foreign meddling in Singapore's affairs that was the problem.

The most controversial action against the press was directed toward the *Singapore Herald*. Started by veteran Singapore journalists, it was geared to compete with Singapore's oldest and largest English newspaper, the *Straits Times*. By Western standards, its investigative reporting and criticism of government policies were pretty mild, although it did offer an avenue for citizen complaints through its publication of letters to the editor. By PAP standards, it was a disruptive threat to national unity in trying times. Initially, the government tried to shut it down by convincing Chase Manhattan Bank to call in the *Herald's* loans. The bank obliged. The ensuing public reaction was surprising. A "Save the *Herald*" campaign started with a number of Singaporeans donating time, money, and voice to try to keep the newspaper afloat. Chase backed off, and in the end, the government closed the paper down by revoking its license.

Legislation was subsequently passed that gave the government control over the printed media. Ultimately, all the daily papers that remained in Singapore were brought under the umbrella of one company with a government representative sitting on its board of directors. The first such position was filled by a former senior security official.

Search for a Common Destiny

The crackdown on the press was also a recognition that the different races in Singapore did not share common values or agendas. How Singaporeans viewed the components of a national identity was deeply influenced by racial considerations. The role of Chinese language and culture was of great concern to the minorities. Singapore's future relations with Malaysia and the role of the Malays were viewed differently by the three races. These are just two examples of the complexity of the challenge in creating a Singaporean identity.

To the PAP, the control of sources of information was an important building block in the creation of a new national identity. Television, radio, and the press played key roles in molding values and behavior. Examples of this are the periodic campaigns. Anyone who has lived in Singapore over the past few decades is familiar with government campaigns. All the opinion framers on the island focus on some particular aspect of life that needs to be changed or modified. For months in the media and in public places, there are messages such as "Be courteous," "Don't spit," "Don't litter," "Stop at two children," "Speak Mandarin," "Save water," and "Foster strong family values." Usually, the campaign is accompanied by negative reinforcement, such as fines for littering and spitting or a third child not being deductible from income tax. There is a common message — sacrifice individual satisfaction for the good of the greater community.

Singapore leaders felt that none of these campaigns would work if there was more than one political party with access to public opinion and pulling in an opposite direction. Singapore was in a state of crisis. With its exit from Malaysia, a national identity had to be created in a multiracial, multireligious society. Given the political and racial turmoil of the 1950s and 1960s, the government felt that competing views of what defined a Singaporean could only lead to disorder and instability.

Another avenue for creating a Singaporean identity that appeared in the second half of the 1960s was National Service (NS). This was also part of the defense buildup to fill the vacuum left by the British departure. Singapore requires virtually all males to spend two years in the military and then be available for reserve duty for years afterward. The potential benefits of this requirement are great. An experience shared by all races, it fosters patriotism, loyalty, and the belief that all are responsible for defending the country. Sacrificing time and effort to serve in the military has had a big impact on generations of Singaporeans.

The growth of Singapore's military establishment has been impressive. While in the 1960s, the single largest government expenditure was education, by the 1980s, that had changed to defense. Singapore has invested billions of dollars in creating a modern well-equipped military.

With NS and reservists, the size of its military when mobilized is clearly a match for those of its neighbors. Singapore has an army of 50,000 and another 200,000 men on active reserve. Top of the line fighter aircraft from the United States, fast modern tanks from Europe, and a modern navy all give Singapore one of the largest military establishments based on the size of its population in the world. The government adopted what was called a "poisonous shrimp strategy" — "We may be small, but if you eat us, we will make you very sick." Another dimension of the British withdrawal and Singapore's defense buildup was that it truly signified the latter's independence. Singapore was no longer dependent on others for the defense of the island.

Malays in the 1960s and Early 1970s

The military situation compounded the crisis of identity that the Malays were going through at this time. Singapore's exit from Malaysia and the subsequent British withdrawal impacted on the Malay community to a much greater extent than they did on the Indian and Chinese communities. As long as Singapore's future had been tied to merger with Malaya, the Malays had a secure position on the island. Attempts in Singapore to placate Malay opinion in the peninsula had given the Malay community added stature. The Malay language was the national language, a Malay was head of state, and the federal government in Malaysia acted as the big brother by protecting the Malays' special position as the indigenous people. The presence of a friendly federal government had contributed to the Malay community's support of the PAP in the 1963 general election. With separation they were no longer "special," and their position in the new Singapore was uncertain.

After independence, the Singapore government began to use the new public housing built by the HDB to break up racial concentrations on the island. While part of Malaysia, it would have been a dicey proposition to force the Singapore Malays out of their kampungs, since any policies with regard to the Malay community would have needed the approval of the Malay leadership in Kuala Lumpur. For example, the Singapore government had actually built a new Malay settlement in Sembawang to show good faith in preserving the Malay way of life.

With independence, this conciliatory policy changed. HDB became a vehicle for nation building and racial mixing, and the Malay kampung began to disappear. Some Malays gladly moved into the new apartments, but for many, it was a socially traumatic experience. While most Chinese were happy to move out of the urban squalor into overwhelmingly Chinese buildings, for the Malays, moving meant a loss of community and a way of life. Many were not happy, and it took time to reestablish the trust they had shown the PAP in the 1963 election.

The creation of the Singapore Armed Forces (SAF) and the way it was organized and staffed contributed to the growing alienation of the Malay community in the 1970s. Prior to separation, the Malays had made up a disproportionate number of the uniformed services in Singapore. Under British rule, they had been encouraged to find jobs in the police and Singapore's small armed services. They had also served as locally recruited uniformed staff to the British forces. With self-rule, this had not changed much due to the campaign for merger. But when Singapore became independent, it was determined that the military and the police reflect the racial makeup of the island, which was predominantly Chinese. Also, the only two countries that were immediate threats to Singapore were of Malay racial and religious origin, and there was concern that Singapore Malays would not have the will to fight against Malaysia or Indonesia. Because the loyalties of the Malays were in doubt, certain units and jobs in the SAF were closed to Malay participation. Elite units, such as the commandos for example, did not accept Malays. In 1987, in reference to the question of why there were no Malay pilots in the SAF, Brigadier-General Lee Hsien Loong said: "... we don't want to put any of our soldiers in a difficult position where his emotions for the nation may come in conflict with his emotions for his religion."*

This unspoken but widely acknowledged practice began to change that year when BG Lee spoke about the need for change in the armed services. He encouraged the move toward greater integration: "Progress can be made but progress will be made patiently, incrementally, step by step."**

---

*The Straits Times, February 23, 1987

**Quah, 1990, p. 88

In the 1960s, a quota system for call-up into the armed forces was set up to correct the racial imbalance, but the Malays did not get drafted in numbers anywhere near their percentage of the population. A generation of young Malays waited for a call that never came. Many employers did not want to offer jobs to Malays that required any degree of training because they did not know when or if the youths would be called up. Even if they were drafted, Malays claimed they had little access to jobs in the military that would give them better job skills. The quotas and prohibitions implied that the Malays were not to be trusted.

Between the politics of the NS and the British withdrawal, many traditional service occupations for Malay men were no longer available. The early years of independence saw an increase in unemployment and dead-end manual labor in the Malay community. There were serious drug problems and crime among bored Malay youths, and their loss of status led to loss of respect in the community. The income levels of Malays fell dramatically in comparison with those of the Chinese. In the 1950s, the average income of most Malays was relatively equal with that of the Chinese community. By the early 1970s, it was about half that of the other races. Income levels of the Malays did rise at this time but not nearly as impressively as the incomes of the other races.

As Singapore reordered its priorities in the first two decades of independence, the economic and social problems of the Malay community continued to remind the nation that there was a downside to forming a common vision of the future.

Relations with Indonesia and Malaysia

Singapore's defense buildup was indicative of the problems it faced in its new relationships with Malaysia and Indonesia. Many leaders in the area were baffled by the size of Singapore's defense establishment. Who would this army fight? The treatment of the Malays in the SAF reinforced the belief that this new military had only two potential enemies, both of whom could see no reason why they would want to attack the island country. High speed tanks, supersonic fighters, and modern ships were not conducive to building trust among its neighbors. For example, the only reason for high speed tanks would be to drive them up Malaysian roads.

Added to this was that the SAF had adopted an Israeli model and had turned to the Israeli defense forces to help institute it. Indonesia and Malaysia wondered if Singapore, like Israel, saw itself as an embattled country in a world of enemies. Would it adopt the Israeli practice of attacking first and asking questions later? There was a religious dimension as well. As countries with large numbers of Muslims, Malaysia and Indonesia sympathized with the Arab and Palestinian causes. Having Israeli advisors in the neighborhood was a hard pill to swallow. Singapore was sending the message that it could be tough, could make difficult decisions, and could follow a course based on what it saw as its national interests.

Suffice it to say that Singapore's relations with its neighbors in the first years of independence were testy at times. An example of this was an incident that took place between Singapore and Indonesia in 1969. During Confrontation, Indonesian commandos were sent to Singapore on sabotage missions. The one successful group placed a bomb in the elevator of MacDonald House along Orchard Road, which resulted in fatalities. The saboteurs were caught and sentenced to death. By the time the executions took place, it was 1969. Confrontation was over, and President Suharto had taken over from Sukarno. The public and government in Indonesia felt that these men had been sent in wartime, and surely in peacetime, their lives could be spared. Added to this was that they had been sent by Sukarno, who was no longer on the scene.

Suharto appealed for understanding and that good neighbors would spare the commandos' lives. The reply from Singapore was that its legal system had taken its course and that it was an internal matter. Singapore then hanged the two marines. The reaction in Indonesia was loud and swift. Anti-Singapore demonstrations broke out in Jakarta and other cities. A crowd attacked the Singapore embassy, forcing the ambassador and staff to run for their lives. The executions would be remembered by Indonesians with anger for some time to come.

The drama over this incident highlighted Singapore's problems in the area. It was a country that was never meant to be, young and determined to be treated with respect by its neighbors. Singapore's relations with Malaysia were summed up by a Malaysian cabinet minister in 1990.

He compared it with two families who lived in semi-detached houses. They shared the same roof, wall, and yard. It was true that both had ownership of their property and could legally use it as they pleased, but if one came home late at night making noise and waking up the other, the neighbor would quite rightly be upset.

Singapore's defense buildup aside, after separation from Malaysia, the island's view of and role in the region were ambiguous and contradictory at times. In its first six years of self-rule, its leaders had seen the island's economic and political future as part of the future of Malaysia. After 1965, this changed. Lee Kuan Yew, Goh Keng Swee, and their colleagues believed that Singapore had to chart a future that was not dependent on its neighbors. Separation had deprived Singapore of the markets of the former British Malaya. The economic downturn that took place as a result of the Confrontation between Malaysia and Indonesia had taught Singapore a lesson in how frail its regional position was in the post-colonial world. Singapore was a Chinese island in a Malay ocean, and this reinforced its insecurity as a regional player. The answer was to create a global city, to offer a base for multinational corporations of the world, and to prosper from markets in the United States, Europe, and Japan. This is evidenced by the fact that close to three-fourths of Singapore's exports to the United States come from American-owned companies in Singapore. Significant portions of the exports to Europe and Japan also come from their own companies in Singapore.

Singapore's tremendous economic success in the first few decades of independence added to an identity different from the countries around it. Singapore enjoyed a much higher standard of living than its neighbors. Its population was more Westernized and spoke a common language from outside the region — English — that reinforced its ties with the world beyond Southeast Asia. Singapore citizens were urban and reflected the values of city dwellers and modernization. Its neighbors still felt the pull of rural and traditional values in their institutions and world views. Many of Singapore's policies and values seemed to stress its separateness from the region and made cooperation difficult between the island and the rest of Southeast Asia.

The flip side is the reality that Singapore is dependent on its neighbors. Half its water supply comes from Malaysia; when an airplane takes off, it is immediately in the airspace of Malaysia; and Indonesia and Malaysia control Singapore's lifelines of trade, the Melaka and Sunda Straits. Yet, Singapore's dual role as an entrepôt and regional financial center continues to be a major factor in its economic success. For example, about one-third of Malaysia's exports still flows through the port of Singapore, as well as some 10–20 percent of Indonesia's exports. Singapore's businessmen are deeply integrated into the network of Chinese business communities in the region and have significant investments in the area.

Over the past three decades, reconciling Singapore's position in the region has posed a tremendous challenge for its decision makers. Singapore is viewed with mistrust by some politicians in the region who question its desire for cooperation. Its success and modernity have bred an attitude that is at times interpreted as arrogance. Some see Singapore as crass and materialistic, having little understanding of the traditions and values of the people who live in Southeast Asia.

Attempts to create a greater regional cooperation that included independent Singapore formally began in August 1967 with the creation of the Association of South East Asian Nations (ASEAN). The founding members were Malaysia, Indonesia, Thailand, the Philippines, and Singapore. In its early years, ASEAN was a hollow organization that represented an ideal rather than reality. Until the mid-1970s, there seemed to be more that divided the countries than what brought them together. Malaysia and the Philippines were still quarreling over Sabah. Relations between Singapore and Indonesia were strained over the executions of the marines and the aftermath of Suharto's rise to power, which had resulted in the killing of hundreds of thousands of ethnic Chinese. Singapore and Malaysia were behaving like a recently divorced couple, arguing over who was to blame. The breaking up of common institutions, such as their currencies, border controls, the national airline (there was an airline called Malaysia-Singapore Airlines), and common newspapers, were all fuel for acrimony.

By the mid-1970s, the climate for cooperation and greater unity began to improve. Some of this came about because of better personal relations between the leaders themselves. Lee Kuan Yew and Suharto began to develop a closer working relationship, which was strengthened by Lee's trip to Jakarta in 1973 and his visit to the memorial for the executed marines. The rise of Tun Hussein Onn and later Mahathir Mohamad to power in Malaysia brought to the fore leaders who did not carry the hard feelings caused by Singapore's separation from Malaysia. President Ferdinand Marcos in the Philippines seemed willing to let the Sabah issue fade. More important were geopolitical considerations that brought the countries together. Singapore saw that Thailand and the Philippines could act as counterweights to the suspicious Malay nations in a regional grouping. Most significant was the withdrawal of the United States from Vietnam and the subsequent North Vietnamese victory. The ASEAN countries drew closer together in the face of what they saw as a potential threat to their security from the Vietnamese communists. This was evidenced by the common stand ASEAN took in opposition to the Vietnamese invasion of Cambodia in 1979. ASEAN's active diplomacy in the United Nations and physical support for the Cambodians who were fighting the Vietnamese-backed regime in Cambodia were key ingredients in denying Vietnamese control of the country. They were also important to the eventual UN-brokered peace agreement and subsequent elections that ended Cambodia's civil war.

Economics also contributed to greater regional unity. The growing economies of Southeast Asia, especially Singapore, gave the countries greater importance in the eyes of the world. A market of some three hundred million people, part of the world's fastest growing economies, gave the countries of ASEAN greater leverage in their dealings with the United States, the European Union, and Japan. ASEAN recognized that there were great benefits to be derived from acting together. For Singapore, the inflation caused by the oil crisis of the late 1970s and the economic recession of the mid-1980s drove home the message that, when the global economy was unfriendly, there were advantages to having good friends close to home.

In the 1980s and 1990s, ASEAN expanded to include Brunei, Burma, Laos, and Vietnam, and there are plans to eventually bring in Cambodia. ASEAN has become an important avenue for economic cooperation as it works to lower tariff barriers between member states, identify regional industrial projects, and project greater influence on the international scene.

Given the rising power and influence of China and the proliferation of other regional trading blocs, such as NAFTA (North American Free Trade Agreement), this cooperation is especially important.

A Case Study: Population Problems

By the 1980s, Singapore had gone a long way toward addressing the problems faced by an expanding population and by its expulsion from Malaysia. Singapore had a standard of living that was fast approaching the levels of developed Western nations. Household incomes had almost tripled in two decades, unemployment had been virtually eliminated, and the majority of Singaporeans had built assets as homeowners. HDB and NS had provided the vehicles for Singaporeans to feel they had a stake in the country and owed it loyalty. Economic development had remade the island; shop houses and kampungs were replaced by skyscrapers and HDB communities.

Generally, the PAP had delivered on its part of the social contract. In the interests of stability and economic growth, Singaporeans had sacrificed a competitive political system, workers' rights, and individual freedom and in return had obtained a successful economy and better living standards. The progress from two decades of PAP rule was mind-boggling, but its very success created new problems for the future and exposed the weaknesses of a contract based almost solely on material well-being.

Singapore's attack on the problem of overpopulation is an interesting case study of how the government of Singapore was able to change people's behavior in the 1960s and 1970s. It, however, brought about totally unintended consequences in the 1980s and 1990s. There is little doubt that Singapore's progress was dependent on lowering the birth rate, which was one of the highest in the world. In the 1950s and early 1960s, much of the effort to bring down population growth had been in the hands of a volunteer organization, the Singapore Family Planning Association. This group had seen some success in educating and encouraging Singaporeans to have fewer children. In the 1960s, it was taken over by the government. The birth rate was too important an issue to be left in private hands.

To address the problem, a government agency called the Singapore Family Planning and Population Board was set up. Campaigns began to encourage correct behavior, and disincentives were established to punish incorrect behavior. On television and over the radio, Singaporeans were admonished to stop at two children. The country was inundated with literature proclaiming the benefits of small families. Pamphlets even appeared with water bills. Posters decorated government offices, and schools delivered the message that families must have fewer children. The government established family planning clinics throughout the island, which provided assistance in avoiding pregnancies. Voluntary sterilization was encouraged. Between 1970 and 1977, over fifty thousand Singaporeans went through medical procedures that made conception impossible. Abortion was legal and available on demand. In the same period, over fifty thousand abortions were performed. For people who continued to have too many children, disincentives were put in place. In government hospitals, the cost of having a baby was increased after the second child. Tax deductions for children were decreased for the third child and subsequent children. In a society that valued education, priority in admission to most schools was determined by birth order. Employers did not have to pay for maternity leave for the third child.

The campaign, along with the natural decline in birth rates that comes with growing affluence, resulted in a dramatic fall in Singapore's population growth. The new challenge was that its very success created a serious population problem for the future. Singaporeans were no longer replacing themselves and faced the consequences of a population growing too slowly.

One result is the greying of Singapore. The falling birth rates of the 1960s and 1970s and the general rise in health standards means that the society as a whole is growing older. With each passing decade, the percentage of Singaporeans over the age of sixty-five rises. Sometime around the year 2020, the percentage will reach crisis proportions. By that time, there will be 117 retired people for every 100 who are working. The post-war baby boomers will retire in the new millennium, and the subsequent generations might not be large enough to support them without a reduction in living standards or sacrificing high growth.

There are numerous ramifications. The cost of living in Singapore has gone up significantly with economic growth. Many of the retirees contributed to CPF when income levels were much lower, and as a result, in the absence of any social security programs, there will be insufficient funds for a comfortable retirement for some. Much of the older generation's retirement resources are tied up in their homes as their CPF contributions were used to purchase HDB apartments. If they sell their homes to retire, where will they live? In larger countries, you can sell your home and move to areas with lower costs of living. As the value of property has risen in Singapore, there are few affordable housing alternatives. Health care costs have skyrocketed, and there is no publicly funded program to meet this need. For example, between 1982 and 1987, the inflation rate averaged 3 percent, but health care costs rose at a rate of 21 percent.

Beyond this, CPF has provided a huge pool of national savings that the government has drawn on to build expensive infrastructure projects such as the Mass Rapid Transport system. The day may come when more is taken out of CPF by retired people than what goes in from workers' contributions, thereby lowering the amount of savings that can be used by the government to build a better society.

This problem is faced by many affluent nations, such as Japan and the United States, and is a price paid for post-war economic success. For Singapore, the options are not very attractive. A law has been passed that permits parents to sue their children for support in their old age. It is unlikely that this will have much of an impact given the shame that would accompany this kind of action. The government could change the age at which money may be withdrawn from CPF from fifty-five to sixty, but when this idea was floated, there was a public outcry. People had paid into CPF on the understanding that the money was theirs at fifty-five and did not like the idea of waiting another five years. Contributions to CPF can be increased, but that would lower current living standards. This will be one of the most pressing problems facing Singapore in the next two decades.

A further dimension to this problem of underpopulation has to do with Singapore's manpower needs. As the economy grew and birth rates dropped, Singapore was increasingly forced to depend on outsiders to provide its labor needs. In the country today, there are close to four hundred thousand guest workers. The economy has become increasingly dependent on low-skilled workers from Bangladesh, Indonesia, India, Sri Lanka, Thailand, the Philippines, and Malaysia to do the jobs Singaporeans cannot or do not want to do. With economic expansion, skilled workers are also in demand.

As can be attested by many countries in Europe, large numbers of guest workers create the potential for social and racial problems. Singapore is small and as a result can regulate these foreign workers, but it is still early to ascertain the repercussions of the large numbers of workers in the country. As Singapore continues to grow, it will be increasingly dependent on people who have no roots or loyalty to the country.

A further complication to the population concerns was the view by the PAP that not only were Singaporeans having too few babies, the wrong people were having them. Analysis of the birth rate figures showed that there was a direct correlation between educational levels of women and the number of children they were having. This is not surprising data. As women become better educated, they are freed from dependence on marriage for economic support. Many educated women postpone or decide against having children to further their careers. The Singapore government felt that this trend had dangerous implications. The argument was one of genetics, that better educated women produce brighter, more capable children. If only the poorly educated replaced themselves, then Singapore would become a nation of low achievers. In his National Day speech of 1989, Lee Kuan Yew lamented offering such good economic opportunities to women because of its impact on the future population. The genetic argument seems out of place for a country of immigrants. Somewhere along the line, virtually every family in the country can trace its roots to an uneducated laborer who got off the boat in Singapore looking for a better life.

Another fear was that the Malays were reproducing faster than the Chinese. This was understandable given that Malays tend to have lower average incomes and lower educational qualifications than the Chinese. The leaders of Singapore foresaw that a change in the racial balance would affect the political chemistry of the island. If the racial numbers began to show more equality, this could cause instability. As long as the population was overwhelmingly Chinese and dispersed throughout the island, it was impossible for non-Chinese politicians to posture for votes along racial lines. But what if in the next twenty or thirty years, the Malay population grew and constituted 30 to 40 percent of the population? This would be a new political ball game, especially given the unity in the Malay community because of Islam and its minority status. Politics could become racially based, a troubling future for the shapers of Singapore's destiny.

How would a rising Malay percentage affect relations with Malaysia? Singapore's planning had been based on a certain racial mix, and this was a troubling trend. A case could be made that the unequal racial birth rates were a further casualty of policies put in place in the 1960s and 1970s, which had especially impacted on the Malay community. The economic position of the Malays and their suspicion of government policies made them less than keen participants in buying into the national agenda.

In the 1980s, a new campaign was started to increase the population, especially by women who were well-educated. Of all the attempts the government had embarked on to change the behavior of Singaporeans, this was the most sensitive. The government was basically asking some people to have more children and others to have fewer, drawing value judgments on the worth of females based on their educational levels. Poorly educated women were offered financial incentives to be sterilized after two children. The money would go into their CPF accounts. University graduates were offered $20,000 tax rebates for a third child. The government also proposed that the children of university graduates be given preference in admission to schools.

A Social Development Unit (SDU) was established as a dating service for better educated Singaporeans. Serious money was invested in programs such as sea cruises for single graduates, a kind of government "love boat." Parties were organized for the same purpose, and computerized dating services set up for the graduates.

The Singapore of the 1980s was a different place from that of the 1960s. Most Singaporeans did not see the population problem as a crisis. Affluence had reduced the need for large families as a source of labor and retirement support. Women enjoyed the freedom and independence that came with rising living standards. The sterilization proposal and school admission policy were dropped in the face of strong public reaction. They smacked of racism, elitism, and downright unfairness. The campaign became more general. Television advertisements sold the virtues of family life and child rearing. Incentives were instituted for those who had three or more children. The SDU continues to function but with limited success.

A Crisis of Identity?

By the 1980s, Singapore's success in modernizing its society and developing its economy had created a discernible pride among Singaporeans. That success had required dramatic changes over the years in the lives and habits of the people. As Singapore entered the ranks of the economically developed world, there was uneasiness in the minds of many Singaporeans. The sacrifices made to achieve material well-being had been fairly straightforward. The tradeoff had been made — restrictions on social and political freedom in return for higher standards of living. In the area of culture and values, things were not quite so clear-cut. In the fast-paced drive to modernization, what traditional values had been lost along the way? On what cultural foundation did the new Singaporean base his or her life? What non-material values did the national identity reflect?

For the political leadership, Singapore's national identity was framed by a conflict between Asian and Western values. Singapore needed to identify and reinforce those Asian values that had led to its success. The Asian quality of its economic success was shared by the other rapidly developing economies in the area — Taiwan, South Korea, Hong Kong, Malaysia, and Thailand. This view is part of a debate that is taking place among academics, politicians, and the media over how much the Asian economic "miracle" is attributable to some kind of shared Asian values.

Lee Kuan Yew and Mahathir Mohamad believe that the twenty-first century is going to be an Asian one. The social/political stability and economic power of Asia will shift the center of global economic dominance away from the West to Asia and the Pacific. Reasons for this belief are inherent in why the leaders think the Asian countries are succeeding — that the Asian model is on an ascending course because its people are willing to sacrifice individual rights for the success of the larger group. This belief effectively takes Singapore's social contract out of the context of a material agreement and places it in the discussion of core values and a national identity.

The argument for the group versus the individual goes beyond questions of workers' rights and the freedom of speech and the press into the underpinnings of the legal system. This was reflected in the debate over the abolition of jury trials in Singapore in 1969. The government proposal provoked the final great public debate between David Marshall and Lee Kuan Yew. In the committee hearings over the legislation, the two founding fathers of Singapore clashed over fundamental social values. Marshall argued that jury trials were essential to protect the individual from the tyranny of the state. Lee argued that clever lawyers often led juries astray and made it possible for the guilty to go free. Lee's point was that by protecting the individual, society suffered from the presence of lawless elements. The issue was decided by the fact that the PAP held all the seats in parliament.

The continued use of the ISA was couched in the same terms. The PAP argued that many times it was difficult in a court of law to prove that people were a threat to social peace and order, and thus in the interest of society, there had to be a way to control them. To this end, changes were made in the ISA that eliminated any judicial review of detentions under the act. People who threatened the good order of Singapore society were problems for the police and politicians to solve, not judges who were concerned with legal niceties. The most prominent cases of people detained without trial have been politicians, but less noticed were the hundreds of secret society members who were taken off the streets. The contention is that Singapore would have never been able to gain the upper hand in its battle against gangs and crime had it followed the due process of Anglo-Saxon law.

Asian leaders pointed at social problems in the West and blamed them on the glorification of the individual. High crime rates were symptomatic of a legal system obsessed with individual rights. Divorce rates, riots in the streets, ineffective government, and a lowering work ethic were the result of the erosion of group values and signs of the decline of the West.

If these observations are valid, they then lead to a rejection of the Western democratic political model. In the eyes of the PAP, Singapore's success is based on a no-nonsense legal system and a political system that can make hard decisions about the future of the group without catering to the special interests of the minority. The majority elects the PAP, and it produces safe streets, a stable and peaceful society, and a passive workforce — all keys to attracting the necessary investments for economic growth.

Some would argue that these values are not uniquely Asian but are authoritarian and traditional and that the rationalizations for what are termed Asian values are nothing more than an excuse for maintaining one political party's dominance. The argument for the group is fascinating because of the great contradictions it presents about modern Singapore. On one hand, there is the call to reinforce Asian communitarian values, but much of Singapore's success is due to policies and goals that promote Western influence and individual success. Some of the attractiveness of Singapore's labor force is that it is educated in English and uses a Western educational model borrowed from Britain. While only about a quarter of Singaporeans speak English at home, a significant part of their socialization takes place in English and gives them further access to Western influences, such as popular culture. One cannot avoid the fact that language communicates values.

Singapore has sold itself as a global city. In competition with its neighbors for foreign investment and trade, it emphasizes its position as a center open to the world. Many businesses come to Singapore because it is seen as a modern, Westernized city compared to its neighbors. Singapore wants to be the Southeast Asian information hub, a center for communication and interaction. It actively pursues Western investment, and as a result, some tens of thousands of Westerners live on the island. It is difficult to reconcile these goals with a desire to de-emphasize the values that come with the business people, their money, and their culture. If the message of the Western media, Western popular culture, and Westerners in general is the importance of the individual, Singaporeans have had more than their share of exposure to it.

Beyond this, government policies to fulfill the social contract have in some ways contributed to the weakening of many traditional Asian institutions and strengthened the emphasis on individualism. CPF savings reduced the need for families to take care of their parents after retirement, and many of the elderly are independent of family ties. It encouraged individual saving rather than saving for the family or clan. The HDB program contributed to loosening of family ties by dispersing family members in different communities and by encouraging the existence of the nuclear family over the extended one. The need for educated women in the workforce liberated many women and radically changed traditional Asian gender models. To keep women in the workforce, children were turned over to day-care centers or looked after by foreign maids, both encouraged by the government although destructive of traditional family ties and values. Malay and Chinese kampungs were torn down to create multiethnic communities, weakening the ability of each community to pass on and reinforce values. The point is that to build a modern capitalist society many group-oriented values are diluted. The extended family as an economic unit and the kampung as a social unit are detrimental to building a prosperous society. Capitalism depends on individual drive and individual rewards as the foundations for its progress.

Related to this question of individualism is a dilemma Singapore faces in its educational system. As Singapore becomes more affluent, there is the need for the economy to change. Because of high educational standards and high wages, Singapore is no longer an inexpensive place for manufacturing. Singapore must soon make its living in competition with Japan and the West. Less wealth will come from assembling other people's products and more from solving problems and coming up with new ideas to sell. This requires an educational system that is less dependent on examination-based rote learning and encourages creativity. The government has recognized this but faces a dilemma. If a society and educational system are to produce more creative thinkers, then the individual must have more freedom.

Western Influences

Singapore's political leadership had addressed the problem of Western-ization and its downside in the past. When the PAP took power in 1959, they banned *Playboy* and *Cosmopolitan* magazines, branding them examples of decadent Western "yellow culture." Jukeboxes and pool tables were also banned as symbols of loose living.

In the 1970s, the government's anti-Western targets were long hair, drugs, and rock 'n' roll music. Fearful of Western popular culture, a campaign against long-haired males was instituted. In all government offices signs went up, declaring that males with long hair would be served last. At the airport and borders, long-haired males were told to get a haircut or not to visit Singapore. There are stories about how the police and immigration authorities actually forced haircuts on those who did not cooperate.

It is interesting that the Singapore Tourist Promotion Board (STPB) advertised Bugis Street, a hangout for transvestites, as a tourist attraction. Long hair on males seemed to be condoned if they were in drag and performed for tourists.

Many discotheques were closed as they were seen as gathering places for the drug culture and anti-social behavior. Numerous popular songs were banned, such as "Lucy in the Sky with Diamonds" by the Beatles, as they were said to have lyrics that promoted drug taking.

The Ultimate Campaign

In the 1980s and 1990s, the attack on Westernization took on a different emphasis. The government wanted to reinforce and re-instill in Singaporeans those values that seemed to be disappearing as a result of modernization and development. In the closing years of their political careers, some leaders in the PAP, such as Goh Keng Swee and Toh Chin Chye, lamented that the overemphasis on economic development had been at the expense of culture and values. This time the government attempted to create a national ideology that could stand up to the assault of Western values. The problem was defining exactly what values were Asian and shared by the three main communities.

The government defined four core values. The first two are somewhat universal and the last two a little controversial:

- The family is the basic unit of society.
- There is a fundamental belief in racial and religious harmony.
- The community takes precedence over the individual.
- Singapore is a society based on consensus, not contention.

After the announcement of the core values, public concern about individual rights led to a fifth core value — community support and respect for the individual.

In the 1990s then, there comes to the fore the ultimate campaign. This time, rather than controlling behavior, it is defining the citizens' view of the relationship of the individual to society. Whether this is possible in the age of mass communication, the Internet, and globalization remains to be seen.

The values campaign has a number of components. In the educational system, it constitutes using core values as the basis for inculcating a national identity. Initially, compulsory courses in Bible knowledge, Buddhist studies, Islamic knowledge, Hindu studies, and Confucian ethics were offered in the belief that they would reinforce the core values and promote universal moral principles. The move was an interesting experiment in a multireligious, multicultural society. Many religious leaders supported the program as a way of reinforcing the beliefs of their adherents, but over time, opposition to the classes grew among the public and within the ruling party. Some parents thought that the program smacked of propagating religion in the schools and could cause disharmony rather than harmony. About a fifth of the Chinese community claimed to have no religious affiliations at all, and many of them thought the classes were a waste of good school time. For others, the program reinforced the specter of the growing popularity of Christianity. In Singapore, the number of Christians has more than doubled in the past few decades, and the figure is approaching 20 percent of the population. The rising influence of Christianity was resented by some who did not like the possibility of the school system encouraging conversion.

Within the PAP, there were two concerns. It had been hoped that the classes would help propagate Confucian values, but this was not successful because about three-quarters of the Chinese signed up for the Buddhist and Christian courses. This in part led to a second concern. By reinforcing the strength of organized religion, the government could inadvertently create alternative forces that might influence public opinion and culture. In the end, the courses on religion were no longer compulsory, and the emphasis was placed on the creation of a national ideology based on the core values as part of the general curriculum and specific civics classes.

Another attempt to reinforce Asian values in education comes from a late 1970s requirement that all students study their mother tongue as a second language. This is especially evident in the push for the Chinese to learn and speak Mandarin, which is seen as a way to promote greater racial unity and identity, as well as transfer Chinese values. A newspaper advertisement in 1992 sponsored by the government read as follows:

"Mandarin allows you to effectively communicate with other Chinese in one language. More importantly, it gives you a deeper understanding of your cultural heritage. So why not speak Mandarin and stay in touch with your culture?"

The government campaign to encourage Mandarin is viewed with unease by some Singaporeans, both Chinese and non-Chinese. To the non-Chinese, it poses the potential of a return to Chinese chauvinism. It seems to be a move away from the multicultural model that has been the hallmark of Singapore society. After three decades of policies in education and housing that were meant to break down racial differences, the government now appears to be encouraging them. To some Chinese, such as those who speak English and dialects in their homes, it is an intrusion on socializing their children to their own values.

Mandarin has also added another component to an educational system that is already a pressure cooker. For Chinese students, passing the Mandarin examinations is a prerequisite for entry into junior college, the preparatory stage for university admission. Students from non-Mandarin speaking homes, especially the English-speaking ones, have another hurdle in their climb to the top of the educational pyramid. And to some, such as sociologist Geoffrey Benjamin, it is the question of what has motivated the PAP to endorse the campaign. He believes it is intended to weaken the traditional Chinese culture passed on via dialects because those traditions focus on loyalty to the family and clan rather than to the state. Mandarin in China is the language of government and defines the citizens' relationships and responsibilities in the public domain.

A final thrust of the values campaign is an attempt on the part of the political leadership to show that there is a "Singapore model" that is the underpinning of its success. This is a combination of the social contract, Asian values, and a national identity. Through whatever means possible, the leaders hope to convince Singaporeans of the uniqueness of what they have done and that it is the foundation of a common view of the future.

New Political Directions

A minority of Singaporeans do not fully accept the direction this country is taking. For some the social contract that was the basis for the Singapore model is outdated and needs to be renegotiated. High educational standards and economic success have convinced many that there is a need for a more open society and more diverse opinions. When Singaporeans went along with the PAP's model for governing, the country was facing a political and economic crisis. By the 1980s, the crisis seemed far away. Singapore had overcome the challenges, and it was time for the government to loosen up and provide for more freedom.

Along with this, there was a new generation entering adulthood, a generation that could not remember the Singapore of the 1950s and 1960s. They had not experienced the civil disorder caused by racial and economic divisions in society. As a result, many among them did not see the need for the political control and social regimentation that their elders had agreed to in the 1960s and 1970s.

The first evidence of change in the political climate appeared in the October 1981 by-election in the Anson constituency. J.B. Jeyaretnam, a lawyer and former magistrate, won the election and ended almost fifteen years of PAP monopoly in parliament. Jeyaretnam had rebuilt David Marshall's old party, the Workers' Party, and represented a new kind of opposition. English-educated, moderate, and middle class, Jeyaretnam and people like him could not be branded as communists, socialists, or as threats to peace and order. Some saw his victory as a freak result that reflected the peculiarities of the Anson district, but this was not true.

In the 1984 general election, two opposition candidates were elected to parliament. Jeyaretnam retained the Anson seat and increased his majority significantly. Joining him in parliament was the founder of the Singapore Democratic Party, Chiam See Tong, who won the Potong Pasir seat.

The PAP's percentage of the electorate dropped from 75 percent in the 1980 general election to 62.5 percent in 1984. In subsequent elections in 1988 and 1991, the downward trend continued, and although it did not translate into more than four opposition seats in parliament in 1991, the message was clear. A significant number of Singaporeans wanted to hear more than one voice in the political arena, and they wanted to be more involved in the decisions that shaped their lives.

The PAP was openly shocked by the 1984 results. Outside observers had a hard time understanding how the opposition winning two of seventy-seven seats in parliament was such a major issue, but it was. In the West, 60 percent of any vote is seen as a landslide but not in the Singapore of the 1980s. The PAP's reply to criticism of restrictions on freedom in Singapore had always been that free and open elections were held and that the people overwhelmingly endorsed its policies by voting for it. The legitimacy of the social contract was based in part on huge majorities in the elections. When four in ten voted against the PAP, the claim became somewhat murky.

The PAP's reaction to the political changes of the 1980s was mixed. Lee and his party believed that a more open and competitive political system would be a stumbling block to future growth and prosperity. To ensure that the government and its policies could proceed without serious challenge, the rules of the political game were redefined. The PAP wanted to ensure that opposition voices would not get in the way of the orderly process of legislation. To this end, positions for nominated members of parliament (NMPs) were created. These were members of parliament who did not belong to a political party and had limited voting powers but could take part in debates. The candidates would be selected from nominations to a parliamentary committee. Chosen from the professions and trade unions, this group would be a responsible alternative voice. The message was that if people wanted more than one voice in parliament, this could be provided without the disruption of party politics.

Another new position created was the non-constituency member of parliament (NCMP). Once again, this member of parliament would have limited voting power, that is, he or she could not vote on budget bills or constitutional amendments. These NCMPs appeared from the best losers in the general election. For example, if a party won all the seats in parliament, then the three losing candidates who garnered the highest percentages of the vote could become NCMPs. The rationale was that this would ensure an opposition voice from other political parties. Thus, people could freely vote for the PAP knowing that some opposition would exist. NCMPs also meant that it would be difficult for the opposition to build power bases in any particular area of the island, as Chiam had done in Potong Pasir.

A final and more significant change was the creation of group representation constituencies (GRCs). Four to six parliamentary constituencies were grouped together, and the MPs in those constituencies were to run as a team. The group with the greatest number of votes won all the seats. The rationale was that if Singapore was going to have competitive party politics, then something had to be done to ensure that members of minority groups got into parliament. The former constituencies had ensured that every parliamentary seat had a sizable Chinese majority, and there was a possibility that the minorities would be shut out completely. To this end, each new GRC had to include as one of its candidates a Malay or an Indian. Opposition politicians claimed that the GRCs were merely a way to ensure PAP control since the districts to be grouped together were determined by a PAP-dominated parliament. The government could easily ensure that districts with high opposition support were married to PAP strongholds, thus making it difficult for opposition candidates to enter parliament as full MPs.

Outside parliament, the PAP's reaction to organized opposition was to discredit its opponents and discourage Singaporeans from joining them. This is a strategy of political parties in all democracies, but in most democracies, the ruling party does not have the influence over the media that the PAP has. While there is no direct control over the editorial policies of the media, the boundaries of political discourse and the role of the media as a supporter of government actions and policies are well understood. Opposition politicians claim that the media's self-censorship and understanding of government sensitivities make it possible for the PAP to attack its opponents with little opportunity for rebuttal. Government access to information makes it possible to publish on occasion people's credit card transactions, examination results, personal problems, and youthful indiscretions. The message is that the opposition is made up of a bunch of incompetent, unprincipled opportunists, and if anyone is considering joining them, he or she had better be squeaky clean.

Participating in opposition groups can be an expensive proposition. On numerous occasions, members of the opposition have been sued by PAP leaders for remarks made in the heat of a campaign or political debate. Invariably, the suits are won by the PAP leaders. The government's position is that it is duty bound to defend the reputation and integrity of the nation's leaders. The opposition claims it is merely an attempt to curtail free speech and stifle criticism of the government.

The government also narrowed the boundaries of the political arena to ensure that those who did not have the inclination to enter the world of party politics did not make common cause with the opposition from the sidelines. When the law society made critical comments on legislation to further control publications, it was attacked by the government for entering partisan politics. Its charter was changed, the society reorganized, and a message sent to other professional organizations to stay out of politics.

Another example of the attempt to limit the participants in the political debate took place in the late 1980s. A group of Catholic lay workers had set up a shelter for abused foreign maids. Many of these guest workers were Filipino Catholics who lived with their employers and had little recourse when mistreated physically or emotionally. The leaders of the effort to help the maids were arrested under the ISA. They were accused of being part of a Marxist plot to destabilize the government. The basis of this accusation was their connection to Catholic movements outside Singapore that practiced "liberation theology." The government had no problem with religious organizations helping the needy. In fact, given the low levels of public funds to support the disadvantaged, the government encouraged their assistance. It is one thing to help the poor and the abused, but it is an entirely different issue to become their advocates. Questions of class and injustice could easily turn into political agitation, but this was not the role of religious organizations. Eventually, in 1990, the Religious Harmony Act was passed, which defined the issues that religious groups could raise. For example, the question of poverty and its causes was out of bounds. The message was that in a multicultural, multireligious society, religious groups should stay out of politics.

The issue of maids highlights one of the problems faced by employing guest workers. Singaporeans employ about forty thousand maids from the Philippines. Their conditions of employment vary from home to home, but some do face ill-treatment from their employers. Some employers do not know how to coexist with foreign maids in their homes and tend to look down on them because of their low wage status. If groups in Singapore publicize the problems faced by these women, it could hurt friendly relations between the two countries, especially in the Philippines with its free and vocal press.

A New Generation of Leaders

The 1980s also saw a change in the political leadership of the island state. As Singapore moved into its third decade of PAP rule, there arose a need to bring to the fore a new generation of political leaders.

By the mid-1980s, most of the leaders who had been instrumental in engineering Singapore's impressive progress were either fading from the political scene or being nudged aside. Goh Keng Swee, who had been the mastermind of the economic blueprint and who had overseen the creation of Singapore's armed forces as defense minister, retired from active politics in 1984. Goh continued to advise the government on monetary and investment policies but spent most of his time as a consultant in China as it moved to a more open economy. Rajaratnam, who had been vital in helping the government put its message out to the people as minister of culture and then served ably as foreign minister, also stepped down. He spent his retirement as a lecturer, commentator, and academic.

The passing of Toh Chin Chye and Devan Nair from the scene was not quite as smooth. By the early 1980s, Toh had been replaced as party chairman and no longer held any ministerial responsibilities, but he did not go quietly. Through most of the 1980s, he remained in parliament and became a vocal critic of government policies and style. Toh argued for a more open political process, insisting that Singapore's success had created the opportunity for less government control over people's lives. In the 1988 general election, the constituency that Toh had represented for almost thirty years was abolished and merged into other electoral districts. Toh accepted the writing on the wall and left political life.

Nair, who had been a key player in taming the labor unions and creating a partnership between the NTUC and the government, was made president of the country in 1981. At that time, Singapore's presidency was a purely ceremonial position and carried with it no political power. Singapore's first two presidents, Yusof bin Ishak and Benjamin Sheares, had not been politicians and had assumed the role of head of state with grace and ease. Nair had been a jailed radical, trade union leader, and member of parliament in Malaysia and Singapore, so he had difficulty adapting to this new role. The greeting of foreign dignitaries, opening social and charitable events, and the generally passive nature of the job did not sit well with the man's temperament. In 1984, Nair resigned from the presidency due to his problems with alcohol. In the ensuing years after his resignation, an unseemly public discourse took place between him and the government, especially with Lee Kuan Yew. Arguments over his pension, the reasons for his resignation, and the public disclosure of his medical records and personal life all made for an ugly debate many Singaporeans would rather have not heard. Nair became a fierce critic of Lee, accusing him of hypocrisy and duplicity. Lee responded with lawsuits and stories of drunkenness and cruelty. Eventually, Nair settled in the United States and accepted a teaching position at an American university.

Lee Kuan Yew gave up the prime minister's position in 1990 but did not leave politics. He remains in parliament and in the cabinet as senior minister. It is not unlike the CEO or president of a corporation relinquishing the day-to-day direction of the company but staying on as chairman of the board. As long as Lee remains in the cabinet, his intellect, experience, and the respect he holds will continue to give him a strong voice in the direction of the country and the party. In his national day speech of 1988, Lee made his intentions quite clear:

> "and even from my sickbed, even if you are going to lower me into the grave and I feel that something is going wrong, I'll get up. Those who believe that when I have left the government as prime minister I've gone into permanent retirement really should have their heads examined."

The second generation of PAP leaders, who were groomed through the 1970s and 1980s, are quite different from those who led Singapore to independence. They are for the most part technocrats and bureaucrats whose paths to positions of responsibility have come through the civil service, the army, and large government-linked or private corporations. The first generation were activists and builders; the next generation are the managers of their success. The nature of the men and their backgrounds reflect the primary assumption of Singapore's future — the need for a well-run, efficient government that will provide the infrastructure and climate for continued large-scale foreign investment. Over half the paid-up capital of Singapore's private sector is foreign owned. The revenue, jobs, and CPF provided by these investors have become the lifeblood of the standard of living that Singaporeans enjoy today. This reality is evidenced by the large percentage of graduates from Singapore's institutions of higher learning brought into government service and the financial rewards they received. Singapore's political leaders and top civil servants are some of the best paid in the world. For example, the prime minister of Singapore receives a salary more than twice as much as the president of the United States.

Goh Chok Tong, who became prime minister in November 1990, went from the civil service to head the government-established shipping lines and then to parliament and ministerial responsibilities. S. Dhanabalan, who replaced Rajaratnam as foreign minister, started out as a civil servant and then went on to help establish the government-sponsored bank, DBS, before entering politics. Lee Hsien Loong, who oversaw the planning unit that led Singapore out of the recession of the mid-1980s and then went on to become deputy prime minister, spent thirteen years in the army before moving to parliament. When the presidency was made an elected post with limited political and veto powers, it was filled by Ong Teng Cheong, who was a city planner before his foray into politics. Tony Tan, the only major second-generation leader who did not come from government service, had run one of Singapore's major private banks before being asked to stand as a PAP candidate for office. These leaders attended Singapore's premier schools and hold advanced degrees from prestigious foreign universities.

GOH CHOK TONG (1941–)

Like many young Singaporeans, Goh Chok Tong chose to bond himself to government service in return for higher education. He attended Raffles Institution and the University of Singapore and joined the Economics Planning Unit (EPU) of the government. Williams College in Massachusetts then offered him a fellowship, and he agreed to work for the civil service for five years after his return. At Williams, he earned a masters in economics (1966) before returning to the EPU.

Goh Chok Tong in high spirits after his reelection to parliament in 1988.

From there, he went on to manage Neptune Orient Lines Ltd and finally, in 1976, was persuaded to run for election. He was not particularly interested in politics but felt that the country needed young, able leaders to succeed the retiring political leaders.

He was elected a member of parliament in 1976 and became senior minister of state for finance in 1977. He continued to be appointed to positions of ministerial responsibility and in 1982 was appointed defense minister as well as second minister in the Ministry of Health. In the 1984 election, voters indicated the need for more open, less paternalistic and younger leaders. The younger-generation core group of PAP members voted unanimously for Goh, and he was appointed first deputy prime minister. He became prime minister in 1990, succeeding Lee Kuan Yew. To date, Goh has worked to fulfill the pledge he made to the nation:

"My mission is clear — to ensure that Singapore thrives and grows after Mr Lee Kuan Yew; to find a new group of men and women to help me carry on where he and his colleagues left off; to build a nation of character and grace where people live lives of dignity and fulfillment and care for one another."

In the 1980s and 1990s, there has been an effort by the PAP to develop a more consultative style and to seek greater input into the decision-making process. A government feedback unit was established to set up lines of communication between citizens and government. The unit attempts to establish vehicles, such as discussion groups, where people are free to speak their minds about current issues. HDB has been being decentralized and town councils created. The PAP hopes that giving the individual estates control over their community services will offer an avenue for greater participation and input into the workings of government. A youth PAP and a women's PAP have been established as avenues for people's participation in the ruling party as well as to cater to a wider variety of viewpoints. MPs have been instructed to spend more time in their constituencies, seeking opinions and feedback from the voters.

These efforts represent a realization by the PAP that the people of Singapore want more control over their lives now that they have succeeded economically. They also indicate that the PAP does not want the underlying structure of government decision making to change dramatically. In the eyes of the PAP, abandoning the Singapore model would mean abandoning the basic reason for Singapore's success.

How much substantive political change the second generation of PAP leaders is willing to institute remains open to debate. Two opinion pieces written by local author Catherine Lim in the *Straits Times* in 1994 are good examples of the present political climate in Singapore. The first article was titled "The PAP and the People: A Great Affective Divide." Her thesis was that while the people of Singapore recognize the effective job the party does in running Singapore and providing for its prosperity, many of them do not like their leaders very much. For instance, on National Day, many Singaporeans do not fly the flag because of the connection between the party and the state. Somehow flying the flag indicated you were a PAP supporter or liked the party, which in many minds was different from respecting what the leaders had done. In her second article, Lim questioned whether any significant political change had taken place with the handover of power from Lee Kuan Yew to Goh Chok Tong. She argued that the recent large salary increase for government officials was an example of the continuing top-down style of government. In a way, the government's response to these articles proved her correct. The immediate reaction was that local writers had no business involving themselves in political issues. If they wanted to do so, they should join a political party and not give opinions from the sidelines. The argument was the same one used almost a decade earlier against the law society and against the churches. While there had been an attempt to obtain more feedback from people, there was still a deep feeling among PAP leaders that public political debate must be limited. Even in the mid-1990s, there was still a belief that too broad a discourse would threaten Singapore's success.

Politically, the people of Singapore face a dilemma. Most are willing to give the PAP credit for the country's success. On the whole, they believe the PAP does a good job running the country. Most see the men and women brought into government as honest and capable. On the other hand, Singapore society has become affluent, well-educated, and cosmopolitan. Singaporeans want the PAP to continue to run the country but in a more open and democratic way. Perhaps it is the role of the third-generation leaders to recognize this, and find the right formula to effect it.

BIBLIOGRAPHY

Abas, Salleh. *May Day for Justice*. Percetakan A-Z: Kuala Lumpur, 1989.

Abdullah bin Haji Ahmad Badawi. *Malaysia-Singapore Relations*. Institute of Policy Studies. Times Academic Press: Singapore, 1980.

Andaya, Barbara Watson, and Leonard Y. Andaya. *A History of Malaysia*. Macmillan Press Ltd.: London, 1982.

Arasaratnam, Sinnappah. *Indians in Malaysia and Singapore*. Oxford University Press: Kuala Lumpur, 1970.

Asher, Mukul G. *Social Adequacy and Equity of the Social Security Arrangements in Singapore*. Times Academic Press: Singapore, 1991.

Bastin, John and Harry J. Benda. *A History of Modern Southeast Asia*. Prentice-Hall Inc.: New Jersey, 1968.

Benjamin, Geoffrey. "The Unseen Presence: A Theory of the Nation State and Its Mystifications." Working paper no. 91, Department of Sociology, National University of Singapore, 1988.

Brown, C.C., trans. *Sejarah Melayu or Malay Annals*. Oxford University Press: Kuala Lumpur, 1970.

Brown, David. *The State and Ethnic Politics in South-East Asia*. Routledge: London, 1994.

Cady, John F. *Southeast Asia: Its Historical Development*. McGraw-Hill: New York, 1964.

Chai Hon-Chan. *The Development of British Malaya 1896-1909*. Oxford University Press: Kuala Lumpur, 1967.

Chen Ai Ju and Gavin Jones. *Ageing in Asean*. Institute of Southeast Asian Studies: Singapore, 1990.

Chew, Ernest C T, and Edwin Lee, eds. *A History of Singapore*. Oxford University Press: Singapore, 1991.

Chia, Felix. *The Babas*. Times Books International: Singapore, 1980.

Chua Beng Huat. *Political Legitimacy and Housing*. Routledge: London, 1997.

Cleary, Mark, and Peter Eaton. *Borneo: Change and Development*. Oxford University Press: Oxford, 1992.

Clough, Shepard et al., eds. *Early Modern Times*. D C Heath & Co: Lexington MA, 1969.

Clutterbuck, Richard L. *The Long Long War*. Frederick A. Praeger: New York, 1966.

Coedes, G. *The Indianized States of Southeast Asia*. University of Malaya Press: Kuala Lumpur, 1968.

Comber, Leon. *13 May 1969*. Heinemann Asia: Kuala Lumpur, 1983.

Crouch, Harold. *Government & Society in Malaysia*. Allen & Unwin: Australia, 1996.

Da Cunha, D., ed. *Debating Singapore*. Institute of Southeast Asian Studies: Singapore, 1994.

Dartford, G. P. *A Short History of Malaya*. Longmans of Malaya Ltd: Kuala Lumpur, 1958.

Deutsch, Antal, and Hanna Zowall. *Compulsory Savings and Taxes in Singapore*. Institute of Southeast Asian Studies: Singapore, 1988.

Diller, Anthony. "Sriwijaya and the First Zeros." *J MBRAS*. Vol LXVII, part I. MBRAS: Kuala Lumpur, 1995.

Farwell, Byron. *Armies of the Raj*. W.W. Norton & Company: New York, 1989.

Fisher, Charles. *South-East Asia*. Methuen & Co: London, 1964.

Fong Sip Chee. *The PAP Story — The Pioneering Years*. Times Periodicals: Singapore, 1979.

George, T.J.S. *Lee Kuan Yew's Singapore*. Eastern Universities Press Sdn Bhd: Singapore, 1973.

Gomes, Edmund Terence, and K S. Jomo. *Malaysia's Political Economy*. Cambridge University Press: Cambridge, 1997.

Gullick, J.M. *The Story of Kuala Lumpur (1857–1939)*. Singapore: Eastern Universities Press Sdn Bhd, 1983.

Hall, D.G.E. *A History of South-East Asia*. Macmillan Press: London, 1955.

Hill, A.I., ed. "The Hikayat Abdullah." *J MBRAS*. Malaya Publishing House: Singapore, 1995.

Hill, Michael, and Lian Kwen Fee. *The Politics of Nation Building and Citizenship in Singapore*. Routledge: London, 1995.

Information Malaysia 1997 Yearbook. Kuala Lumpur: Berita Publishing Sdn Bhd, 1997.

Jawan, Jayum A. *The Iban Factor in Sarawak Politics*. Universiti Pertanian Malaysia Press: Shah Alam, 1993

Josey, Alex. *David Marshall's Political Interlude*. Eastern Universities Press Sdn Bhd: Singapore, 1982.

Kanapathy, V. *The Malaysian Economy: Problems and Prospects*. Asia Pacific Press: Singapore, 1970.

Kassim, Ismail. *Race, Politics and Moderation*. Times Books International: Singapore, 1979.

Khoo Kay Kim, ed. *Malay Society*. Pelanduk Publications: Kuala Lumpur, 1991.

Khoo Kay Kim. "Malaysian Immigration." *J MBRAS*. Vol LXXI, part 1. Kuala Lumpur: MBRAS, June 1998.

_____. "Sea gypsies of the magic circle" *Sunday Star*, Oct 19, 1997.

_____. "Training at English schools" *Sunday Star*, Nov 22, 1997.

King, Victor. *The Peoples of Borneo*. Blackwell Publishers: Oxford, 1993.

Lau, Albert. *A Moment of Anguish*. Times Academic Press: Singapore, 1998.

Leifer, Michael. "Politics in Singapore." *J Commonwealth Political Studies*. Centre for South-East Asian Studies: University of Hull, United Kingdom, 1964.

_____. "Communal Violence in Singapore." *University of Hull Asian Survey*. Vol IV, no. 10. Centre for South-East Asian Studies: University of Hull, United Kingdom, 1964.

Li Dun Jen. *British Malaya: An Economic Analyais*. Institut Analisa Sosial, Kuala Lumpur, 1982.

Li, Tania. *Malays in Singapore: Culture, Economy, and Ideology*. Oxford University Press: Singapore, 1989.

Lim, Catherine. "The PAP and the People — A Great Affective Divide." The *Straits Times*. September 3, 1994.

MacDonald, Malcolm. *Borneo People*. Alfred A. Knopf: New York, 1958.

Mahathir bin Mohamad. *The Malay Dilemma*. Asia Pacific Press: Singapore, 1970.

Major, John S. *The Land and People of Malaysia and Brunei*. HarperCollins: New York, 1991.

Makepeace, W. et al. *One Hundred Years of Singapore*. Vols I and II. John Murray: London, 1921.

Manchester, William. *A World Lit Only by Fire*. Little, Brown and Company: Boston, 1992.

Manguin, Pierre-Yves "Palembang and Sriwijaya: An Early Malay Harbour-City Rediscovered." *J MBRAS*. Vol LXVI, part 1. MBRAS: Kuala Lumpur, 1993.

May, Reginald Le. *The Culture of South-East Asia: The Heritage of India*. George Allen & Unwin Ltd: London, 1954.

Mestrovic, Matthew. *Southeast Asia*. Scholastic Inc.: New York, 1974.

Meyer, Milton W. *Southeast Asia: A Brief History*. Littlefield, Adams & Co.: USA, 1971.

Mills, L.A. *British Malaya 1824–67*. Reprinted in *J MBRAS*. Vol XXXIII, part 3. MBRAS: Singapore, 1961.

Mohamed, Masnah. "The Origins of Weaving Centres in the Malay Peninsula." *J MBRAS*. Vol LXVIII, part I. MBRAS: Kuala Lumpur, 1995.

Morison, Samuel et al. *The Growth of the American Republic*. Oxford University Press: New York, 1980.

Muthulingam, M., and Tan P. C. *The Certificate History of Malaya, 1400-1965*. Preston-Times Printing: Singapore, 1988.

Neilands, Robin. *A Fighting Retreat: The British Empire 1947–97*. Hodder and Stoughton: Great Britain, 1996.

Newbold, T.J. *British Settlements in the Straits of Malacca*. Vol. I and II. Oxford University Press: Kuala Lumpur, 1971.

Ohmae, Kenichi. *The End of the Nation State*. The Free Press: New York, 1995.

Ong Chit Chung. *Operation Matador*. Times Academic Press: Singapore, 1997.

Paul, E.C. "Obstacles to Democratization in Singapore." Working paper. Centre of Southeast Asian Studies, Monash University, Australia, 1992.

Pearson, H.F. *A Popular History, 1819-1960*. Eastern Universities Press Ltd.: Singapore, 1961.

Pelras, Christian. *The Bugis*. Blackwell Publishers: Oxford, 1996.

Png Poh Seng. "The Straits Chinese in Singapore," *J SEA History*. Vol X, no. 1. MPH Printing: Singapore, 1969.

Poh Wong Kum. *Essays on the Singapore Economy*. Federal Publications: Singapore, 1982.

Pringle, R. *Rajahs and Rebels: the Ibans of Sarawak under Brooke Rule*. Cornell University Press: Ithaca, 1970.

Purcell, Victor. *The Chinese in Southeast Asia*. Oxford University Press: London, 1966.

_____. *The Chinese in Malaya*. Oxford University Press: Kuala Lumpur, 1967.

Quah, Jon S. T. et al., eds. *Government and Politics of Singapore.* Oxford University Press: Singapore, 1990.

Quah, Jon S. T. *In Search of Singapore's National Values.* Times Academic Press: Singapore, 1990.

Raja Aziz Addruse. *Conduct Unbecoming.* Walrus: Kuala Lumpur, 1990.

Rao, Chandriah Appa et al. *Issues in Contemporary Malaysia.* Heinemann Educational Books: Kuala Lumpur, 1977.

Ratnam, K. J. *Communalism and the Political Process in Malaya.* University of Malaya Press: Kuala Lumpur, 1965.

Regnier, Philippe. *Singapore: City-State in South-East Asia.* Hurst & Company: London, 1991.

Reid, Anthony. *Southeast Asia in the Age of Commerce, 1450–1680.* Yale University Press: New Haven and London, 1988.

Robinson, R. et al, eds. *Southeast Asia in the 1980s: The Politics of Economic Crisis.* Allen & Unwin: Sydney, 1987.

Roff, William R. *The Origins of Malay Nationalism.* University of Malaya Press: Kuala Lumpur, 1967.

Runciman, Steven. *The White Rajahs.* Cambridge University Press: Cambridge, 1960.

Ryan, N.J. *The Making of Modern Malaysia and Singapore.* Oxford University Press: Kuala Lumpur and Singapore, 1970.

Sandhu, K.S., and P. Wheatley, eds. *Melaka.* Oxford University Press: Kuala Lumpur, 1983.

Saw Swee Hock. "Population Trends in Singapore 1819–1967." In *J SEA History.* Vol X, no 1. MPH Printing: Singapore, 1969.

Sheppard, Mubin, ed. *Singapore 150 Years.* Times Books International: Singapore, 1953.

Silcock, T.H. and E.K. Fisk, eds. *The Political Economy of Independent Malaya.* Eastern Universities Press: Singapore, 1963.

Steinberg, D.J. et al. *In Search of South-East Asia: A Modern History.* Oxford University Press: Kuala Lumpur, 1971.

Swettenham, Frank. *British Malaya*. John Lane: London, 1907.

Tamney, Joseph B. *The Struggle Over Singapore's Soul*. Walter de Gruyter: Berlin, 1996.

Tan Chee Beng. *The Baba of Melaka*. Pelanduk Publications: Kuala Lumpur, 1988.

Tan Liok Eee. "Descent and Identity: The Different Paths of Tan Cheng Lock, Tan Kah Kee and Lim Lian Geok." *J MBRAS*. Vol. LXVII, part 1. MBRAS: Kuala Lumpur, 1995.

Tan, Thomas Tsu-wee. *Your Chinese Roots: The Overseas Chinese Story*. Times Books International: Singapore, 1986.

Tarling, Nicholas. *British Policy in the Malay Peninsula and Archipelago, 1824-1871*. Oxford University Press: Kuala Lumpur, 1969.

_____. *A Concise History of Southeast Asia*. Donald Moore Press Ltd.: Singapore, 1967.

_____. "Malaya in British History." *J. MBRAS*. Vol LXII, part I. MBRAS: Kuala Lumpur, 1989.

_____. "The Singapore Mutiny, 1915." *J. MBRAS*. Vol LV, part 2. MBRAS: Kuala Lumpur, 1982.

Tregonning, K.G. *A History of Modern Sabah 1881–1963*. University of Malaya Press: Singapore and Kuala Lumpur, 1965.

Turnbull, C. Mary. *A Short History of Malaysia, Singapore and Brunei*. Graham Brash: Singapore, 1980.

_____. *A History of Singapore 1819–1988*. Oxford University Press: Singapore, 1989.

Vatikiotis, Michael R.J. *Political Change in Southeast Asia*. Routledge: London, 1996.

Vaughan, J.D. *The Manners and Customs of the Chinese of the Straits Settlements*. Oxford University Press: Kuala Lumpur, 1971.

Wang Gungwu "Migration Patterns in the History of Malaya and the Region," *J MBRAS*. Vol. VIII, part 1. MBRAS: Kuala Lumpur, 1985.

Winstedt, Richard. *The Malays: A Cultural History.* Routledge & Kegan Paul Ltd: London, 1947.

_____. *Malaya and its History.* Hutchinson University Library: London, 1948.

Wolters, O.W. *The Fall of Srivijaya in Malay History.* Oxford University Press: Kuala Lumpur, 1970.

Wazir Jahan Karim, ed. *Emotions of Culture: A Malay Perspective.* Oxford University Press: Singapore, 1990.

Yusop, Mohamad "The Malaysia Plan and Brunei." *J MBRAS.* Vol LXXI, part 1. MBRAS: Kuala Lumpur, 1998.

INDEX

412

CREDITS

PHOTOGRAPHS
Arkib Negara Malaysia: 89, 128, 149, 208, 259,
     329 (top)
Imperial War Museum: 205, 228, 246, 261, 322
Library of Congress: 16, 160, 162, 177, 224
Lim Kheng Chye's Collection at the National
Archives: 100
National Archives of Singapore: 24, 270, 272,
     301
New Paper: 399
Straits Times: 327, 366
Tourism Malaysia: 329 (bottom)

MAPS
Cleary, Mark and Eaton, Peter, Borneo: Change
     and Development: 157, 171
Dartford, G.P., A Short History of Malaya: 39, 46,
     57, 72, 114
Fisher, Charles, South-East Asia: 14, 21, 174, 181
Muthulingam, M and Tan P.C., The Certificate
History of Malaya: 61, 66, 74, 80, 131, 133, 140,
     221
Reid, Anthony, Southeast Asia in the Age of
Commerce, 1450–1680: 12
Turnbull, C.M., A Short History of Malaysia,
Singapore and Brunei: 69

TABLES
Crouch, Harold, Government and Society in
     Malaysia: 356
Li Dun Jen, British Malaya: An Economic Analysis:
     187, 236
Purcell, Victor, The Chinese in Malaya: 106, 183,
     227
Tan, Thomas Tsu-wee, Your Chinese Roots: 104

ABOUT THE AUTHOR

Jim Baker came to Singapore in 1950 at the age of two and has lived in Penang, Riau, Kuala Lumpur, and Melaka. He is now a Singapore permanent resident. Baker teaches history and economics at the Singapore American School. He has a bachelor's degree in history and a master's in education from American University in Washington, D.C.

Jim Baker